Developmental Disabilities
NO LONGER A PRIVATE TRAGEDY

Lynn Wikler and Maryanne P. Keenan, editors

Copublished by
National Association of Social Workers,
Silver Spring, Maryland, and
American Association on Mental Deficiency,
Washington, D.C.

Library of Congress Cataloging in Publication Data
Main entry under title:

Developmental disabilities.

(Readings in social work)
1. Mentally handicapped--Services for--United States--Addresses, essays, lectures. 2. Social work with the mentally handicapped--United States--Addresses, essays, lectures. 3. Family social work--United States--Addresses, essays, lectures. 4. Social group work--United States--Addresses, essays, lectures. 5. Community organization--United States--Addresses, essays, lectures.
I. Wikler, Lynn. II. Keenan, Maryanne P. III. National Association of Social Workers. IV. American Association on Mental Deficiency. V. Series.
HV3006.A4D478 1983   362.3'8   83–17405
ISBN 0-87101-117-4

Printed in U.S.A. 3

Preface

The publication of a new professional anthology is an important event for its sponsors and for the readers it will serve. The publication of this particular anthology is especially significant because it represents the first collaborative publishing project of the National Association of Social Workers (NASW) and the American Association on Mental Deficiency (AAMD). Both these organizations are committed to the goal of an increased awareness and recognition of developmental disabilities among professionals and the general public. Close collaboration between the two editors of *Developmental Disabilities: No Longer a Private Tragedy,* Lynn Wikler (Vice President of AAMD for Social Work, 1980–1982) and Maryanne P. Keenan (NASW Senior Staff Associate), should be seen not only as a continuation of several joint efforts between NASW and AAMD but also as a clear reminder of the important place for social work in the developmental disabilities field.

NASW, a 90,000 member professional organization for social workers that was established in 1955, has shown an explicit interest in developmental disabilities throughout its history. As the first NASW publication devoted exclusively to developmental disabilities, this volume joins a long list of recent association accomplishments in the field, including NASW's Standards for Social Work in Developmental Disabilities, participation in the activities of the International Year of Disabled Persons, and involvement with the Accreditation Council for Services for Mentally Retarded and Other Developmentally Disabled Persons.

Established in 1876, AAMD is the oldest professional organization in the field of mental retardation and the only one of its kind.

Its 10,000 members are professionals in many disciplines dedicated to a broad range of specialties in service to those persons who are labeled mentally retarded or developmentally disabled. AAMD is international as well as interdisciplinary, containing members from throughout the United States, Canada, and several other countries. Its close ties to the social work profession are reflected in the fact that the organization contains a Social Work Division among its major structures.

This volume represents a major contribution to the literature because it serves a dual purpose in explaining the many roles social workers assume in the field of developmental disabilities. The anthology provides generic social workers with an introduction to the needs of developmentally disabled clients, and it broadens and reinforces the knowledge base of professional social workers already in the field. In all cases, the ultimate goal is to improve the lives of developmentally disabled individuals and their families through the promotion of sophisticated social work skills and values as applied to their unique needs. It is our hope that, because of the quality and relevance of its contents, this volume will find a place in reference libraries and in the personal collections of all social workers as well as other professionals in the field of developmental disabilities.

ALBERT J. BERKOWITZ
Executive Director, AAMD

JOHN E. HANSAN
Executive Director, NASW

August 1983

Foreword

When I was at the University of California's School of Social Welfare in Los Angeles, I was told by Professor Mary Duren that what was taught in schools of social work varied greatly from the practice of social work, especially as it was seen in public welfare agencies who, after all, were responsible for the majority of social work practice in this country. What Professor Duren impressed upon me was that social workers needed to know about a great number and variety of interventions as they went about their business.

When I arrived at the School of Social Work in Madison, Wisconsin, I met Virginia Franks, who had conceptualized what I learned in California and fashioned it into a curriculum plan. Professor Franks did not like the term "generic," which was current at the time. She favored the methodology of analyzing social problems and then developing a treatment plan by using whatever social work resources were available. This approach became known at Madison as the social problem–multimethod approach. It meant that we taught students about various kinds of social problems, including mental retardation, and that we also taught them various kinds of social work interventions. Clearly, this was a far cry from the standard approach of teaching social casework, social group work, or community organization. We taught them all. In many ways, this began new patterns of social work curriculum development.

In the present collection, *Developmental Disabilities: No Longer a Private Tragedy,* the editors have organized their selected readings on a social problem that draws upon all the social worker's knowledge of intervention. Developmental disabilities certainly represent a significant problem for our society, one regarding which the social work function of enhancing the fit between society and the developmentally disabled individual is critical. The social issues related to the problem of developmental disabilities include the disabled person's own adaptation, support for the families of the disabled, the use of groups to accomplish these tasks, and the organization of community and legal supports to alleviate the stresses of this population.

The organization of this book, which reflects my own perspective on social work education, is therefore particularly appropriate for the subject at hand. The book concerns itself with four levels of intervention: there are articles on how to bring about change on the level of the individual, the family, the group, and the community. In any collection, there are topics that remain neglected. However, the strength of this collection lies in its making available to the reader interested in both developmental disabilities and social work a wealth of information organized in a way that emphasizes the unique perspective of our profession —a commitment to the amelioration of social problems using various types of strategies.

MARTIN B. LOEB
Emeritus Professor of Social Work
School of Social Work
University of Wisconsin–Madison

March 1983

Contents

Introduction

Recognition of the rights and needs of the developmentally disabled is a recent phenomenon in our society. This recognition has been heightened by innovations in service delivery over the last ten years. Federal legislation mandating deinstitutionalization and the subsequent development of community living arrangements and other alternatives has meant that more developmentally disabled people now live, work, and receive social services in the community than ever before. Social workers in particular have been aware of mainstreaming's impact on both the developmentally disabled population and the community. Frequent contact with developmentally disabled people, an interest in person-environment interaction, and the ability to offer support and assistance to vulnerable citizens provide the basis upon which social work professionals form working and helping relationships with developmentally disabled individuals and their families.

Our belief is that social work practice should address social problems and that the social worker is a capable and knowledgeable advocate for change. Developmentally disabled individuals and their families experience multiple problems, and they therefore constitute a particularly vulnerable group in American society. They may be isolated or denied personal rights available to other members of society, and they are more likely than other individuals to be poor. Families with a developmentally disabled child often suffer more stress than do other families and need outside support. *Developmental Disabilities: No Longer a Private Tragedy* describes the ways in which social workers can support families and help them find solutions to these problems.

Purpose and Organization

Social work services to developmentally disabled people and their families have undergone major changes in the last decade. Programs such as residential, vocational, and educational services, which were once delivered in large institutions, are now being provided in the community. Descriptions of recent developments in social work practice should help service providers recognize the significance of the social work role in community-based services and better utilize the new resources available to the developmentally disabled.

The individuals who are providing services have also changed. For many years, there have been specialists in the field of developmental disabilities in the social work profession. However, virtually all social workers now come into contact with developmentally disabled people and their families, and they need to be familiar with the most current literature to be able to respond to the new demands being placed on them. Moreover, as a result of federal funding in the 1970s that encouraged the proliferation of new services and research in the area of developmental disabilities, innovative social work approaches and programs were developed. Descriptions of these programs should be shared with all social workers.

This collection of articles on practice with the developmentally disabled is therefore intended to meet a definite need within the social work profession for a single source that brings together descriptions of the various approaches that have been used to aid and support the disabled in a community setting. Twenty-six of the articles are reprints and have been published previously; they appear

1

as in their original form. Five of the articles consist of original material and have never been in print before. For those who have specialized in developmental disabilities, this volume pulls together a selection of the current literature. For those practicing in a setting not typically associated with the developmentally disabled, it provides the background and basic information needed to serve developmentally disabled clients. The articles were chosen to provide concrete, practical techniques for working with a variety of clients and families in a wide range of settings. Given its combined focus on social work and developmental disabilities, this volume as a whole updates and supplements but does not duplicate the literature in the field.

Because of the interest in developmental disabilities that has grown within academic programs, this collection should be useful to educators who recognize a need for more content related to developmental disabilities in their curriculum. The volume discusses social work practice in the areas of direct services, community organization, and policy and should therefore be helpful to students, educators, and administrators regardless of their particular focus of concentration or work setting or the methodology they employ.

The anthology is organized around four levels of intervention: work with the individual, family, group, and community. For the most part, the selections emphasize the application of sound social work principles. In general, they suggest how social science data may be used to promote mutual adjustment between people and their social environment. Other sources can be consulted for the theoretical background that lays the groundwork for the methods social workers use to bring about change. This collection does not present research findings but instead focuses on how to apply theory and research to clients' needs in such a way as to better serve those needs.

The articles in the first section describe the various aspects of the field of developmental disabilities as well as the role of the professional social worker and recent advances made by social workers in this field.

Within the next section, which deals with social work with individuals, several techniques for working with developmentally disabled children and adults are discussed. These include a task-focused approach, a psychotherapeutic approach, and a casework approach. In most instances, case studies are used to illustrate the techniques. In the third section, the family is considered the target for change. Parents, siblings, grandparents, and the family over the life span of the developmentally disabled individual are dealt with in turn. Solutions to frequently encountered family problems are presented.

Strategies that use groups to bring about change are outlined in the fourth section. These include the use of therapy and behavior modification groups with parents of developmentally disabled children. Groups focusing on foster parent training and the special needs of siblings of the disabled are also described.

In the last section, the target for change is the community. Public policies affecting the disabled and detailed roles for social workers in implementing and influencing these policies are suggested to assure the continuation of professional involvement in the field.

Because this volume is organized around levels of intervention, the approaches outlined are described as they have been used with developmentally disabled people in general. Had the anthology been organized in terms of specific disabilities, recent articles on social work practice with people with epilepsy, hearing impairments, cerebral palsy, and learning disabilities would have been included. This collection focuses on the details of levels of practice with the developmentally disabled, rather than on the specific implications of each unique disability for social work interventions. Another volume should address this other equally important perspective.

During the compilation of this volume, an important criterion used for selection was whether an article contained a description of exemplary social work practice with illustrative case material. Applying this standard often led to the exclusion of articles by nonsocial workers as well as to the omission of research reports that did not portray the process and details of the intervention being tested. Although we attempted to survey and select from the universe of published articles, we have no doubt that excellent practice papers by social workers were overlooked. In addition, space limitations restricted the number of articles we could include in each section. For these various reasons, important articles concerning social work and the developmental disabilities field will undoubtedly be missing from this collection. We hope that a future volume can remedy that situation.

Focus for the Future

Social workers in the field of developmental disabilities have greatly expanded their roles in the past decade. Professionals need to be sophisticated about medical advances, federal policy, ethical issues, and the latest social work practices. All social workers need an understanding of the multiple needs of the developmentally disabled population. This is especially crucial now that deinstitutionalization is a reality and the profession of social work has made a long-term commitment to the principles of normalization and community care. The Standards for Social Work in Developmental Disabilities approved by the National Association of Social Workers (NASW) specify the knowledge base and principles that should underlie practice, a commitment to prevention and to an interdisciplinary approach, and the skills needed to provide appropriate professional services. This volume complements the standards by presenting the most current literature to aid social workers and inform others of advances in social work practice. It should help social workers focus on approaches through which the professional standards can be fulfilled.

In sum, *Developmental Disabilities: No Longer a Private Tragedy* is offered as a resource for advancing the knowledge and practice of social workers in the developmental disabilities field. The vital contribution by the authors whose writings are contained in this volume is self-evident. We would also like to express our gratitude to Albert Berkowitz, Executive Director of the American Association on Mental Deficiency, C. Annette Maxey, former Executive Director of NASW, and the faculty of the School of Social Work and the Waisman Center on Mental Retardation and Human Development of the University of Wisconsin-Madison for their vision and support of this project. We must thank Jacqueline M. Atkins, Director of NASW's Department of Publications, Natalie Hilzen, Senior Editor, and the rest of the staff of the Department of Publications for their patience and guidance over the course of many months during the production of this book. We are also indebted to our assistants, Erin Parnigoni and Carol Betts, for their humor and vigilance while typing and performing other support services for us. Finally, we must acknowledge the outstanding efforts of Doris R. Parker, special consultant to NASW, without whose energy, creativity, and industry this volume simply would not have been possible.

Lynn Wikler
Maryanne P. Keenan

August 1983

Part One

Introduction

Introduction to Part One

The purpose of this introductory section is to define the population to be served in the field of developmental disabilities and raise some of the more salient issues to be considered in working in the field. The selections in Part One outline both traditional and contemporary social work functions that are being adapted and used in the provision of services to the developmentally disabled and their families. These articles also contain basic information on the history of social work's involvement with the disabled, including material on legislation, court decisions, and other national events that have initiated action, sparked controversy, and deeply affected the profession's interest and participation in this rapidly expanding field.

In the opening article, Wikler and Berkowitz present social workers with a new perspective on mental retardation. Specifically, retardation is viewed as a social problem rather than as a private, often invisible family tragedy as it has frequently been in the past. Wikler and Berkowitz discuss how this changed view of disability has enhanced the social work profession's contacts with the mentally retarded and their families on every level of intervention, from individual counseling and referral to policy development and professional education. Next, Gelman goes on to describe the expanding opportunities for practice with the developmentally disabled now available to social workers as a result of the legislative and judicial trends that have occurred over the past two decades. Horejsi then further defines how the traditional functions of family support, protection of rights, and coordination of services have taken on new dimensions for social workers as a result of deinstitutionalization.

The next two selections in Part One are based on invited addresses by the respective authors to members of the American Association on Mental Deficiency (AAMD), and they have not been previously published. Adams's remarks on ethical issues were delivered at the 1981 Annual Meeting of AAMD as a special addition to the association's program acknowledging the International Year of Disabled Persons. In this presentation, Adams encourages professional awareness of recent medical advances and social changes that raise and complicate many ethical considerations surrounding the birth and subsequent societal support of a developmentally disabled individual. Begab presented his remarks before the Social Work Division at AAMD's Annual Meeting the following year. He describes the ongoing debate in the field of developmental disabilities concerning genetic versus environmental influences and stresses the importance of the psychosocial issues involved in providing optimum services to the developmentally disabled in the community.

In the last article in the section, Keenan presents an overview of a joint project between AAMD and the National Association of Social Workers that resulted in the promulgation in 1982 of standards for social workers in developmental disabilities. The purpose of the standards, the process of their development, and their anticipated impact on the field of developmental disabilities are described in this final selection.

Through these readings we hope to introduce social work practitioners, administrators, and other concerned professionals to the unique and sometimes complex challenges encountered in meeting the needs of the disabled and their families. It should be evident that regardless of the individual social worker's job setting, area of concentration, or level of involvement with the disabled, the profession has a responsibility to understand the problems faced by developmentally disabled people and to assist in their resolution.

LYNN WIKLER
NORMA NESBITT BERKOWITZ

Social Work, Social Problems, and the Mentally Retarded

Mental retardation, which has until very recently been considered by society as a private tragedy striking individuals in random fashion, is now widely recognized to be a social problem. This relatively new look at an old phenomenon has had important implications for the social work profession in the past decade and will continue to do so throughout the coming one.

Neither the causes nor the symptoms of retardation can be eliminated by a vaccine. The condition, then, is not likely to be stamped out as a result of a scientific breakthrough. Poverty, one of the major correlatives of mental retardation, will still be with us in the 1980s. Future cuts in housing, medical care, education, and welfare programs may very well increase the number of mildly retarded individuals who need social work assistance. Depending on the outcome of controversies about abortion and euthanasia, the number of severely and profoundly mentally retarded may also increase. Policies which inhibit the development of a safe environment, one free

of chemical and nuclear hazards, are also altering the composition of the mentally retarded population.

Indeed, the interplay of value and economic decisions in American society today is changing the number and type of people being diagnosed as mentally retarded and the nature of social work practice in the field of mental retardation. Before the advent of the deinstitutionalization movement, the enactment of supplemental social security legislation, and the commitment to "mainstreaming" handicapped children into the regular school system, the mentally retarded were members of a largely hidden population. Social workers who worked with them and their families helped them to cope with their institutionalization and their isolation.

However, initiatives by the Kennedy Administration and new research findings about the cause of retardation in the 1960s brought the plight of the mentally retarded into the consciousness of the American public. By the late 1960s, it had been illustrated that mental retardation met all of Becker's criteria for social problems; it had been defined as an "objective condition," clearly identified and classified by the American Association on

Mental Deficiency. The National Commission to Combat Mental Retardation publicized the scope of the condition, not only focusing on the stress on individuals and their families, but on the costs to society. It was beginning to be viewed as a deterrent which kept a sizable part of our population from living up to the expected norms and roles, thus diminishing their contribution to society. Most importantly, people finally had information which indicated that this condition could be alleviated or prevented.

Who Is Mentally Retarded?

There are approximately six million Americans who are considered mentally retarded. The majority of these, about 80 percent, are mildly mentally retarded due to unknown causes. A disproportionately high number come from the ranks of the poor and isolated. Poor nutrition and medical care, stimulus deprivation, as well as some multifactional inheritance, all contribute to mild retardation. The *potential* level of adult functioning for this population includes reading at a fourth or fifth grade level, managing a paying job, and living in an independent setting with help available for crisis intervention. This level of coping is obviously not so different from the normal expectations of socio-psychological functioning. However, this potential can only be reached with appropriate programs, supportive services, proper expectations and support of family and others in their social milieu.

The severely/profoundly handicapped, which comprise 20 percent of the mentally retarded population, are found equally distributed across all socio-economic classes. The cause of retardation is sometimes drawn from the array of 200 known causes of mental retardation, but nonetheless, for the majority of those diagnosed as mentally retarded, no definitive cause can be established. Most severely retarded need sheltered living environments and daily supervision; the most profoundly retarded need nearly complete care.

Because of the diversity in their levels of functioning and their potential for growth and development, the mentally retarded can be found in nearly all service systems and can be encountered by social workers serving nearly any agency.

Establishment of a legitimate diagnosis of mental retardation (even if cause cannot be determined) is a key to obtaining, advocating for, and delivering appropriate services for this population. Criteria used to establish a diagnosis of mental retardation are: a measured delay in intellectual development that is two standard deviations below the norm (an intelligence quotient of 70 or below), a deficit in adaptive behavior, or the manifestation or onset of both of these between birth and age 18.

Social Work Interventions in Mental Retardation

Until the last 10 to 15 years the mentally retarded were considered unworthy of individual interventions. Now it is agreed that, although the standard clinical social work approach must be modified, it can be effective in the treatment of the mentally retarded.

Recent clinical research indicates that psychotherapeutic approaches can be effective with the mildly retarded adult when there is an understanding of the cognitive impairments. Via reassurance, advice, supportive counseling, etc., social workers can help mentally retarded individuals to alleviate the daily stresses encountered in their adjustments to community living. Behavior modification techniques have proven to be successful in attempts to build skills which enable the individual to function more independently. Such techniques as modeling, behavioral rehearsal, and shaping can make the difference between a recently deinstitutionalized person staying in the community or returning to the institution. Group counseling for transition to and maintenance in the community appears to be effective both as a type of social support network and as a means of improving specific skills.

Social work with families of the mentally retarded has always been directed toward adjustment to diagnosis or to placement. With the trend toward deinstitutionalization, however, interventions must be developed by social workers which anticipate the crisis faced by these families, crisis caused by the stress of stigma, isolation and the burden of constant care. For instance, organized respite care services for these families and supportive counseling for siblings, as well as parents, can help prevent family breakdown or initiation of institutional placement.

While there is an important role for clinical social work and intervention planning to directly serve the mentally retarded individual and family, there is also an increased demand for social workers in the community planning and policy areas. The development of apartment living programs requires social work expertise—in their development, their supervision, their management and their evaluation. Growth in the number of small group homes makes demands on social work personnel for consultation, program development and staff training. The skills of social workers are needed in the planning of public housing, zoning, recreational and environmental health programs —all of which have a profound impact on the mentally retarded population. Traditional community organization skills can be used in the development of self-help, community development, and consumer protection programs.

Social Work Training in Mental Retardation

If our perception of the mentally retarded has changed so much in the last decade or so, it is not surprising that the education sector has also shifted gears. A significant development in educating the broad array of disciplines which serve the mentally retarded was the establishment of the University Affiliated Programs under Public Law 88–164, passed in 1967. These affiliated programs have the goal of competent disciplinary and interdisciplinary training, and are making their mark on the specialized mental retardation labor force in the United States.

A recent follow-up study of social work students in the Wisconsin University Affiliated Program showed that 88 percent of social work students completing training at this facility (1975–1979) were employed providing services to the developmentally disabled; 29 per-

cent of these were in private agencies and 24 percent in community agencies. The skill areas most frequently perceived by the employers of these students as particularly relevant to their jobs were: agency consultation, community needs assessment, and assessment/evaluation of client needs. And, given the necessity for interdisciplinary contact at their jobs, students reported their training in that area to be invaluable.

With social workers' increased exposure to the mentally retarded population, there has been an increased demand for mental retardation content in the curriculum offerings of schools of social work. A national survey of course offerings in 1978 found that of the 71 graduate schools of social work, 36.4 percent offered a minimum of one course devoted to this social problem area. Fourteen percent of those schools offered more than one course. A large percentage of those schools which provide such courses are connected with federally funded, university-affiliated training institutes (78.5 percent).

Training for Generalists

Interestingly, federal seed money for these programs has had the effect of promoting opportunities for specialist social workers in mental retardation. This does not, however, address the pressing need for training social workers who do not specialize and yet need exposure to mental retardation problems. Such general curricula might include training on referral services, and/or provision of appropriate intervention techniques. Generalists who find themselves practicing in communities which will be asked to handle more and more members of the mentally retarded population may also turn for training to specialists who provide consultation, in-service training, or continuing education courses.

In the next 10 years, the profession will be in a double bind. Demands for professional accountability will occur simultaneously with a decrease in available resources.

Efforts to effect primary and secondary prevention will continue, with a growing focus on the environmental causes of mental retardation. Although new knowledge will enhance prevention programs, it will toughen the choice between spending limited resources on the already afflicted and spending on prevention.

Social workers will either rise to meet the challenge through client advocacy and creative use of resources, or will burn out in disillusionment as they become "gate keepers" who determine access to a shrinking pool of funds. The outcome will largely depend on the quality of training and the degree of commitment which the profession is willing to make to this target population and their families. This population no longer suffers alone, in silence and in isolation. The mentally retarded are with us, in and of the community, and they must receive their fair share of community resources and professional services.

Lynn Wikler, MSW, Ph.D., is an assistant professor at the University of Wisconsin-Madison School of Social Work. Norma Nesbitt Berkowitz, MSW, is head of the Social Work Section at the Waisman Center on Mental Retardation and Human Development at the University of Wisconsin at Madison.

SHELDON R. GELMAN

The Developmentally Disabled: A Social Work Challenge

To the social work profession, the increased emphasis on rehabilitation and community-based care for the developmentally disabled represents both the promise of greatly expanded practice opportunities and the burden of a serious professional responsibility.

In the April 1980 issue of *NASW NEWS*, Lynn Wikler and Norma Berkowitz presented a state of the art message on mental retardation and their views on the role social work education and practice play in the care of the mentally retarded. Social work involvement in the field of mental retardation and the broader domain of developmental disabilities remains one of changing knowledge and expectation. The past 20 years have brought a dramatic turnabout in thinking, policy, and programs, and a shift from the automatic segregation of individuals identified as mentally retarded and/or developmentally disabled to a concerted effort to bring them into the mainstream of community life.

In the years since the initiation of legislative reform which refocused the attention of the nation from institutional to community-based care, much has occurred. The Maternal and Child Health and Mental Retardation Planning Amendments of 1963 (P.L. 88-156), the Mental Retardation Facilities and Community Mental Health Centers Construction Act of 1963, the Elementary and Secondary Education Act of 1965 (P.L. 89-10), and the Vocational Rehabilitation Act Amendments of 1965 (P.L. 89-333) and 1973 (P.L. 93-112) have greatly expanded opportunities and services for mentally retarded persons. The Developmental Disabilities Services and Facilities and Construction Amendments of 1970 (P.L. 91-517), the Developmentally Disabled Assistance and Bill of Rights Act of 1975 (P.L. 94-103), and the Education for All Handicapped Children Act (P.L. 94-142) have refined the nation's goals and set a definite course for the future.

An emphasis on the rights of potentially vulnerable populations and the coordination of services has been an integral part of the legislative evolution. Along with the new philosophies of normalization and advocacy, service innovations designed to improve the quality of life and treatment of developmentally disabled individuals have rapidly gained acceptance.

These legislative mandates have broadened the base of potential recipients of services. The subsequent passage of the Rehabilitation, Comprehensive Services and Developmental Disabilities Amendments of 1978 (P.L. 95-602) made the categorical approach to service delivery for those with "substantial handicaps" extinct. The legislation's definition of these individuals reinforced arguments for a generic rather than a specialized approach to the needs of the developmentally handicapped.

The definition of developmental disabilities since 1970 has expanded from mental retardation, cerebral palsy and epilepsy, to include in 1975 autism and dyslexia, and, finally, in 1978, the following: a developmental disability is a severe, chronic disability attributed to a mental and/or physical impairment, manifested before the person reaches age 22, which is likely to continue indefinitely. It also

1. Results in substantial functional limitations in three or more of the following areas of major life activity:
- self care
- learning
- mobility
- self-direction
- economic sufficiency
- receptive and expressive language
- capacity for independent living

2. Reflects the person's need for a combination of individually planned and coordinated care, treatment or other services which are of extended duration.

The inclusiveness of this definition has important implications for social workers. The need for a range of available and accessible services will bring to traditional social services agencies in increasing numbers those identified as having substantial handicaps. These agencies oftentimes are not accustomed to handling a great many of the developmentally disabled, but are geared instead to what may be called generic services, i.e., a broad range of services rendered by public welfare agencies, schools, children's service agencies, counseling centers, community recreational programs, services which would incidentally include services for the developmentally disabled. The agencies, however, must now be prepared.

A shrinkage of funds for services, demands for normalization and mainstreaming, and the nature of many of the services provided to the developmentally disabled leave little doubt that the traditional social service agency is the most appropriate avenue of assistance for this population. Requests for government resources to develop specialized services designed to meet the needs of a substantially handicapped individual, when existing generic services could address such needs, will not be honored. The more accessible a variety of services become, the less is the need for specialized services.

Supportive services required for the maintenance of handicapped individuals in communities, as well as for bringing individuals currently residing in institutions back into the community, currently exist within our social service agencies. Social workers in those agencies possess the knowledge of the community, skills in problem assessment and resolution, expertise in organizational management, service coordination skills, and a grasp of legislative and funding mechanisms.

The 1978 amendments are of special significance to social work professionals because they require that 65 percent of all federal monies spent by the states must be for services in the following areas: (1) case management, (2) child development, (3) alternative community living arrangements, and (4) nonvocational social developmental services. The desired effect is to expand the traditional generic service base, but once more, these four mandated areas of service, as well as the means through which they are to be shaped into a comprehensive service network, fall within the domain of social work.

Legislation is not the only instrument of policy making which has changed the relationship between the profession and the developmentally disabled population. As the judicial branch of government has increasingly been called upon to review the activities and performance of welfare agencies and institutions, social workers as well as other professionals have been drawn, directly or indirectly, into the process. The courts have established a constitutionally protected right to treatment, set up conditions for confinement, required the preparation of individualized treatment plans, set staffing ratios, and mandated that care and treatment be provided in the least restrictive manner.

In *Wyatt v. Stickney* (1971), now *Wyatt v. Ireland,* Judge Frank Johnson recognized a constitutional right to treatment in the least restrictive setting and ordered the adoption of a series of standards for adequate habilitation. The standards included the specification of social work qualifications and worker caseloads.

The Willowbrook Developmental Center case, *New York State ACR and Parisis v. Rockefeller* (1972), now *New York State ACR and Parisis v. Carey,* was an upshot of a campaign by physicians and social workers to bring to the attention of parents and the community the unacceptable conditions which existed within the institution. In many respects, the court action was a vindication of traditional social work responsibility to advocate on behalf of clients.

In *Halderman v. Pennhurst* (1977), Judge Broderick ordered the closing of another institution and the relocation of residents in appropriate community settings. Although portions of the judge's order were overturned by the federal district court, whose ruling has been accepted on appeal by the United States Supreme Court, the implications for social workers and social work activities are clear.

The growing emphasis on client rights in court decisions as well as in mental disabilities legislation generates constraints on certain types of professional behavior and sets new requirements and procedures for professionals to follow. The social work profession, in turn, will have to adjust its training and agency practice accordingly.

The traditional role of social workers as mediators and advocates of human dignity places them in a unique position. In order for the courts to fulfill their function, they will be dependent on the expertise of various professionals and their professional organizations. Social workers, as expert witnesses, as planners, and as service providers, have important roles to play in this process. Since major portions of court orders involve the provision of social services, family involvement, and community integration, primary responsibility for implementation will fall on those who have been trained to meet the identified needs and who possess appropriate skills.

The current emphasis on generic training of social work professionals, particularly at the baccalaureate level, should better prepare social workers who encounter developmentally disabled individuals in their agency practice to be able to relate and respond to the range of needs that are presented. The growing emphasis in social work curricula at both the graduate and undergraduate levels on social policy and on legislative and judicial processes should also help prepare graduates for the demands of changing practice. In-service and continuing education programs sponsored by educational institutions and professional organizations for those currently in practice will need to be developed. The increased emphasis on rehabilitation and community-based care, as well as the need for generic community support systems, make it absolutely essential that the social work education process continue to be responsive and innovative.

Those involved in the provision of services to the developmentally disabled should follow the activities of the joint NASW-AAMD (American Association on Mental Deficiency) Task Force on Linkage. This joint task force is attempting to better identify and articulate the relationship, roles and educational needs of social workers who are identified with both professional organizations.

Sheldon R. Gelman, Ph.D., ACSW, is associate professor of social welfare at Pennsylvania State University, and director of the Undergraduate Social Work Major.

CHARLES R. HOREJSI

Developmental Disabilities: Opportunities for Social Workers

The social work profession as a whole has demonstrated little concern with the field of mental retardation and developmental disabilities, allowing itself to be represented by a relatively small number of standard-bearers. In the early 1960s, Dybwad expressed his dismay over how slow the Child Welfare League of America and the Family Service Association of America had been in responding to the concern generated by the 1961 President's Panel on Mental Retardation. He went on to write:

> The same unresponsiveness was encountered from the National Association of Social Workers whose staff stoutly maintained, all through the nationwide mental retardation planning effort initiated by President Kennedy, that this problem was outside their sphere of activity.[1]

A similar viewpoint was expressed by Adams, who stated:

> The mainstream of social work in America has not demonstrated a concern for retardation and its social implications commensurate

with that given other problem areas or with the needs of this client group.[2]

The lack of response on the part of the social work profession is mirrored in the paucity of articles on mental retardation that have appeared in *Social Work*. The dramatic changes in this field over the past ten years have not been reflected by this representative social work journal. Between 1956 and 1965, *Social Work* published 515 articles, of which 7 —or approximately 1.4 percent—were on mental retardation. From 1965 to 1975, 10 of the 652 articles (1.5 percent) focused on mental retardation. In the 6 issues of *Social Work* that were published in 1976, 1 full article and 1 brief item were on developmental disabilities.

The terms "mental retardation" and "developmental disability" are often used as if they were synonymous. However, it should be noted that although all persons who are mentally retarded are developmentally disabled, not all persons who are developmentally disabled are mentally retarded. The concept of developmental disabilities originated in the early 1970s and is officially defined in P.L. 94-103. In general, it refers to disabilities attributable to mental retardation, cerebral palsy, epilepsy, autism, and certain other conditions closely related to retardation in terms of intellectual and adaptive problems and the types of services needed.

Past Contributions

The fact that a small number of social workers, with little support from their professional organization or from schools of social work, did commit themselves to the field of mental retardation is remarkable. An examination of the literature indicates that contributions by social workers in terms of both practice and research have been made in the following areas: (1) the provision of individual and group counseling to retarded persons, and, more recently, to their parents and siblings in an effort to treat the entire family system, (2) the provision of social evaluations as part of the interdisciplinary diagnostic process, (3) the development of alternative living arrangements, especially various types of foster homes, (4) the development of protective services and the provision of social brokerage and case advocacy services designed to assist families and retarded persons in obtaining the services they need, (5) intake, prerelease, discharge planning, and case management activities related to the retarded individual's placement and movement within a service network, and (6) community organization, social planning, and administrative activities.

If social work had not played a part in the area of mental retardation, one would notice the dramatic absence of "boundary work" or intervention at the interface of social systems. Much of social work practice focuses on modifying the way in which one system interacts with other systems. Social work intervention frequently takes place at the point at which one system meets or establishes a link with another system. Helping a family (one system) to become involved in an association for retarded citizens (another system) is boundary work. Helping a retarded person to leave the institution and enter a community group home is boundary work. Helping an individual to obtain Supplemental Security Income is boundary work. Helping one agency to coordinate its services with those provided by

another is boundary work. Tasks such as intake, discharge planning, placement, case coordination, information and referral, and such roles as social brokerage, mediation, and advocacy involve boundary work or intervention at the interface of systems.

If one views social work as boundary work, the field of mental retardation is both stimulating and challenging. The needs and concerns of the mentally retarded person and his or her parents and siblings are constantly changing, and nearly every human service program—health care, counseling, income maintenance, education, legal assistance, housing, self-help groups, mental health, employment, vocational training—will have an impact on their lives. Building linkages between all these systems is a monumental task. Even more challenging is the fact that the condition of mental retardation is usually a life-long one. Thus, the social worker must be concerned about the mentally retarded infant, the elderly person who is mentally retarded, and all age groups in between.

During the past twenty years, both the social work profession and the field of mental retardation have undergone rapid change. Because of these developments, the next quarter century could bring about significant contributions on the part of the social work profession to the field of mental retardation. This is because developments in social work practice and trends within the field of mental retardation have been moving in parallel and converging directions. Potentially, this convergence could draw the mainstream of social work closer to the problems of mental retardation and generate a demand for social work.

Changing Definitions

Modern definitions of mental retardation, like traditional conceptualizations of social work intervention, underscore the reciprocal relationship between the individual and his social environment. As is shown in the following comment by Gordon, social work has always maintained a dual focus on man and his environment:

This focus has been concentrated at some times on the side of the...[person] as interpreted by psychological theory and at other times on the side of environment as interpreted by sociological and economic theory. The mainstream of social work, however, has become neither applied psychology nor applied sociology...Emphasis has been on individualizing the person-situation complex ...[and] intervening by whatever methods necessary to help people be in situations where capabilities are sufficiently matched with the demands of the situation....

The central concern of social work technology is therefore the matching of people's coping patterns with qualities of impinging environment.[3]

The theme of the interrelationship between the individual and the environment is seen as well in the following paragraph by the Accreditation Council for Facilities for the Mentally Retarded:

The service delivery system mediates between the client and his cultural environment to mitigate and compensate for the abnormalizing effects of disability...by improving the client's capabilities to provide for himself, and by modifying environmental conditions to bridge remaining gaps between personal resources and the normal fulfillment of need.[4]

Thus, there is a striking similarity between the conceptualization of social work practice and how the profession has come to view service delivery in the field of mental retardation.

The landmark definition of mental retardation, which was adopted by the American Association on Mental Deficiency (AAMD) in 1961, incorporated the concept of "adaptive behavior" to highlight the distinction between an IQ score and general social adjustment. The focus on adaptive behavior was further accentuated in the AAMD definition formulated in 1973.[5] In 1959, the same year that Heber confirmed the importance of adaptive behavior, Boehm published his notable description of the purpose of social work as the enhancement of social functioning.[6] The two concepts of social functioning and adaptive behavior are highly compatible. Both are based on role performance, like tasks, social and cultural norms, and the notion that expectations change throughout the life cycle. Thus,

a conceptual bridge has been built between the two fields.

The attention given to adaptive behavior has highlighted a number of types of behavior or areas of performance that are of special concern to social work. These include, for example, social interaction, community orientation, domestic behavior, money management, and leisure-time activity. The recent emphasis on adaptive behavior presents social work with a clear rationale for intervention, specific targets of intervention, and an opportunity to achieve a precisely defined role with this multidisciplinary field.

Many social work scholars have struggled with the following question: What is the role and function of social work in society? There is reason to believe that the profession will begin to respond with answers that are especially relevant to the field of mental retardation. Morris, for example, believes social work will begin to place increasing emphasis on the functions of care and maintenance—functions that it abandoned in the 1920s but that are highly valued by society and are still unclaimed by any other profession. He writes:

Social work needs to assert that its main responsibility includes the personal and physical care of [persons who are dependent and cannot function independently]. This ranges from the provision of specialized housing (halfway houses, group homes, etc.), location of satisfying occupational activity (not only training and counseling, but actually finding jobs, including protected jobs where necessary), the provision of home helps and chore services where necessary to buttress independent living, and even the...hand-holding and moral supportiveness which [may be required by some individuals]—not [with the expectation that] they will become completely independent of all others but are capable of continuing to function even in an assisted capacity.[7]

Morris's statement describes activities that already apply to social work practice in the field of mental retardation. If, as he predicts, the function of social caring becomes central to social work, it will do much to clarify the focus and tasks of the profession and will ultimately draw the mainstream of social work closer to the field of mental retardation.

Approaches

Accompanying the changing function of social work is the development of the social treatment method of working with individuals and families. Siporin described social treatment as the "new-old helping method." By this title, he wished to emphasize that the profession's new approaches to intervention and its current research on the type of assistance people really want and can use are causing it to return to some tasks that were common to the profession prior to the 1920s when its focus was narrowed by Freudian theory. Siporin states:

> Today the revived term social treatment is again an attempt to distinguish a pattern of direct service quite different from psychotherapeutic casework....The return to the concept of social treatment marks a major shift back to traditional perspectives....
>
> This traditional model offers a more suitable alternative to the medical symptom-illness view of social problems.[8]

The field of mental retardation is also moving away from the medical model and toward multilevel or generic models of intervention. New approaches in social work merge the roles of therapist, advocate, ombudsman, teacher, counselor, and service broker. In comparison with other models of intervention, the social treatment approach is particularly useful to the social worker in the field of mental retardation.

Applied behavior analysis, or behavior modification, is the most effective mode of intervention with persons who are moderately to profoundly retarded or with those who have limited skills in communication. However, because schools of social work have not emphasized techniques based on learning theory, many social workers do not possess this important knowledge base and technology.

It is encouraging to note that programs of social work education are moving toward the teaching of behavior technology and that numerous texts on behavior modification have been prepared by social workers for social workers. An example of this trend is the recent formation of the Social Work Group for the Study of Behavioral Methods. In addition, a large number of workshops are being conducted for social workers wishing to acquire skills in behavior technology. On the basis of this, one can conclude that social workers are giving increasing attention to a body of knowledge that is especially useful in working with persons who are mentally retarded. Training in behavior technology will greatly expand the social worker's role in this field.

Ever since the social work profession became involved in the field of mental retardation, much of its attention has focused on the parents and siblings of the mentally retarded person. Today, family considerations have taken on a new importance. Whereas the concern used to be about the psychosocial reactions of family members, there is a recent realization that parents and siblings can be powerful resources in habilitation. For example, infant stimulation, preschool programs, and various other forms of early childhood enrichment emphasize that parents must be actively involved with their children and must learn to be interveners. The data indicate that these family-oriented programs are effective. Their major limitation centers on the difficulty of obtaining the involvement of some parents.

The multiproblem family or the one that is overwhelmed by economic and environmental pressures presents a special challenge. However, it is these same families that are most in need of early intervention. More than any other profession, social work has experience with the economically deprived and the multiproblem family, and has a professional literature that describes techniques for working with these families. Thus, the family of the mentally retarded person presents a real opportunity for the application of social work knowledge, especially various outreach skills.

Recent standards of the Accreditation Council for Facilities for the Mentally Retarded and the mandates of P.L. 94-103 require that the client and the client's family participate in development of an individualized habilitation plan. These guidelines are an embodiment of two traditional social work principles—those of self-determination and client participation. The emphasis on client and family participation provides a fertile area for the application of social work knowledge and skill. The profession has had long experience in the area of total family intervention and has acquired skills important in helping families overcome the barriers in their environment.

Community Services

The movement toward deinstitutionalization and the accompanying expansion of community-based services have created a complex service network and have succeeded in multiplying the number of system boundaries. Now, more than ever, there is a demand for social work's boundary skills.

Retarded individuals, like all people, have different abilities, interests, values, and needs. Each is a unique individual with a unique potential for development. Therefore, services, opportunities, and responsibilities must be individualized and flexible. Each retarded person requires a changeable combination of services throughout his or her life span. The following case shows the variety of services that a retarded individual may need:

> John is 19 years old. After many years in an institution for the retarded, he is about to be placed in a group home in the community. In addition to a place to live, he needs a sheltered workshop where he can learn some basic work skills. There he would make some money but, as it would not be enough to live on, he needs financial assistance, such as Supplemental Security Income. John enjoyed the bowling program at the institution, and would make use of similar forms of recreation in the community. He also needs transportation to get back and forth to work and to recreation activities. During his years in the institution, he had little opportunity to learn to handle money, to care for his clothing, or to learn to use public transportation. Therefore, he needs training in personal care and "survival" skills. He also needs additional education in reading and arithmetic. Because moving into the community will require many personal adjustments, he may need counseling in addition, of course, to ongoing medical and dental care.
>
> By the time John is 22, he may have acquired sufficient skills to make it possible for him to leave the workshop and to move to a sheltered work station in a local factory. At that time, if he requires less supervision

in his daily life, he will be ready to move to a different type of group home or to a semi-independent living arrangement. As John moves within the total service system, follow-along, guidance, and advocacy are needed to insure that his programs are appropriate, coordinated, and in keeping with his human and civil rights. These services must be coupled with an ongoing evaluation of John's progress, needs, and desires.

In view of the complexity of service delivery for the mentally retarded and the variety of specialized services involved, there is a clear need for a case coordinator with a family orientation. A study by Fox concluded:

> The family must be made the central object of concern. Parents (and siblings) must have access to a central coordinator who can act as interpreter between them and the specialists who are trying to help the handicapped child. The coordinator's job will be an immensely difficult one.[9]

The emerging role of case coordinator requires a high level of boundary skills, and is closely related to the profession's traditional area of activity. Because of its expertise, the social work profession has an opportunity to take a major part in this area of work.

Social work is probably the only helping profession that has traditionally given attention to both clinical considerations and to the aspects of social policy and organization that affect service delivery. In the past ten years there has been an explosion of social work literature in the area of social planning and community organization. Here, too, is an opportunity for social workers to take what has been learned about strategies used in community organization and to apply that knowledge to the expanding programs in the field of mental retardation.

Human Rights

Society has tended to view retarded persons as less than human. The institutionalized person, in particular, has been subjected to oppression and discrimination. Skarnulis observed that the mentally retarded have been denied their human and civil rights, not only by the public but by professionals, including social workers.[10] Reflecting society's value system, social workers have participated in practices that have permitted, or at least contributed to, the dehumanization of persons who happen to be mentally retarded. Litigation is forcing the profession to reexamine its practice, its attitudes, and its beliefs. A degree of conflict and even bitterness has been generated by the movement toward deinstitutionalization and by bureaucratic competition between institutions and community-based programs. Because social workers are at the boundaries of these systems, they often find themselves in the middle of the struggle. Unless the social worker is deeply committed to human rights, he or she can become a pawn in the conflict.

Concern over the quality of services available to handicapped persons, the basic human rights of the handicapped, adherence to the principle of normalization in service delivery, and the growing militance on the part of handicapped persons have created an atmosphere of rapid social change. Given social work's rich tradition in the fight for human rights, the profession has an opportunity to lend support to this struggle for dignity.

Charles R. Horejsi, DSW, is Professor of Social Work, University of Montana, Missoula. A version of this article was presented at the Fifth Biennial NASW Professional Symposium, San Diego, California, November 1977.

Notes and References

1. Gunnar Dybwad, "Prevention as a Goal for Social Work: Is Social Work Ready To Meet the Challenges of Mental Retardation?" in Meyer Schreiber, ed., *Social Work and Mental Retardation* (Scranton, Pa.: John Day Co., 1970), p. 739.

2. Margaret Adams, *Mental Retardation and its Social Dimensions* (New York: Columbia University Press, 1971), p. 53.

3. William Gordon, "Basic Constructs for an Integrative and Generative Conception of Social Work," in Gordon Hearn, ed., *The General Systems Approach: Contributions toward a Holistic Conception of Social Work* (New York: Council on Social Work Education, 1969), pp. 6–10.

4. Accreditation Council for Facilities for the Mentally Retarded, *Standards for Community Agencies* (Chicago: Joint Commission on Accreditation of Hospitals, 1973), p. 1.

5. Herbert J. Grossman, ed., *Manual on Terminology and Classification in Mental Retardation* (Washington, D.C.: American Association on Mental Deficiency, 1973).

6. Rick F. Heber, *A Manual on Terminology and Classification on Mental Retardation* (Washington, D. C.: American Association on Mental Deficiency, 1959); and Werner Boehm, *Objectives of the Social Work Curriculum of the Future* (Vol. 1; New York: Council on Social Work Education, 1959).

7. Robert Morris, "Social Work Function in a Caring Society: Abstract Value, Professional Preference, and the Real World." Paper presented at the Annual Program Meeting, Council on Social Work Education, Philadelphia, March 1976.

8. Max Siporin, "Social Treatment: A New-Old Helping Method," *Social Work,* 15 (July 1970), pp. 16-17.

9. A. Mervyn Fox, "The Handicapped Family," *Lancet* (August 30, 1975), p. 401.

10. Ed Skarnulis, "Noncitizen: Plight of the Mentally Retarded," *Social Work,* 19 (January 1974), pp. 56–62.

MARGARET ADAMS

Ethical Issues in Work with the Developmentally Disabled and Their Families

In order to appreciate the relevance of ethics to the field of developmental disabilities and to the social worker's role in the management of developmental disabilities, it is important to have a rudimentary understanding of what the term "ethics" implies in this context. Often it and the adjective "ethical" are used as convenient shorthand for a complex of confused ideas, usually with a strong flavor of discomfort or disapproval. When, for example, a physically gross, mentally retarded, inarticulate adult is paraded before medical students to demonstrate a condition such as Apert's syndrome or Hurler's disease, some may feel a gut protest that something is wrong about exposing to such indignity a fellow human being who has almost no understanding of why he is in the situation and who is unable to defend himself by refusing to participate.[1] Underlying this immediate sense of distaste for such an affront to personal dignity is an awareness of the more fundamental ethical issues that concern the patient's right to give informed consent and the questionable morality of exploiting his misfortune for ends that yield him no benefit.[2]

However, the ethical issues do not end there. Juxtaposed to the humane argument against the abrogation of this particular patient's rights is a different but also valid claim that exposing the patient's disorder to medical students is important, even necessary, for the development of scientific knowledge whose ultimate benign end is promoting the health and welfare of individuals at future risk. If a doctor is able to recognize Apert's syndrome or Hurler's disease—both rare, inherited conditions—in a young baby, he or she could make an early diagnosis that would eliminate prolonged clinical uncertainty and allow the child's family to receive genetic counseling and perhaps forestall the birth of subsequent similarly disabled children.

This brief illustration has revealed a number of ethical questions, demonstrating the complicated nature of the topic of ethics and the imperative need for a clear, common understanding at the outset of any discussion. Ethics represent the body of ideas and knowledge that attempts to delineate the science of moral duty and the moral ends of human actions, the word "moral" in this context meaning the assignment of rightness and goodness to human behavior in its widest sense. In more practical parlance, ethical systems are a set of ideas or rules designed to provide a rational analysis of good and bad behavior, resulting in a blueprint for decisions and actions that has applicability in most situations at most times.

Ethical Relativity

There is, however, another facet of ethics that is often unacknowledged but deserves mention here because it has considerable relevance in regard to the ethical dimensions of professional practice today. This frequently unrecognized issue is that ethics are not a supraforce regulating individual and social behavior but are a product of the society whose morality they influence. They are themselves therefore subject to the dominating forces within that society.[3] This interpretation of ethics helps explain why different ethical norms are in the ascendant in different places and cultures at different phases of history. An obvious example is the notion of the sanctity of human life, which is a predominant feature of the ethical code of Western society.[4] This notion does not have the same significance in certain villages in India, where judicious infanticide is practiced on "surplus" girl infants or among Eskimos, who at one stage, if not now, solved the problem posed by their nonproductive dependent elderly by exposing them on isolated ice floes to anesthetizing cold and the eventual predations of the polar bear.[5] In both these instances the economic resources and structure of the prevailing social system could not support the extravagant ethic of maintaining life at all costs without regard to its social value.

The different ethical and social philosophy illustrated by these two examples gives rise to interesting speculation. What hidden forces underlie the Western ethic that vigorously supports the notion of the value of life in our society at the same time that many of our actual policies and practices demonstrate a commensurately strong disregard for it? On a grand scale this discrepancy is demonstrated by the nuclear arms race, which puts every human being in jeopardy. On another level, the arms race is reflected in the allocation of massive national resources for a futile end instead of for establishing an effective health service and improved living conditions in our deprived cities and rural areas. The impoverished existence of many adults and children that this policy helps perpetuate represents a serious negation of the value of life.

The relative nature of ethics is of great importance to social workers because a great number of the ethical impasses they encounter in their work—and the inequitable and sometimes ludicrous ways in which these impasses are resolved—invariably originate in the anachronistic belief that ethical norms are immutable and must be applied in all circumstances, irrespective of the disruption and harm that may follow in the wake of the decisions they dictate.[6] In Western society, which is the context of this discussion, the two dominant ethical systems are formalism and utilitarianism.[7] Formalism sets out four main principles as the basis of good conduct: (1) acting justly, (2) keeping promises, (3) dealing honestly, and (4) refraining from purposeful injury. These represent the basic ingredients for decent, constructive social interaction that would, if pursued by all members of society, lead to a harmonious and cohesive social order. The social regulation maintained by this ethical system is implicit in its basic principles. Utilitarianism, on the other hand, seeks the same goal of a just and smoothly working social order, but its main tenets articulate this more explicitly and reveal its purpose as the guiding of collective behavior to maximum efficiency. It attempts to do this by determining the rightness of an action or decision by the consequences, specifically, the extent to which an action or decision results in the greatest good for the greatest number or the best balance of pleasure over pain. The difference between formalism and utilitarianism lies in their relative emphases on the rights of individuals versus the good of society. Utilitarianism inevitably subordinates some individuals' needs and claims to the broader exigency and weal.

Formalism and utilitarianism both speak to the principles and practice of social work, which are geared simultaneously to helping individual clients achieve their highest level of personal development and to promoting the most effective interaction between individuals and the social group, system, and institutions that make up the total society.[8] However, the different focuses of these two ethical systems mirror an inevitable feature of social work, namely, the conflict involved in trying to balance fairly the claims of individual clients in need or at risk against the equally valid claims of the social system. This conflict pervades every segment of professional practice. In casework the issue may arise over plans for the care of a severely disabled dependent individual, be it an infirm elderly person, a physically handicapped young adult, a psychiatrically disturbed adolescent, or a severely retarded child, whose needs would best be met by remaining within his or her family in the community but the care of whom would impose far too much strain on family members. It may arise in group work when a disruptive group member, for example, a young retarded adult in a vocational training center, may have to be excluded because his or her behavior upsets the functioning of a program and threatens the adjustment and well-being of the other participants. Finally, this conflict may be provoked in the area of social policy and planning by the perennial dilemma of how to allocate limited resources among a variety of competing services.

Ultimately, the resolution of this conflict must mean that some clients will be better served than others. If, for example, funds were deflected from intensive-care nurseries for newborns in hospitals to community-based services providing antenatal, obstetric, and perinatal care for socially vulnerable families, a greater number of children and adults would benefit.[9] However, some vulnerable newborns with low birth weight, respiratory distress, or neural tube defects might die without intensive intervention. By ethical standards, such a policy decision would fulfill the utilitarian aim of achieving the greatest good for the greatest number. At the same time, it would violate the formalist tenet of refraining from purposeful injury. This is because both clinical experience and documented research have in various instances demonstrated that nega-

tive outcomes can be expected from withholding intervention in certain circumstances.[10]

Social Work Concerns

Dilemmas of the kind just described are encountered by members of every profession involved in the care of disabled children and adults, but they impinge with particular force on social workers for two reasons. The first is that the mandate of social work is much wider than that of its fellow professions, whose concern is primarily, if not often exclusively, the individual presenting a problem. In medicine, the patient has prime place; in education, it is the pupil with whom the teacher is concerned. Social work, in contrast, is equally concerned with the client and the social system in which the client functions, which in the first instance is the family.[11]

The second reason why such predicaments impinge on social workers with such force is that the advocacy role of workers carries with it the obligation to espouse the cause of the individual or group that is most deprived, disturbed, or at risk.[12] In some situations it is extremely difficult to decide which of two contending parties has the primary right to this attention. An example can be seen when the mother of a disabled child becomes ill and would undoubtedly become worse if she had to continue to be responsible for her child's care. Against the obvious need to protect the mother's health must be pitted the unpalatable fact that the only surrogate care available for the child cannot match that provided at home. Thus, the child's slight developmental progress might be checked and his or her potential achievement diminished after placement in a less nurturing and less stimulating environment than that provided by the mother. All these considerations, not just those relating to one party or the other, would be the social worker's concern.

From these preliminary observations it is clear that the field of developmental disabilities is fraught with a formidable array of ethical issues and dilemmas. To reduce the theme of the present discussion to manageable proportions, the rest of this article will be devoted to a single area of practice, namely, the health field and the ethical issues that are emerging in medicine concerning the prevention and management of developmental disabilities. Specifically, the author will examine pertinent ethical and social problems as they relate to different developmental phases of these disabling conditions. Throughout the discussion, the terms "developmental disability" and "mental retardation" are used interchangeably to refer to the same disorder, which involves limited intellectual and social functioning that often originates in neurological impairments.

Prenatal Diagnosis

The first stage of developmental disability to raise serious ethical issues is detectable during pregnancy or the perinatal period and is likely to involve infants with overtly or potentially crippling defects that were (1) genetically determined at conception, (2) developed *in utero,* or (3) acquired at birth or in the postnatal period. These three possibilities are illustrated, respectively, by Down's syndrome or other chromosomal anomalies, neural tube defects, and various perinatal traumas due to difficult delivery, asphyxia, respiratory distress syndrome, or low birth weight.

Two significant questions concerning this early stage of the developmentally disabled individual's career as an object of ethical controversy bear examination. Both of them involve highly emotional issues relating to the concept of human life, the right to have life preserved, and the often unfortunate sequelae of applying these concepts to a seriously damaged fetus with a very poor developmental prognosis. The first question concerns prenatal diagnosis via amniocentesis and the matter of elective abortion; the second relates to the problem of how far to intervene to secure the survival of a severely damaged newborn child.[13]

Prenatal diagnosis is an indisputably effective instrument of preventive medicine that may be used to reduce the number of children born with chromosomal anomalies, neural tube defects, certain metabolic disorders, and a variety of other rare conditions, many of which are seriously disabling and foreshorten the child's developmental prospects as well as create stress for the family into which he or she is born.[14] Forestalling the burdensome existence resulting from such a condition would appear to conform to both the formalist and utilitarian schools of ethics on various grounds. From the formalist standpoint, protecting a fetus from being born with an irremediable disability can be interpreted as fulfilling the ethical obligation to refrain from inflicting injury. Stated another way, this would save the child from enduring what has been termed a "wrongful life," which holds none of the promise of normal development and self-fulfillment that is part of human destiny.[15]

From the different perspective of utilitarianism, preventing the birth of a severely disabled child and its adverse social consequences promotes the greatest good for the greatest number on several counts. First, the unborn child is spared the unenviable fate of coping with a lifelong crippling handicap, and the family who would have been saddled with the responsibility for his or her care are spared the pressures and restrictions on their lifestyle that this kind of responsibility imposes.[16] Second, there is the wider public health benefit to be derived, namely, that preventing the births of defective babies reduces the morbidity in society as a whole.[17] Third, taking preventive measures would enable resources needed to maintain the child and support the family to be rechanneled in ways that would benefit a different but equally vulnerable section of the population.[18] This alternative target of care is the group of socially deprived children who eventually form the ranks of the mildly retarded (who constitute between 75 and 90 percent of the identified mentally retarded population) unless effective intervention is provided early in their lives.[19]

Arrayed against these utilitarian and formalist considerations are constraints relating to ethics, social work, and the law. The first and most formidable obstacle is a proscription on abortion strongly subscribed to by a number of religions and individuals.[20] This proscription is based on the belief that an embryo is a complete human being, the termination of whose existence at any point in development is equivalent to outright slaughter. This attitude brings the sociomedical measure of abortion into the judicial arena of lawbreaking and the religious orbit of sin. From a social work perspective, the option of therapeutic abortion has different but equally important ramifications that present a variety of concerns to the social worker.

First, abortion may threaten the sacrosanct tenet of self-determination and the right of every individual to make decisions about his or her life, some of the most sensitive of which are those affecting childbearing and family planning.[21] From a professional standpoint, the social worker may be very conflicted about what attitude to adopt toward a mother who is reluctant to terminate a pregnancy even though amniocentesis has identified a severely impaired fetus. On the one hand, the mother's right to make this decision demands respect, particularly in view of the deep emotions associated with pregnancy and parenthood. In addition, evidence indicates that pressure brought to bear on an unwilling mother to abort a fetus can lead to psychological disturbance.[22] On the other hand, if the mother has a highly unrealistic approach to disability and a limited appreciation of the problems of giving birth to and rearing a handicapped baby, the social worker has an equally strong obligation to help her understand and foresee some of the pitfalls, difficulties, and heartache that she and her family are likely to face.[23]

A second important consideration for the social worker is the fact that the birth of a disabled child will in all probability have a powerful impact on other family members. Siblings in particular will be affected if the infant's care absorbs an undue amount of parental time and energy to their detriment.[24] As the social worker's professional concern is as much with social systems as with the individual client, there must be a firm commitment to safeguarding the welfare of the family as a whole.

Third, from the angle of social policy,

which is another vital part of social work's domain, the worker must be alive to the question of how society may react to circumstances in which public resources may be required to help subsidize the special care of a handicapped child, whose birth could have been prevented had the parents elected to terminate the pregnancy.[25] Will society's dawning realization that such claims on its resources are avoidable lead to a subtle erosion of toleration and compassion toward all disabled or less well-endowed individuals? Will this in turn eventually lead to a withdrawal of support from this sector of the population as a whole, irrespective of whether their disabilities could have been prevented? This represents a dangerous social and ethical issue that has connotations resembling those associated with the stigma of irresponsibility and accusations of "scrounging" that have been endured by financially insolvent members of society who have to be supported by public assistance.[26]

Intervention: How Far to Go?

When one moves beyond the ethical issues that relate to the time of pregnancy and the fetal stage, other issues arise that relate to the second lap of the disabled child's initial phase of existence. The actual birth of a child with a severe (and perhaps totally unanticipated) disability and a limited capacity for survival creates the clinical and social dilemma of how much should be invested in immediate care to save his or her life. Such situations are becoming more common as expertise in neonatal care develops, and they raise many of the same social and ethical questions that the matter of prenatal diagnosis does: What is the individual's right to life? Should all available treatment be used to preserve life under the precarious circumstances being considered here?[27]

The emphasis with which these questions are asked is slightly different, however, when the object of concern is unquestionably a human life rather than a fetus, to which full human status is not accorded by everyone, including the courts. The legal constraints protecting this life are therefore stronger than those that safeguard the life of a fetus.[28] In addition, the right-to-life argument assumes greater poignancy when it is embodied in a weak infant whose very vulnerability makes claims on everyone's nurturant and medical skills. Indeed, a whole range of new concerns and issues arises in regard to a newborn infant at risk. A basic problem is that it is rarely possible to predict the extent of disability or latent potential accurately in a newborn, and this clinical uncertainty is compounded by a whole spectrum of opinions, feelings, and philosophical thoughts on what constitutes a worthwhile life to be saved as opposed to one with no future.[29] Some parents prefer to have their disabled child survive irrespective of cost and willingly assume the burden of care, whereas others openly question the wisdom and value of intensive medical efforts that leave them with a severely disabled child whose care requires an inordinate investment of their energy and time.[30] A retrospective study undertaken with families of children who had been born with neural tube defects and had been helped to survive through intensive intervention revealed that some mothers expressed open regret about the decision made in favor of survival.[31] Thus, the drama of heroic medical intervention may contrast sharply with the long and often isolated haul of looking after the survivor of such a clinical venture.

This reality brings home the point that social workers should play an essential role in resolving the clinical dilemma of how far survival efforts should be pursued. The worker is in the best position to appreciate the crucial long-term social consequences of survival and to convey these to the family without their assuming that he or she has an inevitable bias toward clinical intervention rightly or wrongly associated with physicians. Some parents feel inhibited about admitting to a physician that they would prefer their child to die, but they may find it possible to confide this socially forbidden wish to the more receptive social worker, whom they may not think of as part of the medical staff. The worker also has the advantage of being able to help parents make a more realistic appraisal of their future plight because he or she is *au fait* with the services that are likely to be available (or, perhaps as important, unavailable) to them in their daunting task.

Ordinary vs. Extraordinary Care

Many of the ethical issues considered in regard to the prenatal and neonatal stages of life also relate to the management of the retarded older child or adult. The question of survival and right to life will crop up whenever the child or adult who is mentally disabled and severely physically impaired develops a secondary illness or condition that can be controlled by normal treatment but whose cure represents the empty prolongation of a vegetative existence. One example in the author's experience was a woman of 26 who had lived in a state school since early childhood and who was blind and emaciated and had a badly twisted physique and virtually no awareness of her environment. This patient periodically developed pneumonia and was admitted to the infirmary for treatment with antibiotics that controlled her illness and staved off death but had no impact on her extensive impairment and primitive functioning.

From one perspective, there would have been little ethical justification for depriving this patient of treatment that was simple and safe and would automatically have been supplied to another patient with a more optimistic prognosis. From the opposite standpoint, it can be argued that this young woman was functioning at such a primitive level and her biological resources were so limited that it was counter to nature to help her foreshortened life continue when a natural solution would have been at hand if only officious medical technology had not intervened. Besides permitting the cessation of a life-in-death existence of benefit to no one (there was no concerned family in this case), the solution at hand would have meant a saving of time, money, and the professional resources necessary for keeping this patient fed, clean, and comfortable.

Nevertheless, beyond these rational assessments of the case are a number of social and ethical considerations that cannot be lightly dismissed.[32] The first of these concerns the standards governing residential facilities that accommodate severely impaired patients. It is of overriding importance that such facilities maintain and be seen to maintain rigorous ethical standards in their caretaking and treatment policies, for this is insurance against the potential abuse that could (and has been known to) occur within segregated institutions for patients who are inarticulate, seemingly unaware, and totally helpless.[33] Adhering to an unimpeachable standard is also necessary for building up staff morale, particularly staff members' sense of doing a job that is of social value. This is crucial for people who deal with a basically unresponsive patient population, work with whom may sometimes seem unrewarding. Second, it is vital that parents and other relatives who have surrendered a retarded family member to surrogate care feel that their decision will always be in the patient's best interest. Third, it is important for members of the surrounding community to know that the social service represented by residential care, which they have indirectly mandated and financed, is run along lines that are compassionate and humane and reflect unquestioned integrity. An institutionalized population with marked deficits and of low social utility is probably the most devalued of any group in society. Without the ethical safeguards that have been mentioned here, it could be all too easy for the public to slip into a frame of mind in which this population is seen as less than fully human and therefore as not eligible for the consideration automatically given to other members of society.[34]

Advocating medical attention to save a severely disabled adult from pneumonia may seem illogical when juxtaposed to a failure to advocate intensive care for defective newborns. However, withholding medical care from a given individual when it is available to everyone for a specific complaint such as pneumonia represents a deliberate and discriminating act of omission based on a value judgment that the patient's life is useless by all criteria of normalcy and therefore does not merit efforts to save it. Even more significant is the fact that such a decision would exploit a fortuitous medical event—the onset of pneumonia —that is independent of the patient's primary disability. In contrast, the newborn baby with multiple clinical and developmental anomalies originating from congenital neurological impairment presents a different situation. Such a child starts life as a severely damaged biological organism for whom there is little expectation of survival under his or her own steam and who may, even with intensive care, fail to develop to a level of mental or physical functioning regarded as halfway normal.[35] The decision against instituting heroic salvage measures on this child's behalf is therefore not a deliberate omission of normal care but a withholding of extra care of a special kind, and the provision of this care does not appear justified in view of the very poor quality of life that clinical evidence forecasts for the infant's future.[36]

Quality of Life

A different type of ethical problem arises in regard to medical treatment that is necessary for a particular illness but has a number of adverse side effects, such as prolonged pain, discomfort, or changes in bodily function. Such treatment may result in greater harm than benefit for the mentally retarded patient, particularly when its outcome is not certain. Patients of normal intelligence can be given an explanation of possible complications to help them decide whether the adverse features of medical care are outweighed by the long-term prospect of possible success. However, mentally retarded patients are unlikely to achieve an understanding of the experience of pain in the short run or of the possibility of being saved from death or serious illness in the long run. They will thus have no compensatory hope to carry them through the physical misery and mental distress that may accompany treatment. When the chances of beneficial outcome are even or less, one can argue that not subjecting the patient to treatment is in his or her best interest.[37]

This stance may suggest a value judgment that a retarded individual's life is less worthy of preservation than that of someone who is of normal intelligence. In reality it represents a respectful attitude toward those who are retarded and a realistic acceptance of what constitutes quality of life for them, rather than the imposition of an absolute standard that is unrelated to their capacity for understanding experience, enjoyment, distress, or pain. In social work terms this is an instance of individualizing the client's unique needs instead of applying a global prescription to them. It is an important aspect of case management, because the current emphasis on securing the long-overdue rights of the mentally retarded carries with it the risk that the specific nature of these rights may be overlooked. As a result, the rights usually associated with "normality" may be imposed on mentally retarded people without any attempt to accommodate the idiosyncratic characteristics of these individuals.[38] In the type of situations under discussion, ethical standards of practice and patients' rights may be more genuinely pursued by ensuring patients' overall well-being through limiting their exposure to potential distress and pain instead of extending their scope for living.[39]

These issues are illustrated by the case of Joseph Seikerwicz, a longtime resident at a state school, who developed terminal leukemia at the age of 67. Seikerwicz's physician and two close relatives considered appropriate treatment and decided against the administration of a particular drug that might have been effective in controlling Seikerwicz's disease and thus in prolonging his life but would have caused him a great deal of pain. The patient was a strong, heavily built man of very limited comprehension, and it was considered probable that rigorous physical restraint would be needed to contain his reaction to the treatment. Overall, it was felt that the suffering and distress entailed in the proposed treatment would be more harmful to Seikerwicz than withholding the drug would be. However, the local association for retarded citizens was anxious about this apparent violation of the right to treatment and brought the case before a county probate judge, who appointed an advocate. The advocate initially supported legal action to enforce the use of

the drug until he realized the distressful circumstances under which it would have to be administered. At this point he applied to the court for permission to reject this treatment for Seikerwicz, on the grounds that the possible benefit of prolonging the patient's life would be overridden by the suffering he would have to endure in the meantime.[40]

Specialized Treatment

When those who are mentally retarded need complicated specialized treatment that is costly and in short supply, another issue arises. Should such treatment be made equally available to mentally retarded individuals and to individuals of normal intelligence with more promising social potential?[41] As in the case of the institutionalized patient described earlier, there would seem to be no justification for depriving handicapped patients of treatment known to benefit them, and withholding treatment would be an outright violation of human rights. Moreover, from an ethical perspective, determining eligibility for medical treatment on the basis of social characteristics rather than clinical criteria would run counter to the formalist tenet of acting justly because it would be depriving potential patients of their common entitlement to health care.

However, other considerations are relevant. Among them are the utilitarian ethic concerned with how to promote the greatest good for the greatest number, as well as the fact that when dealing with restricted resources—which include professional personnel and skills as well as money—some establishment of priorities is inevitable.[42] Because medical care is basically a social resource whose ultimate end is maintaining the health of a viable society, the assignment of limited resources may have to be related realistically to the longer-term impersonal goal of productivity as well as to the immediate needs of individuals. From a social work perspective, the much more crucial point is not whether selection procedures have to be instituted for medical care in short supply but whether the criteria for determining eligibility for care are based on a rational analysis of the situation and the justice of competing claims rather than on an ill-thought-out prejudice. Stereotyped thinking is apparent in the assumption that there is little or no point in trying to prevent or remedy one type of disorder if a patient suffers from another that is not related to the first and will therefore not be favorably affected by its treatment.

As already indicated, social workers are trained to focus on the social as well as the clinical aspects of disability. They can play an important role in resolving some of the issues described by pointing out the social facets of clinical treatment that may not be immediately obvious, such as the impact that help for a patient may have on his or her family. Even when a particular treatment does not appear able to improve a patient's functioning, the minimal progress it effects may make all the difference in terms of the degree of stress the family is experiencing and be critical in determining whether the patient can continue at home rather than have to be placed in a residential facility.

An illustration of the potentially detrimental effect of disregarding the social components of clinical intervention is provided by the case of a man with Down's syndrome who lived in London and developed a serious hearing loss in his early 30s. The medical center specializing in speech and hearing problems to which he was first referred refused to prescribe the hearing aid routinely available to hard-of-hearing patients through the British National Health Service because of doubts that the patient would be able to understand how to manipulate it properly. This attitude may have been reinforced by the belief that a hearing loss would make little material difference to someone already afflicted with "subnormal" intelligence and limited social competence. Not satisfied with this decision, the patient's family sought a second consultation and found a physician who was prepared to listen to their side of the story. They explained that despite his impaired speech, their son could communicate with them and understand and follow simple instructions very well and that they were convinced he would soon learn how to use the hearing device. They added that

listening to records and music on the radio was one of his principal pleasures in life.

Accordingly, a hearing aid was prescribed for the patient, who soon mastered its intricacies and was thus enabled to pursue his normal pattern of life like any other hard-of-hearing patient fitted with the same device. However, one can speculate on what would have happened had assistance been withheld in this case. The patient would have been deprived of his hobby of listening to music, his social interaction at the vocational center he attended would have been seriously circumscribed, and a hitherto happy, well-adjusted, socially acceptable man might have become withdrawn and unhappy or bored. In addition, emotional or behavioral problems might have developed that could have had a disastrous impact on the patient and family.

This case embodies many of the social and ethical issues that are latent in even seemingly straightforward medical care. First of note are the shortcomings exhibited in the first medical consultation, in which an accurate diagnosis or assessment of the patient's mental ability and his capacity for learning a new and complex task was not made. Second, no consideration appears to have been given to the social implications of the patient's hearing loss, to the restrictions such a loss would have imposed on his social functioning, or to the diminished social status that would have resulted. Third, the patient's basic entitlement to a form of treatment that was appropriate to his condition (as the subsequent outcome showed) and part of a national health service available to everyone was totally disregarded. The earlier management of the case illustrates what can happen when the social and ethical components of treatment are overlooked and ignored. It also points up the vital necessity of having a social worker involved in this and kindred situations to serve as interpreter and advocate regarding aspects of the patient's situation that are outside the medical frame of reference.

However, this would have been a more complex dilemma if the device in question had been in short supply or had been disproportionately expensive. Under such circumstances, it might legitimately be asked whether hearing aids should be reserved for more able-bodied patients who without them would suffer greater hardships and social penalties—such as a university student who would be unable to complete his or her education—or who had social responsibilities whose failure to be discharged would adversely affect a number of other people—for example, a wage earner whose employment would be at risk and who would not be able to support a home and family as before. It would be to society's great disadvantage if patients such as these remained disabled. In the first instance, educational resources would be wasted if the student were forced to drop out of school; in the second, support for the patient and family might well have to come from public funds if the patient were no longer self-supporting.

The author would not consider it a breach of ethical standards to give the treatment of these individuals priority over that of a mentally retarded patient, as long as the decision were based on a rational and accurate assessment of the complex social variables at work and the relative claims for treatment were objectively weighed. This approach recognizes that the provision of medical care must to some extent be cost-effective in terms of how much it promotes the social adjustment and productivity of the individual patient and, from that, the maintenance of an efficiently functioning society as a whole.[43]

Further Considerations

The final point to be made about the relationship among ethics, social work, and developmental disabilities concerns the administrative mechanisms for managing the complex social and clinical problems touched on in this discussion. The effective management of developmental disabilities requires an interdisciplinary team in which the social worker is recognized as having a cardinal role in both assessment and intervention.[44] This social work contribution to the interdisciplinary operation is especially necessary for dealing with the ethical issues that constantly crop up in regard to developmental disabilities. Although

a consideration of these issues is triggered off by clinical events that occur in a medical setting, the immediate crisis of ethical deliberation and decision is generally played out against a complicated background of social expectations, demands, and needs, concerning which the social worker has the sharpest insight and greatest expertise.

An illustration of this point can be seen in the recurrent ethical dilemma over whether to perform surgery for duodenal atresia on a newborn with Down's syndrome if the parents do not wish the baby to survive.[45] If the professionals concerned in such a case decide it is ethically wrong to withhold normal, ordinary life-saving treatment, they also have the responsibility of making certain that appropriate provision has been made for the child's care outside the parental home, in a setting in which the infant will be guaranteed full opportunity for development, happiness, and fulfillment as a human being. In practical terms, this means a vigilant monitoring of the whole spectrum of social services available to the mentally retarded. In this instance it also means bringing constant pressure to bear to ensure that there is an adequate supply of foster homes where children in such circumstances can be placed at birth. Reinforcing this basic service must be a battery of supportive programs accessible to the child during all phases of his or her life.[46] These services would include medical surveillance, special education, vocational training, sheltered employment, and day care, as well as a permanent guarantee of residential care within the community.[47] Without this essential provision of substitute parental care, the ethical drive to secure the infant's survival will result in an empty benefit if the child has to drag out an unfulfilled existence in a sterile institutional setting that has limited facilities for fostering development or observing basic human rights.[48]

This specialized service provision is thus a crucial component in the overall management of the problem at hand because it helps secure for the infant the nurturing environment needed to replace the family home and takes into account all the implications this placement has for the infant's personal and social well-being. On these grounds it falls squarely within social work's domain and highlights the profession's indispensable contribution to the solution of the social and ethical dilemma presented by this clinical situation.

If the situation is viewed from a different angle, another question arises: Is society allocating its resources effectively in saving the life of this individual, whom it then has to support throughout his or her lifetime, when abstaining from intervention would have resulted in death and absolved society of responsibility for his or her ultimate welfare?[49] This knotty question is a good one on which to end on two counts. First, it highlights the conflicting claims of the formalist and utilitarian ethical systems as these are embodied, respectively, in the obligation to safeguard an infant from death and in the need to protect society's right to deploy its finite resources to achieve the greatest good for the greatest number. Second, it illustrates social work's particular dilemma of being caught between a concern for the welfare and rights of the individual and a commitment to the broader welfare of society at large and of the anonymous other clients "out there" who have equally pressing needs.[50] This conflict is not new to social work. It is inherent in the very notion of society and social organization and in the need to strike a balance between the claims of individual and collective justice. For this reason the social worker has an especially important role to play in the field of developmental disabilities in identifying these complex issues, defining their nature, interpreting their implications in the management of developmental disabilities, and helping to achieve an equitable solution to the moral dilemmas raised.

Margaret Adams, MA, is Research Associate, Department of Child Health, University of Bristol, England. An earlier version of this article was presented at the 105th Annual Meeting of the American Association on Mental Deficiency, Detroit, Michigan, May 25, 1981.

Notes and References

1. L. B. Holmes et al., *Mental Retardation: An Atlas of Diseases with Associated Physical Abnormalities* (New York: Macmillan Publishing Co., 1972), pp. 222 and 224.

2. Alexander Capron, "Legal and Moral Rights," in Bruce Hilton et al., eds., *Ethical Issues in Human Genetics: Genetic Counseling and the Use of Genetic Knowledge* (New York: Plenum Press, 1973).

3. Mervyn Susser, "The Works of George Rosen," *International Journal of Health Services,* 10 (1980), pp. 323–328.

4. Arthur Dyck, "The Value of Life," paper presented at the Third Annual Joseph S. Barr Intensive Care Limit Symposium—"The Ethics of Intensive Care," Massachusetts General Hospital, Boston, Mass., February 26, 1974; Harold Himsworth, "The Human Right to Life: Its Nature and Origins," in Hilton et al., eds., *Ethical Issues in Human Genetics;* and Helga Kuhse, "Debate: Extraordinary Means and the Sanctity of Life," *Journal of Medical Ethics,* 7 (June 1981), pp. 74–82.

5. Personal communication, John Wyon, Associate Professor, School of Public Health, Harvard University, Boston, Mass., March 1976.

6. Terry Hamblin, "Withholding Treatment in Infancy," *British Medical Journal* (April 1981), p. 1154.

7. See W. D. Ross, *The Right and the Good* (Oxford, England: Clarendon Press, 1930); and John Stuart Mill, *Utilitarianism, Liberty, Representative Government* (London, England: Everyman University Library, 1972).

8. Carel B. Germain, "The Ecological Approach to People-Environment Transactions," *Social Casework,* 62 (June 1981), pp. 323–331; and Charles R. Horejsi, "Developmental Disabilities: Opportunities for Social Workers," *Social Work,* 24 (January 1979), pp. 40–43.

9. Pamela Davies, "Perinatal Mortality," *Archives of Disease in Childhood,* 55 (November 1980), p. 833.

10. John Freeman, "The Shortsighted Treatment of Myelomeningocele: A Long-Term Case Report," *Pediatrics,* 53 (March 1974), pp. 311–313; and John L. Kiely et al., "Cerebral Palsy and Newborn Care, II: Mortality and Neurological Impairment in Low-Birthweight Infants," *Developmental Medicine and Child Neurology,* 23 (1981), pp. 650–659.

11. Carel B. Germain, ed., *Social Work Practice: People and Environments* (New York: Columbia University Press, 1979).

12. Ad Hoc Committee on Advocacy, National Association of Social Workers, "The Social

Worker as Advocate: Champion of Social Victims," *Social Work,* 14 (April 1969), pp. 16–22; and Mary J. McCormick, "Social Advocacy: A New Dimension in Social Work," *Social Casework,* 51 (January 1970), pp. 3–11.

13. See Tabitha Powledge and John Fletcher, "Guidelines for the Ethical and Social and Legal Issues in Prenatal Diagnosis," *New England Journal of Medicine,* 300 (January 25, 1979), pp. 168–172; Raymond Duff and A. G. Campbell, "Moral and Ethical Dilemmas in the Special Care Nursery," *New England Journal of Medicine,* 289 (October 23, 1973), pp. 890–894; and Michael King, "Defective Babies and Death by 'Natural' Causes," *Guardian,* March 16, 1981, p. 7.

14. Consensus Development Conference on Antenatal Diagnosis Task Force, *Predictors of Hereditary Disease or Congenital Defects* (Washington, D.C.: Public Health Section, National Institutes of Health, 1979), sec. 5, p. 146.

15. Michael Bayles, "Harm to the Unconceived," *Philosophy and Public Affairs,* 5 (Spring 1976), pp. 292–304; and H. T. Engelhardt, "Euthanasia and Children: The Injury of Continued Existence," *Journal of Pediatrics,* 83 (July 1973), pp. 170–171.

16. S. Dorner, "The Relationship of Physical Handicap to Stress in Families with an Adolescent with Spina Bifida," *Developmental Medicine and Child Neurology,* 17 (December 1975), pp. 765–776; and B. Tew and K. M. Laurence, "Some Sources of Stress Found in Mothers of Spina Bifida Children," *British Journal of Preventive and Social Medicine,* 29 (March 1975), pp. 27–30.

17. Consensus Development Conference on Antenatal Diagnosis Task Force, *Predictors of Hereditary Disease or Congenital Defects.*

18. George W. Albee, "Need—A Revolution in Caring for the Retarded," *Transaction,* 5 (1968), pp. 37–42; and Michael Rutter and Nicola Madge, *Cycles of Disadvantage* (London, England: Wm. Heinemann Medical Books, 1976).

19. H. Garber and F. R. Heber, "Effectiveness of Early Intervention in Preventing Mental Retardation," in Peter Mittler, ed., *Research to Practice in Mental Retardation,* Vol. 1 (Baltimore, Md.: University Park Press, 1977).

20. R. M. Hare, "Abortion and the Golden Rule," *Philosophy and Public Affairs,* 4 (Spring 1975), pp. 201–208; and Thomas Hilgers and J. Dennis Horan, eds., *Abortion and Social Justice* (New York: Sheed & Ward, 1975).

21. F. E. McDermott, ed., *Self-determination in Social Work: A Collection of Essays on Self-determination and Related Concepts by Philosophers and Social Theorists* (London, England: Routledge & Kegan Paul, 1975); Donald Brieland, "Bioethical Issues in Family Planning," *Social Work,* 24 (November 1979), pp. 478–484; and Eugene Brody, "Reproductive Freedom, Coercion

and Justice," *Social Science and Medicine,* 10 (1976), pp. 553–557.

22. R. Kuman and Kay Robertson, "Previous Induced Abortion and Antenatal Depression in Primiparae: Preliminary Report on a Survey of Mental Health in Pregnancy," *Psychological Medicine,* 8 (November 1978), pp. 711–715; P. Donnai, N. Charles, and R. Harris, "Attitudes of Patients After 'Genetic' Termination of Pregnancy," *British Medical Journal* (February 1981), p. 282; and E. C. Semay, "Therapeutic Abortion: Clinical Aspects," *Archives of General Psychiatry,* 23 (November 1970), pp. 408–415.

23. Brian Tew and K. M. Laurence, "Mothers, Brothers and Sisters of Patients with Spina Bifida," *Developmental Medicine and Child Neurology,* 17 Supplement 29 (1975), pp. 69–76; David Wilkin, *Caring for the Mentally Handicapped Child* (London, England: Croom Helm, 1979); and Elizabeth Wilson, "Exploited Mothers," *Social Work Today,* 2 (January 1972), pp. 6–7.

24. Ann Gath, "Sibling Reactions to Mental Handicap: A Comparison of the Brothers and Sisters of Mongol Children," *Journal of Child Psychology and Psychiatry,* 15 (July 1977), pp. 187–198; and Diana Pomeroy et al., "Improving the Quality of Life for Families with a Mentally Handicapped Child," *Parent's Voice,* 28 (1978).

25. Anne Fry, "Call for Resources for Those We Keep Alive," *Community Care* (September 17, 1981).

26. Frank Field, "Scroungers: Crushing the Invisible," *New Statesman,* 101 (November 16, 1979).

27. M. Absalon, "The Right to Live and the Right to Die," *British Medical Journal* (August 1981), pp. 611–612.

28. J. A. Robertson and N. Fost, "Passive Euthanasia of Defective Newborn Infants: Legal Considerations," *Journal of Pediatrics,* 88 (May 1976), pp. 883–885.

29. See K. M. Laurence et al., "Reliability of Prediction of Outcome in Spina Bifida," *Developmental Medicine and Child Neurology,* 18, Supplement No. 37 (1976), pp. 150–156; Richard A. McCormick, "To Save or Let Die: The Dilemma of Modern Medicine," *Journal of the American Medical Association,* 229 (July 1974), pp. 172–176; Joseph Fletcher, "Indicators of Humanhood: A Tentative Profile of Man," *Hastings Centre Report,* 2 (1972), pp. 1–4; R. S. Illingworth, "The Right to Live and the Right to Die," *British Medical Journal* (August 1981), p. 612.

30. Carol Hosey, "Yes, Our Son Is Still with Us," *Children Today,* 2 (1973), pp. 14–17 and 36.

31. A. M. Fox, *They Get This Training But They Don't Really Know How You Feel* (London, England: Action Research for the Crippled Child, 1975).

32. Margaret Adams, "Ethical Problems in Mental Retardation—Who Shall Live?" seminar

held at the Walter E. Fermald State School, Waltham, Mass., October 28, 1973.

33. Stephen Goldby, "Experiments at the Willowbrook School," *Lancet* (April 1971), p. 749; and S. Krugman, "Experiments at the Willowbrook State School," *Lancet* (May 1971), pp. 966–967.

34. Leo Alexander, "Medical Science Under Dictatorship," *New England Journal of Medicine,* 241 (February 1949), pp. 39–47; and Joseph Margolis, "Theoretical Difficulties Regarding the Moral Status of the Severely and Profoundly Retarded," paper presented at the Sixth International Congress of the International Association for the Scientific Study of Mental Deficiency, Toronto, Ont., Canada, August 26, 1982.

35. J. Lorber, "Selective Treatment of Myelomeningocele," *Pediatrics,* 53 (1974), pp. 307–308.

36. Kuhse, "Debate."

37. Gunyar Karayalcin, Alan Shanske, and Richard Honigman, "Wilm's Tumors in a 13-Year-Old Girl with Trisomy 18," *American Journal of Diseases of Children,* 135 (July 1981), pp. 665–666.

38. Barry Hoffmeister, "Would You Want to Be Normalized?" *Westminster Institute Review,* 1 (April 1982).

39. Renee C. Fox, "The Sting of Death in American Society," *Social Service Review,* 55 (March 1981), pp. 42–59.

40. Ibid.

41. Ralph B. Potter, "Labeling the Mentally Retarded: The Just Allocation of Therapy," in Stanley J. Reiser, Arthur J. Dyck, and W. Curran, eds., *Ethics in Medicine: Historical Perspectives and Temporary Concerns* (Cambridge, Mass.: M.I.T. Press, 1977).

42. Alastair V. Campbell, *Medicine, Health and Justice: The Problem of Priorities* (Edinburgh, Scotland: Churchill Livingstone, 1978); and Daniel Callahan, "Shattuck Lecture—Contemporary Biomedical Ethics," *New England Journal of Medicine,* 302 (May 1980), pp. 1228–1233.

43. W. I. Card and G. M. Mooney, "What Is the Monetary Value of a Human Life?" *British Medical Journal* (December 1977), pp. 1627–1629; and Victor Fuchs, *Who Shall Live? Health, Economics, and Social Choice* (New York: Basic Books, 1975).

44. Rosalie Kane, "Multidisciplinary Teamwork in the United States: Trends, Issues, and Implications for the Social Worker," in Susan Lonsdale, Adrian Webb, and Thomas L. Briggs, eds., *Teamwork in the Personal Social Services and Health Care: British and American Perspectives* (London, England: Croom Helm, 1980).

45. Christine Doyle, "A Baby's Right to Live—or Die," *Observer,* August 16, 1981; Larry Costin, "Court of Appeals Authorisation of Operation on Infant with Down's Syndrome," *Lancet* (August 1981), p. 467; and "An Authorisation of Operation on Infant with Down's Syndrome," *Lancet* (August 1981), p. 413.

46. Peter Gilbert, "Fostering and Mental Handicap," *Adoption and Fostering,* 102 (1980), pp. 43–46; and Joseph Tavormina, "Examining Foster Care: A Variable Solution for Placement of Handicapped Children," *American Journal of Community Psychology,* 5 (Winter 1977), pp. 435–446.

47. See Margaret I. Griffiths, ed., *The Young Retarded Child: Medical Aspects of Care* (Edinburgh, Scotland: Churchill Livingstone, 1973); R. Faulkner, "Opportunity Classes—A Study of Voluntary Integrated Nursery Classes for Handicapped and Normal Children," *Community Medicine,* 120 (1971), pp. 213–217; A. H. Hayden and N. G. Haring, "Early Intervention for High Risk Infants and Young Children: Programs for Down's Syndrome Children," in Theodore D. Tjossem, ed., *Intervention Strategies with High Risk Infants and Grandchildren* (Baltimore, Md.: University Park Press, 1976); Gene Hensley, "The Contribution of Education," in Richard Koch and James C. Dobson, eds., *The Mentally Retarded Child: A Multidisciplinary Handbook* (New York: Brunner/Mazel, 1971); Peter Beresford and Patience Tuckwell, *Schools for All: Education for Severely Mentally Handicapped Children* (London, England: MIND, 1978); E. Whelan, "Basic Work-Skills, Training and Vocational Counselling of the Mentally Handicapped," in Mittler, ed., *Research to Practice in Mental Retardation,* pp. 377–386; Elias Katz, *The Retarded Adult in the Community* (Springfield, Ill.: Charles C Thomas, Publisher, 1977); *Helping Mentally Handicapped School Leavers,* Pamphlet No. 2 (London, England: National Development Group for the Mentally Handicapped, 1977); Tony Apolloni, Joan Cappucilli, and Thomas P. Cook, eds., *Achievements in Residential Services for Persons with Disabilities* (Baltimore, Md.: University Park Press, 1980); and Alan Tyne, *Residential Provision for Adults Who Are Mentally Handicapped* (London, England: Campaign for the Mentally Handicapped, 1977).

48. Dorothea Braginsky and Benjamin N. Braginsky, *Hansels and Gretels: Studies of Children in Institutions for the Mentally Handicapped* (New York: Holt, Rinehart & Winston, 1971); C. MacAndrew and R. Edgerton, "The Everyday Life of Institutionalised 'Idiots,'" *Human Organisation,* 23 (1964), pp. 312–318; Maureen Oswin, *Children in Longstay Hospitals* (London, England: Wm. Heinemann Medical Books, 1978); and "The Silent Minority," Independent Television Viewing, London, England, June 10, 1981.

49. See Fry, "Call for Resources for Those We Keep Alive."

50. J. Cooper, "The Uneasy Response to Social Problems and Private Sorrows," *Social Work Today,* 6 (1976), pp. 646–650.

MICHAEL J. BEGAB

Psychosocial Aspects of Mental Retardation

The behavior and development of mentally retarded persons, like that of all other human beings, is a product of the interaction of biological, psychological, and social forces operating within the individual's cultural environment. Everyone is shaped by the environment to some degree, especially by his or her family, and, in turn, influences others. For some, the circle of influence is far-reaching; for most, it may be limited to the orbit of family life.

Although everyone is affected by these forces, the nature of an individual's constitutional endowment determines the degree of their impact. Each individual differs genetically in intellect from other individuals. In a highly favorable setting, genetics imposes the ceiling on development and performance; under inadequate or unfavorable conditions, the environment is the factor more limiting to individual growth.[1]

This tenet of behavioral theory seems to be largely ignored by a large number of professionals in the field of mental retardation today. In their zeal and enthusiasm for raising IQs, many practitioners have generated numerous intervention programs, only to be disappointed when early gains were not sustained.[2]

Were Head Start and the other noteworthy programs of the Great Society failures? Probably not. The problem lay in the prevailing expectations, in an extreme environmentalist euphoria, and in a reversion to Watsonian psychology optimistically claiming that if the proper strategies and energies were used, anyone could be molded into anything. Had outcomes been measured and goals set in terms of personal and social behavior rather than intellectual growth, many professionals would conceivably have been more pleased with their achievements.

Nevertheless, the emphasis on abilities rather than disabilities has reflected a positive movement. The potential of retarded persons, even the more severely handicapped, has been grossly underestimated in the past. Today the pendulum is swinging to the other extreme. Individual limitations have been swept aside under the thrust of normalization and "least restrictive alternatives" to the point that the existence of actual handicaps is often denied and needed protections are overlooked.

Similarly, a concern about labeling and the consequent push toward mainstreaming have resulted in the decertification as mentally retarded of many thousands of children who have thereby become ineligible for special services. The jury is still out on this development, but negative changes in classification and diagnosis could create the illusion that the prevalence of retardation in the population has diminished substantially and could thus reduce public support for special programs and increased access to services.[3]

These are but a few of the issues that relate to the psychosocial aspects of mental retardation. Some of them may touch on the total spectrum of intellectual performance, but most are especially pertinent to the mildly retarded. It is important to note that psychosocial factors contribute to the etiology of retardation, have a critical influence on amelioration and treatment, and bear heavily on family stability and community interests. They can be modified, manipulated, and, to some degree, regulated and controlled. Moreover, they fall squarely within the domain of social work skills and responsibility. If current efforts in providing services are to succeed, such as in the areas of classroom integration, alternative community placements, stabilization of the family, and employment and leisure time opportunities for the retarded, social workers must have a better understanding of the nature, origins, and determinants of intelligence, of the issues relevant to programs of intervention, and of the need for professional resolution of the continuing debate on institutions versus community alternatives.

Determinants of Intelligence

The relative contributions of nature and nurturance to the etiology of mild mental retardation, in which central nervous system pathology is not demonstrable, remain an unresolved issue. The influence of both factors has always been recognized, but over the years changes in terminology have revealed significant shifts in the assessment of their comparative importance.[4] Individuals who were mildly mentally retarded were originally classified as "familial defectives," indicating that the condition was considered a family-based genetic trait. Subsequently, the terms used were "cultural-familial defectives," "sociocul-

tural retardation," and "psychosocially disadvantaged," each change reflecting a greater emphasis on the part played by environmental variables.[5]

Research into the origins and determinants of intelligence is inconclusive, partly because of methodological difficulties encountered in studies dealing with human development. In research in which animals are used as subjects, the animals can be bred for specific genetic traits, variables having causal significance can be manipulated, and changes in behavior and brain structure can be measured, but studies of human subjects are largely dependent on naturally occurring circumstances. Adoption and foster family care are cases in point: these are natural occurrences that present an excellent opportunity for empirical investigation. In general, however, educational intervention and early stimulation programs are quasi-experimental, with limited control possible over the range of variables affecting development.

Biological and psychosocial influences on intelligence are not easily isolated from one another in the mildly retarded, who are overrepresented in the lowest socioeconomic segments of society and who come from families in which housing, nutrition, and medical care are frequently inadequate, diseases are common, and children are exposed to poor mental stimulation.[6] However, these conditions are common among poor people generally. The 10 percent of the poor who are retarded differ from the poor in general in regard to maternal education and IQ. Retardation in the families of the retarded poor can be interpreted as being due to polygenic inheritance or, conversely, to an unsuitable learning environment, or to a combination of both these factors.

Genetic Evidence

It is of interest to note that although research on animals assigns a predominant role to genetics in determining level of intelligence, environmental factors are also acknowledged. Experiments have demonstrated that rats placed in an enriched, stimulating setting learned better than rats not exposed to the setting and that their behavioral changes were correlated with structural changes in the brain. Specifically, the brains of the rats placed in an enriched environment contained more enzyme of the kind associated with learning ability, as well as larger cells and a thicker cortex.[6] It cannot be known whether similar chemical or structural changes occur in children, but the implications for human intervention are clear: for animals, and possibly for children as well, the "nature" of the organism is not immutable and can be modified by stimulation.

Nevertheless, the genetic foundation of individual differences in intelligence and in behavioral traits is well established beyond debate. The role of genetics in determining characteristics within various socioeconomic groups is less clear, although assortative mating undoubtedly contributes to observed between-group differences. Geographically isolated groups differ from other groups in regard to their gene pools, and the distribution of gene frequencies is manifest in regard to nearly all anatomical, physiological, and biochemical traits. It is highly plausible to extend the relevance of such findings to intelligence and to properties of the central nervous system.[7]

Despite heated debate, the National Academy of Science has taken the position that a selection program to increase human intelligence would almost certainly be successful to some extent and that the same is probably true for other behavioral traits.[8] Such a program, however, might not be compatible with prevailing values and belief systems. Furthermore, whether general intelligence exists or, if it does, whether it can be precisely measured is still in doubt.

Studies of twins and other individuals related to each other are probably the best natural experiments for evaluating the determinants of intellectual development. The IQs of identical twins reared in the same environment have the highest correlation among IQs of family members. The correlation among IQs is lower for identical twins who have been reared apart, but it is still above that found among fraternal twins. This finding is the most compelling evidence that IQ is largely determined by genetics.[9]

In studies dealing with adoption, critical variables affecting development are difficult to control or measure. Despite this limitation, in a review of seventeen major studies conducted from 1922 to the present, Munsinger concluded that the home environment provided by adoptive parents has little effect on the intellectual growth of their adopted children.[10] This conclusion was based on the finding that the correlation between adoptive parents' IQs and those of their adopted children was $r = .19$, whereas that between the IQs of biological parents and the IQs of their children was $r = .58$. In general, studies dealing with twins and instances of adoption support the hypothesis that the influence of genetics explains individual differences in intelligence.

Environmental Evidence

Somatic elements play an unspecified role in the development of subclinical defects that may impair intelligence. Nutritional factors, teenage pregnancy, noxious agents such as drugs, alcohol, and chemicals, and prematurity are the most common examples of such elements. When their influence has been significant, clinical symptoms are clearly evident. When it has been mild, it may interact with psychosocial forces in more subtle ways to depress IQ.

In the final analysis, however, quality of life is the most crucial determinant of all. The family relationships, child-rearing practices, mental stimulation, and affectional experiences to which the mildly retarded are exposed are often qualitatively submarginal. Furthermore, the parents and siblings of mildly retarded and psychosocially disadvantaged children, who frequently have large families, are generally of low intelligence, with poor communication skills. Adherence to their parents' speech patterns can impede language acquisition in these children, who may consequently not be prepared for the formal speech required of them in school. In addition, family pathology and marital and legal conflicts are common among the families of the mildly retarded. Living conditions may be crowded, privacy rare, and children's exploratory behavior unguided. Within such families, children have limited access to models of adult behavior worthy of emulating.

Taken singly, the effects of these variables on cognitive performance may be negligible. When taken together, their interactive influence may follow geometric rather than additive principles. This ensures that a child's potential, however limited, will not be fully realized.

Models for Change

Attempts to counteract the devastating effects of family pathology and cultural deprivation have led to various studies and, at the same time, to tests of the impact of environmental factors.[11] These studies have followed three basic models:

1. Many have taken the form of child-focused programs oriented toward the acquisition of language, preacademic, social, and personal skills. These programs have varied in concept, underlying theory, intensity, duration, content, structure, and age of entry and of termination for participants. Programs in this category have been the most widely applied and heavily criticized among intervention efforts, and they have been preoccupied with outcomes in terms of IQ. In evaluating their efforts, a consortium report indicated that children exposed to this type of intervention had fewer special class placements and were more likely to be promoted in school. However, no permanent gains of consequence were discernible in participants' IQs.[12]

2. Several other studies have taken the form of parent-child programs, which seem to be more effective than those just described and to produce gains that are sustained longer. However, these experimental programs have been applied to poor rather than retarded parents. Their goal, the modification of parent-child interactive behavior, is a sound concept, but the efficacy of these programs with multi-problem families is still to be tested.[13]

3. Various other studies have adopted an ecological approach. Of the three models described, this approach has generated the largest IQ gains for the longest time, but it has not been applied on a large scale.[14] Implementing the ecological approach may require separating children from their families. It therefore involves ethical problems in selecting families for intervention and may understandably present a threat to parents' self-esteem and result in resistance.

Although finding new families for highly vulnerable children is probably the most effective method of ensuring intellectual growth, it runs counter to deeply ingrained values. There is little doubt that intelligence can be positively altered by relocation, but the strategies for accomplishing this on a society-wide scale remain to be developed. Nevertheless, the changes possible in a given individual are limited, and it has been estimated that moving from the worst to the best possible environment early in life can result in a gain of 20 to 25 IQ points.[15] Such shifts in living conditions rarely occur, however, and it is clear that any approximation of possible degree of intellectual change must take into account every parameter of a child's life experiences and place special emphasis on the family.

As experts on the family, social workers carry a heavy burden of responsibility that demands a realistic appraisal of the retarded person's strengths, weaknesses, and capacity for change; the needs, problems, and modifiability of the family; and the resources, attitudes, and readiness of communities to accept and integrate retarded individuals. It also demands a careful examination of current philosophies and trends, the validity of widely touted opinions, and the impact of all these on the retarded and their families. The psychosocial dimensions of retardation are complex, and dealing with them is an integral part of social work practice.

Current Trends

Contemporary philosophy in the field of mental retardation stresses the concepts of normalization, mainstreaming, and deinstitutionalization. These are valuable concepts but are not new. Historically, to the author's knowledge, at least 95 percent of the mentally retarded have always resided in the community, and placement outside the institution has been an integral part of many programs from the very beginning.[16] Similarly, the great majority of the retarded have always attended regular classes and were, as a rule, not officially designated as retarded.

However, the elevation of normalization and deinstitutionalization to the level of ideology has polarized professionals and parents into two camps: those who believe that these concepts have universal application, regardless of the nature of the individual's handicap or behavior, and those who do not. Although people on both sides of the controversy are well intentioned, self-serving interests contribute to the conflict.

The rapidity of change fostered by these national trends in favor of deinstitutionalization and the often-indiscriminate use of community alternatives have, in numerous cases, proved a disservice to the retarded and their families. In the surrounding debate and courtroom disputes, everything about institutions has been painted as evil, while all aspects of the community have assumed a halo of unblemished virtue. Neither viewpoint is supported by facts, and, unfortunately, although much good has been achieved, what was once the province of professional judgment has been taken over to a large extent by the judicial system.

In general, a zealous concern about human rights, which has more recently been applied to the mentally retarded, has sometimes displaced concern about human needs and protections. Many mentally retarded persons caught up in the fervor to close institutions are being exploited, exposed to stresses with which they cannot cope, subjected to repeated failures and rejection, and led down the garden path—but with their "rights" intact.

The facts about deinstitutionalization are just beginning to emerge. If the movement's success is measured by the rate of readmissions to institutions, it is clear that placement programs today are better than those in years past. Nevertheless, the rate of failure is still much higher than desired, and many retarded individuals experience transfer to community placement as one more rejection in a lifetime of such events.[17]

The record on successful placement lends little credence to the notion that institutions have no continuing role in providing the spectrum of services required by mentally retarded persons. The mentally ill have fared even worse than the retarded. Half of all mentally ill individuals discharged from public mental hospitals return within the first year.[18] Within three years, 65 percent are readmitted. The figures concerning the mentally retarded are somewhat more favorable. In 1974, 34 percent of those discharged from institutions were readmitted, a figure higher than the percentage placed in the community.[19] Over the years, some studies have reported recidivism whose rate has ranged from 13 to 60 percent. Economic conditions, preplacement, training activities, job opportunities, and the availability of community support services are some of the factors contributing to this variation in reported percentages.

However, such statistics are grossly misleading. Although return to the institution is an objective measure, it is an extremely crude criterion. Discharged clients may be returned because of incompetent caretaking, the discontinuation of a program, community intolerance, lack of resources, and other limitations or occurrences having little or nothing to do with the individual's competence or behavior. On the other hand, operators of private group homes who are concerned about maintaining a full complement of residents may limit freedom of movement, prolong dependence, and tolerate bizarre behavior. In short, depending on a range of environmental factors, maladaptive behavior or inadequate social adjustment may sometimes result in readmission and at other times in retention in the community. Statistically, the former situation is rated a failure, but the latter is considered a success. Because follow-up data on community placements indicate that the majority of those discharged do not return and "disappear" from the service system, conventional wisdom has it that the adjustment of these individuals has been satisfactory.[20] Studies based on surveys, however, conceal more than they reveal and indicate little about the nature or degree of adjustment or social integration achieved.

Efforts at Evaluation

A continuing problem in assessing community placement programs is the lack of agreement regarding the relevant variables by which adjustment is to be measured. If retarded adults are to be evaluated by the same criteria that are applied to the general adult population, then severely and profoundly retarded individuals and probably a significant number of the moderately and mildly retarded would fail to meet performance criteria. These individuals would have difficulty maintaining themselves in independent living arrangements without some form of supervision and could neither compete effectively in industry nor manage the complexities and responsibilities of marriage and parenthood. They would also be likely to evidence deviant, bizarre, and socially unacceptable behavior. By the rigorously defined criteria of past decades, many of those presently residing in the community would have to be considered failures. Fortunately for the movement toward deinstitutionalization, far less stringent criteria are now considered acceptable.

Some of the best insights into the life experiences of the mentally retarded are derived from ethnographic research. In participant observation studies, much is learned about the process, problems, and strategies used by the retarded in adjusting to their environment. Findings reported by Edgerton in his classic "cloak of competence" study indicate that remaining in the community is hardly synonymous with success.[21] Out of an original sample of 110 subjects, most of those studied returned to the hospital more than once. Among the sample of 48 subjects followed over several years, one-fourth displayed maladaptive behavior, whether characterized as alcoholic, criminal, or antisocial in nature. The quality of life for the total sample declined somewhat with the passing years, although 3 out of 4 subjects were considered to have adjusted reasonably well.

Still more revealing was another study by Edgerton that dealt with mildly retarded adults who had never been in an institution.[22] These subjects were clients of social agencies and had been selected by the social work staff as most likely to achieve goals related to normalization. They were all Caucasian, of middle-class background, without physical handicaps, and willing to participate in the study.

Out of a group of 48, 18 led relatively trouble-free lives and were model citizens in most areas of major life functioning. For another 20, adjustment was, at best, marginal. The men engaged in fighting, psychotic behavior, passing bad checks, drug and alcohol use, homosexuality, and violence; the women's behavior was marked by promiscuity, suicide threats, adultery, assault, drug use, and fraud. These behaviors were seldom reported to legal authorities and were not looked on as especially deviant or serious by neighbors. The remaining 10 subjects had been arrested for assault, theft, manslaughter, wife beating, robbery, burglary, car theft, and various incidents of violence and alcohol abuse.

These data, on a sample of subjects with presumably excellent potential, indicate that many mentally retarded adults have difficulty in adapting to the stresses of community living, perhaps because of limitations they may have in the areas of problem solving, reasoning, judgment, and impulse control. The data also suggest that for some—a minority no doubt—other resources for rehabilitation and treatment are necessary. Among these resources, short-term residential care for specific purposes may be essential. In the absence of institutionalization, many of the mentally retarded may end up in mental hospitals, hospitals for the criminally insane, or in prison. Their prospects for rehabilitation in these settings is, at best, very poor.

It is noteworthy that in Edgerton's two ethnographic studies, individuals who were previously hospitalized were found to be better adjusted in the community than those who had never been in an institution. One could argue that separation from sources of conflict in the community had a stabilizing effect, helped bring behaviors under better control, and actually had a rehabilitative influence on the retarded persons who had been in institutions. This is a provocative thought, though a not fully substantiated thesis. It is imperative that in working with the retarded, professionals make certain that they are guided by facts and not by opinion, by reality and not by myth, and by clinical judgment and scientific findings and not by philosophy. In this way the needs of the retarded, their families, and their communities will be best served.

Michael J. Begab, Ph.D., is Special Consultant to the President, University Park Press, Baltimore, Maryland. An earlier version of this article was presented before the Social Work Division at the 106th Annual Meeting of the American Association on Mental Deficiency, Boston, Massachusetts, June 2, 1982.

Notes and References

1. D. O. Hebb, *The Organization of Behavior* (London, England: Chapman-Hill, 1949).

2. Urie Bronfenbrenner, *Is Early Intervention Effective? A Report on Longitudinal Evaluations of Preschool Programs,* Vol. 2, U. S. Department of Health, Education, and Welfare Publication No. (OHD) 76-30025 (Washington, D.C.: U.S. Government Printing Office, 1974).

3. D. L. MacMillan, R. L. Jones, and G. F. Aloia, "The Mentally Retarded Label: A Theoretical Analysis and Review of Research," *American Journal of Mental Deficiency,* 79 (1974), pp. 241–261.

4. R. C. Nichols, "Origin, Nature, and Determinants of Intellectual Development," in Michael J. Begab, H. C. Haywood, and H. L. Garber, eds., *Psychosocial Influences in Retarded Performance: Issues and Theories in Development,* Vol. 1 (Baltimore, Md.: University Park Press, 1981).

5. H. Grossman, *Manual on Terminology and Classification in Mental Retardation* (Washington, D.C.: American Association on Mental Deficiency, 1973).

6. D. Krech, M. R. Rosenzweig, and E. L. Bennett, "Relations Between Brain Chemistry and Problem-solving Among Rats Raised in Enriched Environments," *Journal of Comparative Physiology and Psychology,* 55 (1962), pp. 801–807.

7. Arthur Jensen, "How Much Can We Boost I.Q. and Scholastic Achievement?" *Harvard Educational Review,* 39 (1969), p. 80.

8. J. Crow, J. V. Neil, and C. Stern, "Racial Studies: Academy States Position on Call for New Research," *Science,* 158 (1975), pp. 892–893.

9. N. Juel-Nielsen, "Individual and Environment: A Psychiatric-Psychological Investigation of Menozygotic Twins Reared Apart," *Acta Psychiatrica Scandinavica,* Supplement, 183 (1965).

10. H. Munsinger, "The Adopted Child's I.Q.: A Critical Review," *Psychological Bulletin,* 82 (1975), pp. 623–659.

11. For a discussion of some of these studies, see Bronfenbrenner, *Is Early Intervention Effective?*

12. I. Lazar et al., *The Persistence of Preschool Effects,* Final Report, U.S. Office of Human Development Services (Washington, D.C.: U.S. Government Printing Office, 1979).

13. Michael J. Begab, "Issues in the Prevention of Psychosocial Retardation," in Begab, Haywood, and Garber, eds., *Psychosocial Influences in Retarded Performance.*

14. Bronfenbrenner, *Is Early Intervention Effective?*

15. Ed Zeigler, untitled, unpublished remarks before the American Medical Association, Chicago, Illinois, 1977.

16. See *A National Plan of Action to Combat Mental Retardation,* report of the President's Panel (Washington, D.C.: U.S. Government Printing Office, 1962).

17. B. Willer and J. Intagliata, "Social-Environmental Factors as Predictors of Adjustment of Deinstitutionalized Mentally Retarded Adults," *American Journal of Mental Deficiency,* 86 (1981), pp. 252–259.

18. Robert B. Edgerton, "Failure in Community Adaptation: The Relativity of Assessment," in K. T. Kernan, Michael J. Begab, and Edgerton, eds., *Environments and Behavior: The Adaptation of Mentally Retarded Persons* (Baltimore, Md.: University Park Press, 1983).

19. R. N. McCarver and E. M. Craig, "Placement of the Mentally Retarded in the Community," in N. R. Ellis, ed., *International Review of Research in Mental Retardation,* Vol. 7 (New York: Academic Press, 1974).

20. See M. Moen, D. Bogen, and D. Aanes, "Followup of Mentally Retarded Adults Successfully and Unsuccessfully Placed in Community Group Homes," *Hospital and Community Psychiatry,* 26 (1975), pp. 754–756.

21. Robert B. Edgerton, *The Cloak of Competence* (Berkeley: University of California Press, 1967).

22. Edgerton, "Failure in Community Adaptation."

MARYANNE P. KEENAN

Standards for Social Workers in Developmental Disabilities: An Overview

In 1982, the Board of Directors of the National Association of Social Workers (NASW) approved a set of standards for social work in developmental disabilities.[1] This action represented the culmination of a lengthy and cooperative effort between two national organizations, NASW and the American Association on Mental Deficiency (AAMD), and resulted from the shared recognition of the need for standards in an area of mutual concern. The significance of the document that was produced becomes evident when the general purposes and potential uses of the standards that were generated are examined.

Standards as Benchmarks

All professional standards are benchmarks that delineate acceptable professional practice. That is, they describe the minimum level of professionalism generally considered requisite for practice in a given field. Any standard may perform several functions. It can specify a guiding principle ("social workers shall meet the expectations of conduct established by the NASW Code of Ethics"); state educational requirements ("social work services shall be provided by a social worker with a graduate degree from a school of social work accredited by the Council on Social Work Education"); describe functions that must be performed ("social workers shall keep records including statistics as needed for the management, education, and planning of the program"); or identify desired outcomes or any other pertinent condition or requirement ("the worker shall strive to prevent child abuse and neglect"). It is essential that standards be written as clearly and explicitly as possible to minimize the possibility of misinterpretation. Most standards are accompanied by a statement of interpretation to ensure that the criteria outlining what is acceptable are clearly defined.

Professional standards can be described according to their content as well as their function. Those standards that deal with staff qualifications or requirements and program specifications are sometimes referred to as service delivery standards. When standards focus on the quality of activities carried out or on the time or resources devoted to an activity, they are called process standards. Finally, when standards specify desired results, they are labeled outcome standards. The development of various types of standards and

41

a conceptual framework such as the one just described is considered the responsibility of a professional organization. Therefore, although the description of standards presented here is used by NASW, it is also referred to in the literature on standards generated by many other professional organizations.

Standards can be categorized as general or specialized. General professional standards are broad statements that apply to all practitioners, such as a profession's code of ethics. Specialized standards relate to practice within a given area. An example of specialized standards are NASW's Standards for Social Work in Health Care Settings.[2] In some cases, the work of a profession may require standards of varying complexity. For example, because of the diversity of health care settings in which they practice, social workers often need the more specific guidance provided by even more specialized standards, such as the Standards for Social Work in Developmental Disabilities that were approved in 1982. As a rule, each specialized type of standard should refer to but not repeat a profession's more general standards.

Regardless of how they are categorized, all professional standards are sources of information about practice. Standards provide the practitioner with guidelines for action and with a means of evaluating performance. They inform the public about the nature of acceptable practice and can be used as a focal point for public demands to improve services. For example, standards developed by NASW have been used as reference points in allegations of professional misconduct brought forth by clients, agencies, and social workers and in attempts to change state and federal regulations affecting the profession. Standards also inform professionals in other disciplines of the parameters of acceptable performance in a given field. They become a tool for achieving professional accountability and avoiding the duplication of services. Without these explicit guidelines, it is difficult for the public, professionals in other fields, policymakers, or even practitioners themselves to assess the adequacy and quality of services that have been provided.

NASW Standards

Text of the Standards

The Standards for Social Work in Developmental Disabilities were created through collaboration between the AAMD's Social Work Division and NASW, as a result of a shared commitment to establishing a level of competence expected of all social workers practicing in settings in which the disabled are served. A number of individuals reviewed and critiqued the many drafts of the standards as they were produced. An early draft was circulated to AAMD social work regional representatives, state officers, fellows, and other selected AAMD members as well as to social work directors of University Affiliated Programs and to educators who teach course material on mental retardation and developmental disabilities. The next draft was reviewed by NASW's National Committee on Health Quality Standards and was mailed to one thousand members of AAMD's Social Work Division for comment. It was then presented at the division's business meeting for approval and at a general session that was part of AAMD's Annual Meeting in 1982. The final version of the standards was approved by NASW's Board of Directors in June 1982. Although the standards represent a consensus of current social work opinion across the country concerning social work practice in developmental disabilities, it is assumed that they will be revised as necessary in the future.

The standards are accompanied by extensive statements of interpretation. These statements will be summarized after the following listing of the standards themselves:

• *Standard 1.* All social workers working with developmentally disabled clients shall possess or acquire and develop knowledge about developmental disabilities.

• *Standard 2.* All social workers shall subscribe to a set of principles regarding developmental disabilities which should underlie their practice.

• *Standard 3.* Social work practice and research shall seek to prevent or reduce the incidence of developmental disabilities.

• *Standard 4.* All social workers shall participate in an interdisciplinary approach to serving the needs of developmentally disabled people.

• *Standard 5.* The functions of the social work program shall include specific services to the client population and the community.

Statements of Interpretation

It can be seen that Standard 1 indicates social workers should maintain background knowledge about developmental disabilities. This background would include a familiarity with the etiology of developmental disabilities and theories on growth and development, an understanding of family dynamics, an acknowledgment of the kinds of support that may be necessary to enhance the client's functioning, and a grasp of information about resources available to the developmentally disabled. Standard 2 alludes to the general principles regarding developmental disabilities that form the basis for social work practice. These principles include concern for providing support over the entire life span of the client, maximizing the client's potential, and maintaining the least restrictive environment for the client. Standard 3 stresses the need for research and practice aimed at the prevention of developmental disabilities, and its statement of interpretation spells out the ways in which social workers should play a role in primary, secondary, and tertiary prevention. The interpretation accompanying Standard 4 notes how and why social workers should function as members of an interdisciplinary team in order to meet the needs of the developmentally disabled most effectively. Last, the discussion of Standard 5 refers directly to NASW's Standards for Social Work in Health Care Settings in describing the types of services that should be provided to the developmentally disabled. Some of the services mentioned are discharge planning, outreach, advocacy, community liaison efforts, and the identification of individuals who are at risk.

Usefulness for Practice

Social workers who deal with developmentally disabled clients are found in settings that are as varied as the circumstances of the developmentally disabled and their families. Social work professionals practice in community-based residential programs, state and local health departments, schools, nursing homes, and direct service agencies, as well as in medical settings. With increasing frequency, schools of social work offer courses or internships in the field that focus on the needs of the developmentally disabled.

Because the role of social work with the developmentally disabled is expanding, it was essential to establish a baseline for professional functioning and to formulate guidelines for professional practice. NASW's standards guide social work practice and, just as important, demonstrate to the developmentally disabled and others that social workers have a commitment to providing high-quality services. The standards delineate the social work perspective on the interrelationship among individuals, families, and their environment. They also affirm social work's support of the concept of normalization as a means of maximizing each client's potential. Thus, the standards should facilitate the integration of social work practice in the field of developmental disabilities.

It is anticipated that a wide audience will use the standards. Their value for providers of direct services and the recipients of services has already been discussed. The standards can also help social work educators structure courses and field placements in the area of developmental disabilities, and planners and administrators may find them helpful in preparing policies and procedures or program evaluations.

In addition, policymakers should consult the standards as part of the process of developing regulations, and private accreditation organizations should refer to them in formulating criteria for assessing the quality of services provided to the developmentally disabled. Finally, the standards are a tool for educating social workers about their responsibilities to the developmentally disabled and, at the same time, for informing consumers about the services social workers can offer.

A lengthy collaborative process has resulted in the creation of the standards, which are to be used in conjunction with other standards developed by NASW. Their primary intent is to establish a baseline for the delivery of exemplary social work services. NASW and AAMD hope that the standards will be an important addition to already existing standards for guiding professional activity in the field of developmental disabilites and will make a significant contribution to improving social work practice in this area.

Maryanne P. Keenan, MSW, is Senior Staff Associate in Health Policy, National Association of Social Workers, Silver Spring, Maryland, and a doctoral student, School of Hygiene and Public Health, Johns Hopkins University, Baltimore, Maryland.

Notes and References

1. See "Standards for Social Work in Developmental Disabilities," in *NASW Standards for Social Work in Health Care Settings,* NASW Policy Statement 6 (Silver Spring, Md.: National Association of Social Workers, revision in press).

2. See *NASW Standards for Social Work in Health Care Settings,* NASW Policy Statement 6 (Washington, D.C.: National Association of Social Workers, 1981).

Part Two

Social Work with the
Developmentally Disabled

Introduction to Part Two

Only recently have significant numbers of social workers been concerned with working with individuals who are developmentally disabled. Previously, the social worker's role had been limited to effecting changes within groups that ranged from the family to the community as a whole. This shift in focus was an indirect consequence of the sweeping changes in society's treatment of the developmentally disabled brought about by the normalization movement.

As long as the developmentally disabled individual was regarded as fit only for institutionalization, the social worker could safely ignore his or her particular problems and potentialities and deal instead with caretakers. The person who was developmentally disabled figured in the social worker's endeavors primarily in regard to a constellation that included family, institution, and social agencies.

As institutions emptied out, however, and the social worker's time was increasingly devoted to arranging placements in the community, attention was inevitably drawn to the developmentally disabled person as an individual. Experience soon showed that IQ—the primary basis of the label of "developmentally disabled"—was an unreliable predictor of successful community adjustment. However, within limits broadly set by the person's disability, social competence was a powerful determinant of success. Because social skills could be learned, the individual became a fitting subject for intervention.

Thus, social workers developed competence in assessing and modifying their clients' social skills. The establishment of creative programs for training clients in specific social behaviors and for enhancing their self-esteem became a key element in social work interventions.

This transformation of professional attitudes also permitted a rethinking of the needs of developmentally disabled people in the community. The belief that mentally retarded people could not benefit from psychotherapy had prevailed among helping professionals and was common even among social workers. Yet workers have now come to realize that the adjustment problems of the developmentally disabled client are not outside the domain of social work knowledge and skills. Whether the individual is afflicted with epilepsy, hearing impairment, mental retardation, or cerebral palsy, similar problems in psychosocial functioning require similar solutions. Social workers are needed to foster formal and informal support networks, identify and resolve conflicts in cultural values, and assist in bringing about a positive and supportive relationship between the individual and the family.

All the selections in Part Two dealing with social work practice with developmentally disabled clients locate that practice in the community. Each selection emphasizes various approaches to the enhancement of the individual's psychosocial functioning and details the interventions with illustrative clinical examples. The first three articles focus on adults; the next three present strategies for effecting change with children. All comment on the relative neglect of this area by social workers and urge increased commitment by the profession.

In the first selection, Milofsky identifies the needs of developmentally disabled clients in terms of the tasks these individuals need to carry out. These range from mundane daily tasks such as routines related to personal hygiene to what Milofsky refers to as community support and institutional access tasks. He acknowledges the new self-help movement for handicapped individuals living in the community, pointing to ways in which professionals can offer support to this movement by identifying and constructing informal networks of people to assist in the training of new social skills and to serve as advocates for the developmentally disabled.

Walker's focus is on increasing social workers' awareness of the mental health needs of developmentally disabled people. He presents two case examples in which clients who live with their parents are helped with casework intervention and highlights the clients' feelings and needs with the clients' own words. He also recognizes that the family dynamics contributing to the self-concept of the developmentally disabled client powerfully affect the client's behavior.

Another approach is discussed by Selan, who writes about psychotherapy with developmentally disabled adults in an outpatient setting. In effect, Selan "normalizes" the problems of these individuals by outlining the following goals for developmentally disabled clients and making clear that these goals apply to all clients: alleviation of painful or uncomfortable symptoms, realization of intellectual potential, improvement of socially unacceptable behavior, development of emotional maturity, and reinforcement of coping mechanisms. She then proceeds to describe the unique features of the interviewing process and the special skills needed to accomplish these goals with the developmentally disabled. Although Selan encourages social workers to increase their involvement in this kind of practice, she cautions that certain therapeutic virtues are needed in extra measure for effective work with the developmentally disabled population, namely, patience, an ability to provide structure, a specialized knowledge base, and a sense of humor.

The next selection on individual intervention focuses on early detection of the child at risk. Kurtz provides information on the correlations among poverty, child abuse, and developmental disabilities, stressing the urgency of early intervention. Several examples are presented to suggest roles for social workers.

Henry, DeChristopher, Dowling, and Lapham also explore aspects of working with children. Under Public Law 94-142, the federal government requires that schools attend to the individual student who has exceptional needs. At a minimum, the social worker's role in the school requires the collection of a social history. The authors present a structured social history outline, with case vignettes illustrating sociocultural factors that affect the cognitive performance of the child. In addition, they demonstrate the need to attend to the child's feelings and offer suggestions on the use of the outline by interdisciplinary assessment teams in the schools.

Last, Panzer, Wiesner, and Dickson describe innovative intervention modeled after the Big Brothers of America program. The authors' project included poor black and Hispanic children who were mildly handicapped, were from single-parent families, and were drawn from a clinic for the developmentally disabled. These clients were paired with graduate students with the goal of promoting their social development and decision-making skills through a one-to-one relationship and a variety of activities. At the same time, respite was provided for their mothers during their participation in the activities planned. One special issue addressed by the authors was the effect of the difference in cultural backgrounds between the students and the children.

Because this collection focuses on intervention and not on epidemiology, we have, reluctantly, omitted papers on a range of special problems experienced by the developmentally disabled and other people that have to do with such topics as alcoholism, parenting, sexuality, poverty, and juvenile delinquency. In light of this omission, we must emphasize here that the problems of developmentally disabled individuals do not all stem from their disability. There is a great overlap between the populations of the developmentally disabled and the poor. That poor people are disproportionately affected by all kinds of social problems is amply documented. The problem of poverty lies behind many of the gravest presenting symptoms of the developmentally disabled, not excluding intellectual deficits and developmental disabilities themselves. The problems of the disabled client, then, must always be assessed and addressed within the client's social context.

CARL MILOFSKY

Serving the Needs of Disabled Clients: A Task-Structured Approach

Disabilities are increasingly defined in terms of functional limitations rather than as aspects of illness. Treated as illnesses, disabilities are seen as fixed, objective limitations that cause people to be excused or excluded from responsibilities of normal life. These people are considered deviant.[1] Treating disabilities as specific adaptive failures, however, emphasizes the supports or adaptations that would allow disabled individuals to be reintegrated into important social institutions, including the family, the local community, the economic system, schools, and the health and welfare system.

The movement toward deinstitutionalization has stimulated this new perspective on disabilities. As public policy, deinstitutionalization has had uncertain success. In some areas, its pursuit was more a measure of economy than a way of improving care, and some people who were unprepared to care for themselves were turned out on their own nonetheless.[2]

Self-Help Movement

In many areas, however, deinstitutionalization has helped the disabled and their families become aware of possibilities for self-help. Self-help organizations have sprung up among elderly, mentally ill, quadraplegic, deaf, and mentally retarded individuals.[3] Legislative reforms reflect this new activism. Public transportation systems are required to provide kneeling buses, in which entrance steps can be lowered to make climbing aboard easier. The Education for All Handicapped Children Act (P.L. 94-142) guarantees an appropriate and least-restrictive education to all children. Public facilities must be redesigned to provide access for the handicapped.

Although welcome, the self-help movement creates certain problems for providers of social services. Professional assistance must now be less direct and oriented more toward teaching concrete survival skills than toward protecting and caring for clients. The disabled themselves must now perform functions of basic personal care.

Self-help organizations and publications provide disabled persons with support, services, and skills. For example, *the Independent,* a magazine published by the Center for

Independent Living, a collective of multiply handicapped people in Berkeley, California, carries articles on preferred methods for turning over in bed without assistance and for selecting people to provide help with dressing and other necessary functions. The center helps people in Berkeley locate housing, roommates, and jobs and helps them manage relations with social welfare agencies. Gilbert's book, *You Can Do It from a Wheelchair,* gives similarly detailed instructions on such things as how to vacuum from a wheelchair and how to get up after having fallen on the floor.[4] Organizations exist that engineer devices to help the handicapped with specific problems.[5] One device provides greater leverage for turning the starter key in an automobile, a task a woman with rheumatoid arthritis found difficult. The goal of the self-help movement and these organizations is to help the disabled help themselves and each other with a minimum of regular or professional help from the nonhandicapped. Naturally enough, there may even be hostility toward social workers or rehabilitation therapists who traditionally have provided care of the disabled and guidance of their families.

Providing Services

Given this new awareness on the part of the handicapped, one way service providers may contribute is by helping the disabled construct networks of people to assist them with the small but necessary tasks that must be done by all people living independently. If one cannot change a light bulb, pick up bills dropped on the floor, go down a flight of stairs, read the labels on grocery store items, or put on a urinary appliance, for example, one will cease to function eventually. Independence for disabled individuals means that they must learn to accomplish these chores. They may develop adaptive skills for some tasks. Other tasks require that helpers be found. But many handicapped people have limited mobility, maintain few social contacts, and lack needed social skills. For these individuals, service providers must locate helpers. To do so, providers should understand the kinds of tasks disabled

individuals must do and the kinds of helpers, typically "amateurs," who may be recruited to assist them.

Detailed knowledge of the regular tasks disabled individuals must do is presently lacking. This article discusses four areas of functioning with which disabled individuals may have difficulty. With these in mind, social welfare programs must decentralize services to fit the needs of disabled clients that result from their functional limitations.

Activities in general can be categorized by whether they involve autonomous or social tasks and whether they are intimate or impersonal. These variables refer less to the tasks themselves than to their social meaning and the kinds of people who might be recruited to help with them. The degree of disability an individual experiences is related to the availability of people who may provide appropriate help as well as to an incapacity to complete tasks alone.

Autonomous tasks are activities that generally can be done without assistance and that do not imply cooperation from others in their performance. Social tasks are activities that require more than one person to complete. Impersonal tasks are ones that may be carried out by members of general social categories: neighbors, people holding general service jobs, acquaintances, or people with whom one shares interests. Personal tasks are ones that may be completed only by people with whom one has a personal relationship. These include intimate tasks, which carry taboos and may be completed only by close friends, family members, and selected professionals. If these categories are seen as variables, four types of tasks emerge: (1) mundane daily tasks, (2) personal hygiene tasks, (3) community support tasks, and (4) institutional access tasks.

Mundane Daily Tasks

Mundane daily tasks are the numerous minor activities that people perform every day without thinking and that are the foundation of social independence. Most of these tasks are discrete; they have clear beginnings and endings. They are completed in a short period of time and usually require little skill. These tasks can be distinguished in several ways. Some are steps in a chain of tasks: operating the broiler is part of cooking and turning the starter key is part of driving. Some tasks can be eliminated easily—women can stop using makeup when they lose fine motor coordination—and some tasks can be delayed—replacing light bulbs can be delayed until most of the lights in the house are gone. Although small in themselves, some of these routine tasks are so strategically placed that they may block an individual's ability to function. Getting out of bed, going downstairs, writing, or shopping are examples of such tasks. Unless a disabled individual lives with family or receives reliable help with such things, life is almost surely disrupted.

Mundane daily tasks make up the largest number of discrete activities disabled people are likely to find they cannot do. Failure to accomplish some of them has been used to define disabilities in various self-help scales.[6] These tasks are also distinctive because it is often easy to recruit benefactors to help with them, partly because they are easy to do and generally take little time. Someone who stops by the house for a few minutes can accomplish five or ten tasks.

It is easiest to recruit help for mundane tasks. The goal is to generate a sufficient flow of people through the disabled individual's immediate environment so that necessary work can be done. Since helpers are not restricted by skills, age, sex, or other social qualities, people can be identified nearby whose jobs or roles in the community allow them to help.

Family, friends, and neighbors are obvious helpers. Other opportunities for interaction also exist through the various services available in many neighborhoods. Letter carriers, drugstore delivery people, pastors, and local business people who survive on the good will of the community are easy to recruit. They may come by the house for a legitimate purpose unrelated to the help needed and offer their services. One of the major budgeting problems of Meals on Wheels in some areas, for example, is that drivers help clients and talk with them for so long that deliveries fall behind.

Personal Hygiene Tasks

Personal hygiene tasks are those that are considered intimate or that, if neglected, cause people to be unclean. As activities, most of these take little more time or skill than mundane tasks, although lay people may find certain personal tasks, such as administering regular injections, unpleasant.

Part of what defines a task as intimate is the difficulty disabled people have recruiting help. Even for individuals who are successful at recruiting people to help with mundane tasks, personal hygiene tasks are difficult because strangers cannot be asked to assist. Using the toilet, washing, dressing, and eating are basic to independence and yet involve bodily contact that violates the personal distance maintained between strangers in this society. If an individual cannot perform these functions alone, he or she must rely on family members or paid helpers such as practical nurses. Until recently, however, health insurance and public assistance to the disabled did not pay for practical nursing aid, and this was a luxury reserved for the middle class and wealthy.

Occasionally, close friends can be asked to help with personal hygiene tasks. Intimate care is possible if it is consistent with the general dynamics of the friendship. Generally, however, this can be only intermittent or emergency help. Intimate care is also difficult because the tasks must be completed every day. Not only must helpers overcome general prohibitions against intimate contact, but they must be reliable and regular.

Community Support Tasks

Some tasks are inherently social. Their performance requires that one be connected with a group or community of people who share common interests. Local networks are important for protecting people from physical assault, exploitation, and embarrassment. Both Newman and Jacobs distinguish between impersonal and communal neighborhoods on the basis of the degree of mutual protection they offer, and Edgerton notes that one of the important functions neighbors performed for the retarded was protecting them from salespeople who would exploit their incompetence.[7] These neighbors also did their best to protect Edgerton's subjects from having the secret of their incompetence exposed.

Some tasks require that one be tied into networks that exchange information. These pose special problems for the handicapped. For most individuals, finding a nice apartment, a good job, or a sympathetic doctor generally depends on having a network of friends and acquaintances to provide information and to gain entry. The extent to which people are tied into these networks varies greatly, and lacking such ties, some people become segregated from social advantages.

The potential for independence increases when one lives in a congenial community. Living in a small town or in an "urban village" for all of one's life creates a built-in stock of people who know and care about each other.[8] Recruiting help in such neighborhoods is easier than in neighborhoods organized around assumptions of mobility. Suburban developments are often not designed for casual encounters of the kind Jacobs observed in her area of Greenwich Village.[9] If people do not feel a sense of responsibility for what happens locally, the disabled will find it difficult to recruit help.

The social consequences of one's disability will vary according to how connected one is with these networks, to the amount and kinds of help these networks provide, and to the amount of competition one has with other handicapped people for resources. This partly depends on the kind of community an individual is born into and the circumstances causing disability. It is not uncommon for able people who have been severely handicapped in adulthood to continue with their jobs, maintain old relationships, and keep a startling degree of independence.

In many cases, however, disability causes serious disruptions of community support networks. One of the serious consequences of institutionalization is that individuals lose touch with their inherited networks, including their families. This was evident with Edgerton's cohort of retarded people who had no families or noninstitutionalized friends who could help them find housing and jobs following their release from an institution.[10] When they did find work, it was with employers who benefited from hiring people with few alternatives who were used to close supervision. Nursing homes and diners were common employers. Disaffiliated handicapped individuals have similar problems finding housing. Disabled people tend to be concentrated with other unfortunate individuals in areas like rooming-house districts where contacts are reduced and competition is increased, limiting their access to information about improving their social situation.

This is destructive not only because direct access to potential helpers is reduced. Also critical to gaining necessary help are the social skills for recruiting people, maintaining their interest, and increasing their commitment to the helping role. Disabled individuals must use different strategies to improve their use of benefactors: they should not demand so much that people will be scared away; they should not mix requests for functional help with requests for affective support; they should find mutual interests that can enhance their relationships with their helpers; and they might locate benefactors who do not provide help often to disabled people and who therefore can offer important, original information.

Disabled individuals may be taught these skills directly by parents or by concerned friends. Many disabled people must learn by trial and error, however, and segregation from the broader population deprives them of opportunities to make instructive mistakes. In addition, the precariousness of their health may limit the time they have to learn how to cope successfully with disability. Segregation may cause further physical deterioration if it leads to personal deprivation.

Institutional Access Tasks

Disabled individuals frequently require complicated services from insurance companies, doctors, welfare programs, and others, but they lack the personal functioning resources to get help easily. For example, they need information about what programs exist and their rights to these services. Three institutional access tasks are especially important: (1) mastering the complexity of each service system to gain information about good services, the requirements for aid, the logistics of being served; (2) advocating one's rights to services; and (3) managing the demands of complex, overlapping service systems.

Specialization and public funding of service programs make consumer problems formidable for many disabled people. Most people solve such problems by tapping into a gossip network of people sharing information. Housebound individuals may find this difficult to do, however. Additional stress stems from the physical, emotional, and cognitive demands of consuming services. Standing in lines, moving from office to office, waiting on the telephone, and filling out forms are the familiar costs of gaining services from a public clinic or welfare office. Many disabled people find it difficult to do these things and do without services instead. To the extent that others can stand in for them, disabled individuals gain improved services.

Advocacy is a special problem for the disabled. They tend to be dependent upon services for which they have no alternative. They also tend to be considered incompetent to act as their own agents. This has led to a growing emphasis on due process in commitment procedures and other actions that might deny clients services to which they are entitled.

Disabled individuals are likely to find it difficult to disagree with a professional if they fear they may be denied services. This problem is most severe for those who are institutionalized. It is difficult for outsiders to determine what goes on in institutions, and it is difficult for patients to look for alternatives.[11] It also is difficult for individuals living at home to assert their interests. Many service agencies are so complex that the client must take responsibility for determining who is responsible for particular services. Clients may also worry that offending one caretaker will give them a bad reputation among other care-

takers. This fear is not wholly unfounded. Service providers are likely to know if a client has had trouble with others and condition their reactions accordingly. Disabled individuals require special advocacy services to retain maximum independence.

A different order of problem is the complexity of being disabled in itself. If disabled individuals are to be independent, they are expected to pay doctor bills, contest judgments with insurance companies, gain information about the multiplicity of agencies that provide services, wait to talk to bureaucrats about services, or contest claims against family members for nursing home or medical costs. Although these tasks can be handled by a lawyer if an individual has the money or by family members if they are educated, such tasks place a special burden on people from lower-class backgrounds and on people who are isolated from help. Neighbors, friends, and family members may not have the skills to deal with a complex system. Help must be recruited across social class lines, a function social workers may perform.

Conclusion

Changes in the status of disabled individuals have created new challenges for service providers. Disabled people may now be distrustful of those in formal helping roles, such as social workers or physicians. Previously, the orientation of these professionals was toward client protection, which now may inhibit an individual's independence. Self-help groups that clearly serve the interests of the disabled and place less emphasis on professional assistance have been growing. In order to serve this drive for personal independence, professionals must address consumer demands rather than provide services unilaterally. This article suggests two general kinds of services that professionals can provide.

One kind of service supports the informal networks people create. This may involve training disabled people in appropriate social skills, arranging housing that will increase opportunities for recruiting help, or providing assistance to self-help groups.

In the second kind of service, providers may serve as professional advocates, taking a role similar to that of a lawyer in relation to clients. Social workers can help disabled people manage their relations with different social service institutions. They can learn the intricacies of the law, can know what programs are available, can become familiar with people in the system and locate administrative shortcuts so that direct intervention is effective, and, most important, can be prepared to take an unpopular stand on behalf of their client when this is necessary. These are skills many workers learn during routine work at their agency, and such advocacy would not involve much retraining of staff.

Carl Milofsky, Ph.D., is Assistant Professor, Institution for Social and Policy Studies, Yale University, New Haven, Connecticut.

Notes and References

1. *See* Talcott Parsons, *The Social System* (Glencoe, Ill.: Free Press, 1951); and Elliot Freidson, *The Profession of Medicine* (New York: Harper & Row, 1970).

2. H. Santiestevan, *Out of Their Beds and into the Streets* (Washington, D.C.: American Federation of State, County, & Municipal Workers, 1975).

3. *See* Gerald Caplan and Marie Killilea, eds., *Support Systems and Mutual Help* (New York: Grune & Stratton, 1976); and Lowell S. Levin, Alfred H. Katz, and Erik Holst, *Self-Care: Lay Initiatives in Health* (New York: Neale Watson Academic Publications, 1976).

4. Arlene Gilbert, *You Can Do It from a Wheelchair* (New Rochelle, N.Y.: Arlington House, 1973).

5. *See* Kathryn Christensen, "His Simple Devices Widen the World of Arthritis Victims," *Chicago Daily News,* June 22, 1976, sec. 2, p. 13; and Rita Reif, "Home Design Is Life and Death for Disabled," *New York Times,* February 15, 1976, sec. 8, p. 1.

6. *See* R. T. Ross, *Fairview Self-Help Scale* (Fairview, Calif.: Fairview State Hospital, 1969); Kazuo Nihira et al., *Adaptive Behavior Scale* (Washington, D.C.: American Association on Mental Deficiency, 1969); and Sharon Landesman-Dwyer and Timothy R. Brown, "A Method for Subgrouping Mentally Retarded Clients: Functional Skills, Medical Needs, and Behavioral Problems." Unpublished paper, Office of Research, Planning and Research Division, Department of Social and Health Services, State of Washington, Olympia, Washington, undated.

7. *See* Oscar Newman, *Defensible Space* (New York: Collier Books, 1972); Jane Jacobs, *The Death and Life of Great American Cities* (New York: Random House, 1961), pp. 29–54; and Robert B. Edgerton, *The Cloak of Competence* (Berkeley: University of California Press, 1967), pp. 172–204.

8. *See* Herbert F. Gans, *The Urban Villagers: Group and Class in the Life of Italian Americans* (New York: Free Press, 1962).

9. Jacobs, op. cit.

10. Edgerton, op. cit.

11. *See* Alfred H. Stanton and Morris S. Schwartz, *The Mental Hospital: A Study of Institutional Participation in Psychiatric Illness and Treatment* (New York: Basic Books, 1954); Peter M. Blau, *The Dynamics of Bureaucracy* (Chicago: University of Chicago Press, 1955); and David Street, Robert D. Vinter, and Charles Perrow, *Organizations for Treatment* (New York: Free Press, 1966).

PHILIP W. WALKER

Recognizing the Mental Health Needs of Developmentally Disabled People

The term "developmentally disabled" refers to persons who suffer from mental retardation, epilepsy, cerebral palsy, autism, and neurological disorders. The concept of mental health needs, as related to the developmentally disabled and their families, is still emerging as social service agencies make continuous efforts to identify the needs of this particular group of clients. While providing mental health services and short-term crisis intervention for the developmentally disabled, agencies are attempting to deal with questions related to the counselor's roles and responsibilities.

Because of the various services offered by agencies and the wide range of responsibility assumed by counselors, many developmentally disabled clients and their families are denied consistent, intensive, clinical counseling services. Sometimes they are referred to another agency, overlooked, or seen intermittently according to the professional's own priorities.

Historically, the mental health needs of the physically and mentally handicapped have

been dealt with in terms of a restrictive and protective approach. As symptoms were exhibited by these persons, professionals usually responded by withdrawing the disabled from their environment through the use of medication or some form of institutionalization. Frequently, the inappropriate behavioral patterns of the handicapped were excused and minimized because of outward symptoms of "retardedness" or other apparent handicaps. Treatment often involved the manipulation of clients within their environment—usually at the convenience of the family, community, or agency. Although environmental manipulation should not be ruled out as a valid treatment tool, its possible overuse may bypass the developmentally disabled's own input and growth potential in dealing with their problems and conflicts.

Mental health professionals have taken a passive approach in coping with the mental health needs of developmentally disabled clients. They believe that the intellectual and verbal deficiencies of many of these clients prevent the clients from responding well to the traditional methods of clinical psychotherapy. Because of this poor response to therapy, many mental health professionals also believe that the disabled do not require direct services.

Most persons identified as developmentally disabled receive services from large agencies. Although programs for the disabled may be sponsored by private, nonprofit organizations, these agencies may depend on the state for the funding of such programs. This arrangement often causes direct conflict between providing for the direct needs of the disabled client and meeting the increasing demands of the state for the documentation of treatment and the tracking of clients. Thus the clients risk the possibility of becoming lost in the maze of paper shuffling done by workers to provide proof of the effectiveness of services. As a result, professionals functioning within this framework are left with only a limited amount of time and energy to promote preventive mental health services for their clients within the family system. Because of conflicting priorities, those social workers capable of providing mental health counseling to the handicapped are forced either to overlook underlying dynamics or contract out for mental health services, thus limiting or fragmenting the treatment process. It is hoped that, with increasing awareness by professionals in the mental health field, some of these concerns may be adequately dealt with and that resources within the agency responsible for serving the developmentally disabled will be used.

This article presents two case histories that illustrate the types of stress experienced by the disabled. In addition, the author discusses the dynamics often neglected in serving families of the developmentally disabled and makes suggestions for therapeutic intervention.

Case Histories

Case 1

Sandi is a 35-year-old, mildly retarded female (IQ 57). She is fully ambulatory, is in good physical health, and is totally independent in caring for her health and hygiene needs. In addition, she expresses herself clearly and well. Sandi has lived with her parents all her life, with no exposure to other life-styles. Her parents are in their seventies and suffer from various health ailments. Her mother moves

about the house with a great deal of effort and depends on her for the performance of routine household tasks. Her father, however, is more active than the mother is: for example, he does his own gardening. Sandi's married sister is normal and lives in an adjacent community.

Sandi attends an adult activity center for the developmentally disabled and has become increasingly aware of the varied life experiences of those with whom she works. Periodically, she has voiced her concerns to staff members and peers. The major concerns expressed are her feeling of restriction within her home environment and her desire to move away from home. Sandi is fully aware of her parents' dependence on her but feels locked into the family system. Although she loves her parents and feels a strong sense of duty toward them, she faces an equally strong need to be independent of them. She experiences a feeling of guilt for wanting to move away but at the same time is aware of her own rights as an individual separate from her parents. This seemingly insoluble conflict has raised Sandi's level of anxiety, which interferes with her daily activities. At times she is so preoccupied with these thoughts that she becomes tearful, whiny, and ineffective in her work.

Therapeutic Intervention. Initial counseling intervention was directed toward helping Sandi become more assertive. The treatment plan included role-playing, both in one-to-one counseling sessions and with the use of peers in group counseling sessions. Because it appeared that the counseling process would take longer than Sandi could tolerate, the counselor approached Sandi's parents about their daughter's conflict. Neither parent seemed to be aware of this conflict. The mother broke down in tears and reminded the counselor of her dependence on her daughter, saying she did not understand why Sandi wanted to leave home. The father hesitantly suggested that if Sandi wished to leave, she should give it a try. Sandi was informed of the visit, which proved to make the familial situation slightly less threatening yet kept her in control of the decision-making process. She finally confronted her parents, and they painfully consented to let her live in a family care facility in a nearby community.

The mental health component in this case was that of Sandi having to confirm her adulthood, which, at age 35, had never been totally realized. Sandi's familial situation placed her at high risk for developing emotional disturbances. Therefore, it was crucial that those involved with her be alerted to behavioral danger signals.

As with many mildly or borderline retarded individuals, Sandi tends to blend physically into the normal population. She has an accurate perception of society's norms and roles but is limited in the area of problem-solving and in the performance of the practical skills required for fully independent functioning. The search for one's own self-concept becomes elusive at this level of intelligence because of factors that suggest near normality on the one hand and the need for protection and assistance on the other.

This particular set of circumstances promotes a no-win process for the mildly retarded person in the community, which provides little opportunity for the resolution of problems without direct intervention. The handicap alone tends to promote a blanket of overprotection by well-meaning family and community support systems. The overprotection further prevents the person from reality-testing, taking risks, and experiencing failure with the usual pain that accompanies the growth process. A chronic double bind exists for the retarded when the parents relate messages of expectation of higher performance but at the same time promote a life-style for the adult child that communicates dependence and overprotection. According to Bateson et al., this dilemma contributes to the development of schizophrenia.[1] Counseling intervention then should focus not only on helping the developmentally disabled find means of altering their untenable life-style but also on helping the family to reassess its communication patterns. In addition, intervention should promote the extensive retraining of the client's support system and the restructuring of the family's communication process. If the family is willing, this can be done over a period of time through joint family therapy, using modeling, didactic instruction, and reclarification of messages (verbal and nonverbal).

The role then of the family counselor is to become aligned with the client as an advocate in order to penetrate barriers of miscommunication and assist the developmentally disabled adult in reaching a level of self-actualization. This role does not negate the realities of the client's limitations, and a system of community support services may be integrated around the disabled's particular needs without stifling personal growth.

Case 2

This case illustrates the emotional needs of a developmentally disabled adolescent. Chris, an attractive blond-haired, blue-eyed 13-year-old male, was referred for assistance in locating a residential school. He demonstrated some specific learning problems and functioned at the borderline level of retardation, an IQ range of 78 to 86. At the time of referral, Chris ived in the home of his 32-year-old mother and 6-year-old sister. The mother had never married, and the children were products of different fathers whose whereabouts were unknown.

When Chris was approximately 11 years old, he and his sister were removed from the mother, declared dependents of the juvenile court, and subsequently placed in foster homes. The mother had demonstrated abusive behavior toward the children and was admitted voluntarily to the state hospital for the mentally ill, with a diagnosis of a character disorder. She remained in the hospital for one year. During that time, Chris was transferred to two other foster home facilities because of aggressive and unpredictable behavior. His sister remained in the original facility. After the mother completed her treatment and returned to the community, she requested and was granted custody of her two children. During the following nine months, the mother, with limited personal resources, attempted to cope with Chris and his sister. By the age of 13, Chris had developed fairly effective ways to manipulate and control his mother. He attended a mental health facility for out-patient treatment, in conjunction with a class for the educationally handicapped. At the time of referral, however, he had been withdrawn from the mental health program because of such explosive and threatening episodes as throwing things at people, fighting, and rebellious behavior in the classroom. He is currently in a juvenile hall awaiting further disposition.

Such obvious factors as lack of a father model, an early childhood with a mother having limited nurturing abilities, and the final removal from his mother, all took a toll on this young boy. He has now formed in early adolescence a particular pattern of coping that expresses his anger on the one hand and sense of emptiness or "unrootedness" on the other, leaving him with no consistent support system to which he can relate. The on-again, off-again availability of his mother created a negative impact on his sense of family identity. Thus Chris's preadolescent or latency years, during which some degree of stability should be developed to help him weather adolescence, had already been disrupted, leaving him with a decidedly confused set of ego boundaries.

Assessment of Dynamics. In reflecting on the causes of Chris's acting-out behavior, one should immediately sort out whether the behavior is simply a discharge of energy, is unfocused, and derives from no apparent source or whether the behavior expresses an organized process stemming from earlier unmet needs or unresolved conflicts. In either case, the boy's sense of reality is in some way distorted, leaving him with apparent deviant behavioral patterns.

Blos identifies a theoretical formulation that defines acting-out behavior as being in pursuit of personal homeostasis.[2] During this pursuit the acting-out adolescent attempts to reduce tension over an unresolved past by creating activity that serves as a type of restitutional service. The temptation for those around Chris may indeed be to write him off as hopeless or untreatable and place him in a protective, structured facility and wait until he grows out of his problem. At age 13, the boy is unable to communicate with others about his losses and needs. He uses his own crude resources to deal with his emotions.

The growth model outlined by Luthman and Kirschenbaum suggests that to be free of symptoms, a person must be productive and creative in ways that are compatible with his or her needs.[3] According to this model, Chris's aggressive acts release energy, express pain and anger, and allow him to be in touch with himself. The community, however, views such behavior as deviant and therefore abnormal. But in the context cited earlier, Chris's behavior must be seen as a relatively normal response by an adolescent—as a reaction to pain, confusion, and profound loss.

If the threatened community viewed the behavior in a new context, counseling could then be directed toward helping the boy's family find more creative means of coping with maladaptive behavior and thus eliminating power struggles set up by various defensive reactions. Such intervention could promote the community's acceptance of the child's right to choose certain risk-related growth experiences.

Clients' Perspective

Although the professional literature on the mental health needs of the developmentally disabled is increasing, there is little opportunity for one to see the world of the developmentally disabled from their perspective. The following statements were made by Sandi, who expressed her feelings as a disabled person:

> It's very difficult to put my thoughts into words because I'm not sure if I understand all my feelings. Right now, today, I feel like I want to cry. Crying comes easy to me because I have a lot of feelings that are hard to share with people. Sometimes when I think that people are listening to me, they just pat me on the back, tell me to "hang in there," and walk away. Sometimes it seems as though what I have to say to people isn't really important to them, and they try to pass off simple suggestions to my problems and act as though they will all go away.
>
> Why is it, for example, that people always talk to me like I was just a little kid? I'm 35 years old! Why do people always

want to speak for me, rather than wait for me to put things into my own words? Why do people always think *they* know what is best for me? That really gets me! Take my parents, for example. Mom and Dad know that I've taken a lot of responsibility around the house, but they still treat me like I was their little girl. I have to really make a scene with them just to go shopping for a day with my friends. At work people are nice to me, but sometimes things get pretty boring and I feel like I need a change. Other people just assume I can go on forever with my life the way it is without doing anything different. I was climbing the walls last week but nobody seemed to take it too seriously. In one way they tell me to be responsible, yet they say I can't make my own decisions. It's all very confusing.

An example of Chris's attempts to assess his inner experiences follows:

God, do I hate this place! How did I get so screwed up? Why can't I just split and go home to my mom? Crazy things are going on in my head. Sometimes I feel like everything is okay, then all of a sudden everybody's on my case. I mean, how would you feel if you didn't know who your father was and had lived in three different foster homes? Since nobody gives a shit about me anyway, the hell with the house rules. Besides, I seem to be able to cause a lot of excitement over screwing up around here, and what have I got to lose.

It seems like whenever anybody talks to me, it's always to get me to do something or not do something. Nobody ever asks me how *I* feel about things. Maybe I'm not sure myself, and that sometimes makes me want to kick in a wall. Yeah, that's it. I get so angry inside it starts to hurt. I feel like going wild. Sometimes I do, and then there's a big fuss, and I'm back into another foster home. Sometimes it would be neat if things were different though. I'm not sure how, but just different.

The common denominators between Sandi and Chris that are familiar to those working with the retarded and learning disabled are these: (1) the need for someone to listen patiently, (2) the need to make independent decisions, and (3) the need for a support system that is both accessible and tolerant. This list, which can be expanded, touches the needs of all human beings but represents the needs of the disabled that are usually unmet.

Luthman and Kirschenbaum point out that family counseling at almost any level of intervention involves a process of locating and breaking down such defenses as the avoidance of disagreement or conflict and the avoidance of the taking of risks that impede the growth of family members.[4] In a family with a retarded child or adult, these defenses may be even more evident. Pain and need may be expressed directly or indirectly by the retarded person. A healthy integrated family may recognize these messages and attempt to deal with them. Other families, however, may have to be confronted with the problem and may face serious internal reassessment and disruption of the long-established status quo.

Discussion

To remain healthy, the family must function as a unit, with each member performing reciprocal roles. Relationships become distorted, however, when two people cannot agree on a definition of their roles. This distortion brings on a set of dynamics marked by a struggle for control of the relationship. According to Haley, "a relationship becomes psychopathological when one of the two people will maneuver to circumscribe the other's behavior while indicating that he is not."[5] Essentially, the family environment becomes increasingly rigid as parents attempt to meet their own emotional needs. Offspring who are developmentally disabled may be seen as a threat to the parents' equilibrium or self-image, causing the parents to block some of the child's developmental tasks. The families are at high risk for schizophrenia when they fail to carry out the tasks necessary for the development of a healthy personality in their children. Moreover, the child's performance of developmental tasks may be complicated by organic or intellectual deficiencies.

Families of the developmentally disabled are particularly vulnerable to distortions in communication because of their tendency to manipulate the behavior of the handicapped child. An example of manipulation is a mother's attempt to project her feelings of inadequacy and helplessness onto the child. The child may then begin to act out or experience these feelings, thus completing the cycle referred to by Laing as the process of "mystification."[6] This process prevents the child from establishing strong ego boundaries between self and others and consequently places him or her at high risk for psychosis.

Although habitual distortions or denials of reality may serve as a defense against a developmental disability, they may also be seen as a way of perpetuating a particular kind of family system. If there is a lack of acknowledgment of each family member's qualities and behavior, it follows that there may also be difficulty in responding to each other's needs. In families in which feelings are collectively denied, members are at a high risk for developing psychotic behavior, as demonstrated by an absence of genuine warmth and expressiveness in interpersonal relationships. These families expend more energy protecting their disabled member than providing the person with activities that promote growth and involve the taking of risks.

Conclusion

The community is still faced with the responsibility of putting to rest the myth that the retarded do not have the same emotional experiences as those with more highly developed intellectual capacities. The prospect for the disabled to develop healthy personalities depends on a value system which promotes that myth.

The author believes that because the retarded may quickly forget specific information given them in therapy regarding such issues as daily living, they may need more persistent review and assistance in testing what they have learned in various reality contexts. The same principles of counseling and therapeutic intervention techniques used with nondisabled clients can be used with the retarded as well, as long as one realizes that learning is done at a slower rate. Because many retarded persons have experienced more failure than has the average population, it is particularly important that they experience a friendly, supportive, and accepting counseling

experience. The examples of Sandi and Chris reveal that these persons are sensitive to social and family relationships but lack the resources and practical skills to make realistic judgments and decisions.

Most agencies that provide services to the developmentally disabled lack experienced staff to handle cases of severe pathology requiring intensive psychotherapy. If therapy is needed and sought by the family, however, it should then be seen as a continuation of the intake and diagnostic process. If the initial focus of therapy is on meeting the needs of the handicapped family member, other family members might feel less threatened and make themselves available for counseling, thus using the agency in a preventive role.

In terms of dealing with the family as a unit, the use of time-limited therapy might be a feasible way of dealing with the high number of community referrals to public agencies. In essence, a time-limited counseling approach suggests working within a parameter of from six to ten sessions. These sessions, which may involve the client and the family of origin, may extend beyond the traditional hour of therapy. Role-playing, fantasy exercises, and didactic methods may be used. These techniques, as well as others, will help the client and family develop more responsible behavior or deal with the conflicts and stresses of daily living. One advantage of providing counseling to clients within their family milieu is that the counselor serves as a role model to the parents or family care provider.

The setting of time limits on counseling tends to remove the "head-shrinking" stereotype of long-term therapy. When identifying positive aspects of short-term therapy, Weakland and his colleagues reported that the client's problems persist only if they are reinforced by the ongoing behavior of the client and those with whom he or she interacts.[7] (This does not deny the fact that many developmentally disabled persons may require years of periodic supportive counseling to help them cope with problems of daily living.)

Although the developmentally disabled client may exhibit chronic problems related to organicity, he or she may be interacting in a maladaptive family system. If so, this system can be examined and perhaps changed through immediate intervention provided to the client within the family structure.

In families of the developmentally disabled, some degree of stress usually exists. If the family consciously or unconsciously tends to withhold growth experiences from the retarded offspring, a high-risk factor for emotional disturbance is created, suggesting the need for consistent monitoring and evaluation of the client's life experiences when danger signals are apparent.

Philip W. Walker, MSW, is Marriage, Family, and Child Counselor, Central Valley Regional Center for the Developmentally Disabled, Fresno, California.

Notes and References

1. Gregory Bateson et al., "Toward a Theory of Schizophrenia," *Behavioral Science,* 1 (October 1956), pp. 251–254.

2. Peter Blos, *The Young Adolescent* (New York: Free Press, 1970), p. 103.

3. Shirley Gehrke Luthman and Martin Kirschenbaum, *The Dynamic Family* (Palo Alto, Calif.: Science & Behavior Books, 1974).

4. Ibid., p. 98.

5. Jay Haley, *Strategies of Psychotherapy* (New York: Grune & Stratton, 1963), pp. 131–132.

6. R. D. Laing, "Mystification, Confusion and Conflict," in Ivan Boszormenyi-Nagy and James Framo, eds., *Intensive Family Therapy* (New York: Harper & Row, 1965), p. 344.

7. J. H. Weakland et al., "Brief Therapy: Focused Problem Resolution," *Family Process,* 13 (June 1974), pp. 141–168.

BELLA H. SELAN

Psychotherapy with the Developmentally Disabled

Although the developmentally disabled have the same range of psychiatric disturbances as the nonretarded, outpatient psychotherapy with this population was not attempted until recently.[1] In a 1970 survey of the literature, Lott reported generally gratifying results in the field of psychotherapy with mentally retarded persons.[2] Prior to this, Sternlicht, one of the pioneers in the field, had also indicated good results, although he pointed out the relative ineffectiveness of nondirective methods.[3] In 1940, Thorne treated eighty-six retarded children most of whom seemed happier after the termination of therapy.[4] However, all these reports refer to treatment in institutional settings that impose special strictures and limitations on goals.

In 1973 the Psychiatry Clinic of Mount Sinai Medical Center in Milwaukee, Wisconsin, implemented an outpatient mental health program for mentally retarded persons who were 15 years of age or older. These clients— all of whom were in the mild or borderline range of disability—were not in large custodial institutions but were employed in the community or in sheltered workshop settings and lived at home, in halfway houses, or in nursing homes. The program is presently staffed by two full-time psychiatric social workers (of whom the author is one), a part-time rehabilitation counselor, and a part-time psychiatrist.

Like most mental health professionals, the author was ignorant of the specific psychological problems and needs of retarded persons. She was equally uninformed of which particular skills would be required of a therapist, and how these skills differ or coincide with those used in working with the nonretarded. After working with the developmentally disabled for a few months, it became clear that the strictly traditional psychiatric techniques would have to be adapted and new techniques devised in order to reach the same psychotherapeutic goals. These goals, which apply to all clients, can be summarized as follows: (1) alleviation of painful or uncomfortable symptoms, (2) realization of intellectual potential, (3) improvement or eradication of socially unacceptable behavior, (4) development of emotional maturity, and (5) reinforcement of coping mechanisms.[5]

This article will attempt to describe the application of some special skills to the attainment of these five goals. In addition, the author will discuss the personality traits necessary for the social worker who undertakes psychotherapy with developmentally disabled people.

Facing the Problem

Retarded persons who understand neither the nature nor the process of psychotherapy rarely seek it on their own. Instead, they tend to resist change by clinging rigidly to known routines, patterns, and habits. Retarded persons are referred to social workers, psychiatrists, and psychologists by someone close to them who is more disturbed than they are about their pattern of behavior. Thus, the therapist initially forms a contract with someone other than the client—a fact that has important implications for the course of therapy. The client's expectations are minimal or absent, but the person referring him may expect miracles from psychiatric consultation.

Because the developmentally disabled are constantly at the mercy of other people and are reprimanded both overtly and covertly when their symptoms become too disturbing, the therapist is presented with the dual task of trying to ease the client's emotional burden at the same time as he determines goals that are consistent with societal demands. Thus the therapist must carefully select his opening remarks. Slivkin and Bernstein report on the great backlog of distrust and hostility displayed by retarded persons that can be attributed to early disappointments.[6]

These patients find it difficult to believe that someone is genuinely interested in them. Frequently, answers to initial questions are as follows: "I'm okay. It's the others who work with me who have problems. They just won't leave me alone; they tease me and sometimes they call me names." Even though he has not intended to state his problem, the client has just done so, and the therapist can point this out. "I can see that being teased is a problem for you. No one likes to be teased. That could make you less happy." Thus a causal explanation is established for the client who is unable to understand the reason for his unhappiness.

Retarded persons often cannot deal with "effects" like unhappiness unless the direct cause, in this case teasing, is pinpointed. This direct, "here and now" approach usually opens up an active exchange of information. The therapist should try to find out what names the client finds particularly disturbing, whether he is also teased at home, and how he reacts to teasing—does he run, cry, or fight?

In working with developmentally disabled clients, the author was forced to be both active and directive. Therapeutic success with nondirective methods is largely based on the client's ability to perceive subtle cues of the therapist's expectations. This is not possible with retarded persons, however, who often interpret silences as hostility or disinterest on the part of the therapist or who may lose the thread of the conversation. The author also found that the therapeutic hour could last from ten to forty-five minutes, depending entirely on the client's attention span. If this time span is extended, the patient will only be confused with "mental garbage" that he can neither assimilate nor dispose of.

It is usually a good idea to end the first session by summing up what was said and by suggesting definite goals for therapy. Since the developmentally disabled have few, if any, choices about where they will spend most of their days, they must manage to get along with their co-workers. Thus, in the case of the man who complained about teasing, the therapist's first suggestion might be to invite the teasers to come with him to the next session so that he and the therapist could both learn why they always pick on him. This suggestion usually pleases the client, particularly because it removes the onus of being singled out for psychiatric treatment. Once the client has agreed to this suggestion, the problem can be approached on an individual level. "Do you think you could learn to ignore some teasing if people didn't do it all the time? It looks like you are doing these guys a favor when you get so angry. This is exactly what they expect you to do. Maybe you and I could find out a way in which you could disappoint them by not getting angry and not paying attention to them?" Thus the client is given several options that permit him to return to the therapist for further help.

According to Sternlicht, Freud blamed therapeutic failure on the lack of ego-ideal.[7] This notion is particularly applicable to the developmentally disabled. The therapist must assume the leadership by becoming the "fixed star" in the life of the retarded person. The group leader establishes a safe and structured relationship that will eventually permit the client to decide to make some positive changes in his life.

Retarded persons respond well to structure and routine because they lack the ability to understand the future. If even one variable is changed, the skills they have acquired in one situation cannot be transferred to another. Although most workers understand that despite changes in personnel, the work will remain the same and life will go on as usual, to a retarded person the replacement of a workshop supervisor is accompanied by extreme anxiety. The supervisor belongs to the small group of "nonretarded" adults who have daily contact with the retarded, and the retarded individual expends much energy adjusting to his personality. The skills these workers have acquired in dealing with the present supervisor are not automatically transferred to a new person. Whatever time the therapist has spent in assertion training or in teaching communication skills may have to be patiently repeated. The group leader plays an important role as long as he remains receptive to expressions of bewilderment, despair, and concern and can convert negative feelings into positive experiences.

Expression of Feelings

At present, the fashionable trend in psychiatry is to encourage the expression of hostility and anger as a means of achieving catharsis. Social workers who work with retarded clients have learned to respect their reluctance to confess feelings of hostility, rage, and anger. With good reason, many developmentally disabled persons fear the loss of control and the consequences that sometimes follow outbursts.

Loss of control may bring on seizures, tantrums, and abusive behavior that are rarely tolerated and frequently result in suspension from work, school, or recreational activity. Lott cautions therapists to exercise exceptional judgment in eliciting strong impulses, but at the same time warns them not to be overcareful, which could lead to the patient becoming too dependent.[8] The author has solved this dilemma by using various substitute measures that permit the clients to cope with depressed and angry feelings without having to admit to them until they feel secure enough to do so.

One such substitute is the use of special dolls with heads that change from a weepy to a sleepy to a happy face. The client is given the doll and is asked to tell how the doll is feeling. If he shows the weepy face, the therapist wants to know why the doll is so sad. The sleepy face could indicate that the doll is sick and tired of something. The therapist can then safely relate the statement to the client and ask whether he too might be sick and tired of something. Once the client is engaged in discussion, the therapist can use another doll family and act out scenes. In direct contrast to traditional play therapy with children, however, the therapist intervenes frequently whenever the plot swerves too far from the conflict as he perceives it. Retarded persons have few social skills and those they do have were acquired for the most part in the family, which constitutes a single, limited social environment. Therefore, the play family can be used to teach more adaptive behavior and to expand social skills.

The Family

Unless the retarded person is legally, financially, and emotionally independent, obtaining consent from his family for a change of residence involves extensive therapeutic work with all concerned. It is certainly tempting for the therapist to advocate specific changes in the life of a retarded client, especially if these changes appear to offer many advantages. Many retarded adults in their 30s and 40s have aging parents who have not accepted the limitations of their children or who have so overestimated their handicaps that they shelter and protect them excessively. In fact, these parents may refuse to plan for the future of the retarded family member. Parental attitudes of denial on the one hand and of indulgent overprotection on the other evokes ambivalence in the developmentally disabled adult who may strive for independence but feel bound by unusually strong family ties.

In one successful transition from a well-protected home to semi-independent living, social workers at the psychiatric clinic used a combination of individual therapy, medical intervention, family therapy, group therapy, and parent counseling. Medical intervention solved the presenting problem.

Ruth, then 22 years old, was referred to the clinic because of her frequent absences from a workshop due to a variety of physical ailments. Ruth's original complaint to me was that her father never listened to her and always had his head buried in the newspaper. She also felt that no one liked her and that she had no friends. Ruth gave the social worker a clear description of her headaches, and after a complete neurological and physical checkup it was discovered that she had an undiagnosed and atypical case of cerebral palsy. Medication immediately relieved her headaches.

Bernstein makes the point that retarded persons frequently complain about physical symptoms instead of their feelings, because physical illness is taken more seriously by those around them.[9] It is certainly true that many retarded persons complain about a variety of vague symptoms and that asking for an aspirin gets an immediate response. But the careful social worker may discover many undiagnosed medical conditions and should make no psychological assumptions without a medical evaluation. In any case, after the therapist had carefully explained her health condition to Ruth, the young woman stopped concentrating on her body and started dealing with her feelings.

Although Ruth's parents were cooperative and genuinely concerned about her, they had underestimated her capacity to function independently. After a series of trials, the social worker increased her independent actions until the parents agreed to let Ruth have her own living quarters on the third floor of their house. Although Ruth had agitated for that room,

she now found all sorts of excuses not to strike out on her own. Her ambivalence about the situation became obvious by such statements as "If they let me move upstairs, they probably will forget me. They want to be rid of me. They don't really love me or they would let me stay downstairs." If Ruth ever decided to leave home, the therapist would have to deal with the subject of rejection and separation with both daughter and parents. There appeared to be two alternatives: to let Ruth decide when she wanted to move upstairs or to suggest to the parents that they insist that she move immediately. If Ruth were asked to decide, she might delay the move indefinitely and ruminate ceaselessly about it, which would lead to guilt. If the parents insisted on the move, they might feel so miserable that they would renege later.

The therapist finally decided to let the family solve the quandary by saying, "I need help. We all agree that Ruth would be more independent upstairs. Both Ruth and you have said you would enjoy one another more if you were not constantly together. But I don't know how this move can be accomplished if no one makes up his mind to take that first step." Ruth herself found the solution. She suggested that she move upstairs for three days a week to start with and increase her time upstairs by one day each week.

Several months later, after Ruth had worked through her feelings of mourning and loss with the therapist, her transition to semi-independent living was accomplished with much less anguish than the original move upstairs. Ruth now attends a group meeting at the transitional home once a week and is learning skills related to independent living.

Love vs. Rejection

When a retarded person is asked what love means to him, the responses are usually the stereotyped "God is love; love is between husband and wife; God loves all creatures; parents love children; love is taking care of someone." If one pursues any of these answers further, it becomes evident that they have been learned by rote and indicate little actual understanding. Love is an abstract concept and, like most abstractions, is difficult to grasp without empirical experience. The only love developmentally disabled persons experience is in the narrow confines of the family.

The concept that "love is taking care of someone" usually relates to a reality of life. The low self-image retarded persons have of themselves convinces them that unless parents love their children out of a sense of obligation, they might neither take care of them nor keep them. Nonretarded adolescents may have to cope with feelings of rejection even after they have made the decision to leave home for college, for a job in another city, or for marriage. Developmentally disabled persons who can rarely decide independently to leave home cannot always accept the idea that love can also mean "letting go."

In one psychodrama session, the two social workers pretended to be parents who did not want to take care of their children any more and were glad to have them leave home. They intended to act out the secret fears of some of the group members, especially one who had been raped repeatedly by her father. Although unable to accept the massive sense of rejection, the group members joined wholeheartedly in this drama. In the play, several of them attempted to return home, but the leaders had them adopted by an aunt instead. Following this, the entire group observed the session on the TV monitor. The members commented that parents would not be so cruel as to push their children out of the house. Group leaders asked, "Do parents have a right to feel exhausted and exasperated?" "Yes, because they work hard." "Could they be anxious to spend some time alone?" "Well, they have all night alone." "Do you ever behave in a way that might cause your parents to get exasperated?" "We won't do it again—we promise."

Despite the fact that most retarded persons complain bitterly about many aspects of their home life, they feel personally responsible for everything that is undesirable. Whereas nonretarded persons have the emotional and intellectual capacity to handle both confounding and confusing thoughts, retarded persons may give up in desperation unless the therapist offers re-peated interpretations. Working through conflicts entails giving simple explanations of what the conflict is all about. Again, the social workers try to avoid verbalizations as much as possible, using action therapy instead.

Crayons, paint, puppets, balloons, and mirrors are all helpful props in action therapy. Following Sternlicht's suggestion, the social worker uses the balloons to calm tempers.[10] The balloon is pressed against the cheek in a darkened room while the client—and sometimes the therapist too—sits with his eyes closed imagining pleasant childhood scenes. Mirrors are held up for the person to look into and describe himself. Later, others will describe their observations. This kind of exercise and interaction brings about more self-awareness than would many hours of talk. Although the group does talk about love and separation to prepare the members for a change of environment, the social workers have not yet solved the problem of explaining the advantages of independence over dependence.

The Therapist

Therapists working with a retarded population must be able to tolerate more than the average number of frustrations. The attainment of goals and therapeutic success is dependent as much on the therapist as on the client. When therapy fails, psychiatric social workers sometimes tend to adjust the goals to fit the new situation. For example, if a client prematurely terminates therapy, the social worker may rationalize that the client is probably a sociopath and that such antisocial persons are not treatable. Or he may console himself by saying that the client probably has already derived maximum benefit from therapy. When a social worker initiates therapeutic interaction with a retarded client, concrete and narrowly defined goals must be spelled out. A retarded client will either adjust to the workshop routine or he will not; he will either leave his home or he will not; he will control his temper in public or he will not. Practical goals can succeed or fail and no matter how often they are readjusted, a definite outcome can be seen.

Mackinnon and Frederick write that unless a professional person achieves a measure of personal comfort out of working with an irreversible defect and is content with small gains over an extended period of time, he can be most effective by *not* working in the field of mental retardation![11] Although this is an extreme point of view, the therapist must constantly confront his own feelings and the limitations that narrow goals impose on him. Strongly client-oriented therapists sometimes expect parents and co-workers of the developmentally disabled to tolerate bizarre behavior. Such "bleeding-heart" therapists become pained and are usually frustrated in their efforts. They may also confuse clients to the point that therapy becomes too stressful for them to endure. Other therapists expect too much of clients who are verbal and who initially show rapid progress. These therapists are then tempted to take the role of society's agent at the possible expense of the client's emotional health. A delicate balance needs to be maintained between the demands of the outside world and the client's psychological well-being. To achieve this balance, the therapist needs to acquire at least a minimum knowledge of medicine, genetics, personality theory, and developmental psychology.

In addition, it helps if the therapist is patient, diplomatic, and has a sense of humor. The therapist plays a far more important role in the life of his retarded client, whose social contacts are limited, than he would in the life of a nonretarded client who has unlimited choice and variety of social exposure. To insure a degree of continuity from which the retarded client can derive lasting security, the therapist must be prepared to maintain intense and long involvement.

Social workers who accept the challenge of working with the mentally retarded need to thrive on small victories in the face of extreme odds. They must be able to make decisions without regrets and they should be able to accept responsibility for failure. On the other hand, therapeutic work with the developmentally disabled is in a pioneer stage and is therefore both intellectually stimulating and emotionally rewarding.

Bella H. Selan, MS, is Coordinator, Mental Retardation Project, Psychiatry Clinic, Mount Sinai Medical Center, Milwaukee, Wisconsin. A version of this article was presented at the NASW Twentieth Anniversary Symposium, Hollywood-by-the-Sea, Fla., October 1975.

Notes and References

1. Michael Rutter, Philip Graham, and William Yule, *A Neuropsychiatric Study in Childhood* (Philadelphia: J.B. Lippincott, 1970). The reader should note that although the terms "mentally retarded" and "developmentally disabled" are used interchangeably in this article, the latter phrase has won increasingly wide acceptance in recent years because of its greater descriptive accuracy, its allowance of a more diversified approach to treatment, and its relative freedom from the pejorative overtones of "mentally retarded." The term "mentally retarded" sometimes inhibits imaginative planning for persons who may be experiencing difficulty in only one area of development.

2. George Lott, "Psychiatric Approaches to Mental Retardation: Values and Caution," in Frank J. Menolascino, ed., *Psychiatric Approaches to Mental Retardation* (New York: Basic Books, 1970), pp. 220–250.

3. Manny Sternlicht, "Psychotherapy Techniques Useful with Mentally Retarded: A Review and Critique," *Psychiatric Quarterly,* 39 (January 1965), pp. 84–90.

4. Frederick C. Thorne, "Counseling and Psychotherapy with Mental Defectives," *American Journal of Mental Deficiency,* 52 (January 1948), pp. 263–291.

5. Irene Jakab, "Psychotherapy of the Mentally Retarded Child," in Norman R. Bernstein, ed., *Diminished People* (Boston: Little, Brown & Co., 1970), pp. 145–158.

6. Stanley E. Slivkin and Norman R. Bernstein, "Group Approaches to Treating Retarded Adults," in Frank J. Menolascino, ed., op. cit., pp. 435–454.

7. Sternlicht, op. cit.

8. Lott, op. cit., p. 240.

9. Norman R. Bernstein, *Practical Psychiatry,* Vol. 2 (New York: Roehrig Corp., 1974).

10. Sternlicht, op. cit.

11. Marjorie J. Mackinnon and Barbara S. Frederick, "Shift of Emphasis for Psychiatric Social Work," in Frank J. Menolascino, ed., op. cit., pp. 493–503.

P. DAVID KURTZ

Early Identification of Handicapped Children: A Time for Social Work Involvement

The national trend toward setting up normal environments for handicapped individuals is an optimistic and flourishing development [44:259]. Social service agencies are establishing and delivering a range of generic community services to provide a lifetime continuum of care [17:13-23]. In contrast to the fervor and funds stimulating the normalization movement, there has been little awareness and enthusiasm for prevention of handicapping conditions and for early intervention with handicapped children. Nevertheless, Sheridan wrote, "The concept of diagnosis as a result of growing suspicion during the child's early life increasingly replaces the concept of diagnosis as an act when he is older and the full clinical manifestations of his disease are apparent" [37:279]. The report of the Joint Commission on Mental Health of Children declared:

> One of our major thrusts must be identification of mental and physical disorders in the earliest stages of life—ages 1 through 5. We must detect and treat malfunctioning before it freezes into severe disorder. Reaching this

objective will require a total commitment, an entirely new set of resources for all. Failure to provide new and reordered resources will most certainly result in another generation of children with large numbers not able to "make it" [18:12].

Although Sheridan proposed preventive early detection about 15 years ago, and more recently the commission recommended reallocation of resources, the social service field has shown little involvement in early identification or recognition of handicapping conditions in children prior to school age. There is scant literature on early identification of preschool children whose deficits include socioemotional, cognitive, locomotor, sensor, and/or language impairments.

Definition of Early Identification

Early identification is the detection of the child's handicapping conditions prior to participation in formal schooling, so that appropriate services can be provided to the family and child and reduce the impact of the deficit. There are four steps in early identification:

1) *Find the child.* Before children can be screened, someone must bring them to a

screening location or provide their names and a way to contact them. Conventional find procedures rely on parent, physician and social service agency referral of youngsters suspected of having handicaps. This method is of questionable value, particularly in detecting children with less apparent handicaps, such as mild to moderate retardation [26:1–16; 45:76–83]. Parents are understandably reluctant to refer a child and thus admit there is an abnormal condition. Health and social service workers often have minimal training in recognizing handicapping conditions, particularly in mild cases. They are hesitant to refer for fear that the child will be indelibly labeled.

In an attempt to solve the dilemma of how to find exceptional children and link them with available early treatment services, several programs have tried innovative procedures. The approaches range from a statewide mass media campaign [8:1–71], to the federally sponsored Early and Periodic Screening, Diagnosis and Treatment program for Medicaid-eligible children, to comprehensive community-based developmental checkups for all preschool children [24:1–12; 26:1–16; 45:76–83]. The results of these approaches are mixed. The more successful models require substantial community support, organizational effort, and manpower to implement.

2) *Screen the child.* Screening is a procedure that categorizes individuals either as possibly handicapped or developmentally delayed, or as not currently handicapped or delayed. It errs in the direction of false positives, rather than false negatives (i.e., it "fails" children who are not handicapped in preference to "passing" children who are handicapped). Screening identifies children in need of further assessment. Several screening instruments are available [30:1–188]. The Denver Developmental Screening Test [12:181 ff.] is the most widely used device. It consists of 105 items, and measures the child's functioning in four areas: gross motor, fine motor adaptive, language, and personal-social. The test takes about 20 minutes to administer and requires no elaborate materials. Professionals and paraprofessionals can readily learn to administer the test quickly and reliably.

3) *Assess the child.* Assessment involves examination of the child's motor, language, cognitive and socioemotional development to determine if development is delayed; an analysis of family strengths and weaknesses; and the formulation of a treatment plan. A comprehensive multidisciplinary assessment may involve physical and neurological examinations, developmental diagnosis, an assessment of the familial environment [23:1–8], and *in situ* observation of the child in the home and possibly in a potential early treatment program such as a special preschool. The use of standardized tests and *in situ* measures increases the assessment data base and reduces the time required to initiate treatment.

4) *Link the child and family to treatment.* Linking entails using the assessment data to determine the appropriate placement in the existing services. Services for handicapped preschoolers and their families have been proliferating recently. The range includes infant stimulation programs for the severely handicapped such as blind [11:40 ff.] and Down's Syndrome infants [15:193 ff.], as well as for high risk infants [14:1 ff.]; center-based programs for handicapped preschoolers [20:1–11; 41:163–181]; combined center- and home-based programs [16:399 ff.]; home-based programs designed to teach parents techniques for managing their child and facilitating development [25:426–432; 36:210–216]; training groups to enable parents to deal more effectively with the child [33:135–140]; combined home and residential programs for children who can function at home, and whose parents need relief during crises such as self-stimulatory abuse, aggressiveness and tantrums, and respite care during family crises such as death and illness [10:42–45; 32:12–13]; and counseling services for family members to help them deal with psychosocial problems [34:197 ff.; 40:111 ff.].

A major shortcoming in many locations is the scarcity of services for young handicapped children. Fortunately, in 1975 the Education for All Handicapped Children Act (Public Law 94-142) was signed into law. It requires free, appropriate public education and related services for all handicapped children between ages 3 and 21 by 1980. Implementation of the law should decrease the drastic need for early programs in some geographic areas.

The number of programs to serve the target population is growing, and not infrequently they have to seek referrals to fill their programs. For instance, the outreach component of the Regional Intervention Program for handicapped youngsters is exploiting alternative methods for soliciting referrals from social service agencies [6]. Similarly, the HiComp project, a rural center-based program for multihandicapped children, has had to use innovative outreach strategies to complete its enrollment.

Need for Early Identification

Any significant distortion in either constitution or environment can generate developmental and/or social deficits. The earlier intervention occurs, the greater impact it can have in reducing deficits and maximizing the development of handicapped children [4:143 ff.; 5:41–43; 14:1 ff.; 36:210–216]. Despite awareness that early identification promotes early intervention, a high percentage of deficits go undetected until youngsters reach school age [3:98; 19:58–71;21;22]. Apparently some deficits become evident and/or problematic only in environments common to older children, such as schools; some handicaps are the result of detrimental early experiences; others are undetectible at early ages with our present level of screening skills. The results of a survey indicated that labeling children as "mentally retarded" is a function of age, severity of handicap, and diagnostic criteria employed. "With reference to visibility, it is only the child who is at least moderately retarded who is likely to be detected during the early years. At school age he and a previously unidentified less retarded child will both be detected" [2:166]. This finding is particularly striking because estimates place about 90% of all retarded individuals in the mild category.

In a recent countrywide survey to find handicapped preschoolers, it was determined that the rate of deficits increased with each additional year [39:84–90]. The handicaps per thousand children at ages 2, 3, 4 and 5 years were, respectively, 1.9, 4.2, 8.5, and 9.5. (The national rate for school-age children is about 10.6 per thousand.)

A longitudinal study of the development of 1000 children who received good prenatal care in a multiethnic community indicated that physicians were generally able to recognize severely handicapped children who had physical defects, but a special screening was necessary to uncover children judged to be below mental norms but without apparent physical defects [42:1 ff.]. It is reasonable to assume that many potentially identifiable handicapped children who could benefit from early intervention are not now being discovered in the early years.

Role of Social Work

In working with handicapped individuals, the function of the social worker is to provide a range of direct and indirect services [34:197 ff.; 40:111 ff.]. The worker may participate with a multidisciplinary team in diagnosis and treatment planning and may provide casework services to the handicapped person and/or family members to assist with the psychosocial problems that may result from the handicap. Additional roles may include helping the family to manage the child and to facilitate development, enlisting the aid of significant others, and linking the family to community resources. Despite the fact that early treatment programs consider social services to be a major referral source, the literature does not suggest that social workers are actively involved with identification and referral. Social workers traditionally are significant referral sources; however, their role in early detection has been limited. A survey of innovative approaches to early identification indicates that educators, psychologists and, in some instances, health professionals developed and implemented the models; generally, social service personnel have not been significantly involved.

Many social workers work in agencies that serve many infants and young children.

However, studies indicate that referrals from social service agencies are uncommon [26:1–16; 45:76–83]. One can postulate several likely reasons. First, although workers are generally aware of the importance of early intervention, other agency priorities often supersede early identification. Second, most workers have a general understanding of child development but lack specific knowledge and skills to make a judgment, "I think this child may be delayed or handicapped." Next, they may be reluctant to refer a child who they only suspect may be handicapped, as the child may be labeled as a result. Finally, many social workers may be unaware of the services that exist for the target population. For example, in an attempt to engage a rural protective service agency in a child find project, the author found the workers to be enthusiastic and supportive, but generally unaware of the services available. It quickly became evident that due to lack of training and information, the caseworkers had difficulty implementing developmental screenings.

Protective Services

Children from families in which abuse or neglect occur have a high likelihood of being handicapped. Although no comprehensive research has investigated the presence of handicap as a causative factor in abuse and neglect, several studies report findings that indicate a possible relationship. Other investigations suggest that abused youngsters are seen by their parents as different or difficult to rear. In a survey of 14,083 abused and neglected children, preliminary analysis of the data reveals that 1680 of the children had one or more distinguishing characteristics; 195 were born prematurely, 288 were mentally retarded, 234 were physically handicapped, 250 had a chronic illness, 130 were from a multiple birth, 180 had a congenital defect, 669 were emotionally disturbed, and 267 had "other special characteristics." The investigator reported that if the social workers who provided the data received special training in how to screen for handicapping conditions, the percentage of known handicaps could be expected to increase [38:126–133].

A review of the literature [22:2 ff.] found no study establishing a definite causal relationship between handicap and abuse; however, some studies do report a correlation. It is difficult to determine whether the handicap or the abuse came first, but presumably a child who is thought to be different or is handicapped is at risk and more likely to be abused than are nonhandicapped children in the same family.

Fitch discovered that the developmental scores of abused children were significantly lower than those of nonabused children [38: 126–133]. Children diagnosed as neglected had a drop in their developmental test scores between hospitalization and a retest 6 months after their return home. Fitch contends that, due to lack of stimulation, neglected children can incur more severe intellectual deficits than abused children, who can have a warm, stimulating family environment even though at times the parents are unable to control their impulses.

Other research [7:396–408; 9:596–602; 27:48–57; 29:859–866] substantiates the impact of child neglect, but indicates that abuse may be even more detrimental. "The abusive environment, apart from the actual physical trauma, impairs the development of the child neurologically, cognitively and emotionally" [28:25–73]. It is unclear whether abuse or neglect is the more detrimental to a child's development. In either case, the unwholesome family environment can inflict psychosocial as well as physical damage [1:21–24].

Since protective service workers serve a high risk population, they are in an ideal position to find potentially handicapped youngsters. Although it may seem unrealistic to add another responsibility to the already overburdened protective service worker, the goal of protective service is not just to deal with immediate family emergencies, but to enable the family to function continuously in a more appropriate manner. The handicapping condition of the child may be precipitating many of the family's problems. Failure to recognize the handicap and refer the child and family for appropriate services may only compound an already unhealthy family situation. Early detection can lead to specialized assistance to enable the family to understand and deal more effectively with the exceptional child.

To aid workers in identifying problems that may interfere with family functioning, screening instruments such as the Denver Developmental Screening Test are easily accessible, inexpensive, and quickly and easily administered in the office or home. The information obtained from screening can be invaluable in detecting unobtrusive delays, which can then be dealt with by referring the child for assessment and linking the family to the appropriate services.

Family and Children's Services

A range of agencies serves families and young children. Typically, an intake interview is conducted during which all family members are present. If a youngster is involved in the family problems, the intake worker may gather general or random information about the child's development. Emphasis is placed on the child's socioemotional development, particularly as to interaction with family members. A comprehensive, normative evaluation of development is rarely obtained, even though the information may be valuable in diagnosing the family problems and determining the treatment plan and referral resources. Seemingly, it would not be difficult or time-consuming for agencies to adopt more systematic, norm-referenced screening procedures in working with families of problematic preschool children.

In addition to detecting possible handicapping conditions, a vital and sensitive worker role is counseling parents of handicapped children. Wolfensberger's extensive review of the literature on parental reactions to unexpected news that their child is handicapped stresses the importance of the methods used to inform parents [43:356]. There is considerable speculation concerning the exact form of parents' psychological reactions as well as the procedures for assisting them. Regardless of the pattern of the reaction, the situation calls for crisis intervention to alleviate the trauma and enable the parents to deal with the situation. After the initial shock, parents face the challenge of dealing with a life-long situation. Long-term counseling should include dealing with parents' personal affective needs and should give parents information about their child's strengths and limitations and how to rear him/her.

Pediatric Services

A pediatrician not only treats physical illness, but often serves as confidant for parents about problems with their children. Frequently the pediatrician is not well trained to recognize the problems and arrange for treatment [35:4–24]. In addition, parents are often reluctant to pursue a referral for treatment. To reduce failure to follow through with referrals and to utilize the pediatrician's office as a treatment setting, increasing numbers of social workers and psychologists are functioning as clinicians in pediatric settings. The therapists deal with emotional disorders, child-management problems, and developmental delays [31:306–312]. The psychologist or social worker may uncover a child with a suspected delay, and the worker can then counsel the unsuspecting parents and arrange for a thorough developmental assessment.

School Social Work

Several early identification demonstration projects have attempted to develop comprehensive approaches. The model is based on the assumption that just as most children have regular health checkups, preschoolers should also receive periodic development checkups or screenings to increase the probability of early detection.

The school social worker, as part of a pupil personnel service team, can help the school carry out early identification. One approach in which the school social worker can be active is a comprehensive developmental checkup of all preschoolers. Preschool children can readily be located through local school census data. The social worker can solicit community support, coordinate and supervise screening activities, screen children, and communicate the results of screening to parents.

The worker can also insure continuity of followup services, including assessment and treatment [24:1-12].

Another less comprehensive but important role is for the school social worker to advocate early detection and intervention. Lay and professional persons are usually unaware of the significance of early intervention. As an advocate, the worker can create greater understanding of the developmental process in childhood, indicators of possible impairments, and the importance of early identification. The worker can stimulate the implementation of services for the target population and disseminate information to concerned families regarding available services.

At a minimum, the school social worker should attend to the family system, including the preschooler. If dysfunctional patterns are noticed in the early years, early intervention may result in their elimination or mitigation.

Conclusion

During the early years "the child is highly susceptible to developmental deficits resulting from detrimental hereditary and environmental factors. Yet paradoxically, during this same period, society's capacity for identifying and treating developmental disorders is at its weakest" [30:9].

Despite the complexities of the problem, social work has the capacity and responsibility not only to become more active in early identification, but to assume a leadership role. In many cases social workers are the first helping source to have contact with the target population. Agencies serving young children should be aware of the importance of early identification and should train their workers in basic find and screen procedures. Workers should be sensitive to the needs of parents and skilled in counseling and referral procedures. In addition, there are many other roles social workers can perform, such as advocating for early detection; organizing and coordinating communitywide developmental checkups; training professionals, paraprofessionals, and community volunteers in find and screen techniques; and ensuring a continuity of services for the children and their families. The roles described do not exhaust the ways social workers can assist in early detection. In addition, early identification has implications for other child welfare groups such as family day care providers and center-based day care workers, and possibly even homemaker services.

P. David Kurtz, Ph.D., is Associate Professor of Social Work, University of Tennessee, Nashville.

Notes and References

1. Ackley, D.C. "A Brief Overview of Child Abuse," Social Casework, LVIII (January 1977).

2. Baroff, G.S. Mental Retardation: Nature, Cause and Management. Washington, D.C.: Hemisphere, 1974.

3. Bereiter, C., and Engleman, S. Teaching Disadvantaged Children in the Preschool. Englewood Cliffs, N.J.: Prentice-Hall, 1966.

4. Brinkworth, R. "The Unfinished Child: Effects of Early Home Training on the Mongol Infant," in Mental Retardation and Behavior Research, edited by A.D. Clarke and A.M. Clarke. London: Churchill-Livingston, 1973.

5. Bronfenbrenner, U. Is Early Intervention Effective? A Report on Longitudinal Evaluations of Preschool Programs (DHEW Publication No. 75-25), Vol. 2. Washington, D.C.: Office of Child Development, 1975.

6. Buhl, I. Personal communication, 1977.

7. Caffey, J. "Whiplash Shaken Infant Syndrome: Manual Shaking by the Extremities, With Whiplash-Induced Intracranial and Intraocular Bleedings, Linked With Residual Permanent Brain Damage and Mental Retardation," Pediatrics, LIV (October 1974).

8. Child Find: Proceedings From the National Coordination Office for Regional Resource Centers and National Association of State Directors of Special Education Meeting. Washington, D.C.: March, 1975.

9. Elmer, E., and Gregg, G. S. "Developmental Characteristics of Abused Children," Pediatrics,

XL (October 1967).

10. Fingado, M., et al. "A Thirty-Day Residential Training Program for Retarded Children," Mental Retardation (December 1970).

11. Fraiberg, S. "Intervention in Infancy: A Program for Blind Infants," in Exceptional Infant, Vol. 3, edited by B. Friedlander, G. Sterritt, and G. Kirk. New York: Brunner/Mazel, 1975.

12. Frankenberg, W. K., and Dodds, J. "The Denver Developmental Screening Test," Journal of Pediatrics, LXXI (August 1967).

13. Gordon, I. J. "Reaching the Young Child Through Parent Education," Childhood Education, XLVI (February 1970).

14. ———. "The Florida Parent Educator Early Intervention Projects: A Longitudinal Look," University of Illinois, College of Education Publication Office/IREC, Catalog #125 (January 1975).

15. Hayden, A. H., and Dmitriev, V. "The Multidisciplinary Preschool Program for Down's Syndrome Children at the University of Washington Model Preschool Center," in Exceptional Infant, Vol. 3. New York: Brunner/Mazel, 1975.

16. Heber, R., and Garber, H. "The Milwaukee Project: A Study of the Use of Family Intervention to Prevent Cultural-Familial Mental Retardation," in Exceptional Infant, Vol. 3. New York: Brunner/Mazel, 1975.

17. Hersch, A., and Brown, G. A. "Preparation of Mental Health Personnel for the Delivery of Mental Health Services." Community Mental Health Journal, XIII (spring 1977).

18. Joint Commission on Mental Health of Children. Crisis in Child Mental Health: Challenge for the 1970's. New York: Harper and Row, 1970.

19. Karnes, M.; Teska, J. and Hodgins, A. "The Effects of Four Programs of Classroom Intervention on the Intellectual Language Development of Four-Year-Old Disadvantaged Children," American Journal of Orthopsychiatry, XL (January 1970).

20. Karnes, M. B., and Zehrback, R. R. "Curriculum and Methods in Early Special Education: One Approach," Focus on Exceptional Children, V (April 1973).

21. Kirk, S. A. Early Education of the Mentally Retarded. Urbana: University of Illinois Press, 1958.

22. Kline, D. F., and Hooper, M. A. An Integration of the Research Related to Education of Children Handicapped as a Result of Child Abuse (Final Report). Logan, Utah: Utah State University, 1975.

23. Kurtz, P. D. Family Situation Inventory (unpublished instrument). Nashville: University of Tennessee, 1977.

24. Laub, K. W. and Kurtz, P. D. "Finding and Screening Children in Rural Areas: Finding a Needle in a Haystack." Paper presented at the annual meeting of the Council for Exceptional Children, Atlanta, April 1977.

25. Levenstein, P. "Cognitive Growth in Preschoolers Through Verbal Interaction With Mothers," American Journal of Orthopsychiatry, XL (April 1970).

26. Makolin, J. "Project Search" (unpublished report). Carroll County Board of Education, Westminster, Maryland, 1975.

27. Martin, H. "The Child and His Development," in Helping the Battered Child and His Family, edited by H.C. Kempe and R. E. Helfer. Philadelphia: Lippincott, 1972.

28. Martin, H. P., et al. "The Development of Abused Children," Advances in Pediatrics, XXI (1974).

29. McRae, K. N.; Ferguson, C. A., and Lederman, R. S. "The Battered Child Syndrome," Canadian Medical Association Journal, CVIII (April 1973).

30. Meier, J. "Screening and Assessment of Young Children at Developmental Risk," (DHEW Publication No. 73-90). Washington, D.C.: President's Committee on Mental Retardation, 1973.

31. Morrison, T. L. "The Psychologist in the Pediatricians' Offices: One Approach to Community Psychology," Community Mental Health Journal, XII (fall 1976).

32. Ray, J. S. "The Family Training Center: An Experiment in Normalization," Mental Retardation (February 1974).

33. Rose, S. D. "Training Parents in Groups as Behavior Modifiers of Their Mentally Retarded Children," Journal of Behavior Therapy and Experimental Psychiatry, V (September 1974).

34. Schild, S. "Social Work Services," in The Mentally Retarded Child and His Family, edited by R. Koch and J. Dobson. New York: Brunner/Mazel, 1971.

35. Senn, M. and Solnit, A. J. Problems in Child Behavior and Development. Philadelphia: Lea and Febiger, 1968.

36. Shearer, M. S., and Shearer, D. E. "The Portage Project: A Model for Early Childhood Education," Exceptional Children (November 1972).

37. Sheridan, M. D. "Infants at Risk of Handicapping Conditions," Mth. Bull. Minist. Lab. Serv., XXI (1962).

38. Soeffing, M. "Abused Children Are Exceptional Children," Exceptional Child (November 1975).

39. Sower, R. and Covert, R. "Identifying Preschoolers With Special Needs: A Countywide Project to Help Plan Future Special Services in the Public School," Education and Training of the Mentally Retarded, X (April 1975).

40. Thompson, C. R. "Social Work," in Developmental Disorders: Assessment, Treatment and Education, edited by R. B. Johnston and P. R. Magnab. Baltimore: University Park Press, 1976.

41. Weikart, D. P. "Preschool Programs: Preliminary Findings," Journal of Special Education, I (winter 1967).

42. Werner, E.; Bierman, J. and French, F. The Children of Kauai. Honolulu: University of Hawaii Press, 1971.

43. Wolfensberger, W. "Counseling Parents of the Retarded," in Mental Retardation, edited by A. Baumeister. London: University of London Press, 1967.

44. ———— . Normalization: The Principle of Normalization in Human Services. Toronto: National Institute of Mental Health, 1972.

45. Zehrback, R. R. "Determining a Preschool Handicapped Population," Exceptional Children, XLII (October 1975).

DIANNE L. HENRY
JOYCE DeCHRISTOPHER
PAT DOWLING
E. VIRGINIA LAPHAM

Using the Social History to Assess Handicapping Conditions

This article is intended not only to describe the use of the social history with handicapped students and their parents but also to be a model for school social workers to follow in policy planning at the political level and in developing a strategy that can have a beneficial effect on service delivery. The events described here began in 1978. The New York State School Social Workers Association had been attempting to establish a working relationship with administrators in the state's Department of Education. A number of written contacts had been made, a position paper had been prepared, and meetings had been held to discuss mutual concerns and ideas in relation to federal and state legislation, its implementation, and its effect on service delivery to children and their families. Particular emphasis had been placed on Public Law (PL) 94-142. At a meeting between the state association's board and the assistant commissioner of the Office for Children with Handicapping Conditions (a division of the New York State Department of Education), the association was

requested to develop an outline of the type of social history required under the procedures specified in PL 94-142.

There was a certain amount of risk involved, since there was no certainty of how such an outline would be utilized or that social workers would be designated to prepare the social history in school districts. Two important issues in the assignment were: (1) how to develop such an outline in a broad context without being parochial in approach and (2) how to communicate the social work process that takes place in gathering information for a social history.

It was an exciting, challenging, and often frustrating task. A rough draft was written and was sent to a representative sample of the association's membership for comment. At the state's Annual School Social Work Conference, the paper was discussed and input was received from many individuals. A diversity of opinion was expressed concerning the basic issues described above. The original draft was revised to include the input received at the conference, and, in June 1979, the paper was sent to the assistant commissioner of the Office for Children with Handicapping Conditions.

The outline was well received. The assistant commissioner and a colleague expressed enthusiastic approval of the document in a meeting with the authors and agreed to utilize it on the state level. An information bulletin that included the outline was sent to all school districts in New York State. The bulletin included criteria for selection of the professional assigned to prepare the social history within school districts. The state's association of school social workers is now viewed as a credible professional organization to be used for consultation and has been asked to continue its relationship by giving input concerning special education classification.

Through such planned strategies, social workers can make contributions to other disciplines as well as become effective on political and policymaking levels and can ultimately serve their clientele on a broader scale. A version of the material the association presented to the state follows.

Background

In 1975, the Congress of the United States passed PL 94-142, outlining procedures to be followed in the identification, assessment, and education of children who had or were thought to have a handicapping condition. Local educational agencies were charged with the responsibility of providing each handicapped child with a free appropriate education. This emphasizes special education and related services designed to meet the unique needs of handicapped children, and in the state of New York this responsibility is vested in a Committee on the Handicapped in each school district.

Federal and New York State laws also specify the right of parents to be involved at all levels of the process, which includes the right to review their child's school records, to ask for an explanation of the contents, and to receive a copy of such records. The school district must otherwise keep such records confidential and allow them to be used only by professionals on the school's staff and only after obtaining the written permission of the parent. The federal and state laws mandate that the assessment process must include prep-

aration of a social history. However, the law does not define a social history and does not designate who should prepare it.

The following description attempts to define the social history in a way that will be useful to a district committee on the handicapped. It also attempts to demonstrate that the gathering of information for the social history is a process that requires the sensitivity and skills of a person with training in interpersonal relationships—a person such as a school social worker or other mental health professional. The interpretation of this information requires a knowledge of people and systems as well as of laws and regulations.

Obtaining a social history is a process. The product is a tool that aids in finding, identifying, and evaluating a child with a handicapping condition. The social history is also a vehicle for interpretation. It is important that the person compiling the social history should view the process as a joint venture through which the worker assists the parent in participating in the evaluation and in the development of a program for the child. The focus of the process is to provide an assessment and interpretation that will assist the committee in evaluating the needs of the total child—not only the child's needs in relationship to the school.

In the process of obtaining a social history, the social worker serves as a liaison, a facilitator, a mediator, an interpreter, and as a synthesizer. The social worker gathers information and synthesizes it into a meaningful whole to explain dynamic impressions that influence the child's learning and functioning on the interpersonal, familial, and environmental levels.

The beginning relationship that the social worker forms in compiling a social history should continue throughout the implementation of the program. This relationship is part of a continuum of service to the parent and child and generally has a therapeutic effect on the parent. During this process, the social worker helps parents to (1) obtain a clear understanding of their due process rights under state and federal laws and regulations and (2) gain a clear understanding of the assessment. The social worker needs the parents' help in the following areas: (1) providing an overview of the child as a whole person, including strengths and special needs, (2) obtaining a clear view of how the parents perceive the child and how the child perceives himself or herself (where appropriate), (3) evaluating the needs of the parents in relation to the child in terms of such factors as coping skills, realizing strengths and special needs, or support, and (4) assessing needed environmental changes. The social worker continually uses professional judgment to assess the significance of the information gleaned from the parent to help assess the child's special requirements and to define a program that meets the needs of the child in the spheres of both education and related services.

Social History Outline

The following is a suggested outline for a social history. The professional obtaining the data should explore the following eight areas and report only what is significant to the child in the situation.

Family Composition (identifying data)

1. Name of child, date of birth, ordinal position among siblings
2. Home address
3. Current school attended and grade placement
4. Names and dates of birth of parents and siblings.

Family History

1. Significant family dynamics (adjustments such as separation, divorce, death of parent or significant other)
2. Events in the family's health history that may have affected the child.

Child's Developmental History (prenatal to age 5)

1. Mother's medical and emotional status during pregnancy
2. Health complications prior to, during, or after birth
3. Data regarding developmental milestones (walking, talking, toilet training, motor coordination)
4. Early childhood difficulties (enuresis, temper tantrums, disruptions in patterns of eating and sleeping)
5. Parents' description of child's early personality development.

Health of Child (age 5 to present)

1. Diagnosed medical history, with dates and severity of diseases, hospitalizations, operations, and accidents (specifying where treated and names of doctors)
2. Undiagnosed illnesses accompanied by fever or convulsions, speech distortion, hearing or vision loss, or other indications of neurological involvement (interruptions in fine or gross motor coordination).

Family Interaction (including significant others)

1. Parents' description of child's personality
2. Symptoms such as temper tantrums, changes noted in child's personality development, night terrors, phobias, thumb-sucking
3. Child's relationship to various family members and significant others
4. Disequilibrium in the areas of child-rearing practices, family constellation, discipline, nurturance, and so forth
5. Current relationship to peers in and out of school
6. Child's interests, hobbies, and leisure activities
7. Child's self-image as perceived by parents (in case of older child, his or her own self-estimate is considered)
8. Current home situation of the family in relation to sociocultural factors (conflicts regarding language, culture, or religion as they affect family functioning).

School History

1. Child's age at school entrance and schools attended, beginning with nursery school
2. Previous relationship with teachers and peers in school
3. Parents' perception of school adjustment; related factors (excessive absence, poor

health, frequent change of schools

4. Parents' view of educational strengths and special needs of child.

Reason for Referral (presenting problems)

1. School-related problem as described to the parents (specifying who made description)

2. Parents' understanding and description of the onset of child's school-related problems and of the child's current school-related special needs

3. What family believes might be causes or contributing factors to child's special needs (when the evaluation involves an older child, the child's perception and understanding should be explored)

4. What steps family has taken to help the child (such as visits to clinics, professionals consulted, therapy, diagnosis, rehabilitation, education)

5. What family sees as the best plan for the child

6. What adaptations the family has been able to make to meet the needs of the child (installed ramps for child who cannot use stairs, shared experiences with other parents); short- and long-range goals family may be considering to help the child

7. Parents' understanding of the total program's function, parents' rights, or due process.

Evaluation

It is important that the information gained in compiling the social history be synthesized for presentation in such a way that members of the mandated interdisciplinary review committee will get a broad understanding of the total child so they are in a better position to make a differential assessment of each child's needs.

Case Vignettes

The social history outline presented in this article is meant to serve only as a guideline. The professional's skill in obtaining, synthesizing, and interpreting data should be utilized individually in each case to help the particular child and family and to make the circum-

stances clear to the reviewing committee or to others who will be expected to act upon the data in the history.

To illustrate and to clarify the process of compiling a social history, relevant documentation and case history vignettes are presented in the following section. As an administrator has stated:

> In evaluating the total child, it is necessary to consider the family dynamics and home environmental situation influencing a child's learning and behavioral patterns. Such information is invaluable in making a comprehensive appraisal of the child's difficulty. Communication and cooperation with the family must be established and maintained in order to facilitate environmental change necessary to correct learning and/or behavioral problems.[1]

In a related statement, Barsch wrote the following:

> The total investigation sequence has therapeutic significance for most of the parents. . . . The clinical interviews were openly cited by many parents as the "first time they had ever had a chance to systematically review the what and why of their daily relationship with their handicapped child."[2]

The following case history vignette illustrates how the social worker used the case history in helping a reviewing committee determine that a child who appeared to be handicapped in relation to his school functioning was actually not handicapped.

> José, age 7, was referred to the social worker by a teacher who believed the boy might be retarded as were two of his older sisters who were in special classes at the high school. José was having a difficult time in the first grade. He was distractable, had a short attention span, experienced difficulty in reading, and was disruptive in class. During the social worker's interview with one of José's parents it became clear that the boy might be experiencing the effects of an emotionally turbulent history. Until the age of 4, he had lived in non-English-speaking homes, where he had witnessed a good deal of violence, including the death of his father. Subsequently, in three years, he had been placed in three foster homes, in one of which he had suffered severe physical abuse. Even his current foster parents were unaware of all

the events in his background. The social worker scheduled several meetings with the placement agency's caseworker to develop an accurate assessment based on the boy's background. On the basis of the low scores José received on his original psychological tests and unfavorable teachers' reports, he would have been placed in a class for educable retarded children. However, the social worker's understanding of the pressure of José's early environmental background, as revealed from information compiled in the social history, led the evaluating committee to question the appropriateness of special class placement for this child. This case points up the importance of sociocultural factors in assessing handicapping conditions.

In some situations, the information gathered in the social history may indicate that although a child needs assistance, he or she does not have a handicapping condition as defined by law. In this event, the social worker may facilitate the parent's effort to seek assistance from appropriate community resources and may involve school staff in designing educational strategies to help the child. In such circumstances, however, the worker should keep in mind the following statement by Mercer and Lewis:

> Within a social system model, it is more serious to label or diagnose behavior as deviant than to label behavior nondeviant. A diagnosis of deviancy may initiate movement on the part of the labeled individual toward a deviant career which may be difficult to reverse. On the other hand, the non-labeling of behavior as deviant may deprive a child of certain services provided to children occupying deviant statuses. The diagnostician must weigh carefully which course of action will most benefit and least damage the child.[3]

The following casework vignette illustrates how the social worker's intervention reduced a parent's resistance and facilitated placement of a student in a special class. It also illustrates how early history and intrafamily relationships affect a child's functioning.

> Donald, an 8 year old, was in a class for children with emotional problems. He was a youngest child who was born to his mother when she was in her 40s, and his three siblings ranged in age from 22 to 35 years. At the time of Donald's birth, his mother was

suffering from heart disease and was unable to care for him adequately. He received inconsistent care from married sisters who had children older than Donald and who were preoccupied with problems of their own. Donald experienced little care at some times and an overabundance of care at other times. The inconsistency resulted in his lack of control, inability to respond to limits, and general physical acting out, which he displayed from preschool on. With a great deal of effort, the teaching staff, who had aides in the classroom, maintained Donald minimally in a regular class placement through kindergarten. However, when he reached the first grade and attended class for a full day with one teacher who had no assistants, the boy's earlier problems intensified. He constantly provoked fights, and groups of his peers began to pick on him. At first, Donald's mother did not feel her son had any problems. However, through the sensitive and consistent efforts of the social worker, who interpreted the problems Donald was experiencing and also helped the mother work out some of her needs in relation to her health, Donald's mother was able to accept the reality of her son's behavior in school and his special needs. She then gave her consent for him to be placed in a class for children with emotional problems. Progress occurred slowly. Donald was eventually able to take responsibility for some of his actions, and his attention span increased sufficiently so that he learned to read.

Sensitivity to Feelings

During the course of the social history interview, a parent may reveal information and feelings of a delicate or confidential nature. A social worker's preparation, training, and skills include sensitivity to the feelings of parents and children. As one observer has written:

> A great deal of sensitivity to parental feelings is necessary....Parents tend to view the school as an authority over which they have very little control. If one of our stated goals is to encourage parental participation in his child's education, then it is from the initial contacts that the first links must be forged. A sound knowledge of the school's operations and community resources is imperative. Often the Social Worker is the person the parent calls and recalls for help.[4]

The following case history vignette illustrates sensitive material that a parent may share with the social worker during the social history interview.

> Bobby's mother confided that she had conceived Bobby out of wedlock and that she had suffered from a good deal of guilt, feeling that God has punished her by causing Bobby to be born with a cleft palate. Because of this excessive guilt she became overprotective of her son, almost to the point of infantilizing him. This was evident in the boy's enuresis and delayed toilet training and in his inability to dress and feed himself. Because of his extreme dependence, Bobby was being considered for placement in a class for the educable retarded. He was functioning poorly in class, and he found it difficult to work independently. In view of his background, further consideration was given to the possibility that he might be capable of higher functioning in school if his mother could be helped to deal with her feelings of guilt and if Bobby could be made more independent of her. Within a short period of time, Bobby and his mother responded to help and he began to make progress in school.

Frequently, special class placement is only one area of a child's life that might benefit from intervention. In the preceding instance, the child's mother needed counseling to help her understand how her feelings interfered with her role as a parent. It is also extremely important to obtain specific prenatal and perinatal information concerning a child. A study by Hoffman showed each of the following six factors to be significantly correlated with learning disabilities: prematurity, prolonged labor, difficult delivery, cyanosis, blood incompatibility, and adoption.[5] The importance of the child's developmental and health history is illustrated in the following example, in which prenatal and perinatal events were significant in ascertaining the possibility of a neurological dysfunctioning.

> Barbara's mother had a difficult pregnancy, almost losing the baby within the first three months. Barbara was six weeks premature and was jaundiced at birth. Her parents reported that she seldom slept during the first year of life. She was also a "rocker." Although her physical development proceeded normally, she was hyperactive and was always "into things." Barbara had trouble with motor coordination in such activities as tying shoes and using a pencil. She seemed to be intelligent, but she had difficulty in school. There seemed to be enough evidence to indicate she needed a neurological evaluation and possible placement in a class for children with learning problems related to neurological impairment. The neurological examination proved to be positive, and a diagnosis of minimal brain dysfunction was made by Barbara's doctor. In this case, the parents had to be gently guided during the evaluation period to help them understand and accept the fact that their daughter had a neurological problem.

The medical history may indicate past or current health problems that interfere with a child's ability to learn. In some situations, this information can be critical in indicating the help a child requires, as is illustrated in the following vignette.

> Michael, age 13, had been classified as learning disabled in elementary school. He had something of a behavior problem and was always fighting with other children. In the sixth grade, his problems began to intensify. He began falling to the floor from his seat (the teacher thought he was clowning), and he sometimes had a dazed look (his teacher suspected he might be using drugs or alcohol). Michael was scheduled to be screened by the Committee on the Handicapped for possible placement in a class for children with emotional problems. During the social history interview, the social worker obtained the following information. Michael was enuretic. He drank excessive amounts of liquids, had poor eating habits, and seemed to crave sweets. Both his parents had histories of diabetes in their families. The social worker advised the parents to have their son receive a complete physical workup, since the boy's behavior patterns and physical symptoms suggested he might have physical problems. Michael's mother took him to her family doctor, who ordered a series of tests that revealed Michael had a severe case of hyperglycemia. The boy was placed in a special class, but it was expected that once his diet was controlled his behavior would improve. Indeed, once the cause of many of his problems was understood, Michael's parents and teachers related to him more positively.

Conclusion

It is extremely difficult and sometimes traumatic for parents to accept that their child has a handicapping condition. It is understandable that they may feel confused about the condition and be angry with or fearful and suspicious of school personnel attempting to place their child in this category. It is at this beginning stage—when social history information is gathered—that a skilled social worker builds a foundation for the supportive relationship that helps parents deal with their feelings about their child's handicapping condition. Such efforts help the parent cope with and participate in the sometimes overwhelming process of identification, diagnostic evaluation, and educational planning for their child. In essence, the social worker turns an informational assessment tool—the social history—into a helping process for the child. The social history begins a therapeutic process that continues after the child has been placed in a program designed to meet his or her needs.

Confidentiality and the protection of families from the indiscriminate distribution of personal material is extremely important. Only such family background as is necessary to the understanding of the child and his or her special needs should be included in the social history report. This material should be discussed with the parents and included only with their permission. It is important that the task of compiling a social history be assigned to a professional who has training and skills in the areas of interviewing, understanding of human growth and development, and analyzing, synthesizing, and evaluating confidential information.

Dianne L. Henry, MSW, is Social Worker, Long Beach Schools, Lido, New York. Joyce DeChristopher, MSW, is Social Worker, Bedford Central Schools, Mt. Kisco, New York. Pat Dowling, MSW, is Social Worker, Sachem Schools, Holbrook, New York. E. Virginia Lapham, MSW, M.Ed., was, at the time of writing, Coordinator of Research, Planning, and Development, New York Institute for the Education of the Blind, Bronx, New York. A version of this article was presented in 1979 to the New York State Education Department, which distributed it to all school districts in the state.

Notes and References

1. W. W. Wilkerson, "Administrative Requirements and Guidelines for Special Education Programs," Superintendent's Memo No. 6355, Commonwealth of Virginia State Board of Education, Richmond, June 2, 1972.

2. Ray H. Barsch, *The Parent of the Handicapped Child: The Study of Child-Rearing Practices* (Springfield, Ill.: Charles C Thomas, 1968).

3. Jane R. Mercer and June F. Lewis, *System of Multi-Cultural Pluralistic Assessment (SOMPA)* (New York: Psychological Corporation, 1978).

4. Mary Louise Lewis, "Kg. Screening," in Neal S. Bellos, Gerald M. Gross, and Joseph R. Steiner, eds., *Innovative Projects in School Social Work Practice,* Vol. 1, Manpower Monograph No. 7 (Syracuse, N.Y.: Syracuse University School of Social Work, 1974).

5. Mary S. Hoffman, "Learning Problems Index," in William Ferinden, Jr. and Donald Van Handel, eds., *The Handbook of School Social Work* (Linden, N.J.: Remediation Associates, Inc., 1969), pp. 35–42.

BARRY M. PANZER
LESLIE CHABON WIESNER
WILLIAM D. N. DICKSON

Program for Developmentally
Disabled Children

Intellectual limitations are not the only obstacle that children who are mildly developmentally disabled must confront. The social skills of such children are also impaired and often constitute an even greater disability than their intellectual impairment. The authors' clinical experience as well as the professional literature indicate that often intelligence alone does not determine the future job placement and social adjustment of these children. On the contrary, the extent to which sociability, self-awareness, cooperativeness, persistence, and adaptability have been developed in a child's personality is frequently the determining factor.[1] With this in mind, the authors designed a pilot program aimed at enhancing the way developmentally disabled children function in relation to their environment and other people by involving them in one-to-one relationships with caring adults.

The authors' program expanded already existing services at a hospital-based developmental evaluation clinic (DEC) that receives referrals for children up to 16 years of age

Copyright 1978, National Association of Social Workers, Inc. Reprinted with permission, from Social Work, Vol. 23, No. 5 (September 1978), pp. 406–411.

who are suspected of having some kind of developmental disability, such as mental retardation, or of having a psychiatric, neurological, speech, or hearing disorder. Through the use of a multidisciplinary approach, each child and family undergo a full diagnostic evaluation at the clinic, which is followed by the implementation of an appropriate treatment plan. Such a plan may include individual, family, and group therapy for a child and his or her parents, medication for neurological or behavioral disorders, speech therapy, and referral for services not provided by the clinic, such as placement in a special class in school.

Need for the Program

Children who are developmentally disabled are often less equipped than their normal peers to face the maturational tasks of latency and adolescence because their intellectual deficiencies hamper their ability to perfect social and interpersonal skills. Mastering age-appropriate games and materials, following rules, and learning socially expected forms of behavior pose major difficulties for the developmentally disabled child in latency. Many of the DEC's young patients, for example, could not prepare a sandwich, play checkers, or wait patiently on line in a restaurant or movie theater.

For the developmentally disabled youngster in adolescence, body image, peer acceptance, self-awareness, and future aspirations are concerns that are made into problems by the stigma attached to mental and physical disabilities. Many of the DEC's teenage patients had difficulty putting on makeup, conversing with other adolescents in social situations, ordering food in a cafeteria, and formulating realistic career goals. The heightened difficulties the youngsters encountered on attempting these tasks and their consequent lack of success concerning them often contributed to maladaptive behavior such as acting out, withdrawing from relationships, making self-deprecating statements, and avoiding new situations.

In addition to developmental problems, many of the DEC's patients had problems with regard to their families. In the case of at least 50 percent of the patients between the ages of 7 and 16 (the age range of the children in the authors' program), only one parent headed the family, and in most instances, this was the mother. Moreover, a high percentage of the families could be described as multiproblem and disadvantaged.

The single parents of handicapped children are often overburdened by meeting basic survival needs and are frequently physically and psychologically unable to provide the attention, guidance, and stimulation a child needs. The children are therefore unable to realize their potential, and their parents feel guilty and frustrated about not being able to help them. The parent-child relationship may be affected in many adverse ways as a result, and the likelihood of emotional problems in the child, child neglect and abuse, and unnecessary or premature institutionalization of the child may increase.[2] In light of the special difficulties faced by the children and families referred to the DEC, the authors decided that additional intervention was necessary to maximize the social development of the children.

Designing the Program

The DEC's pilot program attempted to provide services similar to those offered in programs run by Big Brothers of America.[3] Children in these programs are given the opportunity to further their growth and development through one-to-one relationships with "big brothers" or adult volunteers who maintain consistent contact with them and offer them warmth, support, and stimulation not ordinarily available to them at home. Under the new program, therefore, the clinic began to recruit caring adults to work with certain children who were already receiving its services. The children came from single-parent families and needed and were capable of benefiting from the stimulation of varied activities and from a sustained interpersonal relationship with a volunteer big brother or big sister.

Despite the ability of many handicapped children, especially those who are mildly disabled, to take advantage of participation in a Big Brothers of America program, the various programs of this type in New York City are reluctant to accept children who have been labeled as mentally retarded, brain damaged, or emotionally disturbed. In the DEC's program, volunteers were therefore recruited from among graduate students in the Department of Special Education of Brooklyn College.

Although the authors initially intended to have the students make a long-term commitment as volunteers, as has been the practice in traditional agency programs, they were advised by the school that the students would be available for only one semester, or a period of approximately fifteen weeks. Moreover, the students' participation was not to be a volunteer assignment but was to serve as a field practicum and a corequisite of an advanced special education course. These changes made it necessary for the authors to rethink their philosophy and institute some basic changes in the structure of the program. Essentially, they were concerned about the effect a short-term relationship would have on the children and whether they would feel abandoned and rejected when the students left at the end of fifteen weeks.

Therefore, after extensive discussion about relationships during later childhood and adolescence and a review of the literature on short-term treatment with children, the following conclusions were adopted as the underlying assumptions of the program:

- Children commonly have short-term relationships with camp counselors, teachers, and other individuals.

- Short-term relationships can provide children with a healthy experience of separating from people to whom they are emotionally attached. This can improve their ability to cope with separation and perhaps help them resolve past conflicts.

- Certain safeguards had to be adopted in the selection of children and students.

- Special importance had to be given to the process and techniques of terminating the relationships between the children and the students.

- To provide continuity, provision for the children's possible reassignment to individuals who would act as big brothers or sisters in the future had to be built into the program.

Implementation

Children were selected to participate in the program after all necessary arrangements with Brooklyn College had been completed. To determine their suitability for the program, the children were screened through the use of interviews and a review of psychosocial data pertaining to them. Those who showed a capacity for sound ego functioning and potential for further growth were selected, and the functions given primary emphasis during the screening process were a child's judgment, tolerance for frustration, and ability to relate to others. Children who had major difficulties relating to or separating from others were excluded from the program.[4]

Group meetings between the parents of the children who had been selected and the DEC's supervising social workers then took place so that ideas and suggestions could be exchanged and possible difficulties anticipated. Although most of the parents were receptive, grateful, and eager regarding the program, a few of them expressed anxieties and doubts. One mother feared losing her child's love and

respect as a result of participation in the program, another doubted that the relationship with a student big sister would effect change in her child, and a third doubted that her child would leave her to participate in activities and establish a relationship.

The dynamics underlying these concerns included the parents' rivalrous feelings toward the students, their feelings of being threatened, their fears that their position was being usurped by an adult whom they perceived as the "expert," and their anxieties regarding separation and abandonment by their child, all of which undermined their confidence as parents. The supervising workers discussed and universalized these reactions with the parents to help them see that their concerns were not unusual or uncommon. The workers also stressed the parents' importance in the success of the program and in helping their children. This was done to minimize the likelihood that some parents would attempt to sabotage the relationship between the student and their child.

During this time, students who had submitted an application form for participation in the program underwent screening. Each student was interviewed so that the DEC's staff could learn his or her conscious motivations. The interview was also used to explore various information contained in the student's application and to discuss hypothetical situations that might arise in the relationship between the student and child. In a description of screening volunteers for Big Brother programs, Royfe made the following points, which the authors found applicable to their program:

> The applicant is encouraged to express his thoughts and feelings about the projected situations, as well as the kinds of circumstances in which he feels he can best function. He is also helped to bring out any doubts and misgivings which he may have about his ability to establish and maintain the relationship....The mere visibility of negative attributes within a volunteer's personality does not necessarily lead to his exclusion. He is rejected if the impact of his particular negatives is so overwhelming as to preclude the possibility of effective functioning.[5]

At this point, the authors decided on

contingency plans for handling unanticipated difficulties that might arise after initial contact between student and child. The importance of quickly assessing the cause and correctability of problems was emphasized, and it was agreed that any assignment requiring termination would be ended as speedily as possible. Such early termination might have reflected some incompatibility between the student and child, the student's unsuitability for the assignment, or the child's or parent's lack of suitability for the program. However, none of the relationships between the students and children had to be terminated in this way.

After the students were screened for the program, the supervising workers matched them appropriately with the children. At this point each child and his or her parents were introduced in the office of one of the workers to the student who would be working with them. Once this meeting took place, each student was expected to make personal contact with the child on a weekly basis for the duration of the term. The kinds of activities carried out each week were to be consistent with the overall goals worked out for the child by the student and one of the workers.

The goals established for the children were limited by the short-term nature of the program and were formulated in terms of social and psychological tasks. They included the following: exposing the child to social activities requiring assertion and decision-making; enabling the child to verbalize his or her needs and preferences; and increasing the child's feelings of self-worth through a relationship with a warm and accepting adult. To implement these goals, students and children engaged in activities such as cooking, learning to apply makeup, ordering meals in restaurants, taking trips to parks and museums, and working on arts and crafts projects. Reimbursement for materials and other costs was provided by the clinic.

The students received supervision in weekly meetings with the social workers, and they were expected to submit reports based on logs. A written evaluation was presented to the student and the college at the end of the assignment. The program was in operation for three school semesters. During this time, approximately twenty students and thirty children participated.

Supervision

In carrying out their supervisory role, the DEC's social workers interpreted the overall treatment goals for the children, discussed the students' day-to-day problems as they related to these goals, and periodically evaluated progress in each case to determine whether the purposes of the assignments were being realized. The workers also made various resources of the clinic available to the students. These included diagnostic reports as well as opportunities to participate in team meetings, consult with professionals in other disciplines, and observe the client's preschool program. In their supervisory relationship with the students, the workers found the following comments by Royfe helpful:

> Supervision must not become a device for transforming the volunteer into a...pseudo-social worker, with the caseworker playing the role of a teacher. Although it is true that the interpretation of any given case situation necessarily entails teaching and learning, the chief purpose of supervision is to enable the volunteer to carry on more effectively with the responsibility he has undertaken.[6]

Although the differences in orientation and training between the social worker and the student in special education might have proved a source of conflict, early recognition of this potential problem and a clarification of roles prevented any such friction from arising. Instead, the diversity provided by the different perspectives of the workers and students contributed to greater understanding of the children and their needs.

Nevertheless, various issues emerged as especially significant during the supervisory process. The first of these related to the need for the students to be sensitive to the children's background and environment. That is, because the majority of the students were white and from the middle class and the majority of the children black or Hispanic and poor, it was necessary for the students to discuss these differences in background with their supervising workers. In many cases they were able to acknowledge their discomfort about becoming involved with a child and family whose orientation differed from their own. In general, they were helped through supervision to recognize the cultural and social differences between the children and themselves, and they were consequently able to minimize possible misconceptions on their part while maximizing their own effectiveness.

In addition, successful relationships between the children's families, especially their mothers, and the students required that the students develop an increased awareness of the important role of the parent and the impact on the family of their relationship with the child. Thus, a significant contribution was made by the social work supervisors in educating the students about the social, cultural, and familial aspects of working with the DEC's population.

Another issue given considerable attention by students and their supervisors was the question of how the students' orientation to the classroom affected their relationship with the children. Since all the students had teaching experience in the classroom and an academic orientation, the anticipation of working in a one-to-one relationship provoked anxieties in them about their unfamiliarity with nonacademic learning and about becoming personally involved with an individual child. Therefore, the supervisors had the important task of helping the students learn about the application of social learning. Through supervision and their involvement with the clinic's multidisciplinary approach, the students' perspective of developmental disabilities was broadened.

Finally, because of the program's brevity, termination of their relationships with the children was an issue of immediate concern to the students, who experienced guilt and anxiety and feared that their departure from the program would be psychologically harmful to the children. The supervising workers viewed these reactions as understandable and realistic and helped the students function effectively by limiting their goals and providing them with specific advice about techniques

and activities to aid in termination. These included a series of planned verbal reminders, discussions in which the children were encouraged to express their feelings, an exchange of photographs, and a jointly arranged farewell party. The workers stressed the importance of the children's active participation in these activities to increase their feelings of mastery and control over their loss.[7] It should be noted that termination was apparently carried out successfully, for interviews conducted with families six months later revealed that the children were having few adjustment problems and that their social functioning had improved.

Evaluating the Program

The program described provided many benefits to the children, parents, and students as well as to the clinic. The children's relationships with the students offered them friendship, affection, stimulation, new skills, and a knowledge of limits and in general contributed to the growth of their ego capacities. These benefits derived from the students' being able to approach their relationships with the children with patience, a sense of the child's individuality, and a dynamic understanding not ordinarily available in the home or school. Also of great importance were the therapeutic and maturational benefits gained by the children through their identification with a positive adult image.

Although the program was primarily directed toward the children, benefits were available to their parents as well. The students provided the parents with physical and psychological relief from the difficulties of raising a handicapped child alone. In addition, the parents' involvement in the program enhanced their ability to cope psychologically and socially by enabling them to perceive their children differently as a result of the children's relationships with the students. Finally, the parents came to view the clinic as a source of help and began to take advantage of its other services.

Their involvement with the program was beneficial to the students also, for they received an opportunity to work directly with a handicapped child in a nonacademic setting. This expanded their concept of working with children and helped them understand the influence of the family and the community on the way a child functions. With this heightened sensitivity to social and psychological issues, the students were able to help the children learn in nonacademic areas.

Last, in regard to the benefits derived by the clinic, the program is, to the authors' knowledge, the first of its kind in the field of developmental disabilities, and it broadened the array of services the clinic was able to offer. In addition, evaluating the children for possible assignment to a student big brother or sister was a diagnostic challenge that required the staff to view them as individuals. To illustrate more fully the program's operation, two cases that exemplify the children's problems will be described.

Case 1

Susan, who is black, is an attractive, well-groomed 8-year-old who functioned on a mildly retarded level and was placed in a special education class. Her behavior in school was immature, impulsive, and unpredictable, yet staff at the school and the clinic felt she was capable of doing her schoolwork. She was placed on medication for hyperactivity, and this course of treatment was somewhat successful.

Susan is the only child of a single mother who works and who attempted to provide many structured activities and a good deal of stimulation for her child. However, she also tended to isolate and overprotect Susan. Whereas the child related to her mother and most adults in a coquettish, playful, and demanding manner, her mother generally responded with restrictions and stern admonitions. Although an absent father, impaired peer relationships, and overprotection by her mother were the source of significant psychological conflicts, Susan's behavior disorder manifested itself only in the classroom.

Susan was considered an appropriate participant for the pilot program because of her impairment in the areas of social learning and psychological and educational functioning. She was matched to Linda, a student who specifically requested working with a younger child and who stated the following on her application: "I hope to be able to enrich the child's experiences by exposing her to everyday situations as well as to academic skills." Linda entered the program with a good degree of self-confidence and motivation that she sustained throughout her participation. She easily established a relationship with Susan as well as a positive and cooperative rapport with Susan's mother.

Linda made use of suggestions offered her during supervisory sessions regarding various problematic situations, explored her own feelings regarding her relationship with Susan and working with mentally retarded children in general, and was able to ask many appropriate and thoughtful questions that revealed her sensitivity to psychological issues. By the end of the term, Linda had matured to the point of being able to anticipate problems, and she would discuss plans for possible interventions. Her past experience as a teacher of mentally retarded youngsters was used to highlight her current experience in a one-to-one relationship and also served as a point of comparison.

Short-term and long-term goals were outlined for Susan, and activities were planned accordingly, with Linda exhibiting creativity and flexibility. For instance, she attempted to achieve the goal of increased self-expression for Susan by having her play-act at being different animals and also as people having various feelings; she pursued the goal of increasing Susan's self-esteem by encouraging her to make decisions, giving her increased responsibility for planning and arranging their activities, and fostering positive interaction between her and her mother; she implemented social and educational goals for Susan by engaging her in activities such as cooking and spending money; and she worked toward the goals of increasing Susan's attention span and tolerance for frustration by planning brief activities that she could master quickly.

The program ended after fifteen weeks and was considered effective and of great value to the child, mother, and student. Linda made full use of the educational benefits of the program, matured professionally in the process, and was able to appreciate the importance of psychodynamics and social factors in understanding a child's behavior. Susan was offered a therapeutic emotional experience that successfully combined psychological, social, and educational goals. Her need to act out in school was reduced, and her behavior improved markedly. Her mother benefited from observing alternative approaches to relating to her daughter, and she gradually relaxed in her manner. It should also be noted that the clinic benefited greatly from the program. By getting to know Susan better, it was able to treat her with more success in the future.

Case 2

Other aspects of the program can be seen in the case of Maria, a 14½-year-old Puerto Rican girl who was mildly retarded. Maria was selected for the program by the clinic's staff, who hoped to provide treatment to her hard-to-reach family. She lived in a housing project with her mother and six siblings, and her retardation was only one facet of her family's many problems. Her mother was physically disabled, her oldest brother had a chronic psychiatric disability, another brother had a neurological impairment, and two older siblings were also mentally retarded. Five out of eight people in the family were receiving federal disability payments, and together they formed an isolated, homebound family unit. Furthermore, each of them tended to view everyone else in the family as dependent and disabled.

Maria's family originally came to the clinic to have her certified as disabled so that she could remain in special classes and begin receiving Supplemental Security Income payments. Although they were satisfied with the status quo, Maria was suffering. She was denied many opportunities to make friends and engage in social activities, and her potential social and psychological strengths remained undeveloped. Frustrated, she became withdrawn and sullen.

Maria and the student who became her big sister in the program spent their first few outings forming a relationship. Although Maria was initially timid and nonverbal, her immediate interest in the relationship was apparent by her actions, for she was ready to leave her home hours before the student was due to arrive. The family in general was so needy that several of them would often vie for the student's attention when she came to the house. Skill and tact were therefore required of her to remove herself and Maria from the family. Through patient firmness, she was able to win their support while maintaining her primary alliance with Maria.

As the term progressed, Maria's outings with the student consisted of shopping excursions, bowling, and trips to the student's apartment, where they would cook and play games together. The student was able to provide Maria with positive and supportive experiences in which she could begin to test those abilities that were discouraged or ignored in her home. These often consisted of basic skills, such as being able to order her own food in a restaurant, and they were frequently practiced in the form of a game or role-playing.

Toward the end of the fifteen-week period, definite changes could be seen. Maria was more assertive about her feelings and needs and seemed more self-assured. However, her mother did not recognize this as an improvement and instead felt that she was becoming a problem. The family's equilibrium was upset. The final blow for Maria's mother came when the girl received a phone call from a boy. This "crisis" motivated her to seek out the clinic's help. She is now being seen for weekly treatment, the goal of which is to help the family reach a new and more appropriate equilibrium.

Conclusion

The pilot project represented a creative extension of social work services to developmentally disabled children and their families. The current trend in this field is toward enabling those who are developmentally disabled to achieve greater autonomy in community life.

The use of a one-to-one relationship was found to be effective in accomplishing this and also in enriching the social functioning of the individual. Overall, those who worked with the program found it to be an easily adapted, highly successful approach to enhancing the psychosocial development of the children it served.

Barry M. Panzer, MSW, is Psychiatric Social Work Supervisor and Clinical Instructor,

Leslie Chabon Wiesner, MS, is Clinical Instructor, and William D. N. Dickson, MS, is Psychiatric Social Work Supervisor and Clinical Instructor, Division of Child and Adolescent Psychiatry, Downstate Medical Center, Brooklyn, New York. Mrs. Wiesner is also Consultant, New York State Office of Mental Retardation, New York, New York. *A version of this article was presented at the NASW Fifth Biennial Professional Symposium, San Diego, California, November 1977.*

Notes and References

1. See, for example, Brian H. Kirman, *The Mentally Handicapped Child* (New York: Taplinger Publishing Co., 1973), p. 82; and Jack Tobias, Ida Alpert, and Arnold Birenbaum, *A Survey of the Employment Status of Mentally Retarded Adults in New York City,* report to the Office of Manpower Research (Washington, D.C.: U.S. Department of Labor, April 1969).

2. See Frank Menolascino, "Emotional Disturbances in Mentally Retarded Children," *American Journal of Psychiatry,* 126 (August 1969), pp. 148-160; Alice Sandgrund, Richard Gaines, and Arthur Green, "Child Abuse and Mental Retardation: A Problem of Cause and Effect," *American Journal of Mental Deficiency,* 79 (November 1974), p. 329; and G. Saenger, "Factors Influencing the Institutionalization of Mentally Retarded Individuals in New York City" (Albany, N.Y.: Interdepartmental Health Resources Board, 1960). (Mimeographed.)

3. See Ephrain H. Royfe, "The Role of the Social Worker in a Big Brother Agency," *Social Casework,* 41 (March 1960), pp. 139-144.

4. See Stephen Proskauer, "Focused, Time-Limited Psychotherapy with Children." Paper presented before the annual meeting of the American Association of Psychiatric Services for Children, Philadelphia, Pa., November 1970. (Mimeographed.)

5. Royfe, op. cit., p. 141.

6. Ibid., p. 143.

7. See Frederick Allen, "The Ending Phase of Therapy," in M. Haworth, ed., *Child Psychotherapy* (New York: Basic Books, 1964), pp. 292-296.

Part Three

Social Work with Families

Introduction to Part Three

Beyond social work's general commitment to supporting the integrity of the family unit, specific factors justify intervention at the level of the family by social work professionals dealing with the developmentally disabled. First, the family is the immediate context in which the developmentally disabled person functions. The social isolation and sometimes lifelong dependence typically experienced by the disabled individual intensify and prolong the impact of the family on his or her development and functioning. Second, the family unit often mediates between society and the developmentally disabled person. Parents are natural advocates for the developmentally disabled, and they may organize groups among themselves to change attitudes and improve services and policies. Third, the family itself is affected by the strains and challenges of raising a developmentally disabled child. Professionals can try to limit the stress experienced by families by linking them with concrete resources and by providing support or help in problem solving during crises. Last, if caretakers in the family become unduly stressed, they may opt for a breakup of the family through divorce or placement of the developmentally disabled child—with subsequent social and financial costs to the family and to society.

In light of the family's pivotal influence, the articles in Part Three highlight complementary perspectives on families with developmentally disabled children and interventions to improve the circumstances of these families. Parks describes the complex reactions and adjustments that parents go through at the birth of a handicapped child and explores how social workers can support parents and enhance their ability to cope by encouraging them to accept and work through their feelings. Wikler summarizes the unique stresses faced by families of the developmentally disabled, but she, Wasow, and Hatfield also point out the importance of recognizing the strengths in these families. Because society stigmatizes the developmentally disabled child and offers only meager supports to the family, we can assume that families who rear their disabled child at home have made a deliberate choice to continue full responsibility for child rearing. Although adverse reactions to this challenge are amply documented, the benefits are rarely explored by clinicians or researchers. In fact, as Wikler, Wasow, and Hatfield indicate, parents' claims regarding the strengths they have discovered as a result of coping with their stresses may be routinely dismissed as defensive reactions.

With a recognition of the positive aspects of raising a handicapped child comes an awareness of the limitations of professional expertise in working with parents of developmentally disabled children. One creative way of supporting parents without substituting professional knowledge for their experience is suggested by Davidson and Dosser, who describe a clinical program in which parents are trained to counsel other parents whose child has been diagnosed as disabled. Similar activities without a professionally based formal training component have been carried out by parents' organizations, but such parent-led efforts underscore the appropriateness of the project described by Davidson and Dosser, in which professionals acknowledge the expertise of clients.

The dimensions of supportive intervention at the family level vary, depending on clinical assessments of need. Traditional social work functions would include linking the family with such resources as financial assistance and respite care services. Counseling of the family might focus on parents' chronic sorrow regarding their child's disability by facilitating the normal but protracted process of grieving. It might also deal with the potential for dyadic enmeshment between mother and developmentally disabled child and with inadequacies in marital communication. Most often, however, the parents of developmentally disabled children seem to request information rather than counseling. Evidence has repeatedly indicated that training parents in behavioral management skills can help in the rearing of their exceptional child. Because the behavioral approach often has not been a standard part of the repertoire of social workers, two articles are included in Part Three that reflect this perspective. Proctor describes this approach and illustrates some methods that may be used in its implementation. Tymchuk also describes an approach in which parents learn to take an active part in the training of their child. Siblings and grandparents as well as parents experience the strains and benefits of close involvement with a family member who is developmentally disabled. Two articles in this section document the vulnerability of these populations. Trevino summarizes the research on siblings of handicapped children in terms of needs and interventions. Berns alerts the practitioner to the concerns of the grandparents of a handicapped child. Siblings and grandparents should also be evaluated as major potential resources helping to facilitate parents' adaptation.

The range of interventions described in the selections is clearly not all-inclusive. Techniques such as family therapy are not specifically addressed, nor are they considered to be primary and essential skills in helping families deal with the social problem of developmental disabilities. Recent publications on this topic generally refer more often to counseling parents on how to deal with a developmentally disabled child than to removing the focus from the disabled child as the source of family stress in order to face other disruptions affecting the family. The family therapy strategies for bringing about change in families of the developmentally disabled would be similar to those used with other families, once the focus on the developmentally dis-

abled child as the major problem is removed.

It should be noted that the articles in Part Three are predominantly oriented toward the circumstances of middle-class families with developmentally disabled children. Although the relationship between poverty and psychosocial retardation has been noted, the literature has unfortunately tended to overlook the population consisting of impoverished families. Reflecting this state of affairs, the articles included here do not touch on the specific needs of poor families with developmentally disabled children or outline interventions to be used with these families.

Finally, several topics related to families of disabled children are not discussed in the selections but should be mentioned, such as the extensive support provided to parents by self-help groups. The self-help network has developed outside any relationship with—and indeed often in spite of—professional social workers. Examples of organizations making up this network include the Association for Retarded Citizens, Association for Parents of Autistic Children, and United Cerebral Palsy. In surveys of their attitudes toward professionals, parents have reported frustration and disappointment with the lack of information and skills exhibited by professionals in regard to their child's specific disability. Perhaps parents have banded together in response to these perceived deficits and with the knowledge that other parents of similarly disabled children face similar struggles. Their efforts have included lobbying for services, policies, and laws of benefit to their offspring, and they have secured funding for specialty training of professionals at university-affiliated facilities to ensure an increased reservoir of skilled practitioners. In addition, some parents have written accounts of their personal experiences that are of value to other parents as well as to professionals and the general public. The supports provided by group activities and the sharing of experiences have been enormously beneficial. Such endeavors should be acknowledged and commended; without them, a far greater number of parents might have placed demands on the limited resources of the service system.

Professionals can enhance the effectiveness of self-help groups in a variety of ways, for example, by contributing to positive relationships between consumer and social service organizations and encouraging mutual referrals. They can also volunteer their professional experience to parents' organizations by supplying training materials or by reaching out to underserved or minority populations. And they can undertake such activities as developing structures through which parental expertise can be integrated into program develop-ment and training programs with volunteers.

The family plays an essential role in the care and well-being of the developmentally disabled individual. Recognition of the family as the immediate context and social mediator for the person who is handicapped and the provision of support needed by the family to cope with the stresses they confront are the entry points for social work intervention at this level. The perspectives and techniques outlined in Part Three should be helpful to social workers as they undertake such intervention.

RONDA M. PARKS

Parental Reactions to the Birth of a Handicapped Child

The future of the handicapped child is brighter and more dynamic today than ever before. Positive attitudes toward the handicapped and advances in educational and behavioral techniques have given momentum to innovative programs to meet their needs. Parents and professionals have joined forces in their attempt to provide a meaningful life for handicapped children.

In the midst of this optimism, however, social workers and other professionals must exercise caution. These parents must face the stark reality of the birth of a physically or mentally handicapped child, a fact that cannot be discounted. The birth of a handicapped child is a stressful event that creates unanticipated crisis. The happy event of birth suddenly turns into a confusing situation for which the parents have not been adequately prepared and for which they may not possess adequate coping mechanisms.

Intervention during the crisis period following the birth, which the hospital social worker is in an ideal position to provide, can

facilitate the grief reaction that the parents are experiencing and enable them to understand and accept their own feelings and to develop coping devices to meet present and future needs. Encouraging the parents to progress through the normal grief process will further their acceptance of the real child and strengthen their commitment to fostering his growth and development.

By integrating theories of crisis with the process of grief and mourning, this article presents a framework for understanding the reactions and adjustments that parents go through at the birth of a handicapped child. In addition, the author presents suggestions on how hospital social workers or social workers in other settings can use this understanding in their work with these parents.

To fully comprehend parental reactions to the birth of a handicapped child, the worker must recognize the anticipatory process that preceded the birth. For parents, a child's birth is generally considered to be a joyous event. They expect to be proud of the child who is a product of their union. They prepare themselves for a normal birth and form expectations of what the child will be like and what his future might be. The mental image that the mother forms during pregnancy, which involves the wish for the perfect child and is reflective of self and other love objects, is discussed by other authors.[1] Also examined in the professional literature is the mother's fear of giving birth to a damaged child.[2] However much parents try to dismiss such fears from their minds, they may, in fact, remain apprehensive throughout pregnancy that they will fail to produce the healthy wished-for child.

The Birth Crisis

When the birth of a handicapped child actually occurs, the fear or apprehension of failure becomes a reality. Not only the parents, but other members of the family as well, receive a threat to their homeostatic or steady state that causes disequilibrium. This disequilibrium is what Parad calls crisis.[3]

Many factors contribute to this state of crisis. Despite the fact that the parents may have considered the possibility of giving birth to a handicapped child, the actual reality is an unexpected and unplanned event. Their expectations for a normal child have not been fulfilled. Even with a normal birth, however, there is often a discrepancy between the fantasy child and the real one. The birth of a handicapped child increases that discrepancy dramatically.

In addition, there are stresses that threaten all aspects of the family's life system. For example, the mother must contend with the physiological changes that accompany pregnancy and birth. Her psychological stress such as depression, which may accompany any birth, is exacerbated by the knowledge that she has given birth to a handicapped child. Furthermore, the parents must face the social reality of the handicapped child and the reactions and suggestions that others will have.

Because the parents have not been prepared for the birth of a handicapped child, they may lack the necessary coping mechanisms with which to face reality. Instead they frequently appear confused, disorganized, and immobilized. These reactions are typical of those precipitated by crisis and stressful events.[4]

Grief

The grief that parents suffer with the birth of a handicapped child and the loss of a fantasy or wished-for child is a characteristic reaction to crisis. In her discussion of crisis events that pose a threat, loss, or a challenge and the principal manifestation of these events, Rapoport writes that "loss is experienced with the affect of depression or mourning."[5] Depression and mourning are a part of the grief response to the birth of a handicapped child and the loss of a normal one.

The literature of the profession provides a discussion of the varied forms the grief process might take. For example, Kennedy identifies three phases of the grief reaction—protest, despair, and withdrawal—and suggests behavioral characteristics for each phase. Table 1 identifies other authors who have discussed similar stages of grief and adjustment. A comparison of these ideas confirms the fact that parents do go through various stages of grief following the birth of a handicapped child and that certain behaviors and physical symptoms are characteristic of each phase. Given time, parents can progress through the stages of grief and mourning. Unfortunately, because of the demands of the real child, many parents do not have adequate time to successfully complete the grieving process.[6] In addition, it is difficult to form a relationship with the real child at the same time that one is withdrawing from the fantasy child.

Does Anybody Care?

Social workers have the opportunity to play a vital and varied role in helping the parents of a congenitally handicapped child to complete the grief and mourning process, to restore the balance of their lives through the development or redevelopment of positive coping mechanisms, and to make realistic plans for themselves, their child, and the family as a whole. Because hospital social workers can generally see the parents immediately after the birth and during the following months when they return for clinic visits, these professionals are in an ideal position to provide assistance and to alert the parents to the availability of other community resources.

Knowing that the birth of a handicapped child presents an unanticipated crisis for the parents, the social worker should arrange to visit the parents as soon as possible. The importance of rapid access is confirmed by Rapoport, who suggests that the energy created when crisis occurs can result in adaptive or maladaptive personality change.[7] Furthermore, Parad observed that a person in crisis is more responsive to therapy. He writes:

> As his defenses are lowered during this temporary period of disequilibrium, he is usually

more accessible to therapeutic influence than he was prior to the crisis or will be following the establishment of a new equilibrium, with its accompanying consolidation of defensive patterns. Hence, as indicated earlier, a minimal preventive or therapeutic force may have a maximal effect during this period.[8]

It is essential that parents are immediately aware that someone—in this case, the social worker—actively and genuinely cares about them and is willing to support them. Providing reassurance and fostering realistic hopes are additional important elements.

During the first meeting with the parents, and in subsequent visits, the social worker should assess the parents' ability to handle

Table 1. Typical Stages in the Grief Process

Kennedy[a] 3 Phases of Grief	Goodman[b] 3 Phases of Grief	Cohen[c] 4 Stages of Adjustment	Solnit and Stark[d] 3 Stages of Reaction to Mourning	Sieffert[e] 3 Stages of Parental Reaction
Protest—shock, numbness, disbelief, evasiveness, anger, and "shopping" for magical cures	*Initial*—shock, disbelief	*Grief*—not hearing, searching for causes, "shopping" for cures, disbelief	*Numbness*—disbelief	*Nonacceptance*—shock, anger, denial
		Anger—questioning why, self-pity		
Despair—disappointment, loss, hopelessness, futility, loss of warmth in relationships, insomnia, loss of appetite	*Awareness*—awareness of loss, sadness, guilt, helplessness	*Arousal of Anxieties*—feelings of personal inadequacy, guilt	*Disappointment*—feeling of loss, physical symptoms	*Acceptance*—accepting the reality of handicap, depression, sadness, relinquishing attachment to fantasy child
Withdrawal—Recall of prebirth longings for idealized infant, evidence of attachment to live infant	*Recovery*—natural mourning continues, but trauma of loss is overcome	*Adjustment to Reality*—begins to act in meeting real needs of child and family	*Reexperience*—Reliving the memory of birth, loss of attachment for fantasy child	*Acceptance of Child*—beginning activity to meet the needs of the real child

[a]James F. Kennedy, "Maternal Reactions to the Birth of a Defective Baby," *Social Casework,* 51 (July 1970), p. 411.

[b]Lawrence Goodman, "Continuing Treatment of Parents with Congenitally Defective Infants," *Social Work,* 9 (January 1964), p. 92.

[c]Pauline C. Cohen, "The Impact of a Handicapped Child on the Family," *Social Casework,* 43 (March 1962), p. 137.

[d]Albert J. Solnit and Mary H. Stark, "Mourning and the Birth of a Defective Child," *The Psychoanalytic Study of the Child* (Vol. 16; New York: International Universities Press, 1961).

[e]Al Sieffert, "Normal Parental Reaction Process to Having a Defective Child," unpublished manuscript, Topeka, Kansas, April 1975.

the crisis situation and to restore their homeo-static balance by their use of realistic coping mechanisms. Although there is no time for a thorough diagnostic study, the skillful social worker can usually gather a reasonably accurate picture. During crisis, the parents' defenses are down and they are often more willing to reveal verbal and nonverbal information than they would otherwise be.[9] Therefore, even without a diagnostic study, the social worker may have much available material with which to begin the therapeutic process.

It is essential to remember the need for differential diagnosis. Each set of parents and each family brings to the situation a different combination of biological, psychological, and social components, as well as individual experiences and coping mechanisms. Although all parents faced with the birth of a handicapped child may need support or guidance, the kind and degree of assistance they require varies. The following are some of the questions the social worker will consider in order to decide what kind and what degree of support is needed:

1. What strengths do the parents have?
2. Do they have any particular limitations?
3. What social and family supports are available to them?
4. Are there immediate concerns other than the birth of a handicapped child?

The family may have other immediate concerns with which the social worker can assist them in order to relieve the pressure. For example, there may be financial concerns that are aggravated by the birth. In such an instance, the social worker can help the couple explore resources that could help them meet their present and future financial obligations. In addition, it is often helpful for the social worker to act as a liaison between the parents and the hospital staff. Frequently, parents become overwhelmed by the number of staff members involved and the information presented and feel lost in the midst of it all. The social worker, who is in close contact with the parents, can alert other staff of the parents' concerns and questions and assist the parents in contacting staff persons as needed.

Tension

One of the primary needs of a person in crisis is to reduce the confusion and bewilderment caused by tension. One way for the social worker to do this is to communicate to the client an explanation of the dynamics of the crisis.[10] This is highlighted by the following study:

> Mr. and Mrs. B reacted with shock and disbelief when their physician first revealed that their second child, a son, was mongoloid. Usually able to cope effectively with life's circumstances, they frantically tried to find ways to meet this unexpected situation. In doing so, they felt bewildered, lost, and helpless. Visits with the medical social worker before they left the hospital provided an opportunity for the parents to express their grief and to understand that their reactions were a natural response to the situation.
>
> Once Mr. and Mrs. B allowed themselves to mourn the loss of the expected child and to redefine their experience, they began to feel better prepared to mobilize their personal strengths to cope with caring for their disabled child. Because of their activity in church and community organizations, the family received immediate support from colleagues, friends, and neighbors. The social worker also acquainted the family with community and state agencies and resources that would be available to them as needed.

Thus, the hospital social worker should share with the parents the reasons why the birth of a handicapped child will disrupt their functioning. In giving this explanation, the social worker should insure that the parents truly understand the events that contribute to the crisis and any subsequent reactions they may have. In line with this, Rapoport suggests that the client be reassured of the legitimacy of his feelings. To accomplish this, the social worker must help him accept his feelings as natural in coping with the stressful situation.[11]

The importance of offering legitimacy to the feelings of parents of handicapped babies is substantiated by Kennedy's observation that a mother may recognize her grief and the reason for it, but may be reluctant to show it because of a lack of encouragement from society.[12] As is seen in the following case, the hospital social worker can and must provide parents with that encouragement to mourn.

> A medical social worker started working with Mr. and Mrs. R during their visits to the clinic shortly after the birth of their son. On learning that their first child had cerebral palsy characterized by severe motor disability, they became angry and evasive. Why had this happened to them? They had only moved to the community a few months before and had no close family or friends nearby to help support them during this crisis. Furthermore, Mr. R was a high school football coach, and the parents were disappointed that their son would not be an athlete as well. They had looked forward to the baby's birth with great excitement and now felt inferior and concerned as to what their new acquaintances and colleagues would think.
>
> The social worker encouraged Mr. and Mrs. R to recognize their grief and to mourn the perfect child they had expected. Together they discussed the parents' prebirth fantasies and how these related to their present feelings. The social worker also helped the parents identify the strengths they could use in coping with the situation. She told them of a community association for cerebral palsy where they could meet other parents with similarly afflicted children. Additional resources were discussed and investigated. As Mr. and Mrs. R became able to respond to the real needs of their child and family, they began to feel more comfortable in their new community and in pursuing present and future child-rearing issues.

Concluding the Grief Process

It is not easy for parents to accept their feelings as natural and to achieve a cognitive grasp of the distressing situation. Clients can master this by being helped to describe, define, and reorder the events of the recent experience.[13] They must learn to recognize feelings and bring them out in the open through such means as emotional catharsis.[14] The hospital social worker must be capable of providing the parents with an opportunity to think, feel, and talk about their prebirth fantasies and their feelings concerning the discrepancy between the imaginary child and the real one.

Parents cannot make an honest attachment to the real, handicapped child until they have withdrawn their affection from the normal, wished-for child. Withdrawal from the fantasy child and the substitute of new attachment for the real child signifies that the grief process is finishing. However, in the course of the grief reaction, protest and despair must occur before withdrawal. As suggested previously, hospital social workers can facilitate the grief reaction by giving the parents permission to mourn and by helping them focus on prebirth fantasies and the relationship of these to present feelings and behaviors. This is superior to having the family face the reality without giving them ample opportunity to reexamine and reorder the birth experience and make a gradual investment of sincere feelings onto the real child. Although the fantasy of the normal child may always be present, cognitive understanding of that fantasy enables parents to deal with it realistically.

The social worker can also help the parents develop or restore adaptive, as opposed to maladaptive, coping mechanisms. This may involve an examination of those coping mechanisms they possessed prior to the crisis. Such examination has the additional advantage of helping the parents regather and mobilize their strengths and contributes insight into whatever growth may be necessary. In addition, the social worker can help the parents find and take advantage of such situational supports as people in work and leisure activities, and church, civic, or craft groups. As the parents reestablish a balance that is acceptable to their homeostatic mechanism and helps them meet their own needs and those of their handicapped child, reality issues come to light. They are now ready to consider and pursue such issues as child-rearing concerns, anticipatory planning, and educational consideration—all facets of their new role as parents of a handicapped child.

The focus of this article has been on the vital role that hospital social workers can play in insuring that parents of handicapped children have an ample opportunity to grieve, to understand, and to cope adequately with the crisis situation. There are additional related areas in which hospital social workers can make worthy contributions and that deserve mention. One of these is that hospital social workers, by teaching classes and presenting informative programs, can help other staff and the community at large to better understand parental reactions and adjustments.

Because they are frequently the first to know about the family and child, social workers can be a valuable link to other community services. They can acquaint the parents with available services and make community agencies aware of the family and child and their needs. Smooth transition from hospital services to outside services will lessen the risk of the family becoming "lost" in the community service network. Finally, hospital social workers can give insight into an ongoing evaluation of needs and facilitate the delivery of present and future community services for handicapped children and their families.

Ronda M. Parks, MSW, is a school social worker, Heartland Area Education Agency, Carroll, Iowa.

Notes and References

1. *See* Albert J. Solnit and Mary H. Stark, "Mourning and the Birth of a Defective Child," *The Psychoanalytic Study of the Child,* (Vol. 16; New York: International Universities Press, 1961), p. 524; and James F. Kennedy, "Maternal Reactions to the Birth of a Defective Baby," *Social Casework,* 51 (July 1970), p. 411.

2. Solnit and Stark, op. cit., p. 524; and Lawrence Goodman, "Continuing Treatment of Parents with Congenitally Defective Infants," *Social Work,* 9 (January 1964), pp. 92–97.

3. Howard J. Parad, "Crisis Intervention," in *Encyclopedia of Social Work* (Vol. 1; New York: National Association of Social Workers, 1971), p. 192.

4. A. G. Zaphiris, "Crisis Intervention with Children and Their Families—An Effective Modality of Treatment," lecture presented at the Kansas Conference on Social Welfare, Wichita, March 17, 1975.

5. Lydia Rapoport, "Crisis Intervention as a Brief Mode of Treatment," in Robert W. Roberts and Robert H. Nell, eds., *Theories of Social Casework* (Chicago: University of Chicago Press, 1970), p. 277.

6. Kennedy, op. cit., pp. 411–412.

7. Rapoport, op. cit., p. 273.

8. Parad, op. cit., pp. 198–199.

9. Rapoport, op. cit., p. 298.

10. Ibid., p. 287.

11. Ibid., p. 289.

12. Kennedy, op. cit., p. 416.

13. Rapoport, op. cit., p. 298.

14. Donna C. Aquilera and Janice M. Messick, *Crisis Intervention: Theory and Methodology* (St. Louis, Mo.: C. V. Mosby Co., 1974), p. 20.

LYNN WIKLER

Chronic Stresses of Families of Mentally Retarded Children

Families with a child who is mentally retarded are more likely to experience stress, all things being equal, than families who have normal children. This stress may lead to family dysfunction requiring societal intervention. Research on families of mentally retarded children has repeatedly indicated three stressful effects of the mental retardation: (a) social isolation (Cook, 1963; Cummings, Bailey, & Rie, 1966; Davis & MacKay, 1973; Erickson, 1968; Farber, 1968; Holt, 1958; McAllister, Butler, & Lei, 1973); (b) increased indicators of stress in the parents (Barsch, 1968; Cummings, Bailey, & Rie, 1966; Cook, 1963; Erickson, 1968; Levinson, 1975); and (c) a greater incidence of problems at school and mental health clinic visits for normal adolescent sibling(s) (Farber & Jenne, 1963; Fowle, 1968; Gath, 1974). When divorce does occur, the burdens of the single mother of the retarded child outweigh those of the single mother of the normal child (Wikler, Note 1). If these problems continue unresolved the fam-

ily frequently turns to institutionalization as a way of coping with the stress (Farber, Jenne, & Tolgo, 1960; Graliker, Koch, & Henderson, 1965; Saenger (Note 2); Stone, 1965).

Historically, clinical interventions have been *reactive* to these problem situations. However, the delineation of types of stresses and pinpointing of high risk periods for families over the life span of the retarded child could provide information which would enable clinical programs to function from a *proactive* stance. By alerting the clinician to those times when families may need additional attention and support, possibilities for *preventing* problems increase.

This paper contains an overview of stresses in families of mentally retarded children, including the manifestation, etiology and temporal pattern of stress. First, stresses which are chronic for families of mentally retarded children are discussed. Second, the series of potential crises which periodically seem to affect these families is sketched. Finally, a brief account of the implications of this theory of chronic stress is presented. Working hypotheses are presented for further research.

Types of Chronic Stresses Unique to Families of Mentally Retarded Children

Parents face stresses that continue over the lifetime of their mentally retarded child. Some are related to the characteristic hardships of mental retardation (stigmatized social interactions and prolonged burden of care) and others are typical parental responses to retardation (realistic parental confusion concerning child care, and periodic parental grieving). All of these are reality stresses resulting from situational demands of raising or caring for a retarded person (Menolascino, 1977).

Stigmatized Social Interactions

Although most mentally retarded people are mildly retarded and eventually function in society with minimal supports, the public (and prior to diagnosis, the parents) stereotype all mentally retarded people as completely lacking in basic competence (Edgerton, 1967). People generally feel uncomfortable with the mentally retarded and strive to avoid interacting with them. Parents must change their own attitudes in order to become advocates for their child. In addition, they must develop competence in managing uncomfortable social transactions (Birenbaum, 1970). They face hostile stares, judgmental comments, murmurs of pity, and intrusive requests for personal information whenever they accompany their child to the grocery store, on the bus, or to the park. Although parents report that they do learn to manage the stigmatized interactions successfully (Voysey, 1972), the growing discrepancy between the child's size and mental functioning tends to increase the number of stressful encounters.

Prolonged Burden of Care

Chronic problems such as managing hyperactivity in a nonverbal child, or lifting a spastic teenager out of a wheelchair are often physically exhausting to the caretakers. As the child grows larger, he becomes more burdensome (Berger & Foster, 1976; Holt, 1958). Even when there are no secondary problems associated with the mental retardation, developmentally delayed children by definition have more prolonged dependency needs than do normal children. Mothers of older retarded children cannot look forward to engaging in activities comparable to those of parents of normal children now adult age (Birenbaum, 1971; Farber, Note 3). In addition, the prolonged burden of care is continuous. There is no respite from the burden since local babysitters are much less available to families who have mentally retarded children (Moore & Seachore, Note 4).

Recent studies of the effects of respite care on family stress have shown that it leads to a decrease in negative maternal attitudes towards the mentally retarded child (Wikler & Hanusa, Note 5) and increased positive family interaction (Cohen, Note 6).

Lack of Information

In response to offers of therapy, parents of mentally retarded children say that they would *rather* have facts about mental retardation and information about what to do to handle specific child management problems (Matheny & Vernick, 1969; Price-Bonham & Addison, 1978; Puescel & Murphy, 1976; Wolfensberger, 1967). Although parents of normal children can rely on their childhood experiences of being parented, and on advice from friends, relatives, and neighbors, these resources are generally inadequate for parents of children with special needs. Even when these parents go to specialists for advice and information they may find that the general principles presented are inadequate for handling the daily practical tasks of child rearing (Waskowitz, 1959). Moreover, professional texts and behavior management programs tend to focus primarily on the early years of development rather than on management issues that arise *over time* (Berger & Foster, 1976).

The potentially richest source of information is another parent of a mentally retarded child, but here too the parent in need of help may be disappointed because retarded children vary so greatly. The parent of a moderately retarded 12-year-old Down's Syndrome boy would have very different accumulated wisdom from that of the parent of an 8-year-old severely retarded child with uncontrollable seizures or that of a 15-year-old mildly retarded girl with poor social skills. Even when parents are fortunate enough to get the data they need to continue with some confidence, those data do not necessarily generalize to the next complicated situation they confront. The critical, on-going need for information which parents encounter as they pursue long-term care of the mentally retarded person at home cannot be underestimated as a source of stress (Berger & Foster, 1976).

Grieving

Grieving is extensively described in the clinical literature in relation to the parents' emotional responses to the diagnosis of retardation in their child. The primary cause for the grief at that time is considered to be the loss of the fantasized normal child (Emde & Brown, 1978; Mandelbaum, 1967; Parks, 1977; Solnit & Stark, 1961; Wolfensberger, 1967). Although the parents will regain their sense of equilibrium, the initial apparent adjustment to that disappointment may be temporary. At various points in time, their loss of the fantasized normal child will be restimulated. Depending on the personal fantasies of the individual parent, these moments may occur during holidays, family reunions, birthdays, the wedding of their normal child, watching normal children play, or hearing mothers of normal children chat about their child's successes or failures.

Most important, there are predictable periods when grieving will be reactivated, periods of developmental and transitional crises (described later) in which culturally assumed enactment of parental roles are not fulfilled. When major discrepancies from these expectations occur, most parents will again experience the grieving that they felt at the time of the diagnosis.

Fathers' vs. Mothers' Stresses

Fathers and mothers perceive and cope with mental retardation in different ways and they may do so at a different pace (Price-Bonham & Addison, 1978). This could be problematic for the marriage. If one parent is grieving and the other is concerned about the burden of care, they are less likely to be responsive to one another. This could also reduce the potential effectiveness of one mate in ameliorating the impact of the stress for the other. Mother's reports of marital satisfaction are highly correlated with her coping behavior (Friedrich, 1979). On the other hand, many families claim that the stress of the mental retardation has brought the family closer together (Grossman, 1972). Overall, the rate of divorce in families of the mentally retarded (when they have been matched for social class) does not differ significantly from families of normal children (Davis & MacKay, 1973; Schufeit & Wurster, 1976).

Mediating Factors

The extent to which families experience crises is seen as being mediated by (a) the familial interpretation of the stressor event, and (b) the familial resources available for managing that stressor event (Hill, 1958). Certain familial resources for managing the various stresses presented will decrease their impact on the family. For example, a family living in a community which is tolerant of a mentally retarded person—such as a rural community (Dunlop & Hollingsworth, 1977) or a strongly Catholic community (Menolascino, 1977; Saenger, 1960, Note 2)—might experience a significantly decreased number of stigmatized social interactions. A family with strong extended family network, including active involvement in the caretaking, would not find the prolonged special needs as burdensome (Farber, 1959; Waisbren, 1980). Similarly, a mother who has a close friend with a similarly afflicted child and who is consulting regularly with an accepting, specialist pediatrician and social worker team, may have an abundance of relevant information on daily management. Finally, access to a supportive marital partner, close friends and relatives, and non-judgmental professionals may enable a parent to express periodic grieving without being considered pathological.

Periodic Potential Crises over Time

Although the stresses above occur continuously throughout the life of the mentally retarded person within his/her family, parental awareness of the stresses is periodically increased. An underlying thesis in this paper is that *when a discrepancy emerges between what parents expect of a child's development and of parenting as opposed to what actually takes place when rearing a mentally retarded child,* a crisis may be precipitated.

The anticipation of a crisis can have an ameliorating effect on its impact (Golan, 1980), but parents of the mentally retarded commonly adopt the coping mechanism of living day to day. Although this proves functional in many ways, it becomes problematic if it inhibits their ability to anticipate potential crisis periods over time.

Professionals, as well, have historically been more sensitized to the immediate crisis surrounding diagnosis, and less concerned with ensuing crises. In fact, most of the clinical literature on familial responses to mental retardation suggests that after parents experience three stages of adjustment (e.g. emotional disorganizations, reintegration, and mature adaptation) they learn to live without undue stress (American Medical Association, 1964). The various emotions that parents are said to experience upon learning that their child is mentally retarded include alarm, ambivalence, denial, guilt, shame, self-pity, sorrow, depression, and a wish for their child's death (Price-Bonham and Addison, 1978; Wolfensberger, 1967). The task of the helping professional is to recognize the "novelty shock" early and to help parents work through that "well circumscribed, definable and time-bound process" (Menolascino, 1977, p. 255).

Although the dominant viewpoint in the psychotherapeutic literature has pointed to a series of stages common to parents' reactions to the diagnosis (Berger & Foster, 1976; Jacobsen & Humphrey, 1979) another view is suggested by a parent of a retarded child.

> Professionals could help parents more—and they would be more realistic—if they discarded their ideas about stages and progress.

> They could then begin to understand something about the deep lasting changes that life with a retarded son or daughter brings to parents and then they could begin to see that negative feelings—the shock, the guilt and the bitterness—never disappear but stay on as part of the parents' emotional life (Searle, 1978, p. 23).

The experience of Mr. Searle suggests that the stresses induced by the addition of a mentally retarded child to the family unit are not one-time phenomenon, and that the stresses cannot be alleviated by a single adjustment. In a pamphlet produced by the National Association of Retarded Citizens on Needs of Parents of Retarded Children, Murray writes:

> After thirteen years experience as the mother of a retarded child and having talked and corresponded with literally hundreds of other parents, I have come to the conclusion that all of our many, many needs can be covered in one sentence and it is this:
> The greatest single need of parents of mentally retarded children is constructive professional counselling at various stages of the child's life which will enable the parents to find answers to their own individual problems to a reasonably satisfactory degree. (Murray, Note 7, p. 11).

An increasing number of clinicians are listening to and supporting the perspective voiced by these parents. Olshansky (1962) coined the term "chronic sorrow" referring to a long term internalization of a depressive mood responding in an understandable, nonneurotic manner to a tragic fact. Farber (Note 3) noted the normality of parental disappointment in response to the tragic crisis, and describes the ongoing disruption of the normal family life cycle resulting from having a mentally retarded child. Menolascino (1977) distinguished three types of crises experienced by parents, including the "reality" crises and the "values" crises that can occur throughout the life span. Peterson & Lippa (Note 8) described seven crises (including diagnostic, informational, socialization, family adjustment, school, social and independence) discussing the parental needs of each one.

What is lacking in these conceptualizations of chronic stresses is an hypothesis for when these crises might occur. The accepted view that a crisis occurs following the diagnosis because of the general disruption of expectancies (Menolascino, 1977) is probably correct; but the conclusion that the gradually regained equilibrium is permanent is probably incorrect. Rearing a mentally retarded child brings with it a whole life of shattered expectations. If tension between what is expected and what occurs produces one crisis (the diagnostic crisis) that dynamic also should hold for later periods of important expectations.

It is hypothesized that ten critical periods are potentially stressful for families of mentally retarded children (Table 1). When these occur, the family would experience a *renewed* emotional upheaval and would need to reactivate their coping mechanisms to reestablish family functioning. Five of the critical periods are defined by the chronological age of the child

and are related to an age which for a normal child is characterized by achieving a major developmental milestone. The other five periods are essentially distinctive events not experienced by parents of normal children. There are several instances in which developmental and transitional crises coincide in time.

Crises Arising from Lack of Normal Developmental Progression

One of the most widely shared parental expectations is for normal developmental progression through certain milestones such as baby's first step or first word. These are symbolic markers of important periods of growth towards independence. In the case of the normal child, parents will recall details about each stage of development from their own childhood, will hear about them from their

Table 1. The Hypothesized Effect of Predictable Crises on Types of Stress

Discrepancy in Expectations	Types of Stress			
	Parenting: No Models	Prolonged Burden of Care	Stigmatized Interaction	Grieving
of Child's Development				
Child should have begun walking (12–15 months)	Increase	Same	Increase	Increase
Child should have begun talking (24–30 months)	Increase	Same	Increase	Increase
Beginning of public school (public label as different in classroom)	Decrease	Decrease	Increase	Mixed
Onset of puberty (tension between physical appearance and mental/social ability)	Increase	Increase	Increase	Increase
21st birthday (symbolic of independence)	Increase	Increase	Increase	Increase
of Parenting Events Experienced Only by Families of the Mentally Retarded				
Diagnosis of mental retardation	Increase	Increase	Increase	Increase
Younger sibling with lower CA has MA matching and then higher than MR sibling	Increase	Same	Increase	Increase
Serious discussion of placement of MR child outside the home (or placement itself)	Increase	Decrease	Decrease	Mixed
Exacerbated behavior, seizure or health problems unique to MR child	Increase	Increase	Increase	Increase
Serious discussion about guardianship and care for the MR child	Increase	Increase	Same	Increase

neighbors, will see them demonstrated on television and read about them in magazines and books on rearing children. Children's normal developmental milestones are available as practical information to anyone who wants to measure their child against normality.

The deviance of mentally retarded children lies in the delayed achievement of the developmental milestones. Their rate of development and the discrepancy of that development from the norm becomes the area focused upon for diagnosis and treatment and, consequently, the source of heightened stress for the parent. The slow development in mental age in retarded children stands in stark contrast to their chronological age. This disjuncture constitutes the underlying common denominator of the critical period which is here called "developmental crises." Each period involves acknowledgement that the child's performance is discrepant from expectations for what should have occurred had the child been normal. The poignancy lies in the gap between what is expected and what occurs.

Five developmental crises, therefore, can be identified on the bases of the normal child's developmental milestones: (a) the child should have begun to walk (ages 12–15 months); (b) the child should have begun to talk (24–30 months); (c) the child should be starting kindergarten in public school (the child is publicly labeled as "different" and belonging in "special classes"); (d) the onset of puberty (tension between physical appearance vs. mental-social ability); and (e) the 21st birthday (symbolic of independence from the family).

Crises Arising from Transitions in Perception and Services

In the same way that parents have expectations that are culturally derived about normal developmental milestones, they also have expectations about the parenting experience. Certain expectations will not be fulfilled in the process of rearing a mentally retarded child. The events that occur only in families of the mentally retarded could be critical periods in which the discrepancy between what was expected of parenting and what happened were the greatest. It is at these points that the clinician would expect the greatest potential for stress in families of mentally retarded children.

The most obvious of these crises (the sixth one) is that of the professional diagnosis of the child being mentally retarded rather than normal. The seventh crisis often arises when the parents consider the possibility of having others rear their abnormal child, i.e., placement. The eighth parental crisis occurs when the normal sibling with a lower chronological age performs at a higher developmental level than the retarded child and the retarded child moves functionally into a different ordinal position within the family (Farber, 1959). The ninth crisis arises from child management problems necessitating professional involvement, such as seizure control, stereotypic behavior, and health issues which are unique to the mentally retarded child. The serious discussion about guardianship of the child as the parents grow older and the possibility of having to relinquish guardianship to an outside-the-family member is the tenth crisis.

This second group of crises involves transitions away from the traditional carrying out of parental responsibilities, shifts away from the family and towards professionals in the assignment of decision-making. The process of negotiating with the social service delivery system and the stigma of that process contributes to the stress of the transitional crises. The parents are reminded at each point that had their child been normal this process would not have been necessary. This, in turn, will re-evoke the disappointment about their situation and about the deviant life which they and their offspring are living together.

In a study which was conducted to ascertain parental perspectives on developmental and transitional crises described in this paper, 30 parents retrospectively described their feelings at the times of the 10 critical periods (Wikler, Wasow, & Hatfield, 1981). Data suggest support for the hypothesis that adjustment of parents of mentally retarded children is one of chronic sorrow rather than time-bound adjustment. The data do not, however, indicate that the sorrow is continuous; it seems, rather, to be a periodic phenomenon. Each of the 10 postulated critical periods appeared to precipitate a period of stress for the families. The parents' reported responses to these periods did not decrease in intensity over time. In fact, following the diagnosis, the 21st birthday was the second most stressful of the 10 crises.

The thesis of this paper is that *the various stresses experienced by families of mentally retarded children are exacerbated over time by unexpected discrepancies between what might have been and what is.* The hypothesized interactions of the developmental and transitional crises with the stresses described in the first section are outlined in Table 1.

Implications for Research and Clinical Interventions

Although retrospective accounts of parents have provided initial support for the 10 predictable critical periods over the life-span, an in-depth current examination of the manifestations of stress within family interaction is needed. A longitudinal study which measured various indices of stress before, during and after the occurrence of these periods in conjunction with similar cross-sectional data would allow one to compare families in the various stressful and nonstressful periods contemporaneously.

Further investigation of these conjectures are important in light of their clinical implications. First, due to past practices of institutionalization of the mentally retarded, the professional community has not been involved with the *ongoing* stresses that are part of rearing a mentally retarded child within the home. With the current shift towards deinstitutionalization and maintenance in the home, as well as the increased exposure of professionals to mentally retarded children in the school system, more professionals will inevitably become increasingly involved with these families. An awareness of the special difficulties encountered by parents rearing their retarded child at home is necessary before the professionals will be able to make appropriate interventions with those families. Parents as consumers of these services should be considered as rich sources of information for professionals (Wikler, 1979).

Second, since anticipation of crises is itself an ameliorating factor, professional as well as parental awareness of the predictable periods of vulnerability may help to reduce the impact of those stressor events on families. Self-help parent groups could be organized to prepare parents ahead of time for the high risk periods. Third, parents would find themselves being less self-critical about their responses to the difficulties of having a mentally retarded child if they were aware of the normality of these disappointments over time and of the chronic sorrow.

Lynn Wikler is Assistant Professor, School of Social Work and Waisman Center on Mental Retardation and Human Development, University of Wisconsin-Madison, Madison, Wisconsin 53705.

Notes and References

1. Wikler, L. *A neglected population: Needs of the single parent of a mentally retarded child.* Paper presented at American Association on Mental Deficiency, Miami, Florida, May, 1979.

2. Saenger, G. *Factors Influencing the Institutionalization of Mentally Retarded Individuals in New York City.* Albany, N.Y.: New York State Interdepartmental Health Resources Board, 1960.

3. Farber, B. Sociological ambivalence and family care: The individual proposes and society disposes. *Family Care of Developmentally Disabled Members Conference Proceedings.* (Available from Department of Psychoeducational Studies, University of Minnesota, August, 1979.)

4. Moore, C., & Seachore, C. *Why do families need respite care? Building a support system.* Unpublished report, 1977. (Available from Montgomery County Respite Care Coalition and Maryland State Planning Council on D.D.)

5. Wikler, L., & Hanusa, D. *The impact of respite care on stress in families of mentally retarded children.* Paper presented at American Association on Mental Deficiency, San Francisco, May, 1980.

6. Cohen, S. *Demonstration model continua of respite care and parent training services for families of persons with developmental disabilities.* Unpublished Annual Report, 1979. (Available from

United Cerebral Palsy Associations, Inc., City University of New York.)

7. Murray, M. Needs of parents of mentally retarded children. *National Association for Retarded Citizens.* (Available from 2709 Avenue East, P.O. Box 6109, Arlington, Texas, 76011, 1970.)

8. Peterson, R., & Lippa, S. *Life cycle crises encountered by families of developmentally disabled children: Implications and recommendations for practice.* Paper presented at American Association on Mental Deficiency, Denver, Colorado, May 1978.

Adams, M. *Mental retardation and its social dimensions.* New York: Columbia University Press, 1971.

American Medical Association. *Mental retardation: A handbook for the primary physician.* New York: Author, 1964.

Barsch, H. *Parents of the handicapped child.* Springfield, IL: Charles C. Thomas, 1968.

Berger, M., & Foster, M. Family-level interventions for retarded children: A multivariate approach to issues and strategies. *Multivariate Experimental Clinical Research,* 1976, 2, 1–21.

Birenbaum, A. On managing a courtesy stigma. *Journal of Health and Social Behavior,* 1970, 11, 106–206.

Birenbaum, A. The mentally retarded child in the home and the family cycle. *Journal of Health and Social Behavior,* 1971, 12, 55–65.

Cook, J. J. Dimensional analysis of child-rearing attitudes of parents of handicapped children. *American Journal of Mental Deficiency,* 1963, 8, 354–361.

Cummings, S. T., Bayley, H. C., & Rie, H. E. Effects of the child's deficiency on the mother: A study of mothers of mentally retarded, chronically ill, and neurotic children. *American Journal of Orthopsychiatry,* 1966, 36, 595–608.

Davis, M., & MacKay, D. Mentally subnormal children and their families. *The Lancet,* October 27, 1973.

Edgerton, R. *The cloak of competence: Stigma in the lives of the mentally retarded.* Berkeley: University of California Press, 1967.

Emde, R., & Brown, C. Adaptation to the birth of a Down's Syndrome infant: Grieving and maternal attachment. *American Academy of Child Psychiatry,* 1978, 17, 299–323.

Erickson, M. T. MMPI comparisons between parents of young emotionally disturbed children and mentally retarded children. *Journal of Consulting Clinical Psychology,* 1968, 32, 701–706.

Farber, B. Family adaptations to severely mentally retarded on family integration. *Monographs of the Society for Research in Child Development,* No. 71, 1959.

Farber, B. *Mental retardation: Its social context and social consequences.* Boston: Houghton Mifflin Co., 1968.

Farber, B. Family adaptations to severely mentally retarded children. In M. J. Begals and S. A. Richardson (eds.), *The mentally retarded and society: A social science perspective.* Baltimore University Park Press, 1975.

Farber, B., & Jenne, W. C. Family organization and parent-child communication: Parents and siblings of a retarded child. *Monographs of the Society for Research in Child Development,* 1963, 7, 28.

Farber, B., Jenne, W., & Tolgo, R. Family crisis and the decision to institutionalize the retarded child. Washington, D.C.: Council for Exceptional Children, NEA *Research Monograph Series,* 1960, No. A-1.

Fowle, C. M. The effect of the severely mentally retarded child on his family. *American Journal of Mental Deficiency,* 1968, 73, 468–476.

Friedrich, W. Predictors of the coping behavior of mothers of handicapped children. *Journal of Consulting and Clinical Psychology,* 1979, 47, 1140–1141.

Gath, A. Sibling reactions to mental handicap: A comparison of the brothers and sisters of mongol children. *Journal of Child Psychology and Psychiatry,* 1974, 15, 187–198.

Graliker, B., Koch, R., & Henderson, R. A study of factors influencing placement of retarded children in a state residential institution. *American Journal of Mental Deficiency,* 1965, 69, 553–559.

Golan, N. Interventions at times of transition: Sources and forms of help. *Social Casework,* 1980, 61, 259–266.

Grossman, F. K. *Brothers and sisters of retarded children: An exploratory study.* Syracuse, N.Y.: Syracuse University Press, 1972.

Hill, R. Generic features of families under stress. *Social Casework,* 1958, 39, 139–150.

Holt, K. Home care of severely retarded children. *Pediatrics,* 1958, 22, 744–754.

Illingworth, R. S. Counseling the parents of the mentally handicapped child. *Clinical Pediatrics,* 1967, 6, 340–348.

Jacobsen, R. B., & Humphry, R. Families in crisis: Research and theory in child mental retardation. *Social Casework,* 1979, 60, 597–601.

Levinson, R. Family crisis and adaptation: Coping with a mentally retarded child. Unpublished Dissertation, University of Wisconsin, 1975.

Mandelbaum, A. The group process in helping parents of retarded children. *Children,* 1967, 14, 227–232.

Matheny, A., & Vernick, J. Parents of the mentally retarded child: Emotionally overwhelmed or informationally deprived? *Journal of Pediatrics,* 1969, 74, 953–959.

McAllister, R., Butler, E., & Lei, T. J. Patterns of social interaction among families of behaviorally retarded children. *Journal of Marriage and the Family,* 1973, 35, 93–100.

Menolascino, F. J. *Challenges in mental retardation: Progressive ideology and services.* New York: Human Sciences Press, 1977.

Olshansky, S. Chronic sorrow: A response to having a mentally defective child. *Social Casework,* 1962, 43, 190–193.

Parks, R. M. Parental reactions to the birth of a handicapped child. *Health and Social Work,* 1977, 2, 52–66.

Price-Bonham, S., & Addison, S. Families and mentally retarded children: Emphasis on the father. *The Family Coordinator,* 1978, 27, 221–230.

Pueschel, S., & Murphy, A. Assessment of counseling practices at the birth of a child with Down's Syndrome. *American Journal of Mental Deficiency,* 1976, 81, 325–330.

Schufeit, L. J. & Wurster, S. R. Frequency of divorce among parents of handicapped children. *Resources in Education,* 1976, 11, 71–78.

Searle, S. J., Stages of parent reaction: Mainstreaming. *The Exceptional Parent,* 1978, April, 23–27.

Solnit, A., & Stark, M. Mourning and the birth of a defective child. *Psychoanalytic Studies of the Child,* 1961, 16, 523–536.

Stone, N. M. Family factors in willingness to place the mongoloid child. *American Journal of Mental Deficiency,* 1965, 72, 16–20.

Voysey, M. Impression management by parents with disabled children. *Journal of Health and Social Behavior,* 1972, 13, 80–89.

Waisbren, S. Parents' reactions after the birth of a developmentally disabled child. *American Journal of Mental Deficiency,* 1980, 34, 345–351.

Waskowitz, C. The parents of retarded children speak for themselves. *The Journal of Pediatrics,* 1953, 54, 319–329.

Wikler, L. Consumer involvement in training of social work students. *Social Casework,* 1979, March, 145–149.

Wikler, L., Wasow, M., & Hatfield, E. Chronic sorrow revisited: Attitudes of parents and professionals about adjustment to mental retardation. *American Journal of Orthopsychiatry,* 1981, 51, 63–70.

Wolfensberger, W. Counseling parents of the retarded. In A. Baumeister (Ed.), *Appraisal, education, rehabilitation.* Chicago: Aldine, 1967.

LYNN WIKLER
MONA WASOW
ELAINE HATFIELD

Seeking Strengths in Families of Developmentally Disabled Children

On Mother's Day, 1980, Erma Bombeck included a supportive poem for mothers of handicapped children in her syndicated newspaper column.[1] In later commenting on the reactions of readers, Bombeck indicated that "never in the sixteen years of [the column's] existence, had there been such a reader response." Most of the letters were written by mothers of handicapped children, who stated a determination to be strong and to feel good about themselves. In contrast to these was a letter from a social worker, which said, "Sure, some gain the strength you talked about. *But tell about the ones who drown.*" [Italics added.] This statement exemplifies the perspective that many helping professionals have toward the parents of developmentally disabled children. This article is a plea to professionals to look instead for families' strengths when working with the families of children who are developmentally disabled.

Clinical intervention and research with the families of developmentally disabled children have consistently focused on the prob-

lems, stresses, and inadequacies of these families.[2] There are at least two reasons why this approach may be detrimental. First, it may be mistaken. Families may have more successes than failures in dealing with their children, and by looking for problems within the families of the developmentally disabled, the clinician or researcher may unknowingly direct attention away from potential positive outcomes. Second, the clinician or researcher may create the milieu that he or she assumed existed. This could come about as a result of insufficient reinforcement being provided to families for exhibiting coping behaviors and because of a focus directed exclusively on the negative.

In the past, when parents insisted on mentioning their strengths, such as by pointing out that they had benefited from the challenges presented by caring for a developmentally disabled child, experts would often interpret these reactions as defensive. Parents' statements of satisfaction or pride were therefore frequently considered to be evidence of denial, sublimation, or overcompensation. In 1981, the authors conducted a study that examined reports of "chronic sorrow"—sadness that did not disappear over time—experienced by parents of mentally retarded children.[3] In part of the study previously unreported, parents were asked whether raising a developmentally disabled child had made them stronger or weaker. The response to the query was surprising. As expected, most parents acknowledged that they felt chronic sorrow, but, remarkably, most of them also indicated they had become stronger people because of their experience.

At the time of the study, the authors discounted these findings. (However, they did *not* discount the data from the rest of the questionnaire.) They decided that methodological reasons accounted for many subjects' apparent conviction that being the parent of a retarded child had been a strengthening rather than a debilitating experience. They now consider this initial dismissal to be another example of a pervasive stance adopted among professionals, in which problems instead of strength and instances of coping are concentrated on in dealing with families of developmentally disabled children. They therefore wish to share their earlier findings with others and to discuss the pertinent clinical implications.

Subjects' Responses

When asked directly, 75 percent of the parents studied ($n = 27$) reported feeling that being a parent of a developmentally disabled child had made them stronger. Forty-six percent felt that the experience had made them much stronger. Although most parents indicated that they experienced chronic sorrow, they also stated that they tried to keep their feelings of sadness under control. They were divided on whether it was better to express their sadness or to control it, but they knew clearly what they wanted professionals to do for them— they wanted to be encouraged to be strong.

The authors also asked workers in a social service agency ($N = 43$) about their perceptions of how parents of mentally retarded children adjusted to their children's illness. The workers' descriptions were in keeping with the parents' responses in several instances. For example, they were aware that parents experience chronic sorrow, that is, that parents' feelings of grief fluctuate over time rather than move in stages from despair to mature adjustment. Specifically, 63 percent of the workers felt that parents experience chronic sorrow, and 65 percent of the parents experienced it.

However, the workers underestimated the extent to which parents felt they had been made much stronger by the experience of caring for a mentally retarded child. Forty-six percent of the parents felt they had been made much stronger, but only 9 percent of the workers believed that parents would feel this way. They also underestimated the extent to which parents wished to be encouraged to be strong and to cope: 67 percent of the parents wished to be encouraged to be strong, and 26 percent of the workers believed that parents wanted this.

Parents shared their feelings to a greater extent than they were asked to as part of the study. A curious combination of sadness and strength appeared in their remarks. Subjects stated that "Yes, we experience a sorrow that does not disappear with time," but "We feel stronger from and even grateful for that experience." The following are typical comments made by the parents in the study:

> As the parent of a retarded child, I believe that it has made me stronger. It has made me much more patient than I was. Even emotionally you get an inner strength to deal with everyday care and problems of the child.

> I don't really know if I am any stronger emotionally or not. I think you learn to accept what you cannot change, and you have to learn to cope and live with it. I comfort myself with the belief that God gives these children to special people. I'm honored He chose me.

> When I first realized my son was lagging, I felt very guilty and wondered if I had somehow caused it. Then I began to tell myself that I can't handle it, I'm too inept to cope with a retarded child—but all the while I was coping with him.

> It has caused us to be more sympathetic toward people with such problems. Our love for this child seems deeper as we realize her need for greater understanding.

Having a retarded child causes you to ask certain questions that perhaps you would never ask and to develop certain values.

———————

We hit many peaks and valleys. I would say that there is some sorrow, but our happy moments overshadow the sad times. Our daughter has been a joy and a sorrow.

Clinical and Research Implications

Clearly, no one elects to have a developmentally disabled child; the events that have such a permanent impact on the course of one's family life seem to strike at random. As indicated earlier, the literature on the adjustment of families of developmentally disabled children focuses on the detrimental impact that such children have on the family. Study after study has been done to determine whether the presence of a mentally retarded child in a family is associated with increased rates of alcoholism, depression, physical illness, or divorce. In each instance, when social class has been held constant, the answer has been no.[4] The only repeatedly observed effects reported in the literature can be summarized as the following: (1) increased risk of social isolation for the family, (2) increased stress experienced by the primary caregiver, usually the mother, and (3) an increased tendency for adolescent siblings who share the burden of care to develop problems.[5]

Intervening variables related to family resources, such as supportiveness between marital partners, religion, and regular contacts with extended family, have been found to reduce the risk of stress.[6] However, even findings such as these have been presented in the literature in a less-than-positive way, for the variables have been regarded as nothing more than mediators of stress rather than as factors contributing to a family's well-being. Overall, the possibility that families who raise a developmentally disabled child might derive some unexpected benefits from their experience is rarely considered.[7]

New perceptions of these families, in which they are seen not as the odd few who somehow survive a calamity but as successful family systems whose strength has been augmented by raising a child with developmental disabilities, call for a new program of research. General understanding of these families' success would be enhanced by detailed studies concentrating on various family relationships and on such questions as these: Are the spouses especially open and intimate, and do they share tasks and attitudes? What is the special nature of the parents' relationship to the handicapped child—are they more nurturing and less judgmental than other parents? Do these families have exceptionally warm and supportive extended families, and do they have unusually frequent contact with them? Although families who have been successful in caring for a developmentally disabled child may not excel in all the areas relating to these questions, surely their strengths derive from or are reflected in more than the individual resources of each family member. Findings from the research proposed here might help clinicians to focus on strengthening certain family relationships and thereby enable the families to profit from raising a child with developmental disabilities. Social policy, too, might be advantageously revised as a result of studies based on this positive new perception. In the present era of retrenchment, the knowledge of which family support services such as respite care, counseling, or medical care are most effective may prove essential to increasing the number of success stories among families of developmentally disabled children.

Given the bias reflected in the clinical literature, it is not surprising that most of the helping professionals in the authors' study underestimated parental reports of the positive effects related to raising a handicapped child. On the basis of their study and their own work as professionals, the authors have derived several clinical recommendations intended to help workers determine and emphasize a family's strengths. They are the following:

1. In general, workers should be aware that although parents of developmentally disabled children are under stress and are grieved, they may benefit and grow in many ways from having an exceptional child.

2. During the initial interview, workers

should ask parents about their child's unique traits that have given them pleasure.

3. Workers should assess parents' strengths by asking for stories of familial successes in coping. Parents can also be asked what they have learned from their experience and whether friends or family have come through for them in unexpected ways. They should be praised for their creative parenting and be given an opportunity to cite examples.

4. Workers should help parents who have been successful in coping to meet parents whose children have recently been diagnosed as developmentally disabled. During this process, a model of successful familial managing can be provided.

The authors' experiences as clinicians and researchers lead them to believe that chronic sorrow and increased emotional strength are by no means incompatible. Parents of developmentally disabled children experience recurring sadness as a natural response to a tragic reality. However, at the same time, most of them also develop increased strength and coping abilities. Social workers should be paying more attention to the latter.

Lynn Wikler, Ph.D., is Assistant Professor, School of Social Work and Waisman Center on Mental Retardation and Human Development, University of Wisconsin–Madison. Mona Wasow, MSW, is Clinical Associate Professor, School of Social Work, University of Wisconsin–Madison. Elaine Hatfield, Ph.D., is Professor and Chairperson, Department of Psychology, University of Hawaii, Honolulu.

Notes and References

1. Erma Bombeck, "God Carefully Selects Handicapped Child's Mom," *Wisconsin State Journal,* May 11, 1980, Sec. 5, p. 7.

2. R. Brooke Jacobsen and Ruth A. Humphry, "Families in Crisis: Research and Theory in Child Mental Retardation," *Social Casework,* 60 (December 1979), pp. 597–601; S. Price-Bonham and S. Addison, "Families and Mentally Retarded Children: Emphasis on the Father," *Family Coordinator,* 3 (July 1978), pp. 221–230; and M. Berger and M. Foster, "Family-Level Interventions for Retarded Children: A Multivariate Approach to Issues and Strategies," *Multivariate Experimental Clinical Research,* 2 (1976), pp. 1–21.

3. See Lynn Wikler, Mona Wasow, and Elaine Hatfield, "Chronic Sorrow Revisited: Parent vs. Professional Depiction of the Adjustment of Parents of Mentally Retarded Children," *American Journal of Orthopsychiatry,* 51 (1981), pp. 63–70. Sample sizes given in the present article are based on responses to a second questionnaire used in the 1981 study that were not reported originally.

4. M. Davis and D. MacKay, "Mentally Subnormal Children and Their Families," *Lancet,* October 27, 1973; S. J. Korn, S. Chess, and P. Fernandez, "Impact of Children's Physical Handicaps on Marital Quality and Family Interaction," in Richard M. Lerner and Graham B. Spanier, eds., *Child Influences on Marital and Family Interaction* (New York: Academic Press, 1978), pp. 299–325; R. Roesel and G. F. Lawlis, "Divorce in Families of Genetically Handicapped/Mentally Retarded Individuals," *American Journal of Family Therapy,* 11 (1983), pp. 45–50; and L. J. Shufeit and S. R. Wurster, "Frequency of Divorce Among Parents of Handicapped Children," *Resources in Education,* 11 (1976), pp. 71–78.

5. Lynn Wikler, "Chronic Stresses of Families of Mentally Retarded Children," *Family Relations,* 30 (1981), pp. 281–288; and Berger and Foster, "Family-Level Interventions for Retarded Children."

6. B. Farber, "Family Adaptations to Severely Mentally Retarded Children," in M. Begab and S. A. Richardson, eds., *The Mentally Retarded and Society: A Social Science Perspective* (Baltimore, Md.: University Park Press, 1975), pp. 247–266; R. Levinson, "Family Crisis and Adaptation: Coping with a Mentally Retarded Child," unpublished Ph.D. thesis, Department of Sociology, University of Wisconsin–Madison, 1975; and P. Petersen, "Stressors, Outcome Dysfunction, and Resources in Mothers of Children with Handicaps," unpublished Ph.D. thesis, Department of Psychology, University of Nebraska, Lincoln, 1981.

7. Berger and Foster, "Family-Level Interventions for Retarded Children."

BERNARD DAVIDSON
DAVID A. DOSSER, JR.

A Support System for Families with Developmentally Disabled Infants

Developmental disabilities are defined as severe, chronic disabilities of a person which (a) are attributed to mental and/or physical impairment; (b) are manifested before the age of 22 and are likely to continue indefinitely; (c) result in limitations in the areas of self-care, language learning, mobility, capacity for independent living, and economic sufficiency; and (d) reflect a person's need for special care and treatment which are of life-long or extended duration. Examples of such disabilities include Down's Syndrome, Mental Retardation, Cerebral Palsy, and Spina Bifida. According to current estimates approximately 3 to 6% of the U.S. population is considered developmentally disabled (Stewart, 1978).

Factors which disrupt a family's adjustment to the crisis of experiencing the birth of a developmentally disabled child may best be viewed from a model such as Hill's (1949) A, B, C, -X family crisis framework. Within this framework, family crises are seen as resulting from the interactions between A (the stressor

event), B (the family's crisis meeting resources), and C (the definition the family makes of the event). For families experiencing the birth of a developmentally disabled child, the stressor event takes on both a normative and nonnormative quality (McCubbin, Joy, Cauble, Comeau, Patterson, & Needle, 1980). The normative event of transition to parenthood is expectable and ubiquitous, and is usually viewed as a relatively short term progression. The nonnormative event of the addition of a developmentally disabled family member is seen as a more sudden and long lasting chronic occurrence. For families already struggling with normative and other expected life changes, the sudden onset of this nonnormative birth can profoundly influence the level of crisis experienced. The family's crisis meeting resources as well as the definition the family makes of this event will determine in large part the family's regenerative power in adapting to this crisis. As Hill (1949) has suggested, the course of adjustment to crisis is seen as involving a period of disorganization, an angle of recovery, and a new level of organization.

It is in the areas of family regenerative power and management of resources that the availability and procurement of community support can directly aid a family's recovery and re-organization to a crisis such as the birth of a developmentally disabled child. McCubbin (1979) has commented that what may be the major determinants of successful adaptation to family stress are the solutions that the community and culture provide.

With society's strong emphasis on admiring those families whose children demonstrate a great physical and intellectual prowess it is no wonder that parents who give birth to a developmentally disabled infant often perceive this event as a great personal failure. Klaus and Kennell (1976) have commented on the disruptive effects upon parent-infant attachment for these families, which often results in an emotional withdrawal from the child and lowered parental self-esteem as the child is perceived as a sign of the parents' own badness. Before a secure attachment can be fostered, parents must accept the death of their idealized infant and accept the reality of their more frail and imperfect child. In addition, formerly contained conflicts can become magnified and interfere with the functioning of the parenting role. For example, the number of separations and divorces for these families is unusually high and the suicide rate for parents of these children is twice the national average (Love, 1973).

The Quality of Present Services Rendered to Parents

According to McCubbin (1979) and McCubbin et al. (1980) families' involvements in collective support groups offer a potent source of resources for the management of stress. The community support group, acting as a unified body on behalf of families in specific crises situations, is seen as offering a facilitation for regenerative power, that could not be accomplished by individual family solutions alone.

At present it appears that the major responsibility of providing for families with developmentally disabled newborns rests with the attending physician. Wolfenberger (1967) has reported that it is the attending physician who almost always conveys the news of an infant's disability, with most families regarding the extent of information supplied and manner in which it is conveyed as unsatisfactory. Parents often report a less than satisfactory attending to their primary emotional needs when the news of their infant's disability is first discovered. In a study of 215 families (Abramson, Gravink, Abramson, & Sommers, 1977), almost all reported having sought advice from their physician concerning their infant's developmental disability. Of these, only 18% believed that they had received informative and sympathetic guidance, while most reported the quality of medical services were good. Zwerling (1954) has suggested that much can be done precisely at the time of diagnosis of a newborn's developmental disability to reduce parental anxiety and promote a satisfactory adjustment and family acceptance of the child's handicap. Zwerling's interviews with families of developmentally disabled newborns confirmed that a large number of parents reported that their physician offered them a shocking and non-supportive diagnosis. How might it have been for these families had someone initially provided for their emotional support? The comments of some couples suggest that a lot of undue anxiety might have been avoided. One couple commented that their mentally retarded son who is five years old is very lovable, can say several words and group some together, and ride a bike. Initially, all of the physicians that saw his family appeared kind, but not one gave a single word of reassurance.

What Is Needed?

In assessing this type of situation, Abramson, et al. (1977) concluded that what is needed for these families is an immediate informative and supportive approach when confronting parents with the news that their newborn is developmentally disabled. These parents need to be provided with an opportunity to confront, work through, and accept their feelings, as well as be informed concerning the availability of community services, clinics, agencies, and parent groups. The way in which these parents make their initial adjustment to this situation can greatly affect the subsequent patterns of attachment that parents and children engage in. As best said by Bruno Bettelheim, "Children can learn to live well with a disability but cannot live well without the conviction that their parents find them utterly lovable" (Bettelheim, 1972, p. 35). The creation, structure, and function of the Parent Helpers Program is based upon all of these aforementioned considerations.

The Structure of the Parent Helpers Program

The Parent Helpers Program is a support service designed to facilitate a positive climate in which parents of newborn developmentally disabled infants are afforded an opportunity to maximize their adjustment to this family crisis. The program enlists parents who have developmentally disabled children and who have made successful adjustments, as evidenced by their acceptance and success in dealing with this situation, to serve as parent-peer helpers for other parents who are initially experiencing this crisis. Parents selected as peer helpers undergo a training program that emphasizes the basic elements of a successful counseling relationship.

The primary assumptions of our program are: (a) since the parent helpers have lived through and adjusted to the crisis of the birth of a developmentally disabled newborn, they are capable of displaying an enormous amount of empathic understanding; (b) the parents selected as helpers receive training in basic counseling skills and attend lectures on the nature of various developmental disabilities which serves to increase their effectiveness in a helping situation; (c) since the parent helpers have been through this crisis and have adjusted to it, they essentially serve as role models conveying the message, "I too have felt like you and thought it unbearable and I have learned to cope and adapt."

In our program, parents who were selected as peer helpers were drawn from a group of volunteers from the Northeast Georgia Parents' Down's Syndrome Congress. These parents received a ten week, 20 hour training program in basic counseling skills (Blakeman,

Smith, & Elmore, Note 1). Through lecture and role play activities, emphasis was directed toward instructing an active listening approach. Skills emphasized included the expression of empathy as evidenced by *attending* to feelings, *discriminating* feelings from content, and developing a sense of *genuineness* as it pertains to being in an intimate interpersonal exchange. Much practice time was provided to allow trainees to role play and experience effective helping in the roles of both helper and helpee. Continuous constructive feedback was provided from experienced trainers as well as from fellow trainees. All parents who have undergone this training have reported that it has greatly facilitated the ease of communication that they have encountered within their own families.

Parent helpers also received additional training concerning the nature of various types of developmental disabilities that may be encountered through referrals. This was accomplished by bringing in professionals such as physicians, nurses, psychologists, and special educators who led discussion and lecture on such topics as the variety of disabilities and the nature of parental reactions to discovering their child's condition.

The primary source of referrals consists of pediatric and nursery nurses, neonatologists and other community physicians, preschool teachers of developmentally disabled children, and social workers associated with various hospitals. Throughout the year we have periodically met with these groups, informing them of our available services, keeping them up to date on our happenings, and inviting any input they might have as to how we may increase our effectiveness. All of these groups have shown us an overwhelming acceptance and have indicated a willingness to seek out our services.

A most likely example of a referral would be when a developmentally disabled child is born, the attending nurses, after consulting with the parents about the child's disability, would offer the parents the opportunity to meet with one of the parent helpers. The new parents would be told that the parent helpers have gone through a similar situation and have also been trained to assist with the emotional adjustment to such a happening. While our parent helpers are assisting other parents, our project staff is available to offer support to the helpers to facilitate their working with these families. The likely alternatives for parents who use our services are: (a) they will make a successful adjustment and will cease to see their parent helper; (b) they will make a successful adjustment and seek to join other support groups such as those to which the parent helpers belong; (c) they will not display a successful adjustment and will be referred to an appropriate agency that can provide them with needed in-depth counseling and other services.

Two Examples of Referrals

Parents of newborn developmentally disabled infants often report great difficulty in having to tell their friends, neighbors, and parents about the condition of their newborn. Usually family and friends await the arrival of a new child with excitement and enthusiasm, and it is of great disappointment and sorrow to have to break this news to loved ones. It was expected that the availability of our initial services would offer support in handling difficult situations as such described. In addition, it was felt that the sooner parents became wholly accepting of their child and his or her handicap, the sooner they would be likely to seek out other services available in the community. Our overall guiding assumption is that if our parent helper services are effective, then this should ease the adjustment of new parents in all of these situations. The success of our program can best be represented by the presentation of two cases.

The Harrisons

This couple in their mid twenties, a housewife and husband who was an officer candidate at a local naval school, had a Down's Syndrome child born to them. The physician who delivered the child was consulted by one of the nurses who was familiar with our program and he agreed that this service should be offered to the parents. The parents had no relatives or close acquaintances in the community as

they had been recently transferred. When offered the parent helper service, they accepted it and a meeting was set up within a few hours after birth. A couple who also had a Down's Syndrome child and was approximately the same age as the new parents and who had been involved with our training program was selected to serve as the parent helpers.

The following excerpt is abstracted from a diary that the parent helpers kept:

> On our first visit they talked about their disappointment, confusion, embarrassment, and grief and especially about their concern over telling other members of their family. They seemed to be fighting to hold back tears. At times I found it hard not to cry with her. On a subsequent visit the mother cried a lot and seemed more open and pleased to see me. She told me about telling her parents. She expressed feelings about not wanting to accept the diagnosis and hoped the chromosome tests would be negative, but she knew deep down that it was true. She expressed fear about the future. I told her I often think that for some reason God gave us a special baby that needs us and our love more than anything. She smiled and cried and told me her husband had said the same thing. She smiled and told me about feeding the baby and how pretty he was. As I left she told me "You have helped me more than anything and one day I hope I can help someone the way you have helped me."

The Harrisons indicated that although they were concerned about how they would tell their parents, it was not as difficult to tell them as they had anticipated. In addition, at two months after the birth of their child the Harrisons indicated that they sought out at least three additional community services, the first being sought within a week after birth. They indicated that they felt the community was very accepting of their situation and would continue to provide support for them. They reported that their physician was unsympathetic and rushed in breaking the news of their child's disability to them. In fact, he did not offer them any initial advice on services available. These parents learned about additional services from the parent helpers. On a subsequent visit to their physician they showed him all the brochures and pamphlets they had obtained outlining available services. He was so impressed that he sent off for copies for himself and other patients.

The Smiths

The second case to be described in this paper concerns a couple in their mid twenties. The child born to them was a girl who had part of her lower left arm and hand missing. At birth, it was the mother who was the first to notice the deformity. An attending nurse asked the mother if she wanted to see a parent helper and an appointment was set up for the following day.

In the mother's initial meeting with the parent helper, she expressed a lot of anxiety and concern over talking to her parents and neighbors about her daughter. She was most concerned about someone reaching for her daughter's left hand and it not being there. The mother continued to see the parent helper for a number of visits and the success of these visits can be best described from comments from an unsolicited diary that the mother kept during her visits with the parent helper:

> In the hospital I had all calls stopped. I became confused when I thought of a lifetime for my child. Even though I have a different problem than Pat, I felt I was helped by her concern. She sat and listened and then began to tell me how there were others feeling like me and I was not alone. She didn't tell me everything is going to be fine and nobody will notice, the things I heard a million times before. She let me talk and led me to realize I had no choice but to face facts. She also has put me in touch with the Crippled Children's Association, something I had heard nothing about. We were really lost until Pat helped us.

The Smiths also contacted various community services and arranged for an artificial hand to be fitted. As we see it, this reflects a deep level of acceptance of the child and the affliction on the part of the parents. The parents have also expressed an interest in joining our parents' group and possibly serving as parent helpers themselves.

A Primary Goal

In establishing the project, the group most enthusiastic and active in supporting our program in its initial stages was the nursery nurses who were very aware of the emotional needs of these new parents. They have served as a liaison between us and the hospital physicians in communicating our goals. They are the primary source of referrals. Since the population to which we can offer direct services is quite limited, our primary aim has been to produce a replicable model to assist others in initiating similar services. It is our conviction that community support networks, such as the Parent Helpers Program, do fulfill a vital need in facilitating the development of family resources necessary for successful coping and adaptation to this particular family crisis.

Bernard Davidson is an Assistant Professor in the Department of Home and Family Life, Texas Tech University, Lubbock, Texas 79409. David A. Dosser, Jr. is an Assistant Professor in the Department of Child Development and Family Relations, North Dakota State University, Fargo, North Dakota 58105. Earlier versions of this paper were presented at the annual meeting of the National Council on Family Relations, Boston, August, 1979, and the annual meeting of the American Association for Marriage and Family Therapy, Toronto, November, 1980. Research for this paper was supported in part by grant 50-P-20742/4-02 from the Office of Developmental Disabilities Region IV, of the Department of HEW.

Notes and References

1. Blakeman, J., Smith, R., & Elmore, R. *Training manual. Systematic helping skills.* 1974, Georgia State University, based on a training model developed by Dr. Richard M. Pierce of Carkhuff Associates, Inc. of Amherst, Massachusetts.

Abramson, P. R., Gravink, M. J., Abramson, L. M., & Sommers, D. Early diagnosis and intervention of retardation: A survey of parental reactions concerning the quality of services rendered. *Mental Retardation,* 1977, 15, 28–31.

Bettelheim, B. How do you help a child who has a physical handicap? *Ladies Home Journal,* September, 1972, 89. 34–35.

Hill, R. *Families under stress.* New York: Harper and Row, 1949.

Klaus, M. H., & Kennell, J. H. *Maternal-infant bonding.* Saint Louis, Missouri: Mosby, 1976.

Love, H. *The mentally retarded child and his family.* Springfield, Illinois: Thomas, 1973.

McCubbin, H. Integrating coping behavior in family stress theory. *Journal of Marriage and the Family,* 1979, 41, 237–244.

McCubbin, H. I., Joy, C. B., Cauble, A. E., Comeau, J.K., Patterson, J. M., & Needle, R. H. Family stress and coping: A decade review. *Journal of Marriage and the Family,* 1980, 42, 855–871.

Stewart, L. G. Hearing-impaired/developmentally disabled persons in the United States: Definitions, causes, effects and prevalence estimates. *American Annals of the Deaf,* 1978, 23, 488–495.

Wolfenberger, W. Counseling the parents of the retarded. In A. Baumeister (Ed.), *Mental retardation.* Chicago: Aldine. 1967.

Zwerling, I. Initial counseling of parents with mentally retarded children. *Journal of Pediatrics.* 1954, 44, 469–479.

ENOLA K. PROCTOR

New Directions for Work with Parents of Retarded Children

Recent advances in the fields of special education and behavioral psychology are paving the way for more innovative social work with parents of retarded children. With new expectations of improvement and equipped with new methods, social work can now move beyond its traditional, often limited emphases to help parents facilitate their children's development. This article, after briefly reviewing some traditional emphases, will explore the unique contribution that social workers can make and some methods which can be employed toward that end.

Traditional Emphases

A common entry point for social workers is the time of diagnosis of retardation, when parents are emotionally upset and their child's prognosis may seem irreversibly hopeless. Accordingly, professional literature has thoroughly documented parents' emotional states and needs. Accounts are presented of parents' experiencing emotions of grief, sorrow, shock,

depression, anger, guilt, and self-pity,[1] and responding by rejecting initial diagnoses, seeking other medical opinions, and searching for a cause of retardation.[2]

This same literature identifies as goals of intervention helping parents to accept the diagnosis, to deal with the accompanying emotions, and to learn to view their child as having a limited potential.[3] Toward these ends, workers have been limited to those methods of support, clarification, and facilitation of the exploration of feelings that are employed in individual casework or group work practice.[4]

Helen Beck suggests that the development of professional practice has been hampered by a "seeming lack of promise of returns from work in the field of retardation."[5] To social work practice and theory, retardation has not seemed very amenable to treatment,[6] and professional involvement has seemed unpromising. Social work practice and theory, then, may not have moved far beyond issues related to diagnosis, and may reflect a view of retardation as an irreversible, relatively static condition to which acceptance and at times resignation seem the only possible responses.

This view, held for so long and perhaps

still prevalent in practice, should be examined in light of current evidence. The assumed irreversibility of the seemingly hopeless condition of retardation is now being challenged by the discovery of ways, some small and some large and dramatic, to reverse the irreversible. Although shock and frustration may still accompany a diagnosis of retardation, the child, the parents, and the professionals can move ahead to deal with issues of growth and development. Technologies in special education and behavioral psychology are being employed to produce advances of a range, degree, and rate that professionals had not previously thought possible due to limitations assumed inherent in retardation. Improvements in level of intellectual functioning and self-help, language, motor, and social skills are now, however, increasingly viewed as possible for even the severely retarded.[7] As management of these symptoms is demonstrated, a contemporary view regards retardation as a dynamic rather than a static condition, one amenable to modification and improvement through casework, counseling, education, and training.[8]

But these advances are usually provided by other specialists, such as teachers and behavioral psychologists. Where are social workers? Have they reflected the dramatic progress that has occurred in special education, and found promise in this field? What implications for social workers, particularly working in conjunction with parents, are raised by advances in child training? Perhaps social workers must embark on a new course —a course marked by knowledge of current behavior change methodologies, new attitudes toward retardation, and new skills to be made available as training for parents.

Need for New Directions

The need for new directions in social work was clarified for the author recently when introducing a rapid toilet training program[9] to the parents of an eleven-year-old, "moderately" retarded boy. The child, who was living at home and was enrolled in a special education school, met the behavioral entry criteria for the toilet training program, and

school personnel were convinced of his suitability for the training. The parents, however, did not believe that their son could profit from the training. Ten years before, they had been advised by a social worker to recognize that their son would never attain certain skills, among them toilet training. They had "accepted" the fact of his retardation and resigned themselves to his limitations. Staff, however, proceeded with the program, focusing on the child's toileting habits and the parents' attitudes of resignation as equally important targets for change. Although the boy learned to initiate proper toileting behaviors at school, he was less successful at home. The parents expressed, at times explicitly, their conviction that the social worker of ten years ago was correct in predicting their son's limitations.

The experience of these parents, unfortunately not unique, makes obvious an important fact: attitudes of resignation, perhaps realistic ten years ago, are both unrealistic and detrimental today. Resignation is unrealistic because advances in knowledge and training methodology expand at such a rate that we can never state with certainty that a child will not surpass a given level of development. Resignation is, in addition, detrimental because negative attitudes may actually prevent a child from reaching his full potential. Charles Pascal observes that when adults define and treat a child as if he is retarded, the behaviors which will be attended to by those around him are behaviors which are expected, namely those compatible with the concept of retardation.[10] Research with mothers of retarded children reveals a tendency for those who describe and view their children as defective to see the child as an infant and to respond by overstructuring the child's environment.[11] Workers' biases or stereotypes, too, may result in self-fulfilling prophecies if their expectations of poor outcomes cause them to feel discouraged about intervention.[12] Negative attitudes in workers and parents may, therefore, result in the retarded child's remaining or becoming less active, less competent, and less self-sufficient than he might otherwise become.[13] Accordingly, acceptance and resignation to limits can no longer be accepted as appropriate goals of casework treatment,[14] and workers must take care that negative attitudes, in parents or in themselves, are not engendered or reinforced, even inadvertently, by sympathetic counseling. Social work's tradition of concern for families of the retarded can be channeled in some new directions.

Proposed New Directions

This article proposes two emphases for future social work practice with parents of the retarded: First, that social workers themselves must adopt and then instill in parents new, healthier expectations toward the retarded; second, that beyond the realm of attitudes, social workers can help equip parents with more effective skills for working with their children.

If expectations are realistic, attitudes toward work with the retarded can remain positive and not become negated by frustration and failure. Although learning may be slow and occur in small increments, retarded children can learn, and those around them must expect achievement. Thus the attention of professionals and parents should be focused neither on upper limits to a child's achievement nor, impatiently, on global learning tasks.

The fostering of positive yet realistic expectations, then, might begin with a reexamination and modification of the attitudes of social workers. Professionals' attitudes are explicitly and implicitly transmitted to parents and affect the quality of services delivered;[15] these attitudes should reflect current progress in the field of special education.

Social workers can then help instill in parents realistically positive expectations toward their children in several ways. First, parents should be encouraged to expect their child to learn only *one skill or behavior at a time.* Such a focus is realistic because it delimits learning to manageable proportions, yet positively identifies a goal to be achieved. Second, parents can be assisted in assessing their child's readiness to learn the identified target skill. Realistically, a child's learning can only proceed on the basis of existing skills; yet

assurance that a child has achieved skills prerequisite to a new task is evidence for optimism. Third, parents should be assisted in identifying and ordering the component substeps of the task to be achieved. Progress will occur in small increments; these increments should therefore be the focus of parents' attention and positive expectations. By directing parents' attention in these ways, social workers can help relieve the parents' sense of frustration, provide a focus for expectations, and contribute to a realistic foundation for confidence that the child can achieve.

Positive expectations of achievement can serve as a basis for a second focus of social work with parents of the retarded, which is the provision of more effective skills for working with their children. Exclusive attention to parents' attitudes and feelings has been recognized as minimal treatment,[16] particularly in light of growing evidence that workers can help equip parents with new ways of responding to their children.[17] In day-to-day tasks, parents can help maximize their children's self-sufficiency[18] and workers can help prepare them to do so. Parents assume a role of teacher to their children, and social workers assume a role of consultant or trainer to parents.[19] These roles present several advantages. Parents are usually the first to encounter and have to deal with problematic behavior, and they can facilitate the transfer of learning from school or treatment to home.[20] In addition, parents of retarded children can gain a great deal of satisfaction from contributing to their child's achievement.[21]

Parental assistance has frequently been employed by social workers to help eliminate problem behavior in their children. However, in the field of retardation, perhaps uniquely, parents can help their children to acquire adaptive behavior, particularly self-help and social skills. Tasks which parents may help teach in day-to-day activities include language acquisition, play behavior, toilet training, dressing skills, feeding skills, attention focusing, and imitation.[22] To guide parents in developing these behaviors in their children, social workers need not become expert speech therapists, psychologists, or special educators.

However, familiarity with learning processes may be required. Social workers may then fulfill their unique and most important role: translating the processes of child education to parents and helping them to generalize these processes within new contexts. In addition to specific adaptive skills, social workers working with parents may also focus on more general problems of behavior management, such as discipline issues or parent-child communication. Skills imparted in counseling may then be individualized and applied in a variety of situations which may later arise in the home.

Methods of Parent Counseling

Social workers may draw on a variety of methods to help provide parents with skills for working with their children. Selection of a method involves consideration of parents' needs and strengths, the problem or task facing the child, and practical considerations of time and economy with respect to the worker's total responsibility. Any one of the methods to be reviewed below may be employed individually or in groups. Individual counseling may be preferable with the child who is acquiring or modifying a unique behavior or when the parent needs individual attention and assurance from the worker. Groups, however, are advantageous and economical if several parents or children have similar abilities and problems. In groups, parents can learn from each other, encourage each other, and offer acceptable suggestions and examples. The parent who shares the "teaching" role can learn and gain self-confidence. For socially isolated parents, the group may be the only audience with whom to share achievements and the only source of encouragement and support.

Didactic Counseling

With a didactic approach, the worker assumes the role of teacher, passing on to parents skills in behavior management.[23] Programmed texts, designed to teach parents principles of behavior change, and the exercises for application are increasingly used by social workers,[24] especially in group treatment. A number of texts are available and applicable to parents on a variety of educational levels.[25] To individualize this approach and for specific skill training, such as toilet training, feeding skills, and attention focusing, the worker may find it useful to write his own material. Text material has two major advantages: procedures and behavior sequencing are clearly presented and may be referred to repeatedly by parents, and application and generalization to situations occurring at home are encouraged, often through "homework" assignments.

Modeling

A second technique effective in parent counseling is modeling, wherein the worker, teacher, or other parent demonstrates correct interaction with a child. Simple advice is seldom sufficient to add skills to a parent's repertoire of behaviors and often leaves parents wondering exactly what they are supposed to do once they are home. Modeling is especially effective when the desired behavior in the child occurs infrequently or when the desired response is new to the parent.[26] The thoroughness of modeling can serve to increase the parent's confidence in knowing what can be done, and then doing it. Seeing is believing.

Rehearsal

A third effective method of parent training is rehearsal, in which the parent performs, evaluates, and repeatedly practices the responses he is to perform at home with his child.[27] The role of the worker, in addition to modeling, is to support, to encourage, and to praise the parent's performance. This method has the advantages of showing the parent not only that his child can perform a new task, but that, in addition, the parent is being instrumental in helping the child, thus demonstrating to the worker an understanding of the desired behavior and appropriate response to the child.

Videotape

For workers with access to videotape equipment, the small investment of time required to learn to use the equipment can produce enormous benefits. In counseling with parents, videotape has at least two advantages: Once on tape, exact model presentation of desired interaction with children can be presented to numbers of parents any time it is needed; specialized personnel, such as a speech therapist, need not be present each time parents meet to learn more about language acquisition. Videotape may be used to provide parents with immediate replay of their filmed interactions with their child; mistakes can be quickly identified and the positive reinforcement of successes can be presented. One father, when viewing the filmed replay of his successful management of lunchtime feeding of his usually troublesome daughter, exclaimed that he would not have believed that he had been so successful without seeing it himself. The replay presented powerful reinforcement, while enabling him to closely examine his successful response to his daughter.

Any method selected for a particular time and task must be augmented by the worker's demonstration of respect for and support of the parent. Counseling should be made relevant to the needs of the parent and child. A clear definition of procedures and goals can serve to minimize parents' anxiety[28]

and maximize the likelihood of parents' successes. And, most important, demonstration of concern and conviction that the parent can be successful must come clearly and frequently. Efforts at behavior management and skill acquisition require considerable investment of parents' time and energy. Frequent phone calls can be effective communicators of the worker's support. That support, in combination with innovative counseling methods, offers to parents of the retarded child positive expectations and specific skills for dealing with a situation for which social workers have too long offered only understanding.

While psychologists and special educators have particular expertise at developing change modalities for retarded children, social workers are uniquely prepared to encourage, train, and support parents in the vital application of day-to-day expectations and guidance.

Enola K. Proctor is research and teaching fellow, George Warren Brown School of Social Work, Washington University, St. Louis, Missouri. This article is a revision of a paper presented at the National Conference on Social Welfare, San Francisco, California, May 11–15, 1975.

Notes and References

1. Pauline Cohen, The Impact of the Handicapped Child on the Family, *Social Casework,* 43:137–42 (March 1962); Ada Kozier, Casework with Parents of Children Born with Severe Brain Defects, *Social Casework,* 38:183–89 (March 1957); Arthur Mandelbaum, The Group Process in Helping Parents of Retarded Children, *Children,* 14:227–32 (November-December 1967); Ann Murphy, Siegfried Pueschel, and Jane Schneider, Group Work with Parents of Children with Down's Syndrome, *Social Casework,* 54:114–119 (February 1973); Simon Olshansky, Chronic Sorrow: A Response to Having a Mentally Defective Child, *Social Casework,* 43:191–94 (April 1962).

2. Cohen, The Impact of the Handicapped Child, p. 137; Murphy, Pueschel, and Schneider, Group Work with Parents of Children with Down's Syndrome, p. 114.

3. Kozier, Casework with Parents of Children Born with Severe Brain Defects, pp. 183–89; Arthur Mandelbaum and Mary E. Wheeler, The Meaning

of a Defective Child to Parents, *Social Casework,* 41:360–67 (July 1960); Helen Perlman, Help to Parents of the Mentally Retarded Child: A Diagnostic Focus, in *Social Work and Mental Retardation,* ed. Meyer Schreiber (New York: John Day Company, 1970), pp. 346–65.

4. Helen Beck, Counseling Parents of Retarded Children, *Children,* 6:225–30 (1959); Kozier, Casework with Parents of Children Born with Severe Brain Defects, p. 185; Murphy et al., Group Work with Parents, p. 117; Mandelbaum, The Group Process in Helping Parents of Retarded Children, p. 231.

5. Beck, *Social Services to the Mentally Retarded* (Springfield, Ill.: Charles C. Thomas Co., 1969), p. 101.

6. Ibid.

7. William Gardner, *Behavior Modification in Mental Retardation* (Chicago: Aldine Publishing Co., 1971), p. 22.

8. Michael Begab, Some Basic Principles as a

Guide to More Effective Social Services, in *Sourcebook on Mental Retardation for Schools of Social Work,* ed. Meyer Schreiber and Stephanie Barnhardt (New York: Selected Academic Reading, 1967), p. 1–4.

9. Nathan Azrin and Richard Foxx, A Rapid Method of Toilet Training the Institutionalized Retarded, *Journal of Applied Behavioral Analysis,* 4:89–99 (Summer 1971).

10. Charles Pascal, Application of Behavior Modification by Parents for Treatment of a Brain Damaged Child, in *Adaptive Learning: Behavior Modification with Children,* ed. Beatrice Ashem and Ernest Poser (New York: Pergamon Press, 1973), pp. 299–309.

11. Sue Seitz and Robert Holkenga, Modeling as a Training Tool for Retarded Children and Their Parents, *Mental Retardation,* 12:28–30 (April 1974); Shlomo A. Sharlin and Norman A. Polansky, The Process of Infantilization, *American Journal of Orthopsychiatry,* 42:92–102 (January 1972).

12. Jean Gottman and Samuel Leiblum, *How to Do Psychotherapy and How to Evaluate It* (New York: Holt, Rinehart and Winston, 1974), p. 21.

13. Seitz and Holkenga, Modeling as a Training Tool, p. 28; Sharlin and Polansky, The Process of Infantilization, p. 93.

14. Edward Fuller and Kieth Kieth, The Social Work Role in Institutions: A Critical Assessment, *Mental Retardation,* 12:61 (June 1974).

15. Begab, Some Basic Principles, p. 3.

16. Norman A. Polansky, Donald R. Boone, Christine DeSaix, and Shlomo A. Sharlin, Pseudostoicism in Mothers of the Retarded, *Social Casework,* 52:643–50 (December 1971).

17. Benjamin Moore and Jan Bailey, Social Punishment in the Modification of a Pre-School Child's Autistic like Behavior with a Mother as Therapist, *Journal of Applied Behavioral Analysis,* 6:497–507 (Fall 1973); Joel Ray, The Family Training Center: An Experiment in Normalization, *Mental Retardation,* 12:12–13 (February 1974).

18. Polansky et al., Pseudostoicism, p. 643; Luke Watson and Joan Bassinger, Parent Training Technology: A Potential Service Delivery System, *Mental Retardation,* 12:3–10 (October 1974).

19. Roland G. Tharp and Rolf J. Wetzel, *Behavior Modification in the Natural Environment* (New York: Academic Press, 1969), p. 206.

20. Sheldon Rose, Ronal Parson, Betty Jarman, and Carol Hethlenthal, Group Training of Parents as Behavioral Modifiers of Their Own Mentally Retarded Children (unpublished paper, The University of Wisconsin at Madison, 1972); Rose, Group Training of Parents as Behavior Modifiers, *Social Work,* 19:156–62 (March 1974).

21. Sandra B. McPherson and Cyrille R. Samuels, Teaching Behavioral Methods to Parents, *Social Casework,* 52:148–53 (March 1971).

22. V. L. Baldwin and H. D. Fredericks, eds., *Isn't It Time He Outgrew This? Or a Training Program for Parents of Retarded Children* (Springfield, Ill.: Charles C. Thomas, Publisher, 1973); Eric Marsh and Leif Terdal, Modifications of Mother-Child Interaction, *Mental Retardation,* 11:44–49 (October 1973); Baldwin and Fredericks, *Isn't it Time?;* Kathleen Jeffords, Leslie Danzig, and Kathleen Fitzgibbons, Group Training of Parents as Behavioral Modifiers of Their Own Mentally Retarded Children, unpublished paper, The University of Wisconsin, 1971; Baldwin and Fredericks, *Isn't it Time?;* William Butterfield and Ronal Parson, Modeling and Shaping by Parents to Develop Chewing Behavior in Their Retarded Child, *Journal of Behavior Therapies and Experimental Psychiatry,* 4:285–87 (December 1973); Jeffords, Danzig, and Fitzgibbons, Group Training of Parents, p. 6; Sebastian Santostefano and Stayton Stayton, Training the Pre-School Retarded Child in Focusing Attention: A Program for Parents, *American Journal of Orthopsychiatry,* 37:732–43 (July 1967); and J. Richard Metz, Conditioning Generalized Imitation in Autistic Children, *Journal of Experimental Child Psychology,* 2:389–99 (December 1965).

23. McPherson and Samuels, Teaching Behavioral Methods, p. 148.

24. Rose, A Behavioral Approach to the Group Treatment of Parents, *Social Work,* 14:21–29 (July 1969).

25. Baldwin and Fredericks, *Isn't it Time?;* Wesley Becker, *Parents Are Teachers* (Champaign, Ill.: Research Press, 1967); Gerald Patterson and M. Elizabeth Gullion, *Living with Children: New Methods for Parents and Teachers* (Champaign, Ill.: Research Press, 1968).

26. Stephen Johnson and Richard Brown, Producing Behavior Changes in Parents of Disturbed Children, *Journal of Child Psychology and Psychiatry,* 10:107–21 (October 1969).

27. Rose, A Behavioral Approach, p. 27.

28. Ibid., p. 29.

ALEXANDER J. TYMCHUK

Training Parent Therapists

Psychotherapeutic intervention strategies with parents of disturbed or delayed children have been of a dynamic, or recently of a behavioral bent.[1] In the former strategy there is generally an emphasis upon the parents' reactions towards their child and an attempt to reconcile dissonance caused when normal parental expectancies are shattered by having an abnormal infant or later, as a suspicion grows in the parents' minds that their child is not as normal as they would like. In this strategy, however, there is little systematic effort made to directly involve the parents in the training of their child even though much of the dissonance felt by the parents is related to the fact that the child is not performing up to his developmental level or even to his possible capacity. The implication is that the reconciliation of the parents' feelings will somehow translate into their acceptance of their child's disordered behavior. Their handling of the child may not be really changed and his potential may not be fully realized.

Copyright 1975, American Association on Mental Deficiency. Reprinted with permission, from Mental Retardation, *Vol. 13, No. 5 (October 1975), pp. 19–22.*

The behavioral strategy, especially where there has been direct training of the parents in the application of operant learning principles, has been to directly change the parents' handling of the child's behavior. The parent is taught to take an active part in the training of the child. A secondary result of the success of the parents in their endeavor is often an improved parental attitude towards their child, usually exemplified by a greater acceptance of that child concomitant with more positive affect towards him.

Although in the training of the parents there is some dealing with the attitudes toward their child within the behavioral strategy, this effort is usually secondary to the behavioral training. This is so despite the fact that parents do not come to a clinic with nothing more than a problem child. The parents come with an entire experiential history of failures, of dashed expectancies, of real or imagined social pressures, of incredibly complex personal feelings and even of family disintegration. Training parents to be trainers of their children when these same parents have come to reject their child may in effect curtail the chances of the success of such training. This may be a reason why some parent training programs have not been altogether successful.

A more effective model would appear to be a combination of the dynamic and behavioral strategies. There are two other major considerations in the treatment of parents of disabled or disturbed children. Unfortunately, there is insufficient accurate information that is disseminated effectively to the public and to people who may already have or will have disabled or delayed children and to people who may be associated with others who may have such children. Such information relates to the diagnosis, prognosis and treatment of each type of child, including the mentally retarded, the autistic and the behavior problem child as well as others. There may also have been inadequate dissemination to professionals who have traditionally worked with these parents.

When an accurate information vacuum occurs, other information may fill it, information that might be inaccurate and therefore hamper the parents' accurate assessment of their child's chances in life. To overcome this deficit, parents should be given such accurate information during the parent therapy process.

Presenting accurate information is the first consideration; the second relates to the information issue, but deals specifically with the parents' knowledge of what constitutes normal child development and how such development is changed as a result of the child's disorder. Parents' unrealistic expectancies of their child place pressure upon the child, the parents and upon the family. Since our society does not educate people to become parents, people, especially parents of delayed children, need accurate developmental information.

What Is Parent Therapy?

Parent therapy is an intervention strategy designed for use with parents of disabled or delayed children:

1. To handle the issues related to their feelings, emotions and attitudes that center around the dynamics of having such a child;

2. To give accurate information regarding their child specifically relating to diagnosis, prognosis, and treatment as well as educational, legal and other service resources available to them;

3. To present a perspective about normal child development with which they can view the delayed or peculiar development of their child;

4. To give them training in the effective use of principles of social learning so that they can take an active role in the education of their child. This training provides them with skills through which they will have success in their parental roles. Table 1 contains a summary of the model of parent therapy.

Training Program

A group of social workers were trained to be parent therapists. The workshop was offered through the auspices of the Center for Training in Community Psychiatry which offers training programs for mental health professionals. There were eight participants from service agencies. The workshop lasted seven weeks with each weekly meeting lasting three and one-half hours and an eighth week follow-up meeting one month after the last training session.

The first three sessions followed a standard format during which didactic information was presented on the parent therapy model and included what was known about parents' reactions towards themselves, towards members of the helping profession and towards their developmentally disabled child; information on resources available to these parents and their children in Los Angeles; information on normal and delayed child development; finally, the group members were trained in the theory and the practical application of operant learning techniques in the training of children. Films and readings were used as well.[2]

At the beginning, the group members were instructed to identify a family in their agency, with whom they could implement the model. During the first session, the mechanics of identifying, interviewing, and selecting parents for parent therapy were discussed. Although parent therapy in groups seems like a more effective use of the trainer's time, both group and individual parent therapy was discussed. During initial training, trainers should work with an individual case before they work with a group; however, as part of their training, they should observe an ongoing group.

During the second session, in addition to the didactic material, each member described his case using questionnaires filled out by the parents. These questionnaires were designed to help the group member structure the interview and to identify problem areas. Several of the cases selected were parents of retarded children, others were parents of behavior or school problem children and one was a mother of a normal girl who felt extremely ineffectual in her parenting role.

After the third session, the members began working with their cases, but they still received additional didactic information during the remaining sessions.

Ten-minute presentations were made by each group member weekly on his case and problems and solutions to those problems were discussed. Members were encouraged to tape record sessions and each week summaries written by the individual group members were shared. In this way, although a particular member worked with a parent of a retarded child, he also had information on how to work with parents of other problem children. The tapes were also played during the meetings.

As problems arose, they were dealt with; and they related specifically to: how to motivate parent training group members; how to determine a fee schedule; when and where to hold meetings; who should practice parent therapy; what about licensing; should there be a co-therapist; how to foster group interaction.

There was particular emphasis upon communicating accurate information in response to questions raised by parents. Although there was not a formal testing of the members of the group before the group began, the infor-

---

Table 1. Model of Parent Therapy

Parental Attitudes
  Reactions to professionals; to child; to self
  Effects on self, family, child, marriage
  Strategies (roleplaying, modeling)

Child Development
  Normal (expectations at various stages)
  Abnormal (possible deviations)

Facts (re: mental retardation;
  emotional disturbance;
  learning disabilities, etc.)
    Diagnosis
    Etiology
    Description
    Treatment
    Prognosis

How Children Learn
  Personality (how anxiety affects learning)
  Cognition (the importance of use of
    verbal labels)
  Learning principles (reinforcement)

Resources
  1. Legal
    legislation (re: education; financial; rights)
    courts

  2. Organizations
    national (Council for Exceptional Children)
    parent (National Association for
      Retarded Children)
    information and research
      (National Institutes of Mental Health)
    state (Department of Health, Education)
    local (Regional Centers; schools; camps;
      respite care centers)

Other Family Members
  Reaction of index child to self and to parents
  Reaction of siblings to index child
  Strategies

mation level of the group members was not high with regards to their knowledge of mental retardation, autism, learning disabilities, parental attitudes, etc. They were encouraged to bring parental questions to each session. Specific questions raised by parents were: Why did this happen to me? Why do I have to work so hard being a parent? Can I use those techniques with my other children? and What is behavior modification?

Case Study

The following case is representative of what each of the group members did.

Sam is a 9-year-old, white male. He lives at home with his mother, and his younger brother, Burt, who is seven.

Sam has had difficulty in school since the first grade. His teachers have consistently commented that his behavior is inappropriate ("acting out," refusing to work, yelling and fighting with his peers). They also report that he is not functioning academically at his expected grade level (fourth grade).

He was given an IQ test by the school psychologist when he was in the first grade. At that time he generated a score within the "gifted range" and was placed in a "gifted supplementary experience" program. He continued to go to his gifted class on a once-a-week basis.

Due to his mother's work situation, he and his brother attend a day care program before and after school during the week.

The parents had been divorced for 5 years and the mother had been involved in psychotherapy off and on since the divorce. She was very concerned about both of her sons, but particularly Sam, the oldest, since he had been a pawn during her arguments with her husband and whose affection she felt she needed. She constantly interpreted in dynamic terms. She did not have any effective way of interacting with Sam and, as a result, his behavior had deteriorated to the point that the mother's work was suffering and she was considering placement for her son. There was no evidence to suggest a med-

ical reason for Sam's behavior based upon a doctor's report the mother brought.

The mother was seen in an initial interview by both the group member and by the author and the entire session was taken up by attempting to resolve her dislike of her son, his apparent dislike for her and her displeasure with herself for being so ineffectual as a parent.

It became apparent that during the period immediately after her divorce she had turned to Sam for support, catering to him in an attempt to keep him on her side. Unfortunately, in so doing, she had inadvertently reinforced him to make demands upon her, and even to make derogatory remarks. Her only social contact was with a neighbor who was having difficulties with her own son, so Sam's mother did not have any suitable models. She was unaware of community resources that were available to her and was reticent to seek help for fear of admitting failure.

To the statement "being the mother of this child makes me feel" on the questionnaire, she responded:

> Sometimes I just want to say, I've had enough. Between the two boys, I really feel that I can't take much more. I want to keep both of them. I don't want them to go to another home, but at the same time I don't know what to do. . . .

Since the mother was in psychotherapy, it was decided not to focus on the dynamics of the situation, but rather to emphasize problem-solving strategies. She was asked to identify those things which were most critical to her which, if resolved, would relieve some of the pressure.

Some of the behaviors were:

Verbal Abuse: directed from Sam to his mother, e.g., "You ---, I'll get my knife. . . ." "I love my daddy and I hate you, I wish someone would cut your face up."

Fighting: (usually instigated the interaction) with his brother.

Not Dealing With or Handling His Hostility: or aggression "properly," i.e., mother would like Sam to talk to her and be able to express his anger to her instead of breaking toys, windows, destroying plants, swearing at her or hitting others.

Poor Academic and Social Behavior: in school. Mother receives reports from Sam's teachers both from his regular class and his day care class that he is not doing his work and is falling behind. They also report that he is "immature," goofs off and gets into trouble.

The mother was then observed and videotaped, both in the home and in the office, attempting to structure a learning situation for Sam with Burt playing separately. This tape was then used to show the mother what had actually occurred. The situation was chaotic. Without any instruction, upon seeing the tape, she recognized what she had done wrong and what she could have done better. Both boys refused to obey commands, neither sat still, they threw things and finally began fighting. Through most of this, the mother, after having given the initial commands, retreated to a chair and sat stoically.

It appeared that she had lost control over the boys, but Sam was being tutored and apparently behaved well in that situation. The group member then spent 1 hour, three times a week in which he tutored while the mother smiled and congratulated Sam for doing well. By the second hour, the mother was able to tutor while the group member sat nearby offering her support. By the third hour, the mother worked by herself with Sam while the group member contacted her by telephone daily to give her support.

Through this initial effort, although it was a small part of the boy's day, the mother gained confidence in herself again and began feeling in command of her home life. It was feared that if too much pressure were placed on the mother, she would balk for she was now in a new role and was assuming more responsibility for her children. Several times, in fact, she complained of being overworked as a parent, so that an arrangement was made with her neighbor that they would babysit for each other when needed. A college student also began coming over twice weekly to roughhouse with the boys.

After the first week, once the boys had begun responding to the mother, a system was set up so that each day the boys were responsible for getting up on time (previously they were late at least twice a week for school), for dressing and washing, for eating breakfast properly and on time. By the third week, the boys began to be responsible for after school behavior including preparing for dinner, cleaning up afterwards, doing their homework and preparing and going to bed on time and appropriately. Each day, the mother simply punched a golf scorer for each of the boys as they completed their work. A system was worked out whereby the boys needed so many points to watch television, to have special foods or toys, to play for a given period of time and so on.

The group member continued meeting with the mother on a weekly basis in an effort to help her problem-solve and to respond to her questions and telephoned her between meetings. Both boys were involved in training to insure their getting "equal" attention. As a result of the program and after a follow-up, the mother felt much more confident, felt positive towards her children, had learned how to restructure her life and to use resources as a means to avoid crises and felt that "the good finally outweighed the bad."

The group member similarly felt confident that great gains were made with this mother and had even begun adopting the parent therapy model with several other of his clients.

The other group members had similar success experiences and in all cases were already adopting the parent therapy model with other clients. In addition several members had had inquiries from colleagues for information about and training in parent therapy.

Discussion

Since parents of developmentally disabled children often come to the clinic with a plea for help in training their child and also with a complex attitude pattern towards themselves, their child and towards other professionals with whom they have dealt, as well as a general lack of knowledge regarding the conditions affecting their child, their child's development and the resources available to them, neither a dynamic nor a behavioral therapeutic approach would be singularly effective. However, a therapy encompassing both dynamic and behavioral principles as well as basic didactic information may have marked efficacy. The dissemination of this model is just beginning; in order to be effective, workers already in the field must be trained in its application as well as currently included in regular training programs.

Alexander J. Tymchuk, Ph.D., Assistant Professor, Department of Psychology and Psychiatry, University of California, Los Angeles 90024. The author would like to thank his colleague, Nancy Brown, M.S.W., for her cogent comments on the present article.

Notes and References

1. The author's work is supported in part by MCH Grant #927. Additional descriptive materials are available. A book on parent therapy is currently nearing completion.

2. A listing of these readings used is available upon request from the author.

FERN TREVINO

Siblings of Handicapped Children: Identifying Those at Risk

The impact a brain-damaged child has on his parents has been well documented! Although much attention has been given in the professional literature to preventive therapeutic intervention with the parents, relatively few studies deal with the repercussions of a handicapped child on his normal siblings.[2] This neglect of the "normal" siblings is reflected in hospital clinics, family service agencies, and schools where, more often than not, these children are excluded entirely from the diagnostic phase and treatment plan. It is indeed surprising that in spite of the available knowledge of family systems, roles, and life cycles, professionals persist in maintaining a fragmented view of families with a handicapped child even when preventive efforts are clearly indicated.

The term "brain damage" is sometimes used interchangeably with retardation; however, for the purposes of this article, brain damage is used comprehensively to include the full range of sensory, mental, motor, and behavioral impairments of which the etiology,

treatment, and prognosis vary extensively. Retardation, seizure disorders, cerebral palsy, and learning disabilities each require a different set of accommodations on the part of family members, which will in turn depend as well on the severity of the particular type of brain damage. However, certain common effects also exist that are independent of the type and degree of brain damage; rather, they are determined by the characteristics of the family system.

The intent of this article is to stress the importance of including the entire family in the diagnostic phase, to consider those effects of a handicapped child on his normal siblings that are independent of type and degree of brain damage, and to suggest as guidelines for evaluating families four important variables that influence the impact on the normal siblings.

Families with a handicapped child are by definition high risk. Threatened by a chronic, often unsolvable predicament, members of these families are prey to a host of situational and emotional pitfalls that undoubtedly affect them. Yet, the specific effects of a handicapped child on his siblings are so elusive that some researchers have concluded that sufficient evidence to support such a hypothesis is not available.[3] One has pointed out that the impact is often described in retrospect and that much of the information in the literature is based on subjective observation and interpretation involving selective populations.[4] The data, for the most part, involve users of available services. Perhaps those who use mental health services are more likely to have been adversely affected by a handicapped child. Presumably a segment of the population is excluded from the statistics, thereby rendering an unrepresentative sample.

Actual studies on siblings of brain-damaged children are relatively few. Only recently have social scientists begun to question the influence "normal" siblings have on each other. Research thus far has been questionable and the difficulties involved in this area of investigation perhaps obviate the possibility of making reliable, valid studies. The multiplicity of variables that affect all children are added to those involved with a disabled child. Therefore, in addition to family resources, values, and interpersonal relationships, the researcher must consider the type and severity of the handicap, attributes of the affected child (age, sex, ordinal position) relative to siblings, as well as the type and quality of services made available to the family. In addition, the range of afflictions classified as brain damage must be considered.

The Variables that Interact to Cause Conflict

Although studies thus far are inconclusive for methodological reasons, the consensus is that the presence of a handicapped child in a family has an adverse effect on his siblings.[5] Based on research as well as personal clinical experience, it is the author's contention that prospects for the normal siblings appear to be the worst for families in which (1) there are only two siblings, a normal and a handicapped child, (2) the normal sibling is close in age to or younger than the handicapped sibling, or is the oldest female child, (3) the normal and handicapped child are the same sex, or (4) the parents are unable to accept the handicap. Individual case assessment and planning for families with a handicapped child would be improved with special consideration of these variables.

Number of Normal Siblings

An atmosphere for normalcy increases with the number of normal siblings.[6] Although not particularly logical, a common reaction of siblings, especially a single sibling of an afflicted child, is a feeling of guilt for having been born normal.[7] Resentment toward the disabled child, particularly if the affliction is a constant impediment to usual family functioning, magnifies the possibility of overwhelming guilt on the part of normal siblings.

The family with limited finances in need of constant supervision for a retardate has little choice but to ask the normal children to share the load. Clearly, the more normal children there are in the family, the more potential help is available. Studies and case histories indicate that the lives of some children with a handicapped sibling, especially an older female or a single sibling, are wasted or devastated.[8] Normal children may be deprived of their childhood and may assume the role of substitute parents. Margaret Adams cautions counselors to watch for the "golden-hearted" sister, the one who establishes a maternal relationship with the afflicted child, a relationship that the family accepts all too easily.[9] Not only may the care be exhausting, the responsibility may be overwhelming or terrifying. In an informal study by K. S. Holt of 138 families with mentally retarded children, the "normal" children were reported to have suffered from unexpected, persistent physical attacks by their afflicted siblings.[10]

In families with a single normal sibling, an imbalance of roles analogous to the scapegoat-idealized child pair is more likely to occur. A normal child may be pushed beyond his or her limits to overcompensate for a sibling who is regarded as a failure. Very often there exists the feeling that the normal child, because he or she is normal, should behave better; that he or she does not need as much attention. Children often cannot understand how consideration can be measured and doled out on the basis of need and, consequently, these children may feel, and many times are, emotionally neglected. Thus, a single normal sibling has a higher risk of emotional problems as a result of having to bear the impact of guilt, responsibility, and parental disappointments alone.

Age of Siblings

Conflicts related to competition, identity, and role are intensified in cases in which the normal child is close in age and/or younger than his or her handicapped sibling or is the oldest female child in the family.[11] Bernard Farber points out that a retarded child alters the family life cycle, which results in role tension for both parents and siblings.[12] In describing the life cycle, he emphasizes that although family relationships change drastically, certain characteristics are similar at each stage. Initially, young children play with their disabled sibling on an equal basis. As they grow older, however, they must redefine their role because eventually they must assume a superordinate position. Normal children may feel badly about surpassing a sibling who is handicapped and older, and prefer to drop behind to ease an overburdened conscience. Parents struggling with denial and guilt may repress the abilities of a younger child so that he or she will not outdo an older handicapped brother or sister, especially if the impairment is a mild one.

Alternatively, normal children may be targets for unrealistically high parental expectations to counteract the frustrated hopes for the handicapped child. Sibling rivalry, known to be greater between children close in age, may escalate to a destructive level in situations involving a handicapped child. Normal children may become bitter over the extra favors and attention given the afflicted child; the handicapped child may be intensely envious of the normality of his siblings.

Children close in age to a handicapped sibling more often experience social discomfort than do children where there is a greater age gap. Children close in age have to deal more frequently with peer reactions. Often, normal siblings have to explain to their friends things that they themselves do not understand or cannot accept. Teasing, taunting, and gossiping about a child with a handicapped sibling is not uncommon among young children. Small children may feel uncomfortable or fearful in the presence of an afflicted child and be reluctant to visit the home. Parents frequently demand that the normal child include the disabled child in peer-group activities; peers may refuse or be reluctant to do so, putting additional strain on the "normal" child. During early adolescence, identity development and separation are especially difficult for children tied to an afflicted brother or sister through such expectations. Francis K. Grossman found that a major concern of normal siblings was how not to identify with their affected siblings.[13]

Gender

Gender is primarily related to conflicts about identification and role.[14] Young children are more likely to be adversely affected by an afflicted sibling of the same sex because of their fear of being disabled also, especially if there is no other sibling in the family with whom to identify.

Females are more likely than males to be adversely affected by a handicapped sibling. Ann Gath found disturbance to be significantly higher in sisters of mongoloids than in the normal children used as controls; however, this was not so for brothers of mongoloid children.[15] Several authors have attributed the vulnerability of the eldest female child in the family to her having to bear much of the responsibility for care and management of the handicapped child.[16] Both Farber and Carolyn M. Fowle found role tension to be higher for the oldest female sibling than for the other normal children in homes with a handicapped child. Grossman's data support these findings.[17]

Parental Reaction to the Handicap

Perception of the handicap rather than the handicap itself is a crucial factor.[18] Thus, a learning disability or controlled epilepsy may precipitate severe circumstances for the family in which the parents are unable to accept their child's mild shortcoming. In situations in which the neurological deficit is not at all severe, parents can more easily deny the situation, which ultimately causes more turmoil for all. Family secrets or implicit rules forbidding the discussion of the problem force normal siblings to constantly pretend that circumstances are other than they seem, a situation that places them in an ambiguous predicament of conflicting demands and expectations. Because children are extensions of their parents, their ability to accept the handicap and cope with the hardship is greatly influenced by, if not a total reflection of, parental attitudes.

Wide variation exists in the reactions of parents to the child and his handicap. Parents who are extremely depressed or overly anxious after the birth of an abnormal child may be emotionally and physically unavailable to their normal children; further, child neglect is known to occur more often in families of the handicapped. Parental guilt is frequently cited as a common response.[19] Parents may have difficulty controlling their hostile feelings toward the afflicted child and in turn may project this hostility and anger onto their normal children. Ambivalence toward the handicapped child is often expressed in alternating exaggerated patterns of overprotection, overindulgence, and rigid authoritarianism. Two completely different sets of rules may exist within the same family, and often intensify sibling rivalry. If the parents are not emotionally stable, their reaction to such an intractable problem is more likely to be unhealthy. Case histories illustrate that these parents often have long-standing adjustment problems that are exacerbated by the arrival of an afflicted child or that the arrival itself triggers maladaptive reactions not previously apparent.[20]

Because the emphasis in this article is on the effects a handicapped child has on siblings, the tendency the parents in afflicted families have to marital conflict will not be discussed except to observe that it seems to be higher and that marital conflict has a noxious effect on children. Therefore, if the parents are unable to accept the handicap, the impact of a handicapped child will be greater for the siblings, the marital relationship, and the family system as a whole.

Case Illustration

The following illustrates that a handicap does not have to be severe to generate a forceful impact. Even though the afflicted child may be far more adversely affected, parallel conflicts are subtly intertwined in the developmental tasks of the normal siblings as well.

Sharon Q was nine years old when Linda, her eleven-year-old sister, developed grand mal epilepsy. Anticonvulsive medication was prescribed. The parents, unable to accept the diagnosis or the stigma it carried, were not open to discussion of the illness. The Q children were merely told that Linda would hopefully outgrow her "fainting spells." Additionally, they were warned not to tell anyone for fear others would think Linda was mentally ill or that she had a hereditary disease. Mr. and Mrs. Q hoped that by keeping Linda's illness a tight secret, they could protect her from being labeled "different."

Mrs. Q explained to Sharon alone that Linda could suffocate if she were to swallow her tongue and that a "fainting spell" while she was swimming could be fatal if no one were nearby to save her. Because both parents worked and Sharon was a dependable child, they enlisted her help in keeping an eye on Linda after school and on outings. The family could be reasonably sure that Linda would not have a seizure at school because Mrs. Q gave her her medication at breakfast. However, sometimes Linda forgot to take her noontime medication and on those days she suffered late afternoon seizures. Warning signs usually allowed her time to lie down in bed before the seizure. But, because she knew that she would be reprimanded for forgetting her medicine, in her confused state she would frequently attempt to hide, hoping no one would discover that she had "fainted."

Even before Linda's illness became apparent, she had experienced noticeable social and scholastic difficulties. Although a bright child, because of her epilepsy and the side effects of the medication, she became impulsive and distractable. For several months she had double vision and vertigo. At an age when children begin to struggle with peer pressures and independence, she was forced to become even more dependent on her family. Her role within the family was a most difficult one. Feelings of guilt, fear, and shame which appear almost universally in parents of the handicapped were reflected in overprotection and false, light-hearted optimism. Linda was aware that she was a source of tension for her family and alienated from her peers. She was defeated even further by Sharon's high marks and involvement in extracurricular activities.

Sharon was fearful of being left alone with Linda and of sleeping in the same room with her. She imagined that Linda might die and that it would be her fault or that Linda, in a trance-like state, might hurt her. When she expressed these fears to her parents, her father became irate, accused her of being selfish, and reminded her of how lucky she was to be normal. Sharon worried increasingly that she, too, would develop epilepsy; she began to watch herself for signs that her own behavior was abnormal. Over the next few years, Sharon's interest in school began to wane. Although she maintained her friendships, she stopped participating in outside activities. Gradually, her grades fell and by the time she reached ninth grade she was a mediocre student.

When Linda reached her late teens, the culmination of uncompleted developmental tasks added to the stress of adolescent conflicts was overwhelming. Having missed an important stage in her life when children develop their social skills and separate identities, she remained shy and insecure; friends and dates were few. In an effort to solve her social problems, Mr. and Mrs. Q pressured Sharon to include Linda in her group of friends. But Sharon, at the age of fifteen, wanted and needed to be separate and different from Linda. To Sharon, insecure in her own identity, Linda's social ineptness was too threatening. Her reluctance to include Linda only confirmed what her father had told her many times before: that she was a selfish and self-centered girl.

Although Linda's seizures at this time were well controlled, Sharon's turmoil continued. Her energies had been consumed with morbid fears, guilt, resentment, and self-control. Unable to discuss her feelings at home or with friends, she tried to suppress them. She started sleeping sixteen hours a day and found it difficult to concentrate. When she began experiencing severe anxiety attacks, she sought individual treatment for herself.

Summary

The literature on families of the handicapped suggests that siblings potentially are adversely affected. Indeed, psychiatrists treat more siblings of handicapped children than handicapped children themselves.[21] Attempts to sort out empirical evidence of the precise effects have to date been mired in the failure to control many variables.

Professionals can initiate a preventive approach at an optimal stage by including the entire family in the diagnostic phase and, when necessary, in the treatment plan. In recognizing the potential for problems that these children have, it is evident that a diagnostic family interview for all situations involving handicapped children should be taken as a preventive, therapeutic, and educational measure as an alternative to the traditional parent-counseling approach. This framework offers a means for evaluating families with handicapped children and for identifying normal siblings at high risk, that is, siblings who fit into one or a combination of the following categories: (1) the only other child, (2) children who are close in age and/or younger than the handicapped sibling, (3) a younger child of the same sex as the handicapped child or the oldest female child, or (4) a child whose parents are unable to accept the handicap. Treatment planning can then be tailored to deal with the pitfalls and conflicts to which these at-risk children are particularly prone.

Fern Trevino is a Clinical Social Worker, Family and Mental Health Services of South West Cook County, Family Service Bureau of United Charities of Chicago, Chicago, Illinois.

Notes and References

1. Margaret Adams, *The Mentally Subnormal* (London: Heinemann Medical Books, 1960), pp. 48–53; Abraham Levinson, *The Mentally Retarded Child* (New York: John Day, 1965), pp. 25–33; and Joan K. McMichael, *Handicap* (Pittsburgh: University of Pittsburgh Press, 1971), pp. 86–98.

2. The content of this article necessitates the use of the singular to refer to the handicapped child and the masculine form of the pronoun has been chosen as less obtrusive.

3. Betty V. Graliker, Karol Fishler, and R. Koch, "Teenage Reaction to a Mentally Retarded Sibling," *American Journal of Mental Deficiency* 66 (June 1962): 838–43; and Howard R. Kelman, "The Effect of a Brain-Damaged Child on His Family," in *Brain Damage in Children,* ed. Herbert Birch (New York: Williams and Wilkins, 1964), pp. 77–92.

4. Kelman, "Effect of Brain-Damaged Child," pp. 79–92.

5. Shelia M. Bergreen, "A Study of the Mental Health of the Near Relatives of 20 Multihandicapped Children," *Acta Paedeatrica Scandinavia* 215 (1971): 1–24; Bernard Farber, "Effects of a Severely Retarded Child on Family Integration," *Monographs of Society Research in Child Development* 24, no. 71 (1959): 46–50; Carolyn M. Fowle, "The Effect of the Severely Mentally Retarded Child on His Family," *American Journal of Mental Deficiency* 73 (March 1968): 468–73; Francis K. Grossman, *Brothers and Sisters of Retarded Children* (Syracuse, N.Y.: Syracuse University Press, 1972), p. 294; K. S. Holt, "The Home Care of Severely Retarded Children," *Pediatrics* 22 (September 1958): 746–55; Mary San Martino and Morton B. Newman, "Siblings of Retarded Children: A Population at Risk," *Child Psychiatry and Human Development* 4 (Spring 1974): 168–77; Ann Gath, "Sibling Reactions to a Mental Handicap: A Comparison of the Brothers and Sisters of Mongol Children," *Journal of Child Psychology and Psychiatry and Allied Disciplines* 15 (July 1974): 187–89; and Elva Poznanski, "Psychiatric Difficulties in Siblings of Handicapped Children," *Pediatrics* 8 (April 1969): 232–34.

6. Grossman, *Brothers and Sisters,* pp. 103, 182; and Adams, *Mentally Subnormal,* pp. 53–54.

7. San Martino and Newman, "Siblings of Retarded Children."

8. Bergreen, "Study of Near Relatives;" Holt, "Home Care of Retarded;" Grossman, *Brothers and Sisters,* pp. 7–22; Poznanski, "Psychiatric Difficulties in Siblings," pp. 232–43; and Adams, *Mentally Subnormal,* pp. 53–54.

9. Adams, *Mentally Subnormal,* p. 54.

10. Holt, "Home Care of Retarded," pp. 246–55.

11. Grossman, *Brothers and Sisters,* pp. 7–24, 182; Adams, *Mentally Subnormal,* p.53; Farber, "Effects of Child on Family Integration," pp. 90–91; John and Nellie Carver, *The Family of the Retarded Child* (Syracuse, N.Y.: Syracuse University Press, 1972), p. 62; and Sylvia Schild, "The Family of the Retarded Child" in *The Mentally Retarded Child and His Family,* ed. Richard Koch and James Dobson (New York: Brunner/Mazel, 1971), pp. 431–45.

12. Farber, "Effects of Child on Family Integration," pp. 49–50.

13. Grossman, *Brothers and Sisters,* p. 182.

14. Ibid., p. 181.

15. Gath, "Sibling Reactions to Mongol Children," pp. 187–89.

16. Farber, "Effects of Child on Family Integration," pp. 78–84; Fowle, "Retarded Child's Effect on Family;" and Adams, *Mentally Subnormal,* pp. 53–54.

17. Farber, "Effects of Child on Family Integration," pp. 78–84; Fowle, "Retarded Child's Effect on Family;" and Grossman, *Brothers and Sisters,* p. 182.

18. Grossman, *Brothers and Sisters,* p. 181; and San Martino and Newman, "Siblings of Retarded Children," pp. 168–77.

19. Schild, "Family of the Retarded Child," p. 434.

20. Holt, "Home Care of the Retarded," pp. 746–55.

21. Poznanski, "Psychiatric Difficulties in Siblings," pp. 232–34.

JACQUELINE HEIBER BERNS

Grandparents of Handicapped Children

Grandparents experience a grandchild as an extension of themselves. A joyful expectation precedes the birth. They hope for a healthy infant, a child who will enhance family life, make up for past disappointments, and help in conflicts with their own children. These thoughts may be projected into the future: grandparents want a child who will continue their beliefs, pursue higher education, surpass their own achievements, or practice a cherished profession.

With the birth of a handicapped child or the establishment of a child's disability, the repercussions on the family are many, subtle, and extensive. All members of the family experience the stress of raising a handicapped child. The relationships of parenthood are ever changing and never ending, and the role of grandparents has traditionally been to keep hope and custom alive. Parents' parents can be a great influence in family life. If the problems of a handicapped child are never far from the parents' minds and hearts, grandparents may be needed to point out what is

Copyright 1980, National Association of Social Workers, Inc. Reprinted with permission, from Social Work, *Vol. 25, No. 3 (May 1980), pp. 238–239.*

best not just for the child but for all members of the family as well.

It is difficult to determine the role a handicapped child's brothers and sisters should take, how a child's sustained dependency will be managed, and how a child's need for both protection and stimulation can be recognized. Parents and grandparents must help each other accept their new reality by drawing on understanding, compassion, and the appropriate sharing of tasks. When a child is handicapped, the anxieties of raising and guiding a new family are magnified. Married children need support before their energies are seriously depleted, not after.

Expectations

The first indication of a child's difference may not occur with birth and often not within the first year of the child's life. Parents may deny the implications of a handicap or be stunned and disbelieving about a child's retardation. Parents may feel deeply sad about the child but hide their fear and dismay by stressing the positive aspects of the child's development. When grandparents finally are told about the handicap, the child's parents may deny their own pain and frustration and yet look to the grandparents for emotional support.

A child with a handicap is not a separate species. The life of a family cannot revolve around his or her unique differences. Nevertheless, all parents must face the problem of accepting a unique child while mourning for the normal child they had desired. This problem may be exacerbated by the reactions of others with whom the parents are involved. The parents may feel unsupported and fearful of their child's rejection by relatives.

Rare are the grandparents who do not themselves experience ambivalence: love for all their grandchildren and yet personal disappointment or rejection of the handicapped grandchild. A different child may appear as a promise reduced in value. At a time of life when their achievements are lessening, grandparents may think they have been given a "bad deal." Resentment, discomfort, and embarrassment may initially take the place of family pride. If feelings of rejection are severe, grandparents may repress them as inappropriate or unacceptable. Their overt behavior may be directed in precisely the opposite direction, for example, becoming oversolicitous and overprotective of their grandchild, reducing stimulation, and impairing the child's growth toward independence.

How can grandparents be positive in the situation when they have their own questions and disappointments? If their feelings are overwhelming, it will be valuable for them to talk about their fears and anxieties. Other people can help. A pediatrician, friend, or social worker who is knowledgeable about the handicapped can answer questions even if the extent of the child's retardation is not known. A fear of the unknown—a child who is described as mongoloid, brain-damaged, cerebral palsied, or retarded—can be alleviated by reading books in the public library that describe the realistic experiences of other parents in similar situations, as well as practical information and advice. Grandparents may begin to notice newspaper and magazine articles that describe programs for handicapped children during infancy, the school years, and adolescence. Although what was successful

for the grandparents in child rearing may not be appropriate for a handicapped child, the parents will appreciate new information about the handicapped brought quietly to their attention. Grandparents will gradually find it easier to extend themselves, neither avoiding nor smothering the handicapped child or the child's parents.

Society tends to view people, including children and grandchildren, in terms of how quickly they achieve and how well they succeed in life. Every human being is unique, however, and can be cherished in many ways. Society's expectations can be revised. Experience with another person's pain increases one's sensitivity and sense of proportion. When a person has experienced retardation or crippling in a grandchild, another child's religion, skin color, or income is less important.

Concrete Suggestions

The grandparents' relationship with a handicapped child can make a major contribution to his or her progress. The child must receive stimulation from others to learn responses to a variety of experiences. The child should visit the grandparents' home, for example. The handicapped child learns as much by imitation as by practice, and repeated praise for a correct response increases learning. The three R's essential to the handicapped child—repetition, relaxation, and reward—can be reiterated frequently by loving grandparents.

Children thrive on attention. A handicap should not separate a child from attention by relatives. Handicapped children should take walks with their grandparents, ride in a car, go to a park, or accompany others to a grocery store. Grandparents have the opportunity to give attention to the handicapped child in the course of daily events, special occasions, or vacations, endowing the child with significance which the child perceives and which the parents yearn for. Other people also learn that normalized relationships not only are possible but are desirable with handicapped children. If the parents often fear that their child will be dismissed as valueless to the family and society, grandparents can attest to the child's worth through their steadfast interest.

Parents often need assistance when they realize their child may outlive them. Grandparents of the handicapped may want to consult a lawyer to write a provision in their will for the time when their grandchild becomes an adult and is in need of income. In planning care for the lifetime of the child, the parents should be helped in discussing guardianship with several family members. Financial assistance for individuals with disabilities can be obtained from a social security office. Information about resources such as residential schools or tax credits can be obtained from social service agencies or through membership in special associations in the community.

Communities also need help with their special children, to promote a better life and greater opportunities for them. Does the child's community have day care centers and special classes in the schools for the physically handicapped, educable, or trainable child? These programs need senior power, and grandparents can be vital in many ways, being available on flexible schedules to offer practical assistance such as supporting special projects, volunteering in classrooms, or driving children to weekly exercise classes. Other vital chores are fund raising and communica-

tion with legislators who prepare tax bills dealing with the needs of disabled children.

Conclusion

The personal involvement of grandparents in exploring opportunities available to the handicapped is critical to their grandchild's well-being. Grandparents need not remain family ghosts, lost and without direction. The doctor who looks after the handicapped child, the educators and psychologists who teach the child, and the social workers who help the family should understand and encourage the grandparents' continuing influence and interest in the family.

Handicapped children want a chance to grow, to have freedom and fun, training and education, and to progress to the extent of their abilities with help from their family, school, and community. Grandparents can be a basic part of the network of resources that form an emotionally healthy, tension-free circle of security all people want for their children and their children's children.

Jacqueline Heiber Berns, MA, is Director, Social Service Department, Community Hospital, Indianapolis, Indiana.

Part Four

Social Work with Groups

Introduction to Part Four

Some of the problems that confront the developmentally disabled and their families respond dramatically to group-level intervention. One such problem is the social isolation often experienced by families of developmentally disabled people. Groups can help overcome that isolation, regardless of their specific focus. Group members can become valuable resources for each other and may make themselves available to one another outside the structured meetings and beyond the life of the formal group. Support comes through the development of new relationships and the normalizing experience of being with others who are in similarly difficult circumstances.

Groups also provide an appropriate context within which the developmentally disabled individual can learn the social skills necessary for community living. In a group, feedback is immediate. Moreover, a group situation offers opportunities for the modeling of specific behaviors by group members and the sharing of reactions to experiences common to members, such as feelings about being stigmatized.

Another issue for both developmentally disabled people and their families is the need for information on how to deal with day-to-day life under exceptional circumstances. Although social workers can provide a great deal of useful information about resources in the community or principles for managing behavior, the details and realism of stories shared by group members carry unique credibility. In groups led by professionals the exchange of information among members can be facilitated and a program including guest speakers, films, or lists of books for the members can be coordinated.

From a professional's point of view, group intervention is often the most effective way to bring about change concerning a social problem. In addition to the fact that groups are fun to lead, the group process sometimes becomes so powerful that the leader may occasionally sit back and simply enjoy the interaction. Finally, groups are an efficient use of professional time.

The articles selected for this section about social work with groups focus on various target populations and several types of group work. The object is to present the dynamics of the group process and the impact of the group on its members and leaders in sufficient clinical detail to encourage the reader to replicate the experience. In the first selection, Davis and Shapiro emphasize the impact that participation in a group has on the self-image and social skills of the members, who are developmentally disabled adults. They also point out the importance of the expectations held by group leaders when working with this population. Sternlicht and Sullivan describe various group goals and corresponding group leadership functions. Although they place these in the context of parents' groups, the principles also apply to groups made up of other populations. Two other articles deal with parents and substitute parents of developmentally disabled children. Rose reports on the effectiveness of behavioral learning approaches in working with both parents and foster parents of disabled children, laying out procedures as well as the types of behavioral problems managed in this structured group process. A group sponsored by a social service agency to train foster parents of exceptional children is then described by Park, who discusses specific topics of concern to the group and makes recommendations concerning the utility of such groups for agencies wishing to promote expertise among foster parents. The siblings of mentally retarded children represent another target population for groups. Schreiber and Feeley discuss the circumstances of adolescent siblings that often make group-level intervention the treatment of choice in work with these youngsters. The authors sensitively portray the feelings that emerged during group meetings in addition to listing common problems with which the group dealt.

Although various types of groups and various target populations are addressed in Part Four, one important type of group is not mentioned—the group of professionals who evaluate and recommend interventions for the developmentally disabled individual and his or her family. In clinics, institutions, and schools, teams of professionals from different disciplines work together to serve the needs of the disabled client. Psychologist, nurse, pediatrician, neurologist, physical therapist, occupational therapist, audiologist, geneticist, special educator, and social worker all contribute their own perspectives to the collection of data on a client. At times their observations and remarks overlap. When they meet as a group to discuss their findings, they have an impact on one another, and they may revise the emphasis of a particular finding in light of various other findings. Their recommendations to clients should be accompanied by realistic expectations regarding how well or completely any such suggestions will be carried out. Therefore, some coordination among team members may be necessary to set priorities.

Gathering data, comparing findings, and collaborating on recommendations are some of the formal tasks of such groups. The group process that emerges is highly variable. Groups characterized by balanced contributions from representatives of different disciplines and by open exchange and understanding of information with occasional compromise by each team member might be described as interdisciplinary.

Federal legislation during the 1960s supported the development of interdisciplinary team treatment for the developmentally disabled as well as interdisciplinary training for future professionals. Model clinics funded through the Federal Office of Maternal and Child Health and the Office of Developmental Disabilities were established for this purpose. Although criticized for being time-consuming, the interdisciplinary group process enabled professionals other than physicians to play significant roles in treating the developmentally disabled and their families. Social workers were active in the movement in favor of interdisciplinary efforts because they recognized that developmental disabilities are a social as well as a medical problem, because they have historically had a commitment to participatory decision making, and because they had skills for facilitating the group dynamics necessary to the success of the democratic process taking place in interdisciplinary groups.

Social workers know about the differences between formal and informal leadership, the distinction between getting things done (which involves instrumental factors) and having people "like" the group (which concerns the affective component of the group process), the positive relationship between participation in a group and feelings of affiliation toward the group, the importance of delegating responsibility in a group, the contribution of sociometric structure to the group process (that is, the impact of friendships and cliques on the process), and the extent to which norms for group behavior (such as punctuality and self-disclosure) can be established. These factors play a part in any group, whether it is composed of professionals, parents, or developmentally disabled people. They can be manipulated by an expert on groups to increase the effectiveness and the nurturance of the group, whether or not the expert is the group's formal leader. The selections in Part Four are intended to illustrate how social workers—who traditionally have been experts on groups—can bring their skills to bear in group intervention in the developmental disabilities field.

KENNETH R. DAVIS
LINDA J. SHAPIRO

Exploring Group Process as a Means of Reaching the Mentally Retarded

From previous clinical experience with the mentally retarded, the authors observed that these clients usually suffer from social isolation as evidenced by withdrawal, depression, confusion, poor verbal skills, poor interaction with peers, and overdependence on authority figures. Furthermore, their socialization skills reflect a lack of autonomy and an absence of gratifying relationships. These characteristics contribute to their poor self-image, manifested by their frequently unkempt appearance, obesity, sluggishness, as well as a blunted sexual identification. For these reasons the mentally retarded are often stereotyped as unresponsive and unattractive candidates for psychotherapy.[1]

This article is a description of the authors' experiences in applying group process skills with women in the Berkeley Center, Berkeley, California, a work-activity program for mentally retarded adults, sponsored by the Alameda County (California) Association for the Mentally Retarded. The group was conceived as a laboratory for promoting the following objectives:

1. Development of verbal and social skills.
2. Effective expression of thoughts and feelings.
3. Identification as a more autonomous person.
4. Increased mutual support and acceptance.
5. Improvement of grooming and hygiene.

If these objectives were moderately realized, clients would not only be in a better position to cope with life's situations, but would also be more likely to benefit from the center's overall program.

Evolvement of Group Treatment Activity

As an outgrowth of working individually with clients ranging in age from eighteen to sixty, the authors were able to identify many commonalities that could more effectively be treated in a group process orientation. A motivating factor for considering group process was the clients' tendency to seek approval and support from authority figures in the Berkeley Center while avoiding peer relationships, which were often fraught with conflict. The authors discovered that they became one more source of authority approval for clients, unwittingly reinforcing the clients' already existing tendency to avoid developing problem-solving skills.

Concurrent with their observations of the need for utilizing group process as a tool for developing socialization and communication skills, the staff at the center wanted to establish groups for similar reasons. The authors, therefore, had the necessary support and cooperation of the agency which was essential in initiating such services.

In 1974, the authors began a weekly women's group with a male and a female as co-leaders. Individual treatment activity with all participants was maintained, frequently as a follow-up to issues raised in the group. As a result of the interest and popularity of the women's group, a men's group was formed in 1975. Although the need for separate men's and women's groups persisted, the potential benefits inherent in a coed group were recognized. In 1976, a combined meeting of the men's and women's groups began on a monthly basis. The women's group was selected as the focus of this article because of its two-and-one-half-year duration and stability of group members in attendance.

Selection of Participants

Although clients had been seen on an individual basis prior to the beginning of the groups, the nucleus of the group was drawn from people recommended by the supportive services coordinator and program staff. Because of the many complex problems faced by these clients, potential members had to meet specific criteria for inclusion in the group. In consultation with center staff, the authors jointly decided on two major categories. First, clients who presented management problems as a result of disruptive, acting-out behavior were believed to be top priority, especially by center staff. Second, clients who exhibited marked withdrawal and were severely deficient in social skills were seen as unable to benefit from the center's program and, therefore, became a second order of priority. These referrals were contingent upon the approval of parents and of those providing board and care for them, whichever applied. Due to lack of funding, home contact was kept to a minimum.

As a consequence of a reported lack of enthusiasm for previous groups at the center, combined with a lack of familiarity with this population, the authors were apprehensive about excessive member attrition. Nine members were selected, a slightly larger number, based on past experience with various types of groups, than believed to be optimum (six to eight). Ages ranged from approximately twenty-two to fifty-five, and although there were individual differences in functioning, levels of maturity did not necessarily reflect chronological age. A racially balanced group was selected, consisting of 60 percent white and 40 percent black, which approximated the ethnic composition of the center. (There were a minimum number of other minority clients —three Asians, none of whom fit into the selection priorities.)

The group was heterogeneous in terms of degree of retardation, ranging from borderline to severe levels. Clients with severe emotional problems (a small number of them manifesting periodic psychotic episodes) resulting in functional retardation comprised a small percentage of the group. This latter population required a significant amount of attention and follow-up services. There was an attempt to create a balance between those participants who possessed verbal skills and were outgoing and those who tended to be withdrawn and less communicative.

Preparation for Group Members

Those clients who were being seen in ongoing individual counseling were prepared informally during the course of their treatment. They were told that group treatment would be an adjunct to their counseling program. Particular care was taken to communicate to both clients and staff that one modality was not necessarily superior to the other, but rather more complementary in nature. Most of these clients responded favorably to the idea of group involvement, however, not without apprehension and anxiety.[2]

On the other hand, the clients who were new referrals required more intensive preparation efforts because of a lack of any established counseling relationship and greater anxiety about what was expected of them in a group context. These clients required at least one month of preparation time on a weekly or, in some cases, more frequent basis. One factor that seemed to prove especially effective in reducing anxiety was the authors' commitment to seeing these clients individually as the need arose in addition to participation in the group. This seemed particularly attractive to those requiring more individual attention than the group could offer. Furthermore, for groups in general, the principle of sporadic follow-up interviews (however brief and occasional) serves to reinforce the treatment relationship and promotes more rapid group cohesion. This is especially effective during the initial phase of the group and tends to subside as a group identification solidifies.

Development of a Group Process

Following screening and preparation, weekly meetings began. The meetings were approximately two hours in duration, allowing some extra time for stragglers and last-minute individual concerns. Co-leadership was established during the first month for several reasons. First, it was believed that it would be advantageous to have male and female leadership and black and white representation. Second, the male leader was familiar to the clients because of his involvement at the center for several years prior to the group's inception. Because the clients already knew him, they were immediately more comfortable and less threatened by the group experience. The female leader was relatively new to the center and, therefore, did most of the individual group preparation. This afforded her the opportunity to become familiar to the clients and establish ongoing treatment relationships.

Ultimately, a transition from co-leadership to individual female leadership was planned. Because the female leader was white, it was believed that it would be more effective to begin the group with one black and one white leader in order to establish modeling for comfortable interracial peer relationships. After five group meetings, the female assumed leadership of the group, with sporadic attendance by the male leader as the need arose.

Initial group meetings took place in an area usually used as the center's sewing room. The group sat around a rectangular-shaped table in a somewhat formal classroom setting. The leaders chose to sit at opposite sides of the table, so as to facilitate eye contact and non-verbal communication. Conflicts in room availability required meetings to be held in a variety of classroom settings during the first month. This created an atmosphere in which clients had difficulty differentiating the group experience from the traditional activities of the center and also raised questions of confidentiality. Members often arrived with notebooks and pencils "at the ready" and directed all attention and comments to the leaders, as they might a teacher. There was obvious avoidance of peer interactions and clients' emotional vocabulary was virtually nil. Issues raised by the leaders were most frequently met with yes or no responses, followed by silence.

Fostering Participation and Interaction

The leaders began by presenting guidelines of what was expected in terms of client participation, emphasizing that, although grooming and hygiene would be an issue, the primary focus of the group was discussion and sharing of thoughts and feelings. They made it clear that members had the option to decline discussing issues that they did not feel ready to handle. Also stressed was the objective of treating the discussions in a manner that would respect the confidentiality of the participants. Because the leaders were not staff members and not perceived as such by the group, it was easier for them to separate the group and its leadership from other center activities and promote feelings of trust.

Beginning discussions were often punctuated by various kinds of diversionary behavior, such as hiding behind notebooks, excessive gigling, frequent trips to the bathroom, and feigning sleep. Despite efforts to informalize discussions, members repeatedly raised their hands fervently when they wanted to speak, and when called on, many responded with completely extraneous material, reminiscent of elementary school "show and tell."

Members persisted in relying on leaders to initiate and maintain group discussion and, although an attempt was made to direct them toward involvement with each other, they continuously directed responses and sought approval from the leaders. Essentially, members regarded the group with such seriousness that they literally became too nervous to participate. Sensing these restrictions, the leaders began using role playing and humor to lighten the emotional tone of the group. For example, during intervals when there were long silences and members were unable to participate, the leaders turned to each other and made comments such as the following:

"Seems like no one feels like talking today. What's happening with you?"

"I'm feeling a little nervous. How 'bout you?"

"Me too. Seems like things aren't interesting enough right now. Maybe you could sing or do a soft-shoe."

"Me? Whatcha' mean me?"

In this fashion, the leaders got members to laugh while they simultaneously role modeled what sharing experiences entailed.

Because one group member was proficient in grooming skills, the group elected to have her preside as the group's beauty consultant. This served to elevate her self-image and encouraged the group to look to their peers for mutual support and assistance. The model of group interaction was repeatedly reinforced by responding to members with phrases like, "Are you talking to me or to the group?" and "What's your reaction to Betty's comment, Barbara?" These efforts quickly resulted in members imitating the leaders' modeling techniques and learning to interact with each other.[3]

Role Responsibilities of Leaders

Leadership responsibilities took on the dual characteristics of educative and therapeutic roles. The following illustration highlights the dovetailing of these roles. In a situation where a client had difficulty controlling disruptive and impulsive behavior, the leaders instituted a system whereby the client sat next to a leader and by means of prearranged nonverbal signals was able to sustain appropriate behavior during the group. This technique of physically positioning the client near the therapist is reminiscent of the control measures long instituted by ordinary classroom teachers to discourage acting-out behavior in grade schools.

Overall, it took approximately three months for the group to become a viable, cohesive unit. This development parallels more traditional stages of group evolution presented by group theorists.[4] One of the early signs of group solidarity was members assuming responsibility for notifying each other of the commencement of group meetings. Frequently, upon the leaders' arrival at the center on group meeting days, it took no more than their presence to elicit a scurrying of bodies into the meeting room. The group members' motivation ultimately progressed to the stage where they assembled on their own ahead of the scheduled time, often engaging in meaningful discussions independent of the leaders. On occasion, the leaders felt as though they had perhaps outlived their usefulness as group leaders.[5]

Contributions from Group Members

Simultaneously, individuals began to assume greater responsibility for the give and take of successful group process. Clients initiated discussion of individual concerns and requested feedback from the group. In addition, they appeared to have discovered the value of reliance on each other for approval and support as opposed to their earlier dependence on authority figures. The level of participation and involvement went from one extreme, of the leaders having to pull for material, to a level where participants frequently competed for the opportunity to share their problems with the group. Often, even before the group commenced, members would chime in with, "I've got something I want to say," or "My mother is making me so mad I feel like moving out."

Individual interviews supported the leaders' observations of client growth as a result of participation in the group. Clients learned to make a distinction between material that could effectively be handled in the group and material that required more individual attention. In addition, the group provided ongoing material that was later used in follow-up interviews. Individual interviews became more productive, thus demonstrating the mutually self-enhancing qualities of individual and group treatment.

Development of Camaraderie

Observations by center staff revealed a progressive development of camaraderie among group members, which manifested itself in all aspects of the center's program. Aside from the benefits of psychosocial development, clients manifested significant improvement in their grooming and personal hygiene. They also evidenced increased self-esteem and elevated social status by virtue of their group identification. These gains were also a result of the center's initial presentation of the group as a positive aspect of their program.

This spirit of camaraderie was manifested during group meetings by a feeling of a sense of purpose. Although interactions were at times light and humorous, the prevailing attitude was one of seriousness, of "taking care of business." From a purely visual standpoint, it was possible to chart the growing solidarity of the group. In initial meetings, some members positioned themselves so as to create distance between themselves and other participants. This behavior indicated ambivalence and detachment from the group. As the group became more cohesive, the circle became tighter and members felt the need for closer physical proximity. There was a growing development of group sensitivity and concern among the members, revealed by comments such as the following: "Yvonne won't be here today. She told me to tell you she has a dental appointment." Or, "How can we stop Audrey from teasing and interrupting while someone else is talking?" Members discussed alternative ways of modifying inappropriate or disruptive behavior.

Concurrently, the group expressed feelings of caring and an interest in each other's welfare. This was demonstrated by recognition of birthdays, illnesses, achievements, and so on. This increased concern extended beyond group meetings to other center activities and on occasion into their home lives. For instance, some members afflicted by various physical maladies had difficulty remembering their medication schedules. In such cases, other group members assumed the responsibility of reminding them. In other instances, members assisted in monitoring each other in regard to hygiene and personal appearance. In general, there was growing awareness and sensitivity in group members to peer relationships.

Termination

Because of problems maintaining funding for the group, the leaders had to terminate their services at the center after two and one-half years. The termination process required taking into consideration the clients' "here and now" orientation to time concepts and frequent inability to comprehend protracted time frames. Therefore, the leaders decided that three weeks was sufficient preparation time for handling termination. In addition to group meetings, individual interviews were used for further self-assessment and resolution of relationships.

Client reaction ranged from unsuppressed feelings of sadness to apparent anger manifested without any overt responses. Several clients, undaunted by the unexpected news of the leaders' leaving, offered to assume leadership of the group. Subsequently, an animated discussion ensued about the particulars of how this objective could be realized. There was no doubt that they were convinced of their ability to run the group without the leaders.

While recognizing the qualities of denial and self-protection inherent in their efforts to continue the group, the leaders were struck by their natural spontaneity and resourcefulness in their quest to seek viable alternatives. This behavior was seen as a healthy reaction to adverse circumstances and an excellent indication of their growth. Although the leaders experienced sadness at the reality of termination, they were heartened by this evidence of the group members' increased self-determination, autonomy, and self-esteem.

Discussion

Realizing that many of the objectives for the group had been accomplished, the leaders began to assess what factors made group treatment activities effective or ineffective and identified some common misconceptions which appeared to hinder the therapeutic process.

The leaders' teaching backgrounds were a distinct advantage in working with this population; it was easier to assess spontaneously individual levels of functioning, rather than having a focus on tasks beyond client capabilities. For example, vocabulary adjustments were made so that interventions were understood by the group, without resorting to "talking down" to them. Initial group meetings required a heavier reliance on instructional techniques that prepared the clients to utilize in a better way the less-structured measures of therapeutic intervention. Consequently, this duality of therapist-teacher roles operated simultaneously.

Prior to intervention, the leaders observed that clients appeared to function significantly below their potential. For example, many group members had not taken responsibility for washing and grooming their hair. An unfamiliarity with this population and a lack of preconceived performance levels serendipitously worked to the leaders' advantage. Leaders' expectations tended to be considerably higher than the clients were accustomed to and, consequently, the clients responded by performing at a superior level. This calls attention to the authors' belief that the concept of self-fulfilling prophesy is no less operative in this population than among nonretarded clientele. Unfortunately, too many helping professionals working with the retarded underestimate the impact of unrealistically lowered expectations on these clients' growth.[6]

The following dramatically illustrates the above issue: The client was a thirty-six-year-old single female who had been diagnosed as suffering from chronic undifferentiated schizophrenia with brain damage. She exhibited marked flattened affect, was severely withdrawn, and communicated by uttering one-word gutteral sounds which were difficult to comprehend. Center staff believed that the group might be a good experience for her; however, her growth potential was believed to be so minimal that the expectations would probably be negligible. Although the leaders initially were influenced by these attitudes, they gradually determined that this client's capacity had been underestimated. During a period of four to five months she progressed from one-word responses to sentence fragments, culminating in the use of clearly comprehensive simple sentences by the end of six months. In addition, her affect appeared more appropriate and she manifested more animated responses. Of equal significance was the development of a greater interest in her peers and, consequently, higher demands on their performance. She became a more active participant in the group and this expanded behavior was generalized to outside situations, resulting in the establishment of a relationship with a man.

Although this is only one example of the range of unexpected capacities many of the clients exhibited, it serves to highlight the need for a flexible working diagnosis in order to take into account their manifestation of multiple and clinical symptoms.

The presence of a nucleus of clients who have already established an ongoing treatment relationship with the therapist served to facilitate a more rapid development of group cohesion. This advantage was not without its hazards. Such issues as reserving emotionally charged material for individual interviews and maintaining the impression of a special relationship with the therapist were common occurrences and had to be resolved.

In reassessing the group's objectives, the leaders became aware of their failure to consider the obstacles inherent in the clients' living arrangements which were counterproductive to more autonomous development. In order to reinforce independent functioning, it is necessary that the home environment be supportive of these objectives. The lack of contact with parents and those persons who supplied board and care to some clients prevented obtaining this support. Consequently, there were some drawbacks in the attempt to promote greater autonomy.

Clinical stereotypes would lead one to expect that these clients would require a great deal of structure and would be unable to engage in open-ended discussion without a predetermined agenda. Although they required training and orientation in order to engage in spontaneous and meaningful communication, after three or four meetings, clients had developed the skills necessary to open group discussion with a minimum of direction. In this respect they appeared indistinguishable from nonretarded clientele.[7] The common belief that this clientele is unable to participate in a group of average duration because of their short attention span also proved to be unfounded.

It is interesting to note that although a large number of referrals were made as a result of acting-out behavior, this behavior was noticeably absent during group meetings. It is the authors' belief that these clients' lack of ability to express their feelings verbally contributed to their frustration and subsequent disruptive behavior. The group provided an atmosphere whereby support was given for more appropriate modes of expression. This obviated the need for disruptive behavior. In addition, clients seemed to respond favorably to the group norms of autonomy and mature behavior, whereas their environment outside the group frequently supported dependency and immature behavior.

Other Considerations

The mentally retarded are distinguishable from others by their spontaneous display of a wide range of emotions. They appear significantly less inhibited in their physical expression of warmth and affection. Although it took a period of time to adjust to this, the leaders grew to accept this physical exchange as an integral part of the treatment relationship. It is vital that those working with these clients be aware of this issue in order to maximize their effectiveness.

In addition, these clients are frequently diagnosed as mentally retarded with little or no recognition given to additional psychological problems. It is essential that those involved with the retarded continually adjust their expectations to insure that clients are constantly striving toward expanding their levels of functioning.[8]

Videotape and cassette equipment was used on several occasions and proved to be very effective in facilitating the group process. Although the group had limited access to this equipment, its leaders were impressed by the advantages of having material instantly available for recall and evaluations. These tools are particularly valuable for treating the mentally retarded because there is no reliance on memory and they minimize the need for abstraction.[9]

Although coed meetings were held for a limited period of time, the effects were quite dramatic. The change of milieu afforded a situation whereby clients could test out newly obtained skills with peers of the opposite sex and acquire greater comfort with their sexual roles and identification. Coed meetings served to expand the socialization process, but it requires further evaluation for potential use.

Conclusion

In reviewing this experience, the authors believe that group process is a powerful tool for the treatment and education of the mentally retarded. Mutual symptoms such as social isolation, a lack of socialization skills, and a poor self-image lend themselves to a treatment modality which is based on peer support, interaction, and conflict resolution. In addition, group interaction fosters the development of peer relationships as opposed to dependent authority relationships and also serves to promote more autonomous functioning.

The overwhelming needs of the mentally retarded, combined with a lack of psychotherapeutic services available for them, resulted in the leaders' efforts having an immediate, dramatic impact on client behavior.

Although psychotherapeutic skills require adjustments in application for these clients, the leaders found treatment techniques virtually indistinguishable from those utilized in the treatment of other populations.

Of particular significance was the realization that, initially, the objectives came nowhere near the client's performance; their growth and development far exceeded expectations. Unfortunately, the expectations were heavily influenced by prevailing biases. Once relationships with the clients were established, the leaders' biases and anxieties began to diminish. As they became more comfortable, they stopped reacting from their prejudices and began reacting to the group members' individual qualities as people. Thus the successes were directly related to the extent to which the leaders were able to overcome barriers they had established.

From a broader perspective, treatment planning must include a consideration of the obstacles interfering with the developmental cycle crucial for self-actualization. It is essential to work toward altering societal attitudes that perpetuate the overall dependency status of the mentally retarded. Only then can the effectiveness of psychotherapeutic intervention be totally realized.

Kenneth R. Davis and Linda J. Shapiro are in private practice in Oakland, California, and act as consultants to public and private agencies. At the time this article was written, Davis was Director and Shapiro on the staff of the People's Consultation Clinic in Oakland.

Notes and References

1. The general skepticism about psychotherapy for the mentally retarded has been well documented. The aim of psychotherapy is not to raise the intellectual functioning of the retardate (although this may occasionally be a by-product) but to deal with emotional conflicts which beset all people. This issue is discussed by R. K. Janmeja Singh, "Psychotherapy with Behaviorally Disturbed Mentally Retarded," in *Mental Health Services for the Mentally Retarded,* ed. Elias Katz (Springfield, Ill.: Charles C Thomas, 1972), pp. 25–37.

2. The value of building the bond between client and therapist (when possible and practical) has long-term benefits prior to involvement in group therapy. The attrition rate is significantly affected. Irvin Yalom discusses this subject in greater detail in *The Theory and Practice of Group Psychotherapy* (New York: Basic Books, 1975), pp. 286–98.

3. See Frank W. Gibson, Jr., Lawrence P. Scott, and Rosemary O. Nelson, "Comparison of Three Training Procedures for Teaching Social Responses to Developmentally Disabled Adults," *American Journal of Mental Deficiency* 81 (January 1977): 379–87.

4. Yalom, *Theory and Practice of Group Psychotherapy,* pp. 331 ff.

5. The level of enthusiasm was such that the group began to exhibit an "atmosphere of fellowship and camaraderie reminiscent of a summer camp" described by Martin Lakin and Philip R. Costanzo, "The Leader and the Experiential Group," in *Theories of Group Processes,* ed. Cary L. Cooper (New York: John Wiley and Sons, 1975), p. 207.

6. See Laurence J. Severance and Lisa L. Gasstrom, "Effects of the Label 'Mentally Retarded' on Causal Explanations for Success and Failure Outcomes," *American Journal of Mental Deficiency* 81 (June 1977): 547–55.

7. This conclusion is corroborated by Charles Moody, "Group Therapy with the Mentally Retarded," in *Mental Health Services for the Mentally Retarded,* ed. Katz, p. 81.

8. For a more comprehensive discussion of problems of diagnosis with this population see, E. L. Loschen, "Failures in Diagnosis and Treatment in Mental Retardation," *Mental Retardation* 13 (June 1975): 29–31.

9. See Karen R. Nash, "The Sequencing of an Audio-Visual Group Discussion Teaching Method as It Relates to Social Adjustment Attitude Change of Junior High School Educable Mentally Retarded Students," *Dissertation Abstracts International* 37 (October 1976): 1964–65.

MANNY STERNLICHT
INA SULLIVAN

Group Counseling with Parents of the MR: Leadership Selection and Functioning

With the current pervasiveness of group process into all aspects of life and with the effective use of groups in working with parents of the mentally retarded, the issue of who should lead the parents group in an agency serving the mentally retarded is at question. Now that the "team approach" has become popularized the effective and imaginative utilization of the agency team members in leading parents groups requires examination.

The literature of parent counseling offers little information. What does appear is often a defense of why one particular discipline is expressly suited to do it all (Rusicka, 1958). Others attempt to define the qualities of personality, training and experience that might be desirable (Thurston, 1963), and how qualities of compassion and sympathy affect parents' understanding and acceptance of retardation (Raech, 1966). Barsch (1961) is helpful in defining the level of goals that parents groups may have.

Groups form and parents continue to at-

tend on the basis of shared need. How much of the need will be fulfilled is based on how far the group leader wishes to take the group and how far the group is willing to be taken.

Most obviously, the members of the group need information, from the leader and from each other. The parents group is a vehicle for that information to be disseminated. The group process of information seeking and information giving is formalized. Workable, practical solutions to problems all have faced or will face are discussed.

Some problems require the expertise of a specialist. For example, it is the community social worker who guides the group in the use of outside resources, the psychologist who discusses the meaning of intelligence, and the psychiatrist who assists with aspects of depression. But groups can have other important goals as well; information seeking on the part of parents and information giving by the group leader provide entree to other levels of objectives from which the parents can benefit in a group situation. It is suggested that the question of who should lead the group can be resolved by determining the needs of the group, and what is required of the leader to meet these needs.

Barsch (1961, p.41) identifies five general levels of goals that will be pursued by a parents group, with each succeeding level requiring more involvement, investment, and psychological risk on the part of the group members.

1. Information seeking is a quest for the tools of parenting from the leader and from each other.

2. Sharing is the exchange of information, opinion, evaluation, clarification, and suggestions among the group members and the leader.

3. Feeling is the exposure and acceptance of emotions and their recognition as forceful determinants of behavior.

4. Generalization is the application of understanding to other behaviors and of their impact on life patterns.

5. Maturity is the insightful ability to effect change for the better in one's life.

It is suggested that a separate and distinct leadership function may correspond to each of the five levels, and that who should lead the group may be determined from these functions and their requirements.

Corresponding to the goal of information seeking is the leadership function of information giving which can be performed by any person with helpful knowledge to impart —teacher, education specialist, physician, social worker, educational or clinical psychologist and so on.

When the group goal is sharing, an assumption is made in the group that much valuable information derives from one another as well as from the group leader, and that a sympathetic sharing among the parents in the group legitimizes and formalizes their attempts to find and apply answers to common problems. The group leader must use encouragement with this group—sharing requires a personal investment on the part of the parents that goes beyond the passive absorption of helpful information. It requires the localizing and acknowledging of the problems, together with the risk of criticism and even ridicule from other group members on the part of a tentative and insecure parent. An understanding professional in any of the mental hygiene disciplines is needed at this level in order to reassure and invite group members to participate.

The goal of feeling requires the group leadership function of support. Feelings can be exposed without earth-shaking consequences if the group can be led to a rational understanding of how feelings influence behavior and, indeed, how behavior can likewise influence feelings. For this function, a mental hygiene professional with at least a theoretical understanding of behavior and a comfortable working familiarity with one system of psychotherapeutic practice and procedure is needed.

For the goal of generalization, the group leader provides insight. At this level, rational understanding is seen through supportive exposure and acceptance of feelings and is skillfully applied to life styles and patterns of adjustment in general. A skilled, experienced group therapist is needed—a clinical psychologist/psychiatrist, or social worker.

The goal of maturity requires the group leader to help in planning for action and to help parents deal realistically with the future and to live maturely. For this function, the trained therapist necessary to provide insight is needed, whatever his or her professional discipline.

The five levels of group goals and corresponding group leadership functions do not necessarily progress from one level to the next. The dynamics of groups and those of individuals do not permit such clear demarcations in group behavior. But the primary objective of the level can be guided accordingly by the group leader with these succeeding levels in mind.

A danger in rendering group counseling services is in viewing the parents one-dimensionally by the fact that they have at least one characteristic in common—a retarded child. It is sometimes difficult to keep in mind that they will be as diverse as any random group of persons. It is these differences that deserve recognition. Because parents comprise a heterogeneous group in many ways, this suggests that not only will their individual reactions to their retarded child be different, but also that their acceptance of the child and the child's impact on their individual life styles will be different. It is this multi-dimensional character of the group that the leader needs to be aware of and to work with whenever the opportunity presents itself.

Though specific tools and techniques can be given to parents of the retarded, the ideal outcome of group meetings is to help parents become able to find their own answers to questions and solutions to problems, to eventually be able to successfully seek out and personally experiment with methods used in helping the retarded.

While it is important to acknowledge the individual differences of participants in the group, it is also essential to work with them as a part of the total group, rather than as individuals. In the parents group, the needs and interests of one parent should not control the group. Rather, the whole of the group exists and is controlled by the interrelationships of all members.

When the group leader is aware of the dynamic interaction and uses it to help propel the group toward its objective, the objective and the means to it have been shared and thus have more impact. A basic understanding of the dynamics of parents groups' needs to be part of the leader's competence, wherever his or her leadership functions will lead. The leader needs to recognize that groups develop through several stages, not in an order of succession, but with considerable overlap and back-and-forth movement. As a group forms, the heterogeneity of the members is apparent, and will even be asserted by the individual members. As a group identification develops, more homogeneous characteristics will be expressed and a singular group culture will develop. At this point, the integrity of the group becomes of great importance and a give-and-take begins between maintenance of that integrity and the accomplishment of the group objectives—whatever they may be. These two forces tend to work somewhat at odds with one another, with individual group members taking roles that advance one or the other, but in pursuit of a balance between them.

Group norms of behavior and group values that will determine group outcomes develop, and some degree of conformity to them is expected. If a group member does not conform, the group applies pressure and may even expel the group member if the nonconformity is so great as to threaten the balance in the group between task accomplishments and group maintenance. The interrelationships in the group become so well established that any attempt of a new member or "outsider" to enter the group is considered highly intrusive.

As group role-taking is established, males may not enjoy taking the comforting, conciliatory role required to resolve emotional content in the group; conversely, a woman may not be satisfied with roles she is "forced" to take. Social roles outside the group enter into the picture as well. Group members will expect task leadership, for example, from someone everyone knows to be a community leader.

These dynamics in the parents group are always present. If they are not, there is another form of human gathering instead—a classroom or lecture situation or an audience to a performance, perhaps, but not a group. Groups are transactional entities wherein the members singly and as a group receive, process, and act upon stimuli bowing in complex patterns among themselves and the group leader.

Summary

In deciding who should lead the parents group, the foremost consideration should be the stated purpose of the group. However, the objectives of the group leader can differ from those of the group members, and individual members' objectives may differ from those agreed upon by the group as a whole. Individual members' objectives will therefore either be pursued, over-ridden, surrendered, or simply held in abeyance. The attendance record of the individual group members will tell how closely individual members' objectives are being met. When overt and covert goals fail to agree or when neither are being met, the individual members will drop from the group.

It is likely that unexpressed, covert individual and group goals will be those further up on the emotional hierarchy. It is likely that an individual with the objective of wanting to express and share emotional feelings in the group will state either that objective or the lower objective of wanting information. Wanting information can carry a multitude of meanings as well and can be used to express the need to know how to handle emotional feelings.

The group leader, too, also will have overt and covert goals in the group. If therapy is the goal, the leader may be seeking the resolution of deep problems and the consequent establishment of mature, healthy behavior. Two agency professionals may wish to work with the same group simultaneously or at separate sessions, depending upon the purpose of the group and the intensity of the interaction, as well as the convenience to the schedules of all concerned.

Another workable arrangement may be for the team members to work in tandem, in a cooperative application of their separate talents. This would be an ongoing team approach, wherein the group purpose could be met by the disciplines working separately with individual members as well as together in the group as dual-leaders. Many group-leader training programs are now featuring use of two group leaders, one to provide instrumental leadership to lead the group toward problem solution, the other to provide expressive leadership to lead the group toward expression and resolution of emotional content.

The talents required of a group leader discussed herein are not likely to be mutually exclusive—one to psychologist, one to social worker, the other to the educator or psychiatrist. The leader should be someone who (a) has had the training and experience in achieving the particular group's objectives, (b) feels comfortable with the purpose of the group and, most importantly, (c) who performs competently in it.

A clinical psychologist may like the teaching role; he may be the ideal person to convey the latest research or practical techniques (information giving) to the parents group; or it may be the social worker or psychiatrist who performs competently as therapist, as the one who can guide the group skillfully to the mature resolution of the problems of individuals within the group.

Expert guidance of the group is needed, and who will do it depends largely upon the purposes of the group and what talents are demanded of the leader in order to accomplish them.

Manny Sternlicht, Ph.D., Deputy Director, Queens Unit, Willowbrook Developmental Center, Staten Island, New York. Ina Sullivan, M.S.W. (Rutgers University), Team Leader at Willowbrook, pursuing a doctorate in social work.

Notes and References

Barsch, R. H. Counseling the parent of the brain-damaged child. *Journal of Rehabilitation,* 1961, 27, 26–42.

Raech, H. A parent discusses initial counseling. *Mental Retardation,* 1966, 4 (2), 25–26.

Rusicka, W. A proposed role for the school psychologist: Counseling parents of mentally retarded children. *American Journal of Mental Deficiency,* 1958, 62 (6), 897–904.

Thurston, J. R. Counseling the parents of mentally retarded children. *Training School Bulletin,* 1963, 60, 113–117.

SHELDON D. ROSE

Training Parents in Groups as Behavior Modifiers of Their Mentally Retarded Children

Training parents as effective behavior modifiers has been demonstrated by a number of writers (e.g. Allen and Harris, 1965; Bernal, 1971; Hawkins *et al.,* 1966; Straughan, 1964; Wahler *et al.,* 1965; Zeilberger, Sampen and Sloane, 1968). A wide range of behavioral changes such as decreasing tantrums, self-destructive behaviors, verbal aggression, excessive crying, thumbsucking and soiling, and increasing self-help skills, verbal behavior, social approach responses, and play with other children have been successfully attained by parents trained as behavior therapists of their own children. Several other authors have reported successful experiences in the group training of parents as behavior modifiers (Walder, Cohen and Datson, 1967; Galloway and Galloway, 1970; Greyerson, 1968; Howard, 1970; Jeffords *et al.,* 1971; Lindsley, 1966; Rose, 1969, Rose, 1974, Rose *et al.,* 1972).

Because of years of frustration in attempting to teach their children even the sim-

plest motor and verbal skills, parents of the retarded are sometimes discouraged and often set too low standards for their children. Often social problems develop because of siblings' and other children's responses to the retarded child's behavior. A method promising to make the learning process more efficient and providing specific means of improving social relations would be highly valued by the parents of the retarded child.

For the above reasons this project was designed to provide training for parents of mentally retarded children in a group setting to become behavior modifiers of their own children and to evaluate whether that training resulted in the modification of their children's behaviors. The group setting was used to facilitate parents' exposure to a wider range of behaviors than those emitted by their own children. Furthermore, the group is a source of exchange of extensive ideas for potential reinforcers and other treatment plans. It also allows for numerous participants in modelling and behavior rehearsal, important training procedures. Finally, parents in groups provide additional sources of social reinforcement for each other's achievements.

Parent Populations: Natural and Foster

One population of parents was recruited by mail from local organizations for parents of mentally retarded children. After the first few groups had been completed, the trained parents informally recruited members of subsequent groups from among their acquaintances. Other parents heard about the groups at various activities for parents of the retarded where I or one of my students was asked to speak. The foster parent population was recruited by social workers attached to a colony for mentally retarded. Over a period of 2 yr (June, 1970 to June, 1972) 33 families in groups were trained during eleven training programs (each lasting 7–10 weeks). Each group met weekly at one of the two major referring agencies.

Training of Parents

At the first meeting parents agreed in writing to attend all (seven to 10) of the 90-min meetings and to complete all home assignments. These included the following: (1) reading behavioral literature and completing exercises on behavioral assessments; (2) weekly monitoring (counting) of behaviors; (3) applying change procedures; and (4) autonomously developing treatment plans. These assignments tended to overlap. Parents were encouraged to negotiate only those home assignments they felt they could readily complete in the course of the week. Although suggestions were given, parents made their own decisions about the content of the assignment. Once a decision was reached, however, each recorded his agreement in writing, one copy of which he kept, and the other he gave to the therapist. Although no specific contingencies were attached to the agreement, it functioned as an unambiguous set of mutually agreed upon expectations for the week. Still later the application of more complex change procedures was assigned along with autonomous development of treatment planning.

Attendance by the foster parents was encouraged by providing travel and baby-sitter money, whereas the natural parents were required to pay a $10.00 deposit which was returned if there was regular attendance. This disparity was justified in terms of the significantly higher income level of the natural parents.

Each member of foster parents groups was visited at home on the average of once every 3 weeks by his social worker who assisted in carrying out programs.

The 21 families in the natural parent groups, on the other hand, received only a total of six home visits by the group leaders.

A pre-treatment check list was used to facilitate problem definition. The children's problem behaviors were defined by the parents in behaviorally specific terms before monitoring and treatment began. Conditions which controlled these behaviors were examined during the initial group meetings. In order to increase the probability of initial success, parents were encouraged to select as initial targets only those behaviors which were readily identifiable, were relatively simple to count, and lent themselves to simple reinforcement and/or time out procedures. It has been observed that early success increases the motivation of the parents to treat more complicated behaviors later on. In all cases, however, the parents themselves selected the behavior to be worked on.

Once a behavior had been identified and carefully defined, the parent developed with the assistance of the other group members a monitoring plan by means of which he counted the target behavior for a period usually lasting 10 days to 2 weeks (the baseline period). If the probability for the occurrence of the behavior was rare (as in cases of enuresis), every observed event was counted. If the probability for the occurrence of the behavior was high as in the case of picking up toys and putting them in the toy box the behavior was counted only during a specified limited time period each day. Parents were also taught to graph the data collected.

Once a behavior had been successfully monitored, a treatment plan was devised which consisted of one or more treatment procedures and instructions on the exact nature of their application. These plans were developed by the given parent with the active assistance of the group members and the group leader. Treatment plans consisted of such procedures as positive reinforcement and shaping, extinction, time out from reinforcement, cueing, modelling, and behavior rehearsal (Bandura, 1969, p. 188; Butterfield and Parson, 1973; Ullmann and Krasner, 1969, Ch. 4).

In order to learn these procedures the parents read a programmed textbook which outlined social learning theory (Patterson and Gullion, 1968) and several supplementary handouts pertaining to child management. Group members were periodically tested on the content of these materials throughout the training program. In spite of the staff's initial hesitancy to test adults, the parents claimed they benefited from the feedback they received about what they had learned, and indicated that the test served as a necessary pressure to read. In addition there were brief lectures (ca. 5–10 min in length) concerning the major concepts and group discussion in which the parents practiced explaining them or giving their own examples. Another set of techniques used by the group leaders was modelling and behavior rehearsal. Group leaders and, at times, the parents themselves served as models for other parents for the purpose of demonstrating various behavior modification techniques. Behavior rehearsal involved the parents practicing these techniques in the presence of other parents before using them at home. Modelling and behavior rehearsal were particularly useful in training parents in the expression of appropriate affect in the application of reinforcement and time out, since some parents tended to praise with too little enthusiasm or to apply time out with too much affect for these procedures to be maximally effective. Leaders also made frequent use of praise to reinforce the group members for their active participation, for task orientation, for reinforcement by one parent of another, for monitoring, and for completion of assigned tasks during the previous week.

All but the first session was used to prepare for weekly home assignments and for feedback concerning the previous week's accomplishments. The progress of treatment was reviewed each week by examining the graphs prepared by the parents.

In order to achieve autonomous treatment planning in the later meetings the group leader, with gradually increasing frequency, began to rely on the members' ideas on procedures to be used rather than provide them himself as he did in the early meetings. As the members developed skill in designing plans for each other in the meetings, the leaders encouraged them to develop entire plans in writing at home and then describe them to the other group members who in turn evaluated them.

Training of Treatment and Research Staff

Since the method was relatively new, a set of procedures had to be developed to train the staff, which consisted of two leaders and several observers. The initial leaders of the first group I supervised directly, at first in the room with the clients and later behind the one way mirror. The first leader eventually shared his responsibility with his co-leader and ultimately withdrew completely from all leadership responsibility. The co-leader, previously an observer, assumed complete responsibility for the group. At the end of each meeting the activities of the leaders were discussed with the entire staff and adjustments were made in the plan for the next meeting. Co-leaders of the first group eventually served as leaders of subsequent groups. Each in turn gradually delegated the leadership responsibilities to the new co-leader who had observed a previous group while he was demonstrating his effectiveness in carrying out limited assignments. By using this method, an increasing number of groups could be led by trained staff members. Parallel to this practical training the writer carried out a theoretical training program for all the participating leaders and observers which was similar to the program developed for the parents, but which also included training in group observation, group discussion procedures, and other didactic techniques.

Children's Behavior Changed by Parents
A total of 33 families participated in 11 groups in this program. The target children in all but one case were either moderately or severely retarded. Except for one 2-yr-old and one 11-yr-old, the children ranged in age from 3 to 8 yr. Of 33 families, 27 modified at least one of their children's behaviors. These 27 families successfully modified 55 of the 58 behaviors for which treatment plans were initiated. Of six families who failed to modify even one behavior, three terminated early. A behavior was considered successfully modified if it reached a frequency acceptable to the parents. A behavior was classified as "discontinued" if the parents discontinued the treatment because the frequency during the baseline period indicated that the behavior was not problematic.

As noted above only three problem behaviors (all enuresis) were not successfully modified by the parents. In a follow-up interview of 21 of the parents 3–6 months following treatment, all gains (except one of the successful enuretics) were maintained, and most parents claimed they were still using increased reinforcement procedures and fewer punishment procedures. Several had designed new programs of their own but none were still monitoring behavior. At the time of the follow-up, one of the parents who failed to change even one behavior during the training period appeared to have become successful in using sophisticated procedures.

In comparing three groups of foster parents with eight groups of natural parents, no differences were observed either in terms of the number of parents who successfully modified at least one behavior or in terms of behavioral changes in the children. One of the groups categorized as a natural parent group consisted of two natural parents and one foster parent. For purposes of comparison, the outcome for this foster parent was included in a foster parent data cell in Table 2.

Most of the parents who remained in the group without modifying successfully even one behavior appeared to be uncommitted to change and unskilled. They were only incidentally involved in monitoring and arranging contingencies for their child's behavior. Regardless of the assignment they agreed to complete, these parents would return the following week with a new behavior to monitor. They would not persist more than a few days at a given task. Since monitoring successfully was a prerequisite for treatment, these parents seldom got to the treatment phase. They would occasionally use unauthorized treatment procedures, however, which

Table 1. Behavioral Outcomes of Retarded Children

	Successful	Discontinued	Unsuccessful
Increasing vocabulary	2	0	0
Compliance	7	1	0
Temper tantrums	7	0	0
Aggression to self (hair pulling, hitting self)	2	1	0
Dressing (zipping, undressing)	5	0	0
Enuresis (diurnal and nocturnal) and toilet training	10	0	3
Preparing for bed (remaining in bed)	2	0	0
Aggression to others (hitting others)	6	1	0
Feeding (chewing, utensil usage)	9	1	0
Picking up toys (picking up clothes)	2	0	0
Other (cooperative play, getting ready for school, sucking)	3	0	0
	55	4	3

would inevitably fail, either because the parents were not yet skilled enough to apply such procedures, or because they did not carry out their own plan consistently. In two cases where no behavior was changed, the parents terminated early, one case being because the child was institutionalized. In three other cases, the parents remained until the end and stated that they had learned a great deal. Perhaps, in terms of their personal goals, they had made substantial gains even though they did not actually achieve observable behavioral changes in their children. One unsuccessful parent was herself borderline mentally retarded, a fact which may account for her inability to complete or even understand assignments.

Discussion

The above findings indicate that training parents of retarded children in groups is an effective endeavour. Not only are parents able to learn the necessary skills to modify their children's behavior successfully, they are able to learn from leaders who have had relatively little training. Moreover, this approach is useful for people in a wide educational range. In this study parents with 10th grade education were as successful as those with college education. Differences in social class also appears to be of no consequence. In another study Rose (1974) also found that welfare mothers could effectively learn the same procedures in groups which include middle and upper class parents although the welfare mothers learned at a somewhat slower rate than the other parents.

In group training a number of problems arise not commonly found in individual training. The first is a discrepancy among members in rate of learning. The rate of the slower learner tends to hold back the rate of the faster learner. This may not be a disadvantage. The more skilled parents in the groups described in this study were reinforced for helping the slower ones in capacities such as models and reinforcers. They demonstrated to the slower parents that the skills are applicable by parents as well as by group leaders, and helped them develop treatment plans. This additional opportunity for the more

Table 2. A Comparison of Foster and Natural Parents

	Foster	Natural	Total
Modified one or more behaviors	10	17	27
Modified no behaviors	2	4	6
Total	12	21	33

Table 3. A Comparison of Behavioral Outcomes of Foster and Natural Children

	Foster	Natural	Total
Successful	16	39	55
Unsuccessful	1	2	3
Total	17	41	58

skilled parent to practice the basic principles should theoretically have resulted in greater stabilization of the learning gains (see Goldstein, Heller and Sechrest, 1965, pp. 212–259).

Another potential problem in groups is a high frequency of arguments, disagreements, punishing statements and outbursts of anger. In the training program outlined here these behaviors rarely occurred. Moreover, in group training, members are not encouraged to state how they feel about one another. Rather, they are exposed to models who praise frequently, and, it has been observed, they tend to imitate that model. Disagreements, of course, do occur on the best strategies for dealing with specific problems, but the parent is always the final judge on the action to be taken with his child, and the outcome provides the criterion for the correctness of the decision.

Does this not then lead to flat and dull meetings? Though never approaching the emotional peaks (or depths) of an encounter group, parents consistently indicated in response to evaluation questionnaires that they enjoyed the meetings, the contact with the other parents, and the task orientation of the leaders. The more objective evidence was the fact that meetings were almost perfectly attended.

Are groups less expensive than individual treatment? Initial observations in a sample of 10 cases individually treated show the time spent with a mother or both parents was consistently less than the 15 hr used in the group to attain the same goals (between three and eight hours). However, even in the small groups the cost in staff time per changed behavior remained substantially less than individual or family treatment, in contrast to the findings of Mira (1970).

Finally, the group approach provides the parents with a much larger number of examples to draw upon in the face of new problems and new areas of skill training. In individual training, clients usually have direct experience with only those behaviors they are working on and the examples provided by the therapist. In the group each set of parents not only has its own experiences, but also becomes intimately involved in the assessment, planning and execution of change procedures for all the other parents in the group. Theoretically, this added experience should strongly facilitate the stabilization of parental learning and its transfer to new situations.

Sheldon D. Rose, Ph.D., is Professor, School of Social Work, University of Wisconsin, Madison. Partial support for this project was provided by University of Wisconsin Research Funds through the Wisconsin Alumni Research Foundation. The writer also gratefully acknowledges the assistance of the Social Work Section of the Diagnostic and Treatment Unit of the University of Wisconsin Center on Mental Retardation and Related Aspects of Human Development, and the Central Wisconsin Colony.

Notes and References

Allen K. E. and Harris F. R. (1966) Elimination of a child's excessive scratching by training the mother in reinforcement procedures. *Behav. Res. & Therapy* 4, 79–84.

Bandura A. (1969) *Principles of Behavior Modification,* Holt, Rinehart & Winston Inc., New York.

Bernal M. E. (1971) Training parents in child management, *Behavioral Modification of Learning Disabilities* (Edited by Brodfield R. H.), Academic Therapy Publications, San Rafael.

Butterfield W. and Parson R. (1973) Use of modeling and shaping by parents to develop chewing behavior in a retarded child, *J. Behav. Ther. & Exp. Psychiat.* 4, 285.

Galloway C. and Galloway K. C. (1970) *Parent Groups with a Focus on Precise Behavior Management,* Institute on Mental Retardation and Intellectual Development, John F. Kennedy Center for Research on Education and Human Development, Peabody College for Teachers, Nashville, Tennessee.

Gardner J. M. and Watson L. S. (1969) Behavior modification in mental retardation: An annotated bibliography, *Ment. Retard. Abs.* 6, 181–193.

Goldstein A. P., Heller K. H. and Sechrest L. B. (1966) *Psychotherapy and Psychology of Behavior Change,* Wiley, New York.

Greyerson F. F. (1968) *Behavior modification training for parents and teachers.* Paper presented at the annual meeting of the National Society for Programmed Instruction, San Antonio, Texas.

Hawkins R. P., Peterson R. F., Schweid E. and Bijou S. W. (1966) Behavior therapy in the home: Amelioration of problem parent-child relations with the parent in a therapeutic role, *J. Exp. Child Psychol.* 9, 27–36.

Holland C. J. (1970) An interview guide for behavior counseling with parents, *Behav. Therapy* 1, 70–79.

Howard O. F. (1970) *Teaching a class of parents as reinforcement therapists to treat their own children.* Paper presented at the annual meeting of the Southwestern Psychological Association, Louisville, Kentucky.

Jeffords K., Danzig L. and Fitzgibbons K. (1971) *Group training of parents as behavioral modifiers of their mentally retarded children.* University of Wisconsin, School of Social Work, mimeographed.

Lindsley O. R. (1966) An experiment with parents handling behavior at home, *Johnstone Bull.* 9, 27–36.

Mira M. (1970) Results of a behavior modification training program for parents and teachers, *Behav. Res. & Therapy* 8, 309–312.

Patterson G. R. and Gullion M. E. (1968) *Living With Children: New Methods for Parents and Teachers,* Research Press, Champaign, Illinois.

Ray R. S. (1969) *Parents and teachers as therapeutic agents in behavior modification.* Paper presented at the second annual meeting of the Alabama Behavior Modification Institute, Tuscaloosa, Alabama.

Rose S. D. (1969) A behavioral approach to the group treatment of parents, *Social Work* 14, 21–29.

Rose S. D. (1974) Group training of parents as behavior modifiers, *Social Work* 19, 156–162.

Rose S. D., Parson R., Jarman B. and Hechtenthal C. (1972) *Group training of parents as behavioral modifiers of their own mentally retarded children.* University of Wisconsin, School of Social Work, mimeographed.

Straughan, J. H. (1964) Treatment with child and mother in the playroom, *Behav. Res. & Therapy* 2, 37–41.

Ullman L. P. and Krasner L. (1969) *A Psychological Approach to Abnormal Behavior,* Prentice-Hall, Englewood Cliffs, New Jersey.

Wahler R. G., Winkel G. H., Peterson R. F. and Morrison D. C. (1965) Mothers as behavior therapists for their own children, *Behav. Res. & Therapy* 3, 113–124.

Walder L., Cohen S. and Daston P. (1967) *Teaching parents and others principles of behavior control for modifying the behavior of children.* Progress Report, U.S. Office of Education, 32-30-7515-5024.

Zeilberger J., Sampen S. and Sloane H. (1968) Modification of a child's problem behaviors in the home with the mother as therapist, *J. Appl. Behav. Anal.* 1, 47–53.

DANIELLE N. PARK

A Workshop for Foster Mothers of Special Children

It is a well-known fact that many of the children placed in foster care today are not "cute" healthy infants or toddlers. Children with very special needs are entering placement more rapidly as the trend toward deinstitutionalization continues. Increased placement of mentally retarded and physically and emotionally handicapped children has created a need for additional training for foster parents. Public agencies in particular are faced with meeting the needs of all children, especially those most difficult to place.

This article describes the efforts of the Division of Foster Home Care of the Department of Social Services, New York City, an agency that has a long history of group services for foster parents, to develop a workshop training program for foster mothers who provide care for special children.[1] *Special*, as it is used here, is defined as any serious mental, emotional, or physical handicap.

Foster mothers were chosen for this workshop on the basis of having special children in their homes and an interest in participating. Eighty foster mothers were invited with the intent of forming as many groups as the need indicated. Twenty-four foster mothers responded and one workshop group was established. The group was lead by the author and another social worker who was also a nurse.

The group met once a week for seven weeks during the spring at the agency. The sessions were held on weekday mornings from 10:00 A.M. to 12:00 noon; this period reflected the result of a written poll in which the group was asked to indicate the most convenient time and place for the workshops to be held. This was a newly formed group of foster mothers; however, some of the members had attended other agency-sponsored group meetings in the past.

Attendance for the most part remained constant. The first meeting was attended by all twenty-four members. The average session, however, was composed of fourteen to fifteen members. The lowest attendance was ten, following a long weekend. Throughout, attendance seemed unusually high for the agency.

Rationale for the Group

The workshop in caring for special children was developed in response to four major considerations. First, a New York State mandate was anticipated in which board rate payments for handicapped and disabled children were discussed. It indicated that foster parents must have training to qualify for extra board rate. The state also indicated that each agency could develop its own training program to teach the principles of caring for exceptional children.

The second consideration was that the foster parents on a curriculum development committee (as set up by Special Services to Children, Department of Social Services, New York City, and four borough offices—Bronx, Brooklyn, Manhattan, and Staten Island) stated that caring for the special child requires knowledge and skills in addition to the basic fostering skills. They felt that a training program could be used to help foster parents better understand their foster child's problems, needs, and potential. They also stated that additional help would be beneficial in connecting parents to the medical, developmental, and community services.

The third and fourth considerations were to avoid institutionalization of handicapped and disabled children and, even though the state mandate was not going to be enforced at the time (because of a fiscal crisis), to recognize that foster parents who have special children are given an extra fostering responsibility and need more specialized training.

The unifying commonality was that all the foster mothers invited would have special children in their homes. The particular handicaps of the children included autism, mental retardation, sickle-cell anemia, cerebral palsy, brain injury, emotional disturbances, epilepsy, Down's syndrome, and so on. The workshop would be a place to work on problems and concerns central to coping and caring for special children and a place to learn, to share, and to grow as foster parents through practical experience. The agency would share its knowledge with the foster mothers, using both a didactic and experiential approach

drawing on the foster mothers' experience. It was hoped that the workshop would broaden both the members' and the agency's knowledge of techniques and know-how in meeting the needs of the special child. The emphasis would be on mutual learning and growth so that all could work more effectively to plan for the children. Certificates would be awarded based on members' attendance at the workshop.

The Workshop Sessions

A curriculum, developed by the curriculum development committee and the author, outlined the seven sessions. It was distributed at the beginning of the second meeting and was well received by the group members. The following is a synopsis of the curriculum and of each workshop session.

Session 1: Purpose and proposed content of the workshop—merging concerns and problems presented by foster parents. On the whole, the group appeared to be receptive to the idea of workshop sessions for foster parents with special children. Initially, the group members were not able to verbalize what they wanted from the group or what their concerns were. The group leaders were able to mirror back some of the concerns and problem areas that they heard the members verbalize and incorporate these into the curriculum. The program plan was instrumental in being a tool that the leaders could refer to whenever it was necessary to get back to the work at hand. It provided a structure for the group. The first session was devoted to setting up a workshop culture of mutual aid and information sharing and to merging the curriculum with the concerns of the foster mothers. This was accomplished through helping them share concerns about their children.

The meaning of the word "special" was explored and defined by the group. A reading was distributed about caring for special children. Because the group leaders failed to indicate a specific number of group meetings a member must attend in order to be eligible for the workshop participation certificate, it was later decided that everyone who attended at least two sessions would be awarded one.

Session 2: The special child in the life of foster parents—how they and others react to the child's disability. The question of whether or not the additional responsibilities and frustrations of caring for a special child changed a family's lifestyle was raised. The foster mothers agreed that the decision to bring a special foster child into a home should be a family decision. They recognized that their lifestyles had to be changed somewhat when the burden of caring for a special child was added to the household. However, the mothers were quite adamant that helping a special child is a job from which they derived great satisfaction and gratification.

Discussion focused on the ability of these foster parents to accept small steps of progress in the children's physical and emotional growth and development and the need to have great patience because the development of a special child is slower and less obvious than that of the normal child. Some of the foster mothers' capacities and limitations in dealing with various disabilities were explored.

There was some discussion regarding negative feelings toward the special child and the foster parents' ability to handle their feelings in this area. The leaders stated that negative feelings are natural and to be expected. The foster mothers were able to admit to having setbacks and second thoughts about their special children, but they all appeared to be strong women who were willing to keep trying. There was little sense of defeatism and the mothers viewed their fostering experience as a challenge.

Session 3: The normal child versus the special child—growth and development. Generally, the group members were extremely aware of their special child's particular development. They were able to express their children's differences from and similarities to normal foster children. Readings and charts on developmental milestones were used to help increase the appreciation. They appeared able to accept that special children were slow developmentally and to work from there.

The foster mothers were eager to help their children make progress and used appro-priate means to help them take the next step. They realized that it is not always enough to know and accept where a child is and that they must help the child to learn and grow to experience his or her full potential. Most of the foster mothers were able to understand and strategically plan the next step in helping the child develop. Several members, however, were overwhelmed by the developmental problems of their special children and were baffled as to what direction to take. The paramount problem centered on handling sexuality, which at times was exhibited in the special child's inappropriate behavior. Much work was done in this area with the foster mothers, and they later acknowledged that the group was helpful by exploring various ways of handling these situations.

It is interesting to note that the group was able to integrate theory and practice in the area of development of special children only when they were able to take the theory and connect it to practical application of their concerns and problems. It was only at this point that the theory appeared relevant to them. Two or three members said they felt stifled and frustrated with their special child's unique and often slow development. These feelings were recognized and some suggestions for alleviating them were worked on.

Session 4: Understanding the child's behavior—dealing with behavior problems and visits with natural parents. This session focused primarily on dealing with specific behavior problems, the underlying cause of the behavior, and the appropriate discipline a foster parent should and could use. It was generally agreed that behavior problems were areas that the foster mothers were most anxious to work on because they caused the most anguish and concern in the home. The group also agreed that the type of discipline used must be appropriate for the child, but that discipline should and must be a sign of caring. A pamphlet on dealing with behavior problems was also used here.

Much time was devoted to how to handle various behavior problems, that is, anger, testing, stealing, bedwetting, hyperactivity, and so on. Many creative ideas were shared and many mothers expressed enlightenment in hearing new and perhaps better ways of handling various behavior problems. It was pointed out that foster parents should not make idle threats, and the group expressed their agreement.

The foster mothers were able to work on why and how behavior problems arise when the natural family visits. Even though they were willing to handle the repercussions of behavior problems stemming from these visits, they felt they often caused regression in the child that was akin to starting all over again.

The group agreed that handling behavior problems and behavior related to natural parent visiting were areas in which they could further benefit from the agency and from sharing among themselves. It was agreed that further work in this area could be useful, and that it was also useful for group members to have a place to come and air their feelings.

It is interesting to note that the behavior problems of the special foster child seemed more extreme and harder to handle than those of the normal foster child. Going easy on the child and not providing the structure so desperately needed because of feelings of making up for and being sorry for were strong themes of the work.

Session 5: Talking to the special child about his or her unique situation. From the verbalizations and intensity of the group's ability to deal with identity it appeared that "specialness," that is, a big head, funny looking, "crazy" acting, braces, crutches, and so on, was a much more difficult area for the foster mothers to deal with in terms of identity than was the natural parent aspect. Some of the foster mothers tended to lecture the children, telling them that they "are better off than most children, so feel lucky!" Others were able to give examples of the specific words they used to help the child understand what is unique about him or her. There appeared to be a sense of pain, denial, and protectiveness in dealing with the specialness directly with the child. They were much less verbal and enthusiastic when this topic was discussed. The group members role played

how to deal realistically and compassionately with the "special" without such massive denial.

The foster mothers could more readily relate to the identity struggle surrounding natural parentage and appeared to be more comfortable in handling this with the children.

Session 6: The foster child and the world about him or her. Throughout the group meetings the foster parent's role in the special child's life was referred to, particularly in that the foster parents experience the responsibility, pain, and pleasure of living with the special child twenty-four hours a day. They appreciated that agency staff acknowledged their struggle with their special children.

Other systems and resources, that is, tutors, special school placements, medical school workers, pediatricians, natural parents, child care agencies, and the court system, were discussed as being part of the special child's world. Some resources were shared among the foster mothers, while staff made them aware of other facilities and aids available to enhance the special child's functioning. There was a free interchange of both complaints about and praise for schools, medical facilities, the courts, and the agency. There were some questions about the legal responsibility of the agency and the foster parent regarding areas such as damages caused by a foster child, baptism, operations, vacations, court, adoptions, and funding. Again, there was a pull to discuss concerns common to all foster children and parents as if these children were not special.

In general, the foster mothers expressed a desire to be more involved in the planning and decision making for their foster children. They were encouraged to speak up to their caseworkers and supervisors, and assured that their impressions and ideas about the foster children were valuable and that the agency wanted them to become involved.

Session 7: Planning for the special child's future and summary and evaluation of the workshop. A discussion about permanent plans for special foster children revealed that these foster mothers felt that institutionalization should be a last resort. In a sense they equated it with defeat—that they had "lost." Upon having this mirrored back, the foster mothers were helped to see that, although in general the staff agreed with their desire to keep the children in the community, in some instances an institution or a residential treatment facility might be in the best interest of the child. They had difficulty with this but were beginning to grapple with their feelings.

The reality of possible adoptive planning not only produced pain and ambivalence, but the feeling that the agency did not feel that foster parents are really interested in the child unless they want to adopt, regardless of the child's handicap. Much work was done in this area interpreting the law, discussing the pros and cons of the situation, and further sharing experiences.

Whatever the plans for the foster child's future were, the foster mothers expressed a desire to be involved with the agency in making those plans. Many members expressed ambivalence regarding the child's future plans and exactly what part they would play. They were encouraged to share and discuss mixed feelings with the caseworkers. Some members were reluctant to do this out of fear that the agency might remove the child if the foster parents did not express an overwhelming desire to adopt.

Conclusion

Generally, the training group went well and the goals of mutual aid, sharing, learning, and teaching were achieved. The group members for the most part were highly positive, eager women who appeared to be coping well. They were open to suggestions and to new child-care techniques. In view of the need and the response to the workshop, it would be worth considering making such a course a requirement for all foster parents of special children.

Those who attended expressed that they got a lot out of the group experience and would like to come back for an ongoing group with the same members. They learned new techniques and ways of dealing with special foster children, as well as being able

to have a place to ventilate and confront various situations. The members were able to sustain a learning relationship and appeared to begin to trust and relate to the social workers leading the group. They were also able to confront the workers regarding agency policies and procedures. The members were genuinely appreciative of the graduation ceremony at the end of the last session, and of meeting the directors. They said that it made them feel closer to the agency and more a part of it.

For the most part, the learning content was appropriate for the members. They expressed a positive attitude toward the material used and the way it was presented. The members appeared to be open to various learning approaches and seemed eager to connect life experiences with book theory.

In order to integrate the learning content, that is, books and articles, into the training groups and also have enough time in which to give the members a chance to share their experiences, it was felt that a longer training session would be necessary, perhaps fifteen sessions, with more "advanced" training to follow for those members who want to continue the process. In this particular training program, staff felt they often had to choose between "didactic"—the giving of more information—and peer-learning—more experientially oriented approaches.[2] Longer training sessions would enable staff to use both to a fuller extent as well as to explore in greater depth the foster parents' difficulties in dealing with the child's specialness, what words to use, and why they feel a need to preach and lecture to the foster children. More time is also needed for in-depth work on behavior problems of the special child, because this is one of the more frustrating and difficult areas for the foster mothers. Other resource people and films could be used in the context of a longer workshop.

The group was heterogeneous in view of the wide differences in the kinds of special children represented. This was positive for the most part as much "cross-fertilization" took place. What may have been sacrificed was the giving and sharing of more information on specific disabilities. For example, there was a problem in choosing a particular disability for the pediatrician to discuss or show a film about. Something could be gained if there had been sufficient numbers to have homogeneous groupings centered on a specific disability, for example, mental retardation or cerebral palsy. Overall, however, the commonality of having a special foster child was strong enough to forge a productive learning situation.

This was a very cohesive group, one in which the members were able to develop appropriate intimacy, which enabled them to "risk" voicing their various problems. As a result of the workshop, many of the members were able to establish a more positive rapport with both the caseworker and the agency and gained more self-awareness and greater knowledge of their special child's needs. It is hoped that foster parent training such as this will become an institutionalized agency service.[3]

Danielle N. Park is Supervisor and Coordinator, Group Services, Division of Foster Home Care, Special Services to Children, Department of Social Services, Human Resources Administration, New York, New York.

Notes and References

1. See for example William Schwartz, "Group Work in Public Welfare," *Public Welfare* 26 (October 1968): 26–31, 35–36; Adolin G. Dall, "Group Learning for Foster Parents: In a Public Agency," *Children* 14 (September–October 1967): 185–87; and Adolin G. Dall and Seymour K. Fass, "Use of the Group Method with Foster Parents," *Staff Development News* 1 (September-November 1963): 65.

2. Judith A. Lee, "The Foster Parent's Workshop: A Social Work Approach to Learning for New Foster Parents," *Social Work with Groups,* in press.

3. Adolin G. Dall, "Instituting Group Work Services for Foster Parents"; and Seymour K. Fass, "The Institutionalization of Group Services through Supervision and Administrative Practice." Papers presented at the Annual Forum of the National Conference on Social Welfare, Dallas, Texas, 1967.

MEYER SCHREIBER
MARY FEELEY

Siblings of the Retarded:
A Guided Group Experience

In the course of providing group work services to retarded children during the past decade, the staff of the Association for the Help of Retarded Children in New York became impressed by the frequent references made by parents to problems these children created for their normal adolescent brothers and sisters, and vice versa. Parents expressed concern, for example, over the normal child's feelings of being overburdened by the care of the retarded sibling, of his overt expressions of hostility and resentment toward the retarded sibling, of responsibility for the retardation, of obligation to make up to the parents for what the mentally retarded brother or sister could not give them, and of guilt for being the normal child.

At the same time, the staff became impressed by the large number of normal adolescents who were taking their retarded brothers or sisters to social group meetings and to special events, and by other indications these young people gave of being able to cope with the fact of their sibling's retardation. Many of them obviously had been able to

Reprinted from Children, Vol. 12, No. 6 (November–December 1965), pp. 221–229. With permission of the authors.

work out their feelings about their retarded brothers or sisters with no major intrapsychic, interpersonal, or intrafamilial strains, by developing healthy defenses and using compensatory mechanisms.

Thus with evidence both of need and strength in the normal adolescent siblings of retarded children, the staff began considering what the agency could do to include such young people in its total efforts to strengthen family life in the families of retarded children.

Consequently, with agreement from the appropriate lay committee, composed in part of parents of the retarded and the agency's board of directors, the decision was made to establish a demonstration program of guided group discussion for selected normal adolescents, through which they could examine, clarify, and understand more clearly a dynamic aspect of their life situation—their role as siblings of a retarded child. The experience in such a group, it was anticipated, would help these young people to become more effective and assured in their intrafamily relationships and responsibilities, and so would enrich the total family life.

More specifically, the aims of the demonstration were delineated as:

1. To assist the individual and the group to identify the nature of their reactions to having a mentally retarded brother or sister—stress, strain, mixtures of affection and antagonism—and the effects of these reactions upon their relationships with their parents, brothers and sisters, peers, and their entire life situation.

2. To help the individual and the group to examine and to clarify strategies for understanding and dealing with their siblings, their parents and peers, and the problems of daily living related to their status as the brother or sister of a retarded child—strategies which would be helpful not only to them but also to others in similar circumstances.

3. To throw light upon the extent to which the concern and reactions of such adolescents represent strength as well as intrapsychic, interpersonal, and intrafamilial strains, and to determine whether their defenses are similar to or different from those of adolescents with no retarded siblings.

Since expressions of interest in the program came from all parts of the city, it was decided to conduct the group sessions at the association's office, which was centrally located. To qualify for admission to the group, an adolescent had to be between 13 and 17 years of age, and be willing to participate in the group sessions every 2 weeks to discuss his problems and feelings in relation to his retarded brother or sister and his life situation.

Twenty-eight adolescents met this criteria. Obstacles to attendance, such as the day, time, and travel involved, reduced the number selected to participate to 10. Twenty other young people were interviewed by staff members and helped to see why they could not be included in the group. These included several who were "pushed" by domineering parents to apply because "this is good for you," others whose parents expected the group to provide a therapeutic experience, and a few whose needs were basically social. For many of these young people, the group experience might have been too anxiety-provoking or otherwise inappropriate. Unfortunately, shortage of staff members prevented followup of those who seemed in need of individual counseling.

The 10 young people who formed the group included 5 boys and 5 girls, mostly from lower middle-class backgrounds. The age spread was from 14 through 17, with the boys generally 1 to 2 years younger than the girls. Six of the participants were in junior high school and four in high school. Judging from their own comments about school, seven could be considered above average in academic ability and three as average students; and seven were involved in extracurricular activities at school. All participants indicated a real desire to participate in this new experience.

All the retarded siblings of these young people were living at home. Some were mildly, some moderately, and some severely retarded. Half were younger and half older than the normal brother or sister.

The Group Process

The group, which its members called the Brother-Sister Group, met every 2 weeks from October 1962 through May 1963, under the leadership of a professional group worker. The first session was devoted to a consideration of the voluntary nature of the group and what the group hoped to accomplish. The adolescents agreed on their own accord to come regularly, and to share their problems and experiences in order to help not only each other but also other teenagers in similar circumstances.

At the end of each session the group agreed upon the focus of the next. In the beginning, the group worker took an active role in suggesting possible subjects for discussion, such as "How do you tell your friends about your retarded brother or sister?" However, as the members became better acquainted and more comfortable with each other and the worker, they began to bring up spontaneously the concerns they wanted to talk about. These included such questions as: "Does the fact that our family has a retarded member lessen our chances of marriage?" "How can we deal with the feelings we get when our friends show us pictures of their brothers and sisters and brag about their accomplishments?"

The participants offered little resistance to telling the group about their experiences with their brothers and sisters, families, and friends.

The worker helped the group look at different aspects of the material under discussion, adding information as needed, or raising questions and suggesting alternative courses of individual and group action. The worker also dealt with problems of individual needs and intragroup relationships. At the same time, she helped the group hold its aims and special function. She filled a variety of "roles"—confidant, leader, counselor, resource person, agency representative, and even parent—as the situation demanded and the group progressed.

By the fifth session a cohesive group had emerged, held together by a common bond and meaningful relationships between the members and between members and group worker. From that point on, the group was largely self-directed, taking major responsibility for the content of the meetings and for individual participation. The group worker became largely a resource person, who provided clarification of points, support for individual participants, and information to indicate alternative courses of action.

Each session lasted an hour and a half, and included a period of light refreshments provided by the agency. At the end of each, the worker summarized the progress made, emphasizing the positive, the constructive, and the realistic aspects. She encouraged the members to share their findings with parents, other normal siblings in the family, and friends; and to feed back significant reactions from them to the group. Such reporting back was frequent.

The group usually stuck with an issue until it reached a termination point. Completion of a subject of discussion sometimes took as many as three sessions. The group worker's attitude of constant acceptance provided a safe climate for the expression of concern and the ventilation of feelings whether these were of hostility, hate or love. The participants also found support and recognition of the right to be different from their peers. They learned a method of analyzing life situations which was not only appropriate to the current scene but which could be used in dealing with future problems as well. Attendance at sessions over the 8-month period averaged 92 percent.

Concerns and Feelings

What were some of the common problems which emerged? The following list was prepared by members and group worker together. The illustrative material comes from the group records.

1. How do you tell your friends about your retarded brother or sister, especially friends of the opposite sex?

> At this point, Bonnie turned to Susan and said, "Should I ask the question?" Both girls giggled, and Susan encouraged Bonnie to ask it. The question was: "How do you tell a boy that you have a retarded sister?"
>
> Mark responded immediately by telling about his experience in telling a girl about his sister. The girls listened attentively, but then Susan said, "It's different telling someone that you really care about."
>
> Susan is "going steady" and she hopes Stanley will never find out about her retarded sister, Gail. Could she tell why? She feels ashamed and embarrassed.
>
> Kenneth said he knows how Susan feels, but he has been trying to help himself by asking whether he would be ashamed if his sister had no arm or leg. He said knowing about this should have no effect on a person who had nothing to do with it, and if the boy really cares about you, this won't change him.
>
> Kenneth told us that a few weeks ago a girl asked about his sister and he did not tell the exact truth. He felt ashamed about the way he acted and made up his mind to tell the truth the next time he saw this girl, but he just couldn't get himself to do it. He knows that it was wrong but he couldn't help himself.

2. How do you deal with your parents who have not discussed the problems of mental retardation in the family and their implications for you?

3. How do you deal with friends and people in school when you are hurt by their talk of the retarded as nutty and crazy?

4. Are these meetings really helpful or are we betraying our families' confidences?

5. Are our parents' expectations concerning our role and their role in continued care of our brothers and sisters real and fair to all involved?

6. What should be our responsibility toward our retarded brother or sister in the event of our parents' deaths?

> Even before the meeting began the teenagers were discussing among themselves the requests made by their parents for the care of the retarded sibling if anything ever happened to the parents. Regina and Diane have promised never to send their retarded siblings to an institution. Bonnie promised to visit her sister Barbara regularly in the institution. She would definitely not care for her if her mother were unable to do so. The other girls laughed at this and told Bonnie that she was "just talking" again, and that she would be the first one to object to having her sister placed in an institution.

7. What are we to do when our parents do not really feel affection for our retarded brother or sister?

8. How can we deal with our feelings when our friends show off their brothers' and sisters' pictures and talk about their accomplishments?

Bonnie broke in here and said:

> It is hard when you hear the other girls boasting how smart their sisters are, and the things they do, and you can't say anything about your sister. In fact, very often I do not admit that I have a sister at all. Some of the girls in school think I am an only child and others want to know if I have a brother or sister since I never talk about mine....

9. Does retardation in our family lessen our chances of marriage, and is it hereditary?

10. How can our parents help us with our problems?

11. What can you do together with your retarded brother or sister in the home or in the community?

12. How does a teenager really accept a problem that he will face the rest of his life?

13. How can a teenager plan for his adult life?

14. What are our hopes for the future?

At this point Kenneth asked why Susan had such feelings about her sister. He thinks that they should all be very happy that they are living now when so much is being done for retarded children. Years ago people would hide retarded children, and nothing was done for them.

Bonnie said that was easy to say but the fact remained that the situation was hard to face. She says that she has heard all these things before. You are supposed to feel good because the President of the United States, who is very smart, has a retarded sister.

Other feelings expressed by participants in the group were: a feeling of not being loved as much as the retarded child; jealousy, resentment, and hostility toward the retarded child; denial of the severity of the retarded child's condition; and guilt about having negative feelings toward the retarded child. Such feelings, however, were not characteristic of the group, and their intensity in the individuals who held them was often repressed. The worker recognized their significance but did not delve deeper or bring them into focus before the group in view of the anxiety that would be evoked. Rather, she held to the group's educational focus, leaving the resolution of deep and involved feelings as the function of individual therapy.

As part of the group's activity, the worker suggested, after about 18 sessions, that the participants might want to consider ways and means of helping other young people who had a retarded brother or sister. This resulted in a group project, the writing of a pamphlet directed to other teenagers.[1]

Some Observations

Over the 8-month period, the experience with these young people led members of the agency staff to make a number of observations. We present them as hypotheses which need further testing with a larger number of retardates' siblings—young adults as well as adolescents:

About the Normal Adolescent

1. It was not the degree or kind of retardation in his sibling which seemed to affect the adolescent's life or happiness as much as

the way he felt about himself and his retarded brother or sister, and the way in which he learned to live with the fact of having a retarded sibling.

2. What the normal adolescents really needed and wanted was accurate, up-to-date information, in language and concepts which they understood, about mental retardation and what they could do to help their families and their retarded siblings. They wanted to know how to manage *now* and what they could look forward to.

3. The young people's attitudes were not consistent at all times.

4. Almost every adolescent in the group brought up the question: *"Why* did it have to happen in my family, to us, to me?"

> He said the question of "Why did this have to happen to me?" comes to him often. I told him this was a natural question, but said I wondered what it meant in the way of his making friends, or in school. . . . He said that it hadn't meant much up to this point but wondered what would happen when he has to tell a girl about his sister. I pondered that question too. (Kenneth is unable to use the word "retarded.") He said he would just say his sister was different.
> Kenneth mused that everyone has something in their family. One of his friends doesn't have a father—parents are divorced. He can see this as a real problem. I asked him if this friend might also ask himself, "Why did this have to happen to me?" and he admitted that this might be so.

5. The sessions helped the teenagers see some of the strengths, as well as limitations, in their brother's or sister's functioning, and in the family.

6. The importance of good communication and feeling between parents and adolescent depended on the existence of the kind of relationship which encouraged the adolescent to go to his parents whenever he felt the need.

7. The teenagers seemed to be helped by the very fact of knowing that the agency was interested in them as well as in their parents and their retarded siblings.

8. The group worker to be helpful had to look at life as far as possible through the adolescents' eyes, show her care and respect

for them, and treat them with dignity and understanding. She had to be careful not to generalize and assume that the problems and feelings of all the siblings of retarded children are the same.

9. The group worker found it important not to underestimate the strength of adolescents or to expect too little of them. It was clear that the young people wanted their parents to involve them in planning for the total family.

About the Group and the Group Worker

1. The experience was appropriate for the adolescents in the group. They were able to express spontaneous feelings, to invest themselves in the experience, and to extract positive help and strength from their contacts with others who are in similar circumstances. For other adolescents such an experience may be anxiety-provoking to the point that the youngster is not able to handle his feelings appropriately. In some instances, such as when family relationships and parental roles were discussed, an adolescent's group experience carried a potential threat to his parents.

2. The meetings had meaning for the group not only in giving the young people help during a period of hardship, but also in helping them to maintain and build healthy family relationships.

3. The support of others—their peers and the worker—was helpful to these young people.

4. The size of the group was important. Ten members seemed about right for providing good opportunities for exchanging experiences and sharing the worker with each other.

5. Timing the meetings in relation to the many pressures on teenagers—school work, social life, family obligations, and work—was important.

Conclusions

Thus we concluded that this short-term group experience was useful to the teenagers involved. The spread of time helped the young people, at an age when it is difficult to put feelings into words, to open up problems, to delve into

into certain aspects of relationships, to pull together and integrate what had been accomplished, and to begin to think more realistically about the future.

The sessions did not always contribute to modification or change of basic attitudes, but they enabled the participants to know that others knew and experienced similar problems and that is was all right to feel the way they did. Although their problems and feelings could not always be resolved since some were "bottled up" inside, for the most part these adolescents gradually became able to express their feelings more fully as meetings progressed and to become more realistic in their appraisal of them. This seemed to result in their being better prepared to see the next steps necessary in their planning. As time went on, they seemed to be able to look at the broader implications of mental retardation not only for themselves but for others who also had retarded brothers and sisters.

Many parents of retarded children are panicked into the belief that their retarded child will adversely affect his normal brothers and sisters. However, in some families where the parents have dealt with the situation constructively, such young people have developed greater maturity, tolerance, patience, and responsibility than is common among children of their age. Our experience suggests that the young person with positive family relationships is often capable of enduring the emotional hurt and anxiety of having a retarded sibling without severe disruption of his family and social life. He needs reassurance and support, but more often his primary requirements are educational: The more clearly normal siblings of the mentally retarded can see the realities of their particular situation, the better position they are in to cope with them. This is the point of a group experience.

As the young people wrote in their pamphlet:

> ...We helped each other. We learned how to "talk" about retardation and felt free to discuss our problems. We helped each other to be better prepared for any unexpected behavior of our bothers and sisters. We knew that we were not alone.[1]

Meyer Schreiber, MSW, is Consultant on Social Services, U.S. Children's Bureau, Washington, D.C. Mary Feeley, MSW, is Director of Volunteer Programs, New York City Department of Welfare, New York, New York.

Notes and References

1. Brother-Sister Groups, Association for the Help of Retarded Children, New York City Chapter: It's tough to live with your retarded brother or sister. New York. 1964.

Part Five

Social Work in the Community: Roles, Alternatives, and Policies

Introduction to Part Five

For many years, social work involvement with the developmentally disabled and their families was limited to providing them with assistance in choosing an institution in which the disabled person would spend his or her lifetime. As society assumed greater responsibility for providing education, habilitation, and protection for its disabled citizens, the social work role became increasingly complex.

Social workers in the field of developmental disabilities are now active in changing public policies, developing local services, advocating in behalf of clients' rights, and working to prevent the future occurrence of disabling conditions. The setting for these activities is primarily the community. Social work intervention in this setting has never been as essential as it is today.

Social work interventions with developmentally disabled individuals and their families as well as with groups take place in the community. In fact, it is at the community level, in such places as schools, clinics, and family service centers, where most of the counseling, referrals, and resource provision undertaken by social workers are performed. The articles selected for inclusion in Part Five, therefore, incorporate the use of some of the practice techniques described in previous chapters of this book. They appear here, however, because they describe one or more roles that social workers have assumed as a result of deinstitutionalization and that involve interaction with a major group within the community, such as a legislative body, a neighborhood coalition, or an active parents' organization. It is at this level of intervention that social workers use their knowledge of community organizing, citizen advocacy, and the political process as well as their sensitivity to vulnerable people in society. These and other skills are essential in building a solid service network for the developmentally disabled population within the community.

As the cost of managing long-term health problems has steadily increased year after year, public concern regarding the prevention of disabling conditions has grown. Genetic counseling and screening are one form of prevention in which social workers have assumed an important role, and this is described in Part Five by Weiss. Although stress associated with genetic disorders is experienced by individuals, couples, and families and is thus a concern of social workers, the ethical and moral issues regarding group screening, public education, and the provision of appropriate services to affected populations require particular attention from the social work profession in the form of a recognition of the potential impact of these disorders on the community as a whole.

At the same time that social workers have taken on new roles in the area of developmental disabilities, they have also continued to perform a wide range of functions long familiar to them. In general, foster care placement has been a traditional function of social workers. Thus, as an alternative to institutional placement, foster care for children is an area of growing interest among many community-based practitioners. Recruiting, training, and matching families with children who are difficult to place because of complicated physical, emotional, or behavioral needs are perhaps the greatest challenges facing professionals in the field of foster care. Coyne presents the results of a survey revealing some of the characteristics of successful foster parents and examining how these individuals became involved in foster care. It is to be hoped that the information gathered and reported therein will be generalized for use in the many community programs that are searching for suitable families to participate in special foster care placements.

Another exceedingly popular approach to providing residential care for developmentally disabled adults and children has been the use of the community group home. Although strongly supported by federal and state governments as well as by advocacy organizations, the development of group home programs has been hindered by a poor understanding and slow acceptance of these living arrangements within local neighborhoods. Planning specific strategies for the location of a home in a residential neighborhood is the focus of the discussion by Weber. For professionals working in community residential programs, his analysis of the variables involved in choosing a site, identifying sources of resistance, and overcoming barriers in establishing community living arrangements for the developmentally disabled should prove pertinent and helpful.

Despite efforts to promote foster care and group homes as alternative placements for handicapped people, as the policies affecting the developmentally disabled have emerged in recent years, it has come to be generally assumed that the most desirable living arrangement for disabled individuals is represented by the person's own home and family. Moroney discusses the difficult issues surrounding the promotion of family care as a panacea. He presents the realities of the financial, emotional, and physical stresses placed on families in the absence of sufficient support services, a situation that, sadly, exists in most, if not all, communities. The social work profession has a responsibility not only to provide a portion of the support needed but also to become active in the larger process that will eventually close the gap between policy and the realities of family care.

Of all the developments in community services of the past ten years, the concept of case management encompasses, perhaps most completely, the values and functions of the social work profession. In her article, which was adapted from a presentation before the Social Work Division of the American Association on Mental Deficiency in 1981, Baerwald examines the case management concept and suggests its usefulness in providing services to clients with complex, long-term, and far-reaching needs. Social workers involved in case management need to communicate their successes and failures so that the profession will maintain its central role in providing coordination, advocacy, and brokerage services to the disabled and their families.

The involvement of social workers in another phenomenon of widespread importance in the community, namely, deinstitutionalization, is explored by Keenan and Parker in a previously unpublished analysis. Making deinstitutionalization work requires a clear set of goals, political and community support of the concept, a plan for implementation, and the funds necessary to carry it out. Social work's contribution to this process has been limited by a lack of knowledge among professionals regarding policy implementation, confusing and contradictory laws governing community services and programs, and the absence of a clearly mandated role for the profession in the development of alternatives to institutionalization. Keenan and Parker outline the history of deinstitutionalization policies affecting the developmentally disabled, discuss the progress and setbacks of the movement, and encourage social workers to take leadership roles in helping their legislators and communities formulate more effective service systems for the disabled.

The articles in Part Five, then, are intended to describe some of the most important issues and practices of relevance to efforts at the community level in the developmental disabilities field. One barrier encountered in attempting to represent a comprehensive range of community interventions was the apparent paucity of literature describing social work activities in many crucial areas of developmental disabilities. By mentioning some of the gaps in the paragraphs that follow, the objective is to provide readers with the impetus to document their accomplishments so that the social work profession as a whole may benefit from the many innovative programs that are undoubtedly in progress throughout the country.

In general, social workers have a significant role in encouraging the examination of family care as an option in their communities through their involvement in developing such family-oriented services as respite care and the adoption of children with special needs. The provision of respite services as a simple, cost-effective alternative to institutionalization is currently receiving more attention as an intervention of choice both for reducing familial stress and for increasing the behavioral competence of the developmentally disabled child. Recruiting, training, and evaluating care providers and ensuring that families receive the kind of respite they require to care for their handicapped relative in the home are functions social workers can carry out to promote family care. Adoption of developmentally disabled children, an area traditionally of concern to the profession, is in great need of being discussed and documented within the literature. Sharing improved techniques in recruiting adoptive families, providing them with support, and following up on their progress is an important step to broader community acceptance of this family care alternative. Personal advocacy programs for the developmentally disabled have increased in number recently throughout the country. As advocates

for all vulnerable groups, social workers have a potentially central role in preserving the individual rights of their disabled clients through active participation in citizen advocacy. More specifically, the particular problems of disabled women need to be addressed in the professional literature, because this population is subject to the multiple institutional biases that exist within our society.

Finally, social workers need to communicate more effectively their efforts in behalf of developmentally disabled individuals in regard to political and social change. Such efforts include professional support for the initiation and expansion of community-based programs and the necessary monitoring related to quality assurance within the service delivery system. Social workers also have an obligation to offer themselves as role models to aspiring professionals with incipient interest in the developmental disabilities field. Through mentor-protégé relationships and the active transmission of the most current practice knowledge, the social work profession can maintain and expand its role in ensuring that developmentally disabled people have their needs for service met in their communities.

JOAN O. WEISS

Psychosocial Stress in Genetic Disorders: A Guide for Social Workers

Everyone is affected by a genetic disorder, not only the person unfortunate enough to have it, but also the person's family and the community in which he or she lives. Personal and social costs of genetic diseases often reach tragic dimensions. Recent strides have been made in medical genetics that ameliorate these costs, and today, people can make better informed choices about their progeny through genetic counseling. However, genetic counseling, the information-giving process dealing with the risk of occurrence or recurrence of a genetic disorder, is often not enough as a solo method. Genetic counseling is often given at times of duress when little information is absorbed or retained, and anxieties and apprehensions may be increased. A social worker can help clarify the genetic counseling information and lessen the impact by dealing with the emotional reactions to the information that has been given. Once a child with a genetic disorder is born, the social and psychological stress which can interfere so easily with family func-

tioning can best be alleviated by the skilled and knowledgeable professional help of a trained social worker. It is hoped that this article will aid social workers in their understanding and treatment of psychosocial problems connected with genetic disorders.

Those with genetic disorders frequently need continuous medical and nursing care, disability benefits, institutional placements, transportation and architectural adaptations, special education and vocational training, and rehabilitation. Individuals and their families are faced with the chronic financial and emotional burden of a genetic disease. A person with a genetic disorder or with a child who has a genetic disorder often feels apart from the rest of the world and longs to be accepted and acceptable. A genetically afflicted person may experience feelings of defectiveness which are often transmitted to the family and to others in his environment. The burden of a genetic disorder or of being a carrier of a genetic disorder is experienced at several levels, and it is important for social workers who will be counseling the affected individual or carrier to be aware of the ramifications of the burden in order to help work through intrapsychic and intrafamilial conflicts, as well as to locate and coordinate appropriate services (Golden and Kamen, 1980).

The Dimensions of Stress

1. Personal Stress: Individual Reactions

A genetic condition is usually a permanent one, one without a cure. Its chronic nature can threaten people at different life stages, especially with the advent of marriage and parenthood. A genetic diagnosis can precipitate a crisis, such as giving up hope of having children or anticipating the premature death of a child, for example, one with Tay-Sachs disease or with the Hurler syndrome (Schild, 1977). The recurrence risk of a genetic disorder may be different than was expected, and reactions to genetic counseling often are quite unpredictable. Some patients are relieved to learn the risk for transmitting a particular genetic defect is minimal while others may see this same risk as being monumental (Weiss, 1976).

Typical questions raised in a genetics clinic by those considering having children are: What risk do I have of producing a child like the person in my family who has a known genetic illness? Could the genetic disease be more severe in my child? Is there any cure or treatment for my genetic problem? Questions raised by those with an affected child include: What is the matter with my baby? What caused this? What are the chances of this happening again? Can anything be done to prevent this from happening again? What treatment is available for my child? Is there any cure? And then there are the unasked questions: Did I do something or take something to cause this to happen? Why did I marry someone with a defective gene? Will our marriage fall apart now? Will my friends, family, neighbors pity me? Will I be condemned for having bad genes?

After receiving genetic counseling, the individual is often in the shock phase of the coping process (Falek, 1977). He or she can absorb little information at this point. Occasionally, the counselees will accept the facts too easily, believing they have been chosen by God to bear this burden. Sometimes religious belief can be unconstructive, as when parents assume that God will find a cure for their child, since then they may discontinue coming to the genetics clinic for medical supervision and follow-up. Often, a patient will seek new information to undo what he or she has been told or will start looking for a miracle cure, wandering from one clinic to another in hopes of hearing what he or she wants to hear. It is important to evaluate whether the denial of the reality of a genetic disorder is impeding the patient's adjustment to it. Fears must be verbalized about being stigmatized, about being ostracized because one has a genetic disorder or because one might produce a child with a genetic disorder.

One may feel defective, just like the gene. "A part of me is bad; therefore I am a worthless person," is a frequent response, although not always verbalized. Latent feelings of unworthiness rise to the surface when a genetic trait is discovered. The knowledge of a genetic problem or the possibility of one is often more emotion-packed than learning that one has a non-hereditary disease, since the knowledge that one's child will be deformed or suffer pain because of an inherited genetic trait is a heavy load to carry (Levine, 1979).

Individuals react differently to a genetic diagnosis, even within the same family. For example, a 23-year-old son of a woman who had died of Von Recklinghausen's neurofibromatosis, a genetic condition involving tumors, reacted to being told that he had inherited the disorder by exclaiming that nothing was going to stand in his way of finishing graduate school. His younger sister, on the other hand, learning that she was affected, became suicidal, sensing there was no hope for her.

A genetic diagnosis may not be the most important consideration for a patient. In one situation a young woman was told that she had XY chromosomes, those typical of males. Her main concern was that if she could not give her husband the children he wanted, they might not be able to adopt children since her husband had been on trial recently for attempted rape. The focus of counseling subsequently was not on the genetics of the situation, but rather around the personal and marital stress caused by the psychopathic personality of the patient's spouse. In another situation, a 21-year-old woman came to the genetics clinic ostensibly to find out if she had neurofibromatosis. An adoption agency had contacted her after her affected twin sister, of whose existence she had been unaware, had died. However, she was more concerned about establishing her personal identity than about obtaining her genetic diagnosis, and she requested help in searching for others in her biological family, although she had been content with her adoptive family in the past.

A genetic disorder may cause stress during specific periods of one's life. A dwarfed child, for example, becomes more self-conscious about appearing different from other children at the onset of school when he or she is stared at, questioned, and teased. Parents need to be sensitive to the child's need for reassurance that he or she can perform adequately, in spite of being short statured. Another difficult period of adjustment for the dwarf is adolescence, when the basic needs for admiration and acceptance are often not met because of exclusion from coed peer group activities (Weiss, 1977). In general, teenagers who appear different from the accepted norm because of a genetic disorder are frequently left out of social functions by those their own age. Often they are reluctant to participate in age-appropriate activities for fear of being rejected.

Another stressful time for those with genetic disorders is young adulthood when employment is sought. If one has a visible genetic problem, is it preferable to tell prospective employers before being interviewed, or will that destroy all hopes for getting a job? Vocational counselors suggest that one should do what feels most comfortable in that situation, that there is no single right way to apply for a job. Of course, if the genetic disorder involves physical disability, it is important to locate work that has no architectural barriers.

Emotional anguish is not necessarily tied to the visible consequences of a genetic disease. A recently married, beautiful young patient with the Giles de la Tourette syndrome, a bizarre neurological disorder, was adamant about not having children if there was any risk at all that they might be affected. She would not want them to suffer the way she had as a teenager when she would emit horrible screams and curse words uncontrollably and was teased unmercifully as a result.

Treatment Implications. Supportive casework is need to ensure that the patient retain a positive self-image in spite of the stress experienced. The principle of self-determination should be held high in order to enable the patient to make his or her own decisions based on the genetic facts given, and the social worker must reexamine his or her own biases. As always, it is essential for the social worker to assess the individual's and family's strengths and vulnerabilities (McCollum, 1979) and level of functioning and also to act as a liaison between the patient, his family, and the rest of the medical team. Preexisting personal problems or problems aggravated by the genetic situation may require ongoing counseling, often necessitating referrals to community agencies or to private practitioners. The social worker should be available to the genetics patient for repeated interpretation and reclarification of the genetic facts given and should evaluate the patient's perception of the burden caused by the genetic defect. Educative and crisis intervention techniques can be used when indicated, with the goal of preserving or restoring the adaptive functioning of the patient. Other treatment modes which can be effective with a genetics patient include group work, self-help groups, and advocacy strategies on behalf of the patient, while helping him to understand his rights.

Family support can be extremely important in relieving stress. In one situation in which a young college student was told that he would have to give up basketball because he had the Marfan syndrome (a heritable disorder of connective tissue which often has cardiac involvement), his younger brother empathized with him about his extreme distress, but encouraged him to become a team manager in order to channel his interest in a constructive way. This boy was helped more by his family than by all the good intentions and medical advice of the clinic staff.

2. Marital Stress:
Reproductive Decision Making

A couple faced with the possibility of having a genetically affected child is under tremendous stress. The potential conflict is around reproductive risks. Sexual relations often become strained because of the fear of having a defective child; reproductive competency is threatened, and sexual urges are often destroyed.

The decrease of sexual activity can be a direct result of feelings of unworthiness and personal damage brought on by a genetic diagnosis. Sensitive attention by a social worker to sexual needs can build rapport and encourage genetics patients and their partners to concentrate on their basic feelings of loss of attractiveness. Some persons with a genetic diagnosis must prove their normalcy, at least in sexual performance, and might select sexual partners at random, if only temporarily, until they feel better about themselves. Other persons lose interest in sexual activities either because they feel less than whole or because they fear the conception of an afflicted child.

There is frequently a breakdown in communication between the marital partners. Labeling each other, either consciously or unconsciously, as genetically responsible for producing a defective baby upsets the equilibrium of the marriage. However, if the marital relationship is a healthy one, it will usually survive and perhaps even be strengthened.

A young couple without children, learning that they are at risk, may take a chance because of their eagerness to become parents. Some couples feel a need to prove that they can produce a normal child, regardless of the risk. However, there is often disagreement. A husband may vote for adoption, while a wife may decide that she prefers artificial insemination or becoming pregnant, regardless of the risks explained to them in genetic counseling. The mother of a child with fibrodysplasia ossificans progressiva, which involves development of bones in extra-skeletal locations, became almost desperate to produce a second child who would be healthy. Perhaps as a result of the marital tension, in addition to the financial strain, her policeman husband

needed psychiatric care. Of course, his breakdown might have been triggered by the tremendous stress of knowing he might lose his treasured little girl. Also, he felt personally damaged.

The extent of the burden often influences a reproductive decision. For example, a cleft palate, to most persons, has far less serious implications than Tay-Sachs disease, but individual reactions are not predictable. Some couples believe that they could cope more easily with the early death of a genetically disabled child than with the ongoing acceptance of a child who has a normal life expectancy but who may look different from others.

In any case, a couple must make its own decisions after being given the genetic risks. There is a relatively new option now for some genetic disorders, amniocentesis, which is not only a physical procedure, but an emotional one as well. Husband and wife share their hopes and apprehensions before deciding whether to have amniocentesis and possible abortion if the fetus is determined to be affected with a genetic disorder.

Treatment Implications. A social worker who is part of a genetics team is in an excellent position to help with family-planning options such as prenatal diagnosis, adoption, artificial insemination, sterilization, contraceptive devices, or taking the risk of having a genetically impaired child. The social worker will take into account the religious and ethnic background of the couple in helping them in the decision-making process.

Marital partners who have just been told what genetic risks to anticipate in their future children need to weigh alternatives about their own life style and make decisions consistent with it (Silverberg, 1979). It is important for the social worker not only to assess what impact genetic counseling has had on the couple, but also to evaluate the strengths and weaknesses of the couple's relationship which existed before the genetic counseling was given to them in order to help them cope with the temporary crisis they face. A shaky marital status threatened by the knowledge of a potential genetic defect can be stabilized by the supportive and problem-solving skills of a sensitive social worker who can offer time-limited sex therapy and marriage counseling. The knowledge of the universality of some marital discord, particularly sexual dysfunction, after a genetic carrier is identified can be reassuring to couples.

3. Parental Stress:
Hopes and Disappointments

Parents who pass on a genetic trait which may cause problems for their child feel responsible for what they have done, even though it was not an intentional act. It is more likely with a recessive disorder than with a dominant disorder that the parents will believe they share the responsibility, since both father and mother are carriers of the determining deleterious gene.

A young couple's hopes can be dashed by the birth of an imperfect baby. They may face tremendous financial and marital stress and shattered self-esteem. Studies by Leonard and Chase (1972) and by Carter and Evans (1971) indicate that persons with low genetic risk tend to wish further offspring. Persons with high (greater than 1 in 10) recurrence risks generally seem not to want more children. However, the stated and actual reproductive plans often differ, suggesting that couples may have difficulty facing the potential long-term burden of genetic disease. Some persons are undeterred in having a child in spite of high genetic risk and expected personal burden. They may deny their first child's genetic symptoms or push aside the statistical risk.

Too often a child with a genetic disorder is viewed as the all important focal point for professional help. Parents are not given the support they need. In one case, a child, stiffened by fibrodysplasia ossificans progressiva, was given most of the attention by the clinical staff. However, when the social worker talked to the mother, it was apparent that she was quite disturbed and did not accept the genetic diagnosis. She believed that her child's condition was brought on by a car accident which had so angered her that she had brought a major suit against the automobile company responsible for the defective car. This mother could not face the reality that the girl's stiffness was caused by her genetic condition, though possibly worsened by the accident. Her family support system was minimal. Her own mother, deserted years ago by her husband, accused her of negligence for not having gotten the little girl out of the car in time, and this fed into the mother's sense of personal damage and neglect. In addition, the child's father, normally an affectionate, giving parent and husband, was in the terminal stage of his own illness. The mother felt helpless and alone.

Sometimes the mother can displace her feelings of ambivalence onto over-nurturing of the child. But what happens to the father? What does he do with his feelings of disappointment? He also needs help with expressing his feelings towards the child and with vocalizing his previous hopes and present disappointments. He may feel even more left out than the father of an unaffected baby because the mother and the genetically impaired child are often locked together in an unhealthy unit. Father needs to be more involved in hospital visits, therapy sessions, feeding the child, and finding community resources. Mother often has too much responsibility, which she resents. She characteristically becomes the family contact person for the medical team, the provider of necessary medical equipment for the child, the chauffeur to and from the hospital, and the family interpreter. Nevertheless, she may, in truth, want to remain emotionally distant from the child for fear of becoming too attached or because of shame. The mother of a girl with the Marfan syndrome was reluctant to get attached to her daughter because she believed that her daughter would die. Therefore, she focused all her attention on her unaffected younger son, causing the daughter to feel unloved and unlovable.

Meetings with other parents in similar situations can be helpful for both father and mother. Many times, group meetings will cause them to feel less alone. Parents can suffer needlessly because the public is not educated and will, for example, condemn them for child abuse when a child bruises easily because of a genetic disorder known as the Ehlers-Danlos syndrome or when a child fractures an arm because of osteogenesis imperfecta, a brittle bone disease.

Parents can be helped to accept a substitute baby for the one they had expected to be perfect, to face the reality that their baby is not their idealized infant, that their baby has a genetic abnormality. Each parent needs to face his or her own disappointment in the child. It is essential that fathers as well as mothers be given this opportunity. The husband of a dwarfed woman could not believe that his infant son was also a dwarf, having never acknowledged his wife's dwarfism. In the social worker's office, he broke down completely, finally admitting that his greatest disappointment was that he wanted his son to be a white collar worker, and now his son would be a disappointment to his own father, just as he had been. He had become a carpenter; his father was a professional man. He had wanted his son to succeed in the grandfather's eyes since he felt that he himself had failed him.

The impact of the genetic diagnosis becomes greater for both parents as the child enters various social life stages, such as school placement, puberty, and vocational planning, or as the parents age and grow concerned about the child outliving them. Parents must always be considered as individuals with their own needs and goals apart from their child's.

Some parents get overly involved because of feeling responsible for their child's genetic disorder, and then the marriage becomes threatened. A guilt-laden mother of a child with a rare form of dwarfism began to worry about her marriage because she devoted so much time and attention to her child that she and her husband seemed to have no time for themselves. She was encouraged by her social worker to find an appropriate, competent mother substitute to enable her to spend more time with her husband.

If another pregnancy takes place after the first child is born with a serious genetic defect, there is occasionally a moral dilemma. Abortion may be construed by the first child as a rejection or a wish that he too would die. However, parents must consider whether or not it would be fair not only to their first child, but also to the rest of the family, to society, as well as to themselves to produce a second child with a severe handicap.

Although the risk may be high and what seems a rational decision not to have children is made, avoiding having children can intensify guilt and create inner tensions. The psychological costs of deciding not to have children can be tremendous. For some, a solution is divorce and remarriage, hopefully to a noncarrier mate so that there is minimal genetic risk.

Treatment Implications. Parents must know that they will not be judged for experiencing negative feelings initially towards their genetically affected child and that these feelings are almost universal in this situation. Their denial of the genetic disability must be confronted, however, so that they will not make blind reproductive decisions in the future. They need to share their grief reactions with each other and sometimes even need to be taught how to communicate.

The social worker should be familiar with grief responses to having a genetically afflicted child and should be aware that these responses do not necessarily occur in any set order or time pattern. Groupwork with parents can be extremely helpful. Often, a social worker can initiate the formation of a parent group and guide it until it takes on its own independent structure.

In order to help the child with the genetic disorder most effectively, the parents, who have the most important role of all, should be considered an integral part of the medical team, once they have worked out their self-blame and projection of blame onto each other and their extended families. It is the parents who will know their child best and who will be able to report what is typical and atypical physical and social development for their child. It is important that they be included in all decision-making processes related to the medical care of their child. They may need supportive counseling by the social worker to help them verbalize their feelings of guilt, anger, isolation, sadness, and helplessness, and they may seek enlightenment as to how to face family, friends, and the world at large. While these parents struggle with their decision as to whether to have more children, the social worker helps them examine their options to test for a prenatal diagnosis, to abort if an abnormality is found in the fetus, or to carry the defective fetus on to delivery. Throughout the decision-making process, it is essential that the couple feels support, rather than pressure, and respect for their opinions and for their final decision, whatever that might be.

4. Family Stress: Concerns and Conflicts

Families with genetically affected children may suffer tremendous emotional strain and bear overwhelming financial burdens. The continual stress on a family with one or more children affected with a genetic disorder is often horrendous. Naturally, the genetic aberrations which do not interfere greatly with family life will not produce much turmoil. The degree of impairment, physical or mental, bears directly on the amount of stress the family will experience. Genetic disorders vary in the extent of visibility, the degree of physical or mental interference, the amount of disruption of routine family activities, and the effect on the nonafflicted members of the family.

A family with a 19-year-old daughter with Friedrech ataxia, a degenerative, neurological genetic disorder, had to help their daughter make her decision about whether to have radical spinal surgery for scoliosis, knowing that she was eager to finish a home study program for college. They had a younger son with the same condition in a less severe stage. Surgery involved a tremendous risk, but the young woman decided to take it and did survive the operation. In this situation, the stress was not only on the family, but also on the physicians, nursing staff, social worker, and the child life staff.

A genetic diagnosis is a family diagnosis (Schild, 1977). The family's ability to cope is often more determined by the resiliency of the individual personalities than by the severity of the genetic burden. (Hsia, 1973). Children were acting bizarrely in a family in which the father, afflicted with Huntington's disease, had been recently placed by his wife in a nursing home. She wanted to remarry, but on legal as well as moral grounds could not bring herself to do so. Their eldest son ran away from home, but because of his anger and frustration, threatened his mother at work in periodic phone calls. Their 13-year-old son was sleeping all the time and failing in school, convinced that he had somehow driven out his father. The 16-year-old daughter had also run away, having been the closest one to their father, but did come back eventually with more understanding of her mother's unmet social and sexual needs. These children did not know if and when they themselves would be affected by Huntington's disease. Often children wait a lifetime in anticipation and dread of the onset of their own genetic disorder (Falek, 1973). A genetic crisis may be remote, but it is often a real threat to future life fulfillment.

Unaffected siblings need support along the way, too. They may feel guilty that they are not affected with the genetic disorder. They may resent being saddled with too much responsibility for their affected brother or sister or for having to stand up for him or for her. They may feel rejected by their parents who must spend endless time and energy on their affected child. Group sessions for these unaffected siblings, such as those held at the annual Johns Hopkins Short Stature Symposium, are helpful. Shared experiences for all family members can help combat feelings of isolation and guilt (Weiss, 1977).

What issues are involved when the carrier children or relatives of the affected person who are interested in marriage or in childbearing come for genetic counseling? The carrier status and genetic risks to future children usually become important in the late teens and young adulthood. For example, a girl may experience the dilemma of whether or not to tell her boyfriend of genetic risks, fearing that he may see her as inadequate or unattractive and reject her. Young people have their own moral standards about bringing children into the world who have a real potential for a genetic disorder. Now, with a decreased population an accepted value, it is easier for them to decide not to have children. It should be determined whether these young adults who come for genetic counseling have been informed by their parents of their reproductive risks. Are they realistic about the recurrence risk? If they are considering marriage, is the family supportive? They should be encouraged to share facts and feelings with their future mates, or their marriages may be doomed from the beginning. Often a young person is relieved to discover, with accurate history taking and a well established diagnosis, that his relative did not have a genetic condition after all, and that, consequently, he himself is not at risk.

The carrier status and the risk of genetic recurrence are important to each family member. Each person in the family should be given the opportunity to express concerns and conflicts about being possibly affected by the genetic disorder, about being angry at the affected person for having a good life disrupted, and about being neglected by parents who must meet the realistic demands of the afflicted child.

Individuals within a family with genetic disorders may shift roles. Wives may become more career oriented, children more adultlike, and the affected person more childish. Father can become the nurturer, mother the doer.

In some families the genetically affected person can be kept a child by his or her anxious parents far into adulthood. For example, a 40-year-old dwarfed woman, who had severe hearing loss and skeletal deformities, was cared for totally by her aging parents. When it came time to decide whether or not to perform surgery on this woman in order to make her more comfortable for the remaining year or so of her life, her 70-year-old mother became hysterical. How could she decide this without her husband being with her? She was tremendously relieved when the social worker insisted on the patient being given the right to decide for herself. In addition, the patient was pleased to be addressed directly by the medical staff and to be recognized as a competent adult, in spite of her genetic disorder and ill health.

Treatment Implications. A holistic approach to the genetics patient and his or her family is the most desirable one for the social worker to take. With a family centered focus, the social worker can reinforce positive family relationships and easily identify patterns of dysfunction and recriminations within the family constellation. Prior to developing a treatment plan, the social worker should weigh intrapsychic and socioenvironmental facts which may be contributing to the increased stress caused by a genetic disorder (Bracht, 1978). It is important for other medical team members to be aware of the level of family functioning, particularly if it is interfering with the medical considerations for the patient. Family support can be enlisted when necessary, once the social worker has informed the family members of the need for their support to the affected family member and has answered individual questions, allaying anxieties as far as possible. Family members may need individual counseling by the social worker. Grandparents and siblings, in particular, are often appreciative of being included in medical discussions about the patient, but may need clarification of the genetic situation and help with their own feelings about it. The social worker should be well-informed about national and local family groups for specific genetic disorders, community resources, and financial eligibility requirements and be prepared to make appropriate referrals in order to ease the burden for the entire family.

5. Group Stress and Ethical Dilemmas

Genetic screening for minority groups (e.g., Tay-Sachs screening for Jews, sickle-cell screening for blacks, and Cooley's anemia for Greeks and Italians), while identifying carriers, can increase feelings of group stigmatizing (Murray, 1979). Who is to decide which groups will be screened for genetic disease? Public education is clearly needed to dispel myths about carrier status and potential labeling of ethnic groups. Some believe that it is unethical, as well as unwise, for genetic counselors to try to improve the genetic makeup of future generations by discouraging reproduction by known carriers of genetic disorders (Murray, 1979). Society is becoming more aware of both the advantages and the pitfalls of mass screening programs.

The social worker must be sensitive to a group's fear of being stigmatized by a screening process, and the entire health staff must be aware of genocidal connotations in screening programs since many genetic conditions are linked to racial or ethnic groups. For example, discrimination in employment can be sparked by the knowledge that the employee has sickle-cell disease, and blacks often fear screening for this reason alone (Headings, 1979). Educational prescreening techniques, such as brochures or lectures, should be geared towards the goal of offering positive options to parents who want to have children free of genetic disease. Viable alternatives for identified carriers include prenatal diagnosis for Tay-Sachs parents and artificial insemination or nonreproduction for parents carrying the sickle-cell gene (Lappe, 1979).

With so much new emphasis on prevention of genetic disorders, will those already born with genetic disorders be neglected? Will there be more demands for genetically unimpaired babies and less interest in varied traits? Even with prenatal diagnosis, there is no guarantee of a nonafflicted baby (Griffin, Kavanagh, and Sorenson, 1977). It is not clear which traits or genes will be regarded as desirable. There is considerable controversy about whether identification of a group of newborn babies having the XYY syndrome, associated with potential antisocial behavior, is warranted, in view of the possible stigmatization and family problems it may cause (Hull, 1979). With new techniques of conception in vitro and the growth of fetuses in surrogate mothers, potential social problems loom ahead to which social workers should stay alert.

The issue has been raised as to whether genetic screening and counseling should be made compulsory for high risk groups (Twiss, 1979). Advances in medicine have enabled many with severe genetic disorders to live longer, thereby increasing the responsibilities of society to care for them. There is greater national and regional interest in genetic service delivery systems and an increase in legislative activity with regard to prevention of genetic disorders. However, there are lobbying groups for certain genetic diseases and not for others to gain public attention and funds for research and treatment. What should we, as social workers, do to help those unable or untrained to speak for themselves? There is also the ethical dilemma of helping persons with genetic disorders choose between reducing the incidence of genetic disease and protecting their right to survive and reproduce (Twiss, 1979).

Treatment Implications. Because genetic illness still remains an enigma to many, the public needs to be educated not only about the medical and social costs of genetic illness, but also about the value of accepting differences. As always, social workers can be patient advocates and continue to help individuals and their families cope with the stress brought on by a genetic diagnosis or by a genetic prophecy. Social workers can identify gaps in genetic services, such as screening programs, prenatal diagnostic centers, and group support systems, and can mobilize local communities to obtain these services with the backing of the patient population. Social workers can determine the availability of appropriate social resources and develop new resources when needed, again with the cooperation of those who need them. Social workers can have a voice in the formulation of new social policies which will support the rights of genetically afflicted groups.

Summary

Three major steps in the process defined by the American Society of Human Genetics (1974) as genetic counseling can best be handled by social workers. These steps involve helping the individual or family who is concerned with the occurrence or risk of occurrence or recurrence of a genetic disorder to: (1) understand the options for dealing with the risk of recurrence; (2) choose the course of action which seems most appropriate to them while considering both the risk and their family goals; and (3) make the best possible adjustment to that genetic disorder which has affected a family member and/or to the risk of recurrence of that disorder. This article has dealt most specifically with the last step, the adjustment process and its stress components. In order to help an individual and his or her family adjust to a genetic disorder or to the threat of one, it is imperative that social workers have a basic understanding of the inherent emotional and social stress.

Joan O. Weiss is Senior Social Worker for the Division of Medical Genetics, the Moore Clinic, the Johns Hopkins Hospital, Baltimore, MD 21205. This paper is derived from a talk given at the Sixth NASW Professional Symposium in San Antonio, TX, November 1979.

Notes and References

Bracht, N. F. *Social Work in Health Care: A guide to professional practice*. New York: The Haworth Press, 1978, 138–139.

Carter, C. O., Evans, K., et al. Genetic clinic: A followup. *Lancet,* 1971, 1, 281–285.

Falek, A. Issues and ethics in genetic counseling with Huntington's disease families. *Psychiatric Forum,* 1973, 4, 51-60.

Falek, A. Use of the coping process to achieve psychological homeostasis in genetic counseling. In H. A. Lubbs & F. de la Cruz (Eds.), *Genetic counseling.* New York: Raven Press, 1977, 179–191.

Golden, D. & Kamen, G. Families of handicapped children: The experiences and needs of a multiethnic population. *Proceedings: Tri-Regional Maternal and Child Health Services Conference,* Raleigh, June 1980, in press.

Griffin, M. L., Kavanagh, M. S., & Sorenson, J. R. Genetic knowledge, client perspectives, and genetic counseling. *Social Work in Health Care,* Winter 1976–1977, 2, 171–180.

Headings, V. E. Psychological issues in sickle cell counseling. In S. Kessler (Ed.), *Genetic counseling: Psychological dimensions.* New York: Academic Press, Inc., 1979, 185–198.

Hsia, Y. E. Choosing my children's genes: Genetic counseling. In M. Lipvin & R. T. Rosley (Eds.), *Genetic responsibility.* New York: Plenum Press, 1973, 73.

Hull, R. T. Why "Genetic Disease?" In A. M. Capron, M. Lappe, R. F. Murray, Jr., et al. (Eds.), *Genetic counseling: Facts, values, and norms.* New York: Alan R. Liss, Inc., for the National Foundation, 1979, 57–69.

Lappe, M. Genetic screening. In Y. E. Hsia, K. Hirschhorn, R. L. Silverberg, & L. Godmilow (Eds.), *Counseling in genetics.* New York: Alan R. Liss, Inc., 1979, 295–309.

Leonard, C. O., Chase, G. A., & Childs, B. Genetic counseling: A consumer's view, *New England Journal of Medicine,* 1972, 287, 433–439.

Levine, C. Genetic counseling: The client's viewpoint. In A. M. Capron, M. Lappe, R. F. Murray, Jr., et al. (Eds.), *Genetic counseling: Facts, values, and norms.* New York: Alan R. Liss, Inc., for the National Foundation, 1979, 123–135.

McCollum, A. T. & Silverberg, R. L. Psychosocial Advocacy. In Y. E. Hsia, K. Hirschhorn, R. L. Silverberg, & L. Godmilow (Eds.), *Counseling in genetics.* New York: Alan R. Liss, Inc., 1979, 243.

Murray, R. F., Jr. Psychological aspects of genetic counseling. *Social Work in Health Care,* Fall 1976, 2 (1), 13–23.

Murray, R. F., Jr. Genetic health: A dangerous, probably erroneous, and perhaps meaningless concept. In A. M. Capron, M. Lappe, R. F. Murray, Jr., et al. (Eds.), *Genetic counseling: Facts, values, and norms.* New York: Alan R. Liss, Inc., for the National Foundation, 1979, 71–80.

Schild, S. Social work with genetic problems. *Health and Social Work,* February 1977, 2(1), 59–77.

Silverberg, R. L. & Godmilow, L. The process of genetic counseling. In Y. E. Hsia, K. Hirschhorn, R. L. Silverberg, & L. Godmilow (Eds.), *Counseling in genetics.* New York: Alan R. Liss, Inc., 1979, 288.

Twiss, S. B. Problems of social justice in applied human genetics. In A. M. Capron, M. Lappe, R. F. Murray, Jr., et al. (Eds.), *Genetic counseling: Facts, values, and norms.* New York: Alan R. Liss, Inc., for the National Foundation, 1979, 255–277.

Weiss, J. O. Social development of dwarfs. In W. T. Hall & C. L. Young (Eds.), *Proceedings, genetic disorders: Social service intervention.* Pittsburgh: University of Pittsburgh Graduate School of Public Health and Maternal and Child Health Services, 1977, 56–61.

Weiss, J. O. Social work and genetic counseling. *Social Work in Health Care,* Fall 1976, 2(1), 5–12.

ANN COYNE

Techniques for Recruiting Foster Homes for Mentally Retarded Children

In July 1971 the Lancaster Office of Mental Retardation (LOMR), a Nebraska community-based agency serving retarded children and adults and their families, began a series of feature stories in a local weekly newspaper distributed free to each household in this city of 150,000. Each week or two a child needing a foster home was described, with a picture and a personal story about what the child had to offer a prospective foster family. Persons were requested to call the agency for more information. The stories were written to appeal to families who already had children, and included such details as the child's favorite vegetable or toy. The objective was to encourage people to talk to the agency's foster care caseworker about the child and foster parenthood.

A second purpose was to introduce retarded children to the community one by one, bringing the community information about the effects of retardation, the differences among such children, and their special needs. It was believed that more knowledgeable

citizens would be more likely to volunteer as foster parents.

After the stories had been running regularly for 3½ years, a survey was made to assess their effect. During that time, while LOMR used mass media, other agencies in the area used word-of-mouth recruiting techniques. This paper reports on the study to determine how the mass media campaign affected the manner in which individuals became aware of the LOMR program and were influenced to become foster parents of retarded children.

Background

Robert D. Abbey completed in May 1974 a study of 256 foster parents serving nonretarded children under the custody of the Lancaster County Department of Public Welfare (LCDPW) [1]. The foster parents were asked when they became foster parents, where they first found out about the program, and who influenced them to become foster parents. Their homes, plotted on a county map to show spatial dispersion, tended to be clustered in particular areas. Families who had been in the foster care program the longest tended to live in the center of the clusters. It was hypothesized that the presence of a foster family in an area made it more likely that neighbors, through contact, would learn about foster care and be influenced to become foster parents themselves. The spatial dispersion pattern was believed the result of this diffusion of information.

Seventy-nine percent of the questionnaire respondents first became aware of the LCDPW program through interpersonal contacts. In other words, mass media had a relatively small influence, even at the awareness stage. Responses to the question about who or what influenced them most to become foster parents also showed that mass media played only a minor role at this stage of decision making. Abbey concluded that "a 'neighborhood effect' is operating in the social process involved in becoming a foster parent [1:69]."

The study reported here was an attempt to replicate the Abbey study using LOMR foster parents, to determine if the mass media recruitment techniques used by LOMR affected how foster parents became aware of the LOMR program, and to determine how they were influenced to become foster parents.

Method

Questionnaires were mailed in January 1975 to all 40 families who had begun foster parenting for LOMR since the mass media recruitment project began in 1971. After a telephone followup, 37 usable questionnaires were returned. The responses were compared with those on the Abbey questionnaire, using the chi-square test.

Hypotheses of Survey

Five hypotheses were tested:

1) LOMR foster parents are more likely to first find out about the LOMR program by interpersonal communication than by mass media.

2) A higher percentage of LOMR foster parents first find out about the LOMR program by mass media than LCDPW foster parents first find out about the LCDPW program.

3) LOMR foster parents are more likely to be influenced to become LOMR foster parents by interpersonal communication than by mass media.

4) LOMR foster parents are no more likely than LCDPW foster parents to be influenced to become foster parents by interpersonal communication.

5) There is no difference in age or educational level between LOMR foster parents and LCDPW foster parents.

Review of the Literature

There is much evidence in the literature that foster parents usually find out about foster care through interpersonal communication. Radinsky, Freed and Rubenstein found that about 75% of new recruitments can be attributed to interpersonal communication. "With due regard to the cumulative impact of the various promotion media, no more than one-fourth of the homes approved last year are traceable directly to community relations activity in the mass media. The rest of the new homes are attributed to various sources, chiefly foster parents, their friends and relatives [6:38]."

According to Day, "Foster parents are a very fruitful source of recruitment [3:40]." She considered recruitment most likely through interpersonal communication with highly credible foster parents. Kadushin stated, "The literature on foster family recruitment suggests ...that special campaigns should not take the place of unrelenting daily recruitment effort [5:367]."

Stone found that "the survey of various methods of recruiting foster parents and how much success agencies have had with each method yielded overwhelming support for the notion that using foster parents to find other foster parents is the most successful method of recruitment [8:37]." Since so many studies found interpersonal channels the most effective, especially if the source is a foster parent, the expectation was that the majority of LOMR foster parents were recruited in this way, even though mass media recruiting was attempted.

Because mass media were available to inform people about the LOMR program, and less available to inform people about the LCDPW program, it was to be expected that LOMR foster parents were more likely than LCDPW foster parents to first find out about their foster care program from mass media.

Rogers and Shoemaker draw the generalization that mass media are relatively more important at the knowledge stage, and interpersonal channels relatively more important at the persuasion stage in the decision process [7:255]. On the basis of their research, it was to be expected that more LOMR foster parents than LCDPW foster parents were first reached by mass media.

Interpersonal communication—face-to-face exchanges between individuals—allows a two-way exchange of ideas and information, and may serve to persuade a receiver of information to take on new attitudes. Mass media are useful in creating initial awareness, but interpersonal communication is more effective in changing attitudes and behavior, especially if those involved are of the same social class [7:Chapter 8].

Individuals contemplating becoming foster parents of retarded children for LOMR could be expected, because of the importance of the decision, to seek information from their friends, neighbors, relatives, acquaintances, other foster parents and LOMR staff. This face-to-face communication is vital at the persuasion stage. To accept a retarded child often requires basic attitude and value changes on the part of the foster parent.

Cox, in his study in Lancaster County, found: "The data indicate that attitudes about the retarded are composed of at least two facets: emotional response and knowledge about the causes and effects of retardation. Emotional responses seem highly influenced by personal information sources. Knowledge about the causes and effects of retardation has been shown to be significantly related to nonpersonal information sources [2:35]."

Since becoming a foster parent involves a basic emotional response to a child, it was expected that LOMR foster parents were influenced to become foster parents more by interpersonal communication than by mass media. It was assumed that LCDPW foster parents also sought out and were influenced by other people during the persuasion stage, and that most information at this stage reached them by interpersonal communication.

The Abbey study found a range of ages and educational levels in LCDPW foster parents [1:55]. Few were over 50, a shift downward in age from the findings of most studies of foster parents. A nationwide demographic study in Britain in 1955–56 showed that 59% of the foster mothers were over 40 years old when recruited [4]. The fairly even spread in age from 21 to 50 in the Abbey study indicated that foster parents of child-bearing age were being recruited by LCDPW. It was believed that this would also be the case for LOMR.

As to educational level, Abbey found that 19% of the foster parents had a college education, 61% had a high school education, and 20% had less than a high school education [1:55].

Foster parents for LOMR were not expected to show a higher educational level. The Cox study found the highest "intention to act favorably" in the group with a high school education [2:25]. Since such intention toward the retarded is an integral part of the decision to become a LOMR foster parent, the high school education class was expected to be overrepresented in the LOMR population (as it was in the LCDPW population studied).

Results

Knowing Other Foster Parents

LOMR respondents were asked, "When did you first become foster parents (of a child from any agency)?" and, "When did you first become foster parents for LOMR?" The findings showed that about half the LOMR foster parents had been foster parents for another agency previously, the rest being new.

LCDPW foster parents were asked, "Did you know any foster parents in Lincoln before you became one?" LOMR foster parents were asked, "Did you know any foster parents before you became one?" and, "Did you know any LOMR foster parents before you became one?"

Thirty-two LOMR foster parents (86%) either knew foster parents or were themselves foster parents for another agency before they became foster parents for LOMR; only 30 LCDPW foster parents (45%) knew other foster parents before they became one. This difference is significant at the 5% level ($x^2 = 16.6$). Only 27% of LOMR respondents knew another LOMR foster parent before being recruited. What seems significant is knowing another foster parent from any agency, rather than specifically knowing one who cares for a retarded child.

Media Differences—Awareness Stage
LCDPW foster parents were asked, "From whom or where did you first find out about the foster care program?" LOMR foster parents were asked, "From whom or where did you first find out about the LOMR foster care program?" Responses were classified as either mass media or interpersonal contacts.

A smaller percentage of LOMR foster parents (59%) first found out about foster care by interpersonal communication than LCDPW foster parents (79%). This difference is significant at the 5% level ($x^2 = 4.42$). With LOMR foster parents this response to media appeared highly influenced by whether they were new, with new foster parents more likely to first find out about the LOMR program from mass media and previous foster parents much more likely to find out from interpersonal sources.

Seventy-three percent of LOMR foster parents who were new to foster parenting and who had been made aware of LOMR by mass media already knew other foster parents before they became one for LOMR.

Media Differences—Persuasion Stage
LCDPW foster parents were asked, "Who or what influenced you most in your decision to become a foster parent?" LOMR foster parents were asked, "Who or what influenced you the most in your decision to become LOMR foster parents?" Responses were classified as either mass media or interpersonal contacts.

No difference was found between the groups of foster parents by agency. Both were highly influenced by interpersonal communication, with 80% of LCDPW foster parents and 83% of LOMR foster parents influenced by interpersonal contacts ($x^2 = 0.17$).

Age and Educational Background
No differences were found in the groups of foster parents in either age ($x^2 = 1.52$) or educational background ($x^2 = 2.59$). Few foster parents were over 50 (13% for LOMR, 9% for LCDPW). The age of LOMR foster parents was fairly evenly spread from 21 to 50. As expected, the high school educated group was overrepresented in both groups (71% for LOMR, 60% for LCDPW). Only 14.5% of LOMR foster parents had a college education, and 14.5% had less than a high school education.

Discussion

It is evident from the study that the mass media recruiting techniques of LOMR are somewhat effective, since significantly more LOMR foster parents than LCDPW foster parents are first reached by mass media, particularly parents who have not been foster parents for any agency before. However, the situation is complex, since LOMR seems to be recruiting from two fairly equal segments: those who have been foster parents before, and those who have not. The effect of mass media on those who have been foster parents before is minor (23%). These persons are most likely to be recruited by interpersonal contacts, frequently either by or at the suggestion of staff of the agency they have been associated with. (Of previous foster parents recruited by interpersonal techniques, 70% were recruited with the assistance of staff of other agencies.)

More new foster parents are being reached by mass media techniques (55%). However, mass media usually are effective only if these persons have had previous contact with a foster parent. The mass media recruitment of LOMR is a two-step process: first, the potential parent must be exposed to another foster family, then the potential parent is more likely to respond to the newspaper stories and to persevere in the process of becoming a foster parent. On the basis of this study, it is unrealistic to expect to recruit foster parents from the general population by mass media if they have not had contact with foster parents.

Implications for Recruiting

To increase the effectiveness of foster parent recruitment for retarded children, the following steps should be taken.

1) Strengthen ties with other agencies in the community so that their staffs will approach their current or former foster parents in behalf of a retarded child needing placement.

2) Use staff from all divisions of the mental retardation agency to recruit foster parents by word of mouth. Such an approach would: a) include information about a child needing placement in the staff news sheet; b) ask directors and supervisors to inform their staffs about the need of a particular child for placement; and c) call staff members on the phone (on a rotating basis) concerning the child and enlist their aid in finding a family.

3) Encourage foster parents to become involved in home finding. Possible techniques are: a) send a picture and story about the child to each foster parent and ask them to circulate the material among friends and acquaintances; b) develop cooperative agreements with other agencies so that information about retarded children needing placement can be sent to foster parents of other agencies with a request that they make the need known among friends and acquaintances.

4) Encourage foster parents to make other persons aware that they are or have been foster parents, thus increasing the number of persons in the general population who know foster parents, and the number of those most likely to respond to mass media campaigns. Techniques for accomplishing this might include: a) organizing a presentation to the foster parent association stressing the importance of foster parents' making their activity known to others; b) encouraging appearances by foster parents at church or club meetings, especially those attended by persons with a high school education, so that people can meet a foster parent and discuss foster parenting; c) writing articles for newsletters read by foster parents, pointing out their pivotal role in recruiting; and d) sending letters to foster parents explaining the findings of the LOMR study and encouraging them to increase their visibility.

5) Continue the newspaper stories and other mass media recruiting techniques.

Ann Coyne, M.S.W., is Assistant Professor, School of Social Work, University of Nebraska at Omaha.

Notes and References

1. Abbey, Robert D. "Spatial Influences in the Decision to Become a Foster Parent," unpublished master's thesis. University of Nebraska-Lincoln, Department of Geography, Lincoln,1974.

2. Cox, Steven. "Community Attitude Toward the Mentally Retarded," unpublished study, University of Nebraska-Lincoln, Department of Marketing, Lincoln, 1973.

3. Day, Gladys D. Home Finding—The Placement of Children in Families. Washington, D.C.: U.S. Government Printing Office, 1951.

4. Gray, P. G., and Parr, E. A. "Children in Care and the Recruitment of Foster Parents," in Some Useful Data When Sampling the Population of England and Wales. London: Her Majesty's Stationery Office, 1957.

5. Kadushin, Alfred. "Substitute Care: Foster Family Care," in Child Welfare Services. New York: Macmillan, 1967.

6. Radinsky, E. K., Freed, B. S., and Rubenstein, H. "Recruiting and Serving Foster Parents," in Mildred Johnson (ed.), Today's Child and Foster Care. New York: Child Welfare League of America, 1963.

7. Rogers, Everett M., and Shoemaker, F. F. Communication of Innovations. New York: Free Press, 1971.

8. Stone, Helen. Reflections on Foster Care: A Report of a National Survey of Attitudes and Practices. New York: Child Welfare League of America, 1969.

DONALD E. WEBER

Neighborhood Entry
in Group Home Development

The development of a new group home program is a study in deferred gratification. Most of the reinforcing events come late in the process. What comes earlier are the tasks of assessing and verifying the need, building community relationships, doing research on licensing standards, finding the money (maybe grant-writing), and that especially trying matter of establishing neighborhood relations.

Little data-producing work has been done on this last task [1]. Most of the comments that follow are based on the experience and observations of those who have been "through the mill." This article seeks to answer the question: "Knowing there is a high incidence of neighborhood resistance to the development of group homes, what information might be helpful to someone doing this for the first time?"

There are three strategies of neighborhood entry. One is the *low-profile entrance,* achieved by "slipping in quietly," the program being developed on a solid legal (usually zon-

ing basis without prior education of neighborhood residents.

A second is the *high-profile entrance,* educating anyone who will have contact with the new group home—(all neighbors, school principals, social agency leaders, politicians, planning commissions, media representatives, etc.). This is usually a planned, intensive, rapidly executed educational effort.

A third is the *combination approach,* which might be called "informing the select few." This is a planned educational program aimed at preselected individuals who either need information (planning commissioner, assemblyman or councilman from the district, human service organizations authorizing the program development, etc.) or those who might obstruct the program (president of the neighborhood betterment council, etc.).

The three strategies are oversimplified, but most neighborhood entry attempts fit into one of them. A general knowledge of the three strategies is helpful in evaluating the variables that make each neighborhood situation unique. The problem of assessing and managing neighborhood entry variables is so complex that the dominant variable may well be luck—good or bad [5;4]. The five major

Copyright 1978, Child Welfare League of America, Inc. Reprinted with permission, from Child Welfare, *Vol. 57, No. 10 (December 1978), pp. 627–642.*

variables concern neighborhood, clients, sponsor agency, facility and legal factors. Depending on the situation, minor variables not listed (such as a recent auto theft in the neighborhood by a delinquent youth) might end up as dominant. There is no formula for ranking variables that permits a sure-fire strategy [2]. Discussions with someone with neighborhood entry experience—euphoric or painful—before the task is undertaken is essential, if at all possible.

Neighborhood Variables

The major variables associated with the neighborhood in which the group home will be located follow.

Residential Quality. Is the neighborhood all single-family households, without apartments, stores, etc.? Generally, the more single-family oriented and attractive the neighborhood is— neat green lawns, well cared for homes—the more resistance is likely.

Family Orientation and Cohesion of the Neighborhood. Is the neighborhood made up primarily of families with children the same age level as the group home clients or younger? Are there block parties and little league ball teams made up primarily of the families in the neighborhood? If so, the home will be seen not only as a threat to property values in the neighborhood, but as a threat to the "wholesome" children in the neighborhood—versus the "unwholesome clients" the families think the group home will serve.

History of Neighborhood Organization. Has the neighborhood developed a "neighborhood betterment association?" Have the residents recently organized against a rezoning request for a bar or possibly another human service program? If they have, they probably know the several alternatives at their disposal to stop the development of any "undesirable business" in the neighborhood [12].

Socioeconomic Class. Is this a typical middle class neighborhood? A lower socioeconomic neighborhood? A high class neighborhood? A transition neighborhood? Neighborhoods in transition sometimes display less resistance to group home development, but then they are seldom ideal locations for group homes. On the other hand, transition neighborhoods that are cohesive can often resist more than other neighborhoods because most of the families' assets are tied up in their homes, and they fear a further deterioration of property values as a result of a group home entering the neighborhood. Some homeowners may feel trapped by inflation and oppose the group home to vent economic frustration. Upper class neighborhoods often cause fewer group home entry problems, presumably because upper class families have greater mobility. Also, they may oppose the group home as not preparing its clients for middle class life through "experience in the real world." Middle class neighborhoods tend to be cohesive, family-oriented and often resistive or concerned about group home development, although some families may be neutral or support the home.

Race Variables. Is the neighborhood racially integrated? Is it unintegrated? The group home will probably serve all races, and may be seen as an "integration" threat. Minority middle class neighborhoods can be just as resistive to a group home as white middle class neighborhoods.

Other Human Service Programs Nearby. Does the neighborhood have other group homes? If it does, what has the neighborhood experience been with them? Do the residents fear their neighborhood may become a "human service ghetto?" This is sometimes the case when zoning ordinances are restrictive elsewhere, or when most large homes suitable for group homes are in one neighborhood. Other programs nearby, if successful and unintrusive, may prove an asset. Negative experiences with human service programs will usually heighten resistance.

Leadership. Are there acknowledged leaders in the neighborhood? Are they positively or negatively oriented? Do neighbors respond to their leadership? Neighborhood leadership can work for or against the development of the group home. Cohesiveness for or against the home is more likely to develop if there are acknowledged leaders.

Mobility of Families in the Neighborhood. Is there a rapid turnover of families? If so, the neighbors are used to seeing new faces, are less cohesive, and have probably developed a tolerance for neighborhood changes.

Size of City or Town. Is the neighborhood in a large city? In a small town? Large cities usually force families and neighborhoods to develop higher tolerances to change. Residents of small and middle-sized towns, however, often value knowing what is going on in town, and especially their neighborhood. They place a higher value on the "purity" of their neighborhood or town.

Other Variables. Are the tax rates in the neighborhood high, and will a tax-exempt organization be developing the group home? Has there been a recent neighborhood or community debate about community-based programs? Many other variables might be listed. An assessment of neighborhood variables before an entry plan is developed is essential.

Client Variables

Many important variables relate to the clients who will be living in the group home. Although the facility implies a threat primarily to neighborhood property values, the problems of the clients often imply a threat to the well-being of the neighborhood residents, especially the children [9:8–10].

Size of the Client Group. Will there be six or eight clients? Will there be as many as 10 or 12? If the program is to be family-oriented, there should be no more than seven or eight clients in the facility; otherwise neighbors' family-oriented arguments are difficult to defend against.

Age of the Clients. Will clients be infants? Everyone likes babies. On the other hand, if clients are delinquent adolescent boys, apprehension runs higher, especially if there are many teen-age girls in the neighborhood.

Sex. Is this home for boys, girls, or boys and girls? A home for girls seems to cause less anxiety than a home for boys. Experience in several areas, however, shows a decidedly negative neighborhood reaction against a

co-ed home. After the neighbors have had a chance to observe a well-run, single-sex group home, and it proves not to be a disruptive influence, they are much more tolerant of a co-ed home.

The Label the Clients Will Have. Are they delinquents? Are they emotionally disturbed? Are they poor, neglected waifs? Most professionals realize it is behavior that counts, rather than the label placed on the client; however, neighbors do not, and their stereotypes often come from sensational newspaper stories. A "delinquent," especially if he is an older adolescent, will almost always cause apprehension, and if a group of them is going to be living in the neighborhood, you can count on neighborhood concern.

Race. Will there be black clients? Indians? Race is rarely used as an open objection. Negative or confused racial attitudes, however, are almost always present in the neighborhood.

Visitors to the Home. If the clients are youths, will the parents of the clients be coming to the group home frequently? Will their other children be "turned loose" in the neighborhood? Will their cars be blocking the street? Will the girlfriends or boyfriends of the youths be hanging around? Parking problems often may be an important variable.

Other Client Variables. Has there been a recent neighborhood "scare" related, for example, to a mentally unstable youth's behavior? Has a politician from the neighborhood just been elected on the basis of "putting delinquents in institutions where they belong"? Many neighbors see human service clients as somehow "abnormal," even though several neighbors may have received social services in the past. Other variables are possible with respect to how clients are perceived by neighbors.

Sponsoring Agency Variables

Most neighbors do not like faceless bureaucracies, especially those that are centrally located elsewhere yet planning to aid the disadvantaged by locating a treatment program in their neighborhood. Such programs may not be well received.

Auspices. Is the sponsoring agency a governmental or a local nonprofit organization? A public agency may evoke the "can't fight City Hall" reaction. With a private agency, neighbors may use an indirect approach. With government agencies, neighbors rightfully assume that their own tax money is being used to threaten their property values. The complexity of the local government organization may be a factor in the reaction. As mentioned earlier, group homes in New York City, for example, may be resisted to a lesser degree than in a middle size town.

Agency Credibility. Does the agency have a track record of sensitivity to neighborhood and community needs? Is is new and completely unknown? Are some of the group home sponsors living in the neighborhood or nearby? Does the sponsoring agency have powerful board members, good media connections, high (or low) credibility? The agency's reputation will certainly be a major defense against concern by the neighbors.

Political Vulnerability. If neighbors pull the right strings, can the group home be stopped? Depending on the cohesiveness of the neighbors and the strength of their desire to block the home, they may develop political strategies, soliciting support from the media, organizing confrontations with city council members, influencing politicians living nearby, etc.

Experience in the Field. What experience has the sponsoring group had in developing group homes? Has it done so in other neighborhoods? Would the residents in those areas be willing to talk with residents of the proposed new neighborhood? Experience generally is important to concerned neighbors.

Staffing Plan. What will staff living in the group home be like? Will they be "kids"? Will they look like hippies? Will they have their own children? Will there be seven or eight staff so that parking becomes a problem? A powerful neutralizer of neighborhood anxiety is to have bright, reasonable, enthusiastic group home parents available to answer questions (rather than an agency administrator who is not going to live at the home).

Facility Variables

The facility must be appropriate for the program. Objections may center not only on choice of the neighborhood, but on the facility itself.

Size and Layout. Is the facility big enough to house six or eight clients? Where will the staff couple live? Will additions be made on the original facility? The facility, if it is a dwelling converted to a group home, almost always will be a compromise from what the sponsoring agency wants, but it must always be adequate for the program, and defensible to neighbors.

Yard and Play Space. Is the yard big enough to accommodate the clients? Will the yard and exterior be kept up, the grass cut, the snow shoveled and the house painted as needed? These are legitimate neighborhood concerns.

Vehicle Parking. Is adequate off-street parking available? How will it look when three or four cars are at the home? Nothing detracts from a family neighborhood atmosphere more than inappropriately parked cars. Inadequate parking facilities are often overlooked by planners, but seldom by neighbors.

Neighborhood Standards. What are the standards of the neighborhood with respect to property upkeep and appearance? The group home must exceed neighborhood standards, not just meet them, especially in the initial stages of the program. Plans must be developed for this.

Location from Which Clients Come. Are the clients to be from the neighborhood or from another part of the city? Questions can be raised if one neighborhood is asked to help clients from another neighborhood. If client treatment goals include reunification with the family, a home location relatively near client families is important.

Legal Variables

A group home needs a solid legal base [12]. This is taken for granted by business organizations, but human service organizations at times neglect this variable [6:20].

Zoning. Nearly all cities have zoning ordinances governing group homes [9:11-14; 10:11-9]. The city planning commission is usually responsible for interpreting them. No program should be developed unless it has a legal right to be where it is located.

Licensing. Is the facility licensable in the written opinion of fire, health and social service departments? A concerned lawyer in the neighborhood probably will check on the licensing and zoning requirements [6;12].

Motivations of Objectors

Some objections by neighbors to group homes seem to be fairly universal, and some seem highly personal. There are several general motivations [5].

Concern about Property Values. Most families have almost all of their capital tied up in their house. Energy costs are rising, taxes increasing, expenses related to rearing their children spiraling. The families see a group home in the neighborhood as making their home less valuable, and more difficult to sell.

Concern about Privacy. In a neighborhood where you know everyone, you feel comfortable. You can avoid neighbors you don't like; you have control of your own privacy. On the other hand, a group home in the neighborhood threatens the feeling of personal privacy.

Fear for the Safety and Values of Children. Parents who live in a neighborhood of single-family dwellings are, of course, family-oriented. They have spent years developing the values, skills and positive habits of their children. They see the intrusion of "disturbed people" into the neighborhood as a threat to the values and habits of their children, perhaps adding to the normal conflict of a family's teen-age son or daughter with parents. For families with younger children, increased auto traffic may be a concern.

Worries over property values, privacy and influence on children are well founded, and must be addressed openly. Assurances that the group home will be renovated to make it more attractive help to alleviate property value concern. Reassurances about an emphasis on

respectful, discreet behavior by the home's clients, with prompt discipline and removal from the home if necessary, are helpful. There should be expressions of intention to keep noise down, to restrict loitering, etc.

There will probably be some individual, specific motivations for objections to the home in the neighborhood.

Individual Life Pressures. A neighbor may be concerned about losing a job, the recent theft of a car, or the illness of a child. Individual pressures may build up, so that at a group meeting there may be an emotional outburst due more to personal pressures than to the proposed group home.

Personal Style. Some persons have a negative, angry, aggressive style in stating their opposition to the group home.

Strategies of Neighborhood Entry

In the following section the three strategies of neighborhood entry are discussed in detail.

Strategy 1—Low-Profile Entrance. Any strategy takes into account affects and reactions that may develop in the execution of a plan. In group home development, experience indicates that it is possible to develop a program without prior education of the neighbors [4:87]. One rationale for this strategy is that neighborhood fears and concerns can never be completely quieted until after the program has been in operation for some time, and neighbors can see that it is not disruptive. Some data indicate that after the program has been operating for a few months, anxieties subside and neighbors even generate support for it [4:89]. If such a demonstration is the only effective way to lower anxiety, prior education of neighbors can at best be only a part solution to the problem. Some group home sponsors insist that if they have a legal right to develop their program in an area, they owe no explanation to the neighbors. Although this position can be questioned, since a group home is different from private family homes, it has increasing constitutional validity [6:207; 9:15-19,28;12].

If a low-profile strategy is used, a contingency plan should be developed, relating to the education of neighbors if concern arises. Materials, rationales, persons accountable for presentations, etc., must be developed, even if they are never used. Information about the plans must be given to at least a few important persons related to the project, whatever the strategy used. These persons include the executive director of the sponsoring agency, board members, groups or persons funding the project, the city planning director and possibly the planning/zoning commissioners and the client referral sources.

There is no magic in a low-profile entrance strategy. Where effective, it has made use of thorough knowledge of the neighborhood and the community at large [4:86]. It should be noted that existing data that point to a low-profile strategy as generally effective have not included all the variables in entry situations. Some data reflect a high frequency of "I don't know and I don't care" neighbor responses to development of a group home [8:87–92].

Strategy 2—High-Profile Entrance. This strategy involves an intense pre-entrance educational effort by the home developers. It requires the developers to analyze the neighborhood variables, prepare educational methods and materials, and execute an educational plan. A basic rationale is that the neighbors have a right to know about the development of the program.

There are several problems with this approach. First, since the educational effort takes place before the program has been developed, there is usually more time for concerned neighbors to develop opposition to it. Since, as noted earlier, much of their concern can be alleviated only by observing a nondisruptive program, education is only partly effective. Second, advance education, by its nature, implies that what happens in a group home is different from what happens in other homes in the neighborhood; thus, neighbors are being "warned" (educated), and thereby possibly further alarmed. An educational approach may also imply that neighbors have the option to approve or disapprove of the idea—that they have a chance to convince the sponsors that the group home is not welcome.

Third, the approach consumes an enormous amount of time and energy, perhaps discouraging the sponsors.

At times sponsoring agencies insist that neighbors accept the group home before it enters the neighborhood. Such acceptance is rarely achieved, since the neighbors' concerns for property values, well-being of their children, and privacy can seldom be totally overcome in advance, especially if a neighborhood is cohesive or has strong leadership. A basic assumption of an educational approach is that with reason and facts, most neighbors will accept the idea. On the other hand, experience indicates that neighbors often react emotionally and defensively, rather than rationally. If a high profile approach is used, emphasis should be on calming the major anxieties over property value, children and privacy. Humanitarian rationales are seldom effective.

Strategy 3—"Informing the Select Few." This strategy is actually a part of either of the first two strategies, though it is sometimes classified as separate. In this strategy, a "select few" must be informed of the group home plan. Certain local residents are informed and educated, as well as agency and government officials. Emphasis should be on educating those persons who are the most concerned—those in leadership positions, those living closest to the home, known supporters, etc. Channels should be set up to inform the sponsoring group immediately when someone has a concern, so sponsors can contact that person at once, rather than allow the anxiety to spread to others in the neighborhood. Advantages of a combination strategy include: open acknowledgment that a group home is different and requires some explanation to those concerned; evidence that the developers are not trying to "sneak the home into the neighborhood"; the possibility of asking high-credibility persons in the neighborhood to help interpret the program to neighbors. Disadvantages are similar to those in the high-profile strategy.

Summary Comments

Whatever strategy is used, thorough neighborhood knowledge, excellent contingency planning and the development of accountability for neighborhood education are essential to successful entry.

Major steps are: 1) deciding on an adequate facility; 2) becoming thoroughly familiar with the neighborhood; 3) reviewing relevant variables; 4) selecting an entry strategy; 5) doing detailed planning related to that strategy; 6) executing the strategy; and 7) evaluating its effectiveness.

Neighborhood Resistance

Almost all group home developers are confronted by some level of neighborhood concern and resistance. In about three of four cases moderate resistance (vocal, stopping short of formal petitions and legal action) or intensive resistance (legal action; personal, vindictive, verbal attacks; attempts at changing zoning laws; angry presentations to city councils; etc.) develops [3]. Anyone developing a community-based group home treatment program should expect resistance and prepare for it.

The experience of developers permits description of a typical cycle of neighborhood resistance activity.

At the start, someone hears about the program, and the word spreads throughout the neighborhood. Some neighbors react with concern; anxiety and anger are expressed and quickly shared with other neighbors.

In the next stage, a resistance leader emerges, usually a neighbor who has both anxiety about development of the home and a need (and some ability) to provide leadership. This person takes responsibility for informing all of the neighbors and attempts to organize them to resist. The leader then contacts the sponsoring group and requests a group meeting, perhaps inviting local politicians and others to the meeting without telling the sponsors. If the latter have not already informed these persons of the group home plans, the best outcome may be their neutrality, and the worst their full support of opponents of the home. Although it is important to avoid large group meetings with neighbors (the alternative being to meet with families individually), the neighborhood leader is generally able to bring about at least one large group meeting. From 20 to 75 persons are usually present, many arriving long before the meeting begins and exchanging concerns.

Usually at the start the sponsors are asked to outline the group home program plans. Their presentation is frequently interrupted by questions and followed by blunt and emotional questions and statements. The sponsors generally react with prepared rationales for the location, client group, program components, etc., but this seems to have little impact. Questions such as "Why do you have to locate in this neighborhood?" and "What do you think this is going to do to our property values?" often lead to statements such as "Can't you see we don't want you here?" and "We're going to make sure that you don't get into our neighborhood!"

Group meetings are generally punishing for the home sponsors and cathartic for the neighbors. Politicians or human service leaders present are usually embarrassed and wary. Toward the end of the meeting the sponsoring group usually indicates its intention either to go ahead with the home program or to drop it (the latter course is a bad precedent; other neighborhoods assume that by creating such opposition they can get the same response). It is now up to the neighbors to decide what to do.

It becomes obvious at the meeting that the neighbors vary in the strength of their opposition to the home. Almost all discuss the meeting with their families afterward, and develop individual family positions.

Usually a followup "neighbors only" meeting is scheduled by the neighborhood leader, to decide what to do. Political pressure is usually considered—"Who knows councilman so-and-so?" etc. Legal action is also considered, but usually not taken if the home plan has a solid legal base. Slimmer attendance at the followup meeting may indicate to those present that opposition is dwindling. If serious opposition continues, it usually takes the form of legal action or an attempt to stage more large group meetings. The group home sponsors should not accede to requests for more large group meetings.

If no additional opposition evolves from the followup meeting, the final phase in the cycle is a dwindling of formal, action-oriented, emotional opposition into a thoughtful (perhaps surly) acceptance, even by the neighbors who were most opposed. There is often a "wait and see" attitude by neutral or supportive neighbors [11].

Neighborhood Relations after the Home Is Open

As the program begins to develop, the group home parents will face a coolness in the neighborhood, but supporters and the neutrals will become more social. Skilled group home parents can seize opportunities to return greetings, attend social gatherings, etc., and usually within 2 to 3 months only the neighbors who were most vehemently opposed to the home remain socially distant.

As soon as the group home begins operation, the group home must act to generate neighborhood acceptance and support for the program. They and the clients in the home have to win support by their behavior.

The home parents should teach the clients to avoid certain behaviors offensive to the neighbors (e.g., do not pick their flowers or walk on their grass). They must engage in activities that lead to better neighborhood feelings—having coffee with neighbors, offering them help when it is needed, making sure the home's yard is well cared for, keeping cars off the street, etc. After a strong relationship has been developed, a neighbor might be asked to help build support with other neighbors.

The clients should be taught specific social skills and encouraged to shovel snow and cut grass for neighbors and otherwise help them. These activities might lead eventually to jobs for pay. Clients should not just be told to "be on their toes" with respect to neighbors, but must be taught specific behaviors to do or avoid, and when and how. Normally, neighborhood support dramatically increases once a home is in operation.

Suggestions

Experience in group home development is the basis for the suggestions that follow.

• Know your neighborhood. Keep in mind that in about three of every four group home development attempts, significant neighborhood resistance develops. A major factor in successful entry is thorough knowledge of the neighborhood.

• Make sure you have the legal right to be there. If neighborhood objections arise and you lack a legal base, this will nearly always be used as a way of stopping the program.

• Educate before any rezoning hearing. A public rezoning hearing will be a forum for objections. Advance education of the neighbors is always needed if the property must be rezoned. Knowledge gained in educating neighborhood families before the rezoning hearing may indicate the likelihood of success in rezoning, or at least the major areas of concern.

• Organize a neighborhood educational plan and materials well in advance of entry. Regardless of which strategy is used, an organized plan and materials are important, since immediate response to concerns is central to neighborhood education.

• In educating neighbors, be clear and straightforward. Focus the educational materials on the major concerns of neighbors—property values, well-being of their children, and neighborhood privacy.

• Avoid large group meetings with neighbors. Whenever possible, educate neighborhood families individually to avoid problematic group meeting behavior.

• If possible, assign the group home parents to the job of educating neighbors. This seems to work better than assigning board members or administrative staff. Neighbor concerns are quieted more effectively by those persons who will be living in the neighborhood as new neighbors, than by administrators who will function at a distance.

• Ask high-credibility persons in the neighborhood to help you with neighbor education. A local minister, church board executive committee member, or others might be willing to help if you contact them first and explain the program thoroughly.

• Be careful about the home purchase agreement or lease. Never sign without an "escape clause" releasing you if the program is not developed.

• Don't promise there will be "no problems" from clients. Instead, emphasize the reasons problems will probably be minimal, and stress that immediate steps will be taken if problems arise.

• Educate important persons in advance. Those persons on whom the project depends must know in advance what your plans are and when you intend to execute them. Those involved are the sponsoring board of directors, funding sources, and, if they are close to the neighborhood scene, politicians who may be affected by the program.

• Don't expect complete support at once. Neighborhood anxiety and concern are never completely alleviated until after the program has been operating for a time, regardless of how well organized and executed the advance educational plan.

• Speed the "good neighbor" plan. After the home opens, a well organized plan to "be a good neighbor" must be properly executed by the group home parents and clients, until positive results are achieved.

• Be respectful of neighbors. Throughout the time that the home program is being planned and implemented, the home developers should always respect the feelings and attitudes of the neighbors. The developers must be patient, understanding and empathetic even in the face of hostility. Patience and respect will win over the majority of people. With disrespect, neighbors assume they will be treated in a similar fashion after the home opens, and this intensifies their objections.

Donald E. Weber, M.S.W., ACSW, is Director of Community-Based Programs, Father Flanagan's Boys' Home, Boys Town, Nebraska.

Notes and References

1. A great deal of experiential information must exist, since hundreds of community-based group home programs have been developed; however, little has been published, and still less has been data-based. Statements in this article that are unsubstantiated by data or references are based on the author's direct experiences in the development of 30 group homes in 15 states, and indirect experience in the development of several others.

2. Only one ranking of variables was found (4:83, 84).

3. Taken from an assessment by the author in the 30 cases in which he has had direct experience.

4. Coates, R. B., and Miller, A. D. "Neutralizing Community Resistance to Group Homes," in Closing Correctional Institutions, edited by Y. Bakal, Lexington, Mass.: Lexington Books, 1973.

5. Community Residences Information Services Programs. "Gaining Community Acceptance: A Handbook for Community Residence Planners." New York: Westchester Community Council, 1976.

6. Cupaiuolo, A. A. "Community Residences and Zoning Ordinances." Hospital and Community Psychiatry, XXVIII, 3 (March 1977).

7. Evans, J., Clark, H. B., and Hinman, S. "A Study of Community Reaction to a Treatment Program for Youthful Offenders: Staff Predictions Versus Obtained Consumer Evaluation Ratings," (submitted for publication, March 1978).

8. Harris, V. W., Finfrock, S. R., and Weaver, F. L. "Neighborhood Attitudes and Community Homes for Delinquents," final report for Grant # MH21853 from the Centers for the Study of Crime and Delinquency, National Institute of Mental Health, 1976.

9. Lauber, D., with Bangs, F. S. "Zoning for Family and Group Care Facilities," Report #300, Planning Advisory Service, American Society of Planning Officials, Chicago, 1974.

10. Natavelli, P. "Zoning for a New Kind of Family," Westchester (N.Y.) Department of Planning, October 1976.

11. Seligson, H. "Neighborhood Acceptance of Community-Based Group Homes for Youths," research performed under N.I.M.H. Grant MH25604-02, 1975.

12. Wildgen, J. S. "Exclusionary Zoning and Its Effects on Group Homes in Areas Zoned for Single-Family Dwellings," Kansas Law Review, XXIV, 4 (Summer 1976).

ROBERT M. MORONEY

Allocation of Resources for Family Care

Although the specific focus of this conference is the topic of families caring for developmentally disabled members, the economic issues are better understood within the broader context of policies related to the disabled or handicapped in general. Moreover, since previous speakers have discussed in some detail the financial stresses most families are experiencing when they decide to provide care rather than transfer this responsibility to other social institutions, it would seem to be more useful to touch on a number of other economic issues that have significant implications for these families, as well as the professionals concerned with their problems. For these reasons, I have organized my comments around the more generic problems of the allocation of resources and the ever present competition among human service agencies and professionals for these scarce resources.

My concern and your concern is for those families with developmentally disabled

Reprinted with permission, from Family Care of Developmentally Disabled Members: Conference Proceedings, *Robert H. Bruininks and Gordon C. Krantz, eds. (Minneapolis: University of Minnesota, August 1979), pp. 63–76.*

members. In a sense, we are advocates for these families. We are concerned about them, we are interested in their needs being met. This concern or advocacy is not one, however, that can be isolated from the larger issue of resources to meet the needs of all families with handicapped members, regardless of the type of handicapping condition. If we hope to identify policies that would be supportive to them, these recommendations must be realistic and feasible. To ignore the reality of their interdependence would be dysfunctional. Given the American pattern of decision-making, we are in competition with groups concerned with other handicapped persons. Even within the area of the developmentally disabled, those of us interested in supporting families are competing with those who are attempting to develop high quality institutional programs.

This concern about resource allocation decisions has a number of parts. First is the level of current and proposed expenditures. Given the problem, how adequate are they? Do they reflect a real commitment on the part of society? If we can answer this, we then need to assess the translation of these resources into programs and services. It is never a simple matter of expenditures; the ultimate quality of programs is as important. Beyond these issues, we need to examine very carefully the implicit and explicit intent of these policies and programs. What objectives are they trying to achieve? Do they support families or are they designed to encourage families (implicitly) to transfer the caring function by emphasizing substitute services? Finally, we need to determine the target populations, the actual users, and the potential users. Are certain groups excluded in practice? While some services are universal, i.e., available to all who have a demonstrated need, others are means-tested and exclude those with incomes that are determined to be too high even though they have a need for the service. In some programs consumers are labelled implicitly as good or bad, worthy or unworthy. For years, vocational rehabilitation services were denied those who were high risk in terms of their potential for employment. A major criterion for selection was the likelihood of success for the smallest amount of investment. In manpower programs this is known as "creaming." It is conceivable that a respite care program might exclude families with multiple-handicapped children or children with behavioral problems because they are more difficult to handle. All of these issues—the level of the commitment (resources); the specific types of policies, programs, and services; the implicit and explicit purpose of the services; and the target populations—are issues germane to decisions on resource allocation.

We would like to believe that decisions are rationally made. We would like to believe that the criteria used by the decision-makers are reasonable, clearly thought through, and likely to be agreed upon by most people, consumers as well as professionals. We also would like to believe that decisions are made in the best interest of the disabled person, his or her family if they are providing care, and of society in general and the state in particular in so far as it is responsible for choosing how resources are to be used. In terms of opportunity costs, once expenditures are made to achieve some good, other choices are forfeited. And finally, we would like to believe

that behavioral and social scientists, human service professionals, and consumers participate in this process of decision-making.

However, neither the policy makers nor the professionals concerned with services for the disabled are this rational. This, in turn, has produced some questionable policies and practices that have created tensions in the general system. For those reasons, it becomes important to step back and examine more closely these macro-issues before looking specifically at the micro-issue of family care. As mentioned above, those concerned with the developmentally disabled are competing with others for resources allocated to the handicapped and, even within the narrower field, there is fierce competition about the use of developmental disability resources: Should they be allocated for improving institutions, developing community care services, or supporting families?

Macro-Issues: Resource Allocation and Competition

The social, economic, physical and emotional care of the disabled is and will continue to be a growth industry in this society. The prevalence of disabilities is increasing and will continue to grow at an accelerated rate over the next 25 years. It would appear that the greater our successes in overcoming the problems of infant mortality, in controlling the infectious diseases, in discovering and applying cures, drugs and techniques that have saved lives and increased longevity, the greater has been the spread of long-term disability and chronic illness. In this light, the achievements and the problems are the reverse side of the same coin—the paradox of medical and scientific progress.

In this country, approximately 7% of the population, or 15 million people, are disabled. Of these, an estimated 4 million are handicapped, and of these over 40% are severely handicapped in terms of functional ability. Who are these people? By and large, that sub-group of the population with the highest prevalence rate of disability is the aged and infirm and, within that group, those

75 years of age or older. Two of every three handicapped persons are 65 years of age or older, one of every three 75 years of age or older. Furthermore, recent projections indicate that, while the total population is expected to grow by 10 percent between 1975 and 1985, the population 65 years of age or older will increase by 17%, and those over 74 years of age by 22%. Given these trends and the likelihood that they will continue to grow over the next 25 years, we can anticipate a rapidly growing number of handicapped persons requiring health and special services. It would be an over-simplification to assume that the problems of long-term disability are primarily those of an aging population. It is important for us, though, to recognize that the greatest number are elderly persons since they are competing for resources. A sub-group of the handicapped, the severely mentally retarded, may be of special concern to us at this conference, but they are relatively small in number compared to the aged. Taking the prevalence rate of 3.5 per 1000 population, by the year 1980 there will be fewer than 800,000 so handicapped.

Given the projected increases in the population, what kind of national commitment might we anticipate? How much expansion can we hope for over the next 25 years? While it is impossible to identify current expenditures on behalf of disabled persons, some gross estimates are possible. A recent study by Berkowitz and his colleagues at Rutgers University suggests that approximately $83 billion, or 6.5% of the Gross National Product, was expended in 1973 either through transfers (41%), medical payments (36%), or direct service programs (3%). Federal expenditures represented 49% of the total; state and local expenditures, 14%; and private expenditures 37%. The researchers do point out, however, that they were unable to separate expenditures on long-term and short-term disabilities and conclude that much of these were in fact for the latter. Regardless, their findings are useful in that they show the present scale of commitment. Additionally, they report that in real terms, transfer payments increased by 47% between 1967–1973, medi-

cal payments by 49%, and total expenditures by 54%.

How realistic is it to expect that levels will be increased as the number of handicapped persons grows? What share will the developmentally disabled and their families receive? If agencies find themselves in competition for these resources today, what might we expect in the future? In periods of economic retrenchment, agencies dealing with a particular group of handicapped persons will find themselves at a distinct disadvantage. In some instances the numbers will be small compared to others (e.g., the visually handicapped) or the specific disability will be less attractive (e.g., the alcoholic or drug abuser). Additionally, while some of the disabled and their families are well organized for lobbying efforts, others are not. Unchecked, it is conceivable to imagine a scenario in which advocates for different groups will vie with each other to prove that some disabilities are more important than others, that some handicapped persons are more worthy than others. It may be argued that children should be given priority over the elderly since their lives are just beginning; that the blind or mentally retarded should be favored over the alcoholic and the drug abuser since they themselves were not responsible for their disability; that adults should receive disproportionate amounts of resources since they can contribute to overall economic growth by working while children and the elderly are basically consumers. Although each group is sincere and rational in what they do, the enemy becomes "other disabled" and survival is achieved only at the expense of others.

This interpretation of the present system should not be viewed as a criticism of advocacy as such. I believe that practitioners, analysts and planners are much more effective when they are in an advocacy position, when they identify with and are sensitive to the needs of specific population groups. As opposed to the professional who gives the appearance of being detached and objective, the professional who is committed can argue for more sensitive and meaningful policies and services. But there is a danger that advocates' efforts will become fragmented and, in the long run, all handicapped people will lose. An example of this is a recent experience I had as a member of a task force connected with the President's Commission on Mental Health. In a three-day meeting a number of professionals discussed the particular needs of American families and eventually produced a series of recommendations to the Commission. Each of us had been asked to present for discussion a paper on a particular sub-group of families. Unintentionally, each of us became advocates for "our families" and attempted to demonstrate that their needs were, in fact, the most important. But whose needs were the greatest? Is it the single parent family, families with teenagers who become pregnant, families caring for the handicapped, American Indian families, black families, families headed by Vietnam War veterans? All of these and other categories of families are at risk, but is it inevitable that, in assisting one group, we implicitly do so at the expense of others?

Historically, two fundamental criteria are introduced in setting priorities for the allocation of resources. The first is the notion of "worthy poor," a notion deeply imbedded in our long standing Poor Law tradition. Although we often tend to downplay this criterion, it has been very much a part of our process of decision-making even in this more enlightened period of the modern welfare state. The worthy poor have, over time, included the elderly, the handicapped, and widows with children. They are worthy of assistance because they are dependent through no fault of their own. All others were held responsible for their condition; there was something deficient in their makeup. Those of us concerned with the developmentally disabled and their families fare well under this criterion.

Over the past two decades, another criterion has become the basis for setting priorities —the human investment or human capital perspective. Using benefit-cost and cost-effectiveness approaches, decisions are made on the basis of expected return for the investment of resources. Programs are compared in terms of the return (economic) for each dollar

spent. We have seen this in the vocational rehabilitation effort, we are seeing it in our manpower programs. The rationale is simple and in keeping with certain basic American values. The bottom line is easy to measure— did people, as a result of the program, become independent, become producers rather than consumers, enter or return to the labor force, pay taxes and contribute to overall economic growth? This criterion is not totally congruent with the first criterion of worth vs. nonworth and, I would argue, the developmentally disabled, especially those with severe handicaps, become a lower priority. An investment in a severely retarded child will not produce the same economic return as that in a child with an orthopedic problem or in an adult handicapped through a lack of job skills. I would suggest that in times of economic retrenchment the human investment criterion becomes more commonly applied.

Recognizing these trends, a number of professionals are arguing for a more generic approach towards disability. This position assumes that a fresh look at our service delivery system would permit a more systematic consideration of alternatives which might range from better coordination among the fragmented and incomplete specialties to a more structured and generic approach to the problem. Given our negative experiences with coordination efforts (the current policy thrust), it is argued that only large-scale reorganization can be effective. Two coordination strategies are usually offered. The first involves restructuring agencies in terms of functional needs with emphasis on certain commonalities. All of the disabled have difficulty in performing the major functions considered normal for their age. They also experience financial difficulties, family stress, and a lack of social stimulation. In reorganizing the system along functional lines, high quality specialized services can be offered to all disabled persons regardless of the specific diagnosis. The alternative is to build on the growing pattern of restructuring governmental agencies into umbrella human service configurations. Although the evidence to date is not clearly positive, it is argued that the umbrella concept is appropriate. What is needed is the development of mechanisms to integrate these services at the delivery level. To date, most efforts have emphasized state-level operations with little attention given to changing community structures.

A second concern for proponents of a generic approach is that the fragmented system has dissipated any meaningful effort for community support services that are needed by most disabled persons. While there are agencies, programs, and lobbies for the blind, the mentally retarded, children with cerebral palsy, etc., there are none for Meals on Wheels, home care, or transportation services, and expansion in these areas has suffered. A restructuring along some dimension of a generic approach would highlight these deficiencies and re-establish priorities for scarce resources. Without such an exploration, it is likely that these vital services will continue to be ignored, placing further pressures on the specialized services. In the long run, their effectiveness will be significantly reduced.

The issue of provision of generic services is controversial. While specialized knowledge and skills are essential, it does not necessarily follow that these can only be developed through categorical agencies. The provision of services specifically for the disabled or for a distinct group of disabled tends to isolate them from other people and may deny them equal opportunity. In the past, for example, it has led to the provision of poorly paid jobs that were inappropriate to the potential of the disabled worker. Furthermore, it is interesting to note the demands by parents of mentally retarded children for admission to ordinary schools and for opportunities for their children to interact with non-handicapped children; segregation often reinforces rather than corrects negative attitudes in local communities.

The difficult question remains, however, as to how comprehensive a generic approach should be. It would be easy to destroy the effectiveness of any program by making it so comprehensive that the needs of all the disabled are included, such as housing, income maintenance, medical care, education, reha-

bilitation, and socialization. There are approaches between the extremes of specialized agencies and fully generic agencies and they should be examined more thoroughly. These include programs such as Triage in Connecticut, which provides comprehensive services under a single administration ranging from acute hospital care, through intermediate nursing and home nursing services, to chore and neighborhood support services. Other examples are Personal Care Organizations, Community Care Corps, and Home Care Corps, all of which are organized on relatively generic grounds. These efforts, while building on the common needs of the disabled, do not necessarily imply that all agencies be restructured to meet the functional needs of the disabled. Rather, they are building meaningful bridges with the specialized agencies by creating interfacing mechanisms. These efforts are also realistic attempts to re-examine the relationship between community support systems for the long-term disabled and institutional care. Despite the rhetoric of choice and preferences for the disabled and their families, priority (resources) has been given to institutional care. And yet, the evidence is that most families favor home care over institutional care, that they actually are providing a supportive environment for their disabled members whether they are severely retarded children or elderly parents, and that they are doing so with little support from the organized health and welfare system.

The final issue is concerned with this country's need for a positive, integrated policy stance towards disability and the needs of the disabled. Much of the reluctance to favorably address this issue lies in the fear that when these needs and their mushrooming costs are highlighted, governments will seek ways to retrench. However, there is little evidence to support a position based on the hope that by not raising the issue, resources will be made available. The problem of financing has to be directly confronted if an adequate and effective program for disability is to be achieved. A number of alternatives should be considered and analyzed.

Insuring lifetime maintenance care for

the severely disabled, in much the same way that the acute aspects of catastrophic illness are now insured, is one option. To be feasible, however, greater attention should be given to identifying populations at risk. This task is complex in that there are many technical and clinical differences related to the nature of the condition. Blind persons, retarded persons, individuals with multiple sclerosis, the quadriplegic, the severely crippled arthritic, all have different clinical requirements. There is a need to aggregate disabling conditions across diagnostic categories and yet there are not commonly used or accepted objectives of severe disability. Numerous scales measuring activities of daily living, such as the Barthel's and Pulses, measure not only functional status but also intellectual and emotional adaptability, but none are available to permit comprehensive aggregation of data. Once these aggregations are feasible, it then becomes possible to derive firmer estimates about the range of services or benefits the at-risk population is likely to require and to identify the likely utilization rate.

An approach other than full insurance would involve payment in the form of a demigrant comparable to the disability allowance in the United Kingdom (Constant Attendance Allowance) whereby individuals identified as needing the attention of another person are given a supplementary cash allowance so that they might secure the supportive assistance they require. This allowance is not income-tested but given solely on the basis of disability.

Short of full insurance, the present Medicare and Medicaid programs could be expanded to encourage the provision of less costly and more often desirable home care services. If one chooses a non-insurance route, a variety of existing programs might be considered for expansion into more generic approaches, such as programs for the blind and crippled children. The new amendments to the Social Security Act (Title XX), which provide for personal social services, might be considered as a viable nucleus around which to construct such a system.

Regardless of the specific mechanism,

whether it is the creation of a national health insurance program, some form of guaranteed income related to disability, or the large scale development of various generic supportive services, it is unlikely that such comprehensive policies can be realized unless professionals, agencies, and lay associations come together in a united front. If these organizations continue to act separately and only pressure for distinct categorical groups of disabled, these policy issues will either be ignored or receive low priority.

Micro-Issues: Families Caring for Handicapped Members

The issue of family responsibility for the care of its dependent members has, for three hundred and fifty years, been the subject of almost continuous debate. Historically, most social welfare programs were developed on the premise that the family constituted the first line of responsibility when individuals had their self-maintaining capacities impaired or threatened. It was further expected that families would support these handicapped members until the situation became overwhelming and only then would society intervene.

This approach is based on the principle that family life is and should be a private matter and, as a fragile institution, must be protected. There seems to be widespread agreement that society, through state programming, has the right to step in when individuals can no longer meet their own needs or do not have other resources to fall back on. Children who are neglected or in danger of physical abuse can be removed from their families. The isolated elderly person or the handicapped person needing considerable care and supervision can be transferred to an institutional setting. The emphasis is on the protection of the individual who might harm himself, others, or be harmed.

Intervention usually takes place after a crisis or breakdown occurs and the state's role is seen as marginal and concerned with a small proportion of the population, i.e., those who are unable or unwilling to meet their own needs through the normal mechanisms of the family and the market. Historically, then, the state has been reluctant to intervene if that intervention in any way might interfere with the family's rights and responsibilities, their privacy and self-determination.

While these principles may have shaped our social policies, there has been a growing concern on the part of professionals and practitioners that present-day families are not carrying out their responsibilities. One point of view that appears to be gaining considerable momentum is that as the state assumes more responsibility for assuring that basic social and economic needs are met (a responsibility taken on since the 'thirties), the traditional responsibility of the family to provide for the needs of its members is diminished and the family as a social institution has become less important. It has been charged that children are less inclined to support their elderly parents and parents their handicapped children.

And yet the evidence does not support these conclusions. We are finally beginning to recognize that the overwhelming majority of handicapped people are in the community and are being cared for by their families with various degrees of support from public and voluntary agencies. It has been estimated that 7% of the population is disabled and 2.5% is handicapped. And yet, the institutional population over the past 25 years has remained fairly constant at 1%. Furthermore, it is clear that this institutional population is not made up only of the handicapped. For example, 65% of the severely handicapped are elderly and 34% are over 75 years of age. Even though the institutional rate has increased over the past 20 years (from 4% to 5%), 12% of the elderly (half of whom are over 75) or 2½ million persons, are living as dependents of their children or other relatives. If we can rely on various surveys, we must accept the fact that the majority have some handicapping condition. Furthermore, shifting to another group of the handicapped, the mentally retarded, we know that only 25% of those who are severely retarded are in institutions at any point in time. The remainder are in communities. When we look at severely

retarded children, most are living with their parents.

Because of families, then, admissions to institutions of persons who are severely physically or mentally handicapped have been prevented or delayed. Many families, often with the help of friends and neighbors, have provided what can only be described as a staggering amount of care at significant social, physical and emotional costs. In this sense, the family has been a resource for the handicapped and it is becoming clearer that it has been a major resource for the social welfare system. It is frightening to think of what would happen if these families were to seek institutionalization.

However, the major emphasis in terms of expenditures is on institutional care serving a relatively small proportion of the at-risk population. Butterfield, for example, has estimated that 40% of all mental retardation expenditures are for institutional care. Of the remainder, only a small amount is used to support families caring for their severely retarded children. These families are, in fact, competing for these resources with families with moderately retarded children. Furthermore, community care cannot be equated with services supportive to families. Much of these resources are used for substitute family care, e.g., residential care facilities. In spite of this, families continue to provide care, most want to provide care, and until it is proven otherwise, we must assume that they are providing excellent care at considerable financial, social, emotional and physical costs.

The most common reason given for this emphasis on services that substitute for families, rather than support families, is that we lack sufficient resources. We must set priorities, hierarchies of need, in order to distribute scarce resources; handicapped persons without families are at a greater risk and their needs should be met first; when, and only when, resources are increased can services be made generally available to families providing care. This rationale is simplistic for two reasons. The first is that we are never likely to reach that point when we have enough resources. The second is even more fundamental

—we do not know how to support families as well as we know how to take over the caring function. Because of the way our services have been organized and the way our professionals are trained, we are fairly comfortable in substituting for families and extremely uncomfortable in supporting others who are the primary caregivers.

Professionals tend to be trained in the medical model with its emphasis on pathology. We diagnose problems, develop a treatment plan, and work toward a cure—the reversal of a perceived pathology. Furthermore, professionals are rewarded by their sponsoring agency and receive personal satisfaction when these cures are achieved. This model is clearly inappropriate for most families caring for their handicapped members, and who need support to continue. There is no pathology to be cured in these cases and, to many professionals, they are not interesting.

Even this rationale is incomplete. Preoccupation with a medical model is accompanied with a focus on individuals; most of our policies and programs define the individual as the object of intervention. Moreover, they have been developed for specific individuals, i.e., the elderly, the handicapped, children, expectant mothers, mothers without husbands, and so on. Services are provided to individuals on the implicit assumption that if an individual family member receives this service, the entire family will benefit. Although all of our social policies do affect families, the nature of the impact is basically unknown since the assumption has not been tested systematically. In practice, family members are viewed as resources (caregivers) to the handicapped person or as resources (members of the caregiving team) to the professionals. Rarely are families seen as needing resources themselves because they are providing care. In those instances when the family is the focus of the service, it more often than not has meant that professionals have defined the family as part of the problem, one of the reasons why the pathology exists.

A final reason for provision of services that substitute for family care is related to our approach to planning. It can be argued that it is technically easier to plan for services that substitute for the family rather than support it. These services lend themselves to a structured approach while family support services create all sorts of programming difficulties. For example, over the past fifteen years, heavy reliance has been placed on various national surveys. These studies have taken as the unit of analysis the handicapped individual. The data report on the characteristics of the handicapped: their capabilities and incapacities, the degree of the handicap, their socioeconomic status and their living status. For planning purposes, the handicapped are then grouped by age, sex, and the severity of their condition. These data lend themselves to aggregations and a set of programs can be developed for the sub-groups. Furthermore, handicap is usually defined in terms of the ability to carry out basic functions. How many of the handicapped are mobile, how many can bathe, feed and care for themselves? How many live alone? Given these aggregate data on the handicapped, the planner can begin to translate them into specific service plans. Needs, a vague but crucial conceptual starting point, are thus linked to an identification of tasks or functions necessary for social and physical well-being.

If the handicapped person does not have a family, or in the case of many elderly, the handicapped person lives with a spouse, the planning process is relatively straightforward. If the person is severely handicapped and needs total care, the outcome is likely to be institutionalization where the staff assumes those functions normally carried out by a family. The handicapped person is provided with a room, meals, health and personal care services, and social stimulation in a total caring environment. The residential care facility becomes the home, and the staff and other residents function as a substitute family. The planning task becomes one of estimating the number of handicapped who fall into this category and then designing the necessary services.

If the handicapped person can manage reasonably when certain functions are taken over, the task then becomes one of assessing where the individual is deficient or incapable and then providing what is necessary. Again, the available surveys are quite useful. Once norms or standards are established and functions delineated, needs can be aggregated and services designed systematically.

It is much more difficult to "plan" for those situations in which the handicapped person is living with his family, and the family has assumed the major caring responsibility. First of all, the focus has shifted from the handicapped person, a shift that is more significant than may appear on the surface. The task is no longer one of assessing an individual's capacity to function and then providing services that either totally or partially substitute for the family. What is required now is the provision of services that ease the management task of the family. If planning requires an ability to categorize need and then a capability for aggregation, the process logically begins with a search for similarities between families providing care rather than a focus on their differences. This search for common need is difficult when families are providing care because their support needs vary widely. It has been suggested, furthermore, that an important criterion of a caring society is flexibility, but flexibility is often viewed by planners to be antithetical to the need to structure services.

Is it possible then, to plan collective measures, requiring that need be standardized and aggregated, to effectively meet the needs of individual families? If this is a factor in the limited development of family support services, it should be looked at more closely. It might be necessary to begin to search for "similarities" of need among families even if the idea of similarity has to be stretched. This line of argument would suggest that surveys (even of a small scale) and other types of research should be initiated, but that the unit of analysis should become the family of the handicapped and not the handicapped person. There is much to be learned by systematically asking families themselves what types of support they would find helpful. These data might then provide the categorical and aggregate data required for the planning process. Fundamental to this exercise, however, is the development of a sense of trust in families and a confidence in their ability to know what they need.

Conclusions

I began this presentation with the statement that we would like to believe that policies are developed that are in the best interests of society, handicapped individuals and their families, and human service professionals. As many of you are well aware, this is a utopian goal rather than a realistic objective. More often than not, these policies are incompatible in our present system. In maximizing the benefits to one of these three, another will be penalized. For example, we have been experiencing a considerable effort to deinstitutionalize mentally ill and mentally retarded people. The rhetoric underpinning this policy calls for providing the "least restrictive environment" for the handicapped. Two arguments are usually offered: That it is therapeutically sound and that it is less costly. The first reason emphasizes the benefits to the individual and his or her family; the second emphasizes the benefit to society as a whole. Can both be maximized? We do not really know since we have not tried it.

To some extent, the "therapeutic and less costly" criteria are the same as effectiveness and efficiency. Patients have been discharged in great numbers, resulting in cost savings to the mental health and mental retardation systems. However, these savings are misleading. The reduction of hospital places and discharges to the community have not been balanced with a comparable expansion of community support services. Community care is less costly only when community services are non-existent or inadequate. Appropriate community care might be as expensive, if not more so, than institutional care. Implicitly, our non-action places higher priority on a narrow and short-sighted definition of efficiency (cost) than on effectiveness (therapy).

Families with handicapped members need and have asked for support services. More often than not these needs, as defined by families, are for concrete services. The presence of a handicapped member creates financial stress for most families and yet our income policies offer little support unless the family has a very low income. If the cost of caring for a handicapped child is excessive, it would seem reasonable that this be recognized in our tax policies and yet, all children are treated equally, handicapped or not. If families need to make structural modifications in their homes because a handicapped child or adult lives with them, we might want to provide low-interest loans. Following the experiences of a number of European countries, we might want to develop some form of disability allowances. For example, in 1971, the British initiated their Constant Attendance Allowance program. All families providing substantial care to a handicapped person (certified by a physician) receive a non-means-tested grant. Two arguments have been given for this decision. First, it gives families financial support to help defray the costs associated with caring for a handicapped person. Second, and probably more important, it gives families psychological support, a feeling that someone is interested in them and appreciates what they are doing.

A second type of need expressed by families is for relief in the caring function. Respite care is available in many communities, but provision is usually inadequate. In the United Kingdom, 10% of all beds in nursing homes and community-based residential care facilities (e.g., hostels) are available for respite care. Furthermore, they are protected regardless of the pressure used to free them for long-term patients. Even the mental retardation institutions are used differently. Admissions to these institutions are on the average four times higher than in the United States. Moreover, very young children and infants, a group we will not admit, are admitted. But, in spite of higher rates of admission, especially for young children, 90% of these children remain in the institution for less than three months. In this country, 42% remain five years or longer. Why? The British use their institutions for diagnosis, short-term treatment and respite care. Institutional care is used to support

families in one country, to substitute for families in another.

The list of needed services identified by families of disabled persons also includes transportation, home-making, baby-sitting, appliances, and information. They are tangible, hard services and it may be because of this that these needs cannot be maximized if the needs of the professionals are not met. For any number of reasons, professionals end up advocating for their own programs and agencies and not for families. We have a tendency to define problems in terms of solutions, and often these solutions are the provision of more resources to do those things we are already doing. Professional survival and agency expansion become the major goals. An example of this is the recently published report by the President's Commission on Mental Health. Although the report discussed prevention, family supports, and the need for innovative approaches, the major money recommendations were for expansion of the community mental health centers and training. If these funds are used to experiment with new approaches to mental illness, if they result in services to support families under stress, they might achieve the Commission's objectives. If they are used to continue doing what is presently being done, the major beneficiaries will be the professionals.

Policies are not likely to equally benefit society, families caring for handicapped members, and professionals. There will be trade-offs. Different criteria become critical. As advocates for the developmentally disabled and their families, we cannot make our case using a human investment, cost-benefit, efficiency argument. Our rationale will probably be based on the notion of justice as fairness or equity. We need to argue for a reduction of existing social inequalities through a redistribution of claims and access to resources and social opportunities.

Consistent with this approach, we need to think of choice as a criterion. Twenty-five years ago, parents were encouraged to institutionalize their severely retarded children. They were told that it was better for the child and better for the rest of the family. Those who kept their children at home found few supportive services available to help them. Today, the pendulum has swung to the other extreme. Parents are told that institutional care is not in the best interest of the child or the family, and those who seek institutionalization experience considerable pressure from professionals. In neither situation are families given real choices. Choice is only viable when the available institutional care is superior care and when the community support system is of the highest possible quality. Furthermore, family care is not superior to institutional care in every case. Oftentimes, placement is desirable for the child and the family. What is important, though, are policies that allow for choice —for families to choose the best alternative.

A final comment. The issue of professional "burn-out" is being discussed more and more in the literature. We find, for example, that professionals in direct contact with the mentally retarded burn out sooner than those in management. This makes sense and leads me to ask about families providing care to handicapped persons. Who are closer than they? Can we support them before they burn out? This is our task for the future.

Robert M. Moroney, Ph.D., is Professor of Social Policy and Planning, Department of City and Regional Planning, University of North Carolina at Chapel Hill.

ANN BAERWALD

Case Management: Defining a Concept

The concept and goals of case management are complex. They are further complicated by the characteristics of the systems coordinated by means of case management and the needs of the individuals served within those systems. Case management is a central concept in the state of California's system for serving over seventy thousand people with developmental disabilities, where it is identified as "client program coordination." The mandate for its use is found in legislation; however, the prevailing perceptions of case management vary with the differing perspectives, needs, and expectations of legislators, program administrators, case managers, and those being "managed." Although perceptions based on the perspectives, needs, and expectations of different groups would vary in any event, because case management is in this instance being applied to the field of developmental disabilities, the problems involved in its implementation are exacerbated by the characteristics of the system that it is required to coordinate and the needs of the individuals being served within the system.

Beatrice has summarized the trend that is taking place in favor of case management in the following comments:

'service integration' and 'coordination' have become the modern equivalents of the philosopher's stone, through which social service planners seek to turn the 'lead' of disconnected service programs into the 'gold' of organized, consistent services which address client need and do so without waste. This search for coordination has grown over time, in response to issues such as the increase in services and coverage, the expansion of narrow categorical programs..., the growth in the pool of individuals seeking services, the greater recognition of need and the emergence of social service professionals who see and react to human need and attempt to affect the service system to meet the needs observed.[1]

However, this "gold" referred to by Beatrice will never exist in the form of a single, beautifully wrought piece of jewelry. Case management is expected to resolve major difficulties that include the fragmentation of services and programs, gaps and duplication in services, programs that work at cross purposes, a lack of comprehensiveness in service arrangement and delivery, and the multiple needs of long-term care clients. It has been assigned the responsibility of making the social service system work for the client in a consistent and coherent manner, thus relieving the client and family of some of their burdens. The extent of the intervention undertaken by the case manager will, therefore, vary, based on the fragmentation of the system, the service needs of the individual, and the sophistication of the individual in navigating the system independently. Case management seeks to maximize resources through establishing an integrated, individualized plan for each client in which component benefits are contributed by the use of available means. Social workers, who are equipped with the skills necessary to identify and mobilize resources, are well suited to undertake case management.

Historically, case management has been most extensively used in serving elderly persons and persons with developmental disabilities. More recently, the practice of case management has been applied to serving persons who are chronically mentally ill. Thus, case management is generally used in providing services to clients with complex, severe, long-term (and often life-long) needs that affect many, if not all, aspects of their lives and cut across service delivery systems.

In the area of developmental disabilities, at the federal level the Rehabilitation, Comprehensive Services, and Developmental Disabilities Amendments of 1978 (P.L. 95-602) designate case management as one of the priorities that states should implement in their annual Developmental Disabilities Plans. Case management is identified as assisting developmentally disabled persons and their families in gaining access to needed services, coordinating the services provided, and monitoring clients' progress over time; these services should be provided on a life-long basis, if necessary. The Accreditation Council for Services for Mentally Retarded and Other Developmentally Disabled Persons uses the term client program coordination. Developed by professionals and advocacy groups in the field of developmental disabilities, the council's standards are widely applied in the delivery of services to persons with developmental disabilities.

In addition, case management has been mandated through legislation in many states, such as California. Initially, two pilot programs to provide case management were established in the state in 1966. In enacting the Lanter-man Developmental Services Act of 1977, the legislature indicated that the state would contract with appropriate agencies to provide "fixed points of contact" in the community for people with developmental disabilities and their families so that the developmentally disabled would have access to the facilities and services best suited to them throughout their lifetime. It further required the regional centers so established to assign a program coordinator who would be responsible for implementing, overseeing, and monitoring individual program plans.

Traditionally, whether the developmentally disabled or another population has been involved, certain components have consistently appeared in all case management models, namely, intake, assessment (which includes diagnosis and evaluation), development of a services or treatment plan, referral, coordination, counseling or consultation, advocacy, follow-up or monitoring of the client's progress, and revision of the plan. Nevertheless, there are wide variations in applied case management. It is important to look at certain variables when attempting to define a particular case management model. Three of these variables can easily be identified: the structure of the service system in which case management is undertaken, the functions to be performed for clients, and the form of the case management model itself.

Structure of the System

The structure of the system refers to the environment within which the particular case management model is to be implemented. Because case management is predicated on the coordination and integration of existing services in behalf of clients, it is essential to identify what services actually exist. If a continuum of services is already available, the case manager can focus almost totally on integrating services and helping clients deal with complex and often conflicting entry or eligibility criteria. If, on the other hand, available services are minimal or significant gaps in services exist, the development of resources must be emphasized. This is because the effectiveness of case management depends to a significant degree on the array of services on which the case manager can draw.

It is also critical to analyze the complexity of the system. Significant differences in case management models may depend on such factors as the size and variability of the target population to be served, the complexity of intergovernmental and interagency relationships impinging on the system, the level of consumer advocacy sustained, the number of providers involved and whether they are public, not for profit, or proprietary in nature, and the bases of authority for various agencies in the system.

Finally, the characteristics of a case management model will vary according to the coordination network already prevailing within a given system and between systems. An inverse relationship appears to exist between the intensity of the case management efforts needed and the effectiveness of the coordination found among available services. In a system in which resources are allocated inefficiently or inequitably, the authority of the case manager must be greater in order for him or her to intervene effectively in behalf of individual clients. Case management efforts will be affected if there is duplication within the system, just as they will be affected by fragmentation. In general, the greater the fragmentation, the more extensive the case management role.

Functions to Be Performed

A consideration of the functions to be performed for clients must encompass both the number of people to be served and the extent or scope of the service. Given limited resources, decisions must be made whether to serve more people less intensively or fewer people more intensively.

Any particular model of case management must identify the actual functions to be carried out in the delivery of services, and this effort should be based on an analysis of the environment, including the statutory authority under which the model was established. By virtue of their relationship with individuals in a particular target group, case managers are in a position to collect data regarding the gaps in a particular service system. These data are essential to any planning and resource development that must be undertaken. Thus the link between case management and planning is critical.

In addition to planning, a variety of others functions may be included in case management. For example, a knowledge of available resources enables case managers to serve as educators for clients regarding alternatives. With this knowledge as well as an overview of the system, case managers can act as consultants to others. However, knowledge of this kind extends beyond a familiarity with various options and includes an understanding of the intricacies involved in gaining access to resources. It is in this area that the case manager deals with the issue of the differential access and use of resources and can perform a "triage" function while exerting various degrees of authority. At one end of the continuum the case manager provides extensive information to the client regarding various alternatives, and the client makes the decision about which resources to use. At the other end the case manager actually controls access to certain resources.

The first step in the utilization of resources is an assessment of needs, another function to be performed by the case manager. Such an assessment involves the systematic collection and evaluation of data and must include an analysis of both the strengths and needs of the individual as well as a consideration of his or her support structure. On the basis of this assessment, the most effective service or treatment plan can be developed, and components of the service system can be selected for use as needed. The goal here is to fit services to the client rather than the other way around.

In addition, case management encompasses advocacy. On the systemic level, advocacy involves lobbying legislators, activist groups, and others in order to effect changes in the service system. Advocacy for the individual can include undertaking direct intervention in behalf of a client or assuring due process for him or her.

Last, the follow-up or monitoring of clients' progress and the revision of program plans are an integral part of any case management model. This is because case management is used only to provide services to persons with long-term, complex needs. The frequency and intensity of follow-up may be determined by the nature of the system or may be more individualized, as needed.

Form of the Model

The third major variable to be considered is the form of the case management model itself. Such a consideration will involve answering a variety of questions, such as, What type of authority does the case management system have in relation to clients, distribution of resources, and other segments of the service delivery system? Does it provide information and referrals, act as broker or facilitator, or function as final decision maker in the use of resources? Additional factors that involve funding also determine the form of the model. For example, does the case management system purchase services from providers or exert control over moneys spent in behalf of clients? How are yearly fiscal priorities established regarding the purchase of services?

The location of case management efforts within the overall service system must also be taken into account. Are they linked to an existing agency or other entity, or are they freestanding? Are they centralized at the state level, or are they locally based? If it is freestanding, case management may avoid being "tainted" by any specific part of the system, but it can also become totally estranged from the system. Similarly, decentralization can permit the case manager to identify with local interests and with the individuals being served; however, it can also reduce the manager's impact on decision making at the state level.

What does all this mean for the individual case manager who is providing direct services to the client or family, often in an interdisciplinary setting? Given the complex variables just described, it is easy to see why perceptions of case management vary so widely. If, within a particular model, clear decisions have not been made or, once made, have not been adequately communicated to all involved, one can understand why conflicting messages are received by the case manager. Individual functions may be defined so broadly that the case manager is supposed to be all things to all people. Of course, this is an expectation that cannot be fulfilled.

Focus on the Case Manager

What skills and knowledge are required by a case manager? To answer this question, one can begin by noting these comments by Bertsche and Horejsi:

> Case coordination differs from typical interdisciplinary teamwork...because it is a professional activity which extends beyond the boundaries of a particular agency and involves interorganizational as well as intraorganizational and interpersonal factors.[2]

As perceived by this author, much of case management can be identified with case coordination. This viewpoint is borne out by the use of the term client program coordinator in California and some other states.

All social workers are familiar with the emphasis placed on a detailed written plan as the basis for coordination. The development of such a plan is to involve the client, significant others, and professionals. As Bertsche and Horejsi point out, there has been much more discussion about the content of a good plan than about the process or skills involved in developing and managing the plan.[3] Nevertheless, it may be said that a knowledge of the dynamics of group process, problem solving, and teamwork derived from a social work education is integral to formulating an individual program plan, as is an understanding of the principles of self-determination and increased independence for the client and family.

In general, the case manager must possess knowledge or receive training regarding the target population and available resources. Making certain that such knowledge is available is an important element of in-service training and supervisory responsibility, as well as a professional responsibility of the individual. In a survey of case coordinators, Bertsche and Horejsi identified the following as important areas that should be stressed in the training and supervision of coordinators: advocacy principles, the broker role, mediation, crisis intervention, systems of record keeping, state and federal regulations regarding the handling of client data, the consultation process, informal resource systems in the community, prevailing community attitudes toward various client groups, principles of normalization, public relations, principles of organizational behavior and change, and approaches to organizational management.[4] Skills of particular importance that were mentioned included helping the client to communicate assertively with professionals, writing behavioral goals, preparing written reports, abstracting and summarizing data drawn from diverse sources, public speaking, working with the media, and using supervision and consultation effectively.

Need for Clarity

Social workers involved in case management, whether as line workers or in administrative positions, need to accept the challenge of defining it. The definition that emerges needs to evolve within the context of the individual's own system or agency and then be communicated to other appropriate individuals. Only in this way can professionals unify their perceptions. A case management system readily comprehensible to all will assure common understanding and expectations and avoid the development of unnecessary pressure and tensions. It is critical that a precise definition of case management be communicated to clients and to others to ensure clear expectations and a common comprehension of relationships and obligations. In addition, the present economic and political environment requires that social workers convey their concerns to legislators and other leaders to provide input into decisions affecting funding and the service system. In the area of case management, social work stands at the crossroads of change in a changing world, and workers must collectively address an appropriate definition.

Ann Baerwald, MSSA, is Associate Director, Client Management Services, North Los Angeles County Regional Center, Panorama City, California. An earlier version of this article was presented before the Social Work Division at the 105th Annual Meeting of the American Association on Mental Deficiency, Detroit, Michigan, May 27, 1981.

Notes and References

1. Dennis F. Beatrice, "Case Management: A Policy Option for Long-Term Care," in *Major Reforms in Long-Term Care: A Systematic Comparison of the Options,* Center for Health Policy Analysis and Research, February 1980, p. 71.

2. Anne Vandeberg Bertsche and Charles R. Horejsi, "Coordination of Client Services," *Social Work,* 25 (March 1980), p. 95.

3. Ibid.

4. Ibid.

MARYANNE P. KEENAN
DORIS R. PARKER

Deinstitutionalization:
A Policy Analysis

Public recognition of the rights and needs of persons who are developmentally disabled is a relatively recent phenomenon in this nation's history. The types of services and the methods of service delivery targeted for any population are based on commonly held beliefs. Prior to World War II, the developmentally disabled were labeled "subnormal" or "incurable" and were segregated from society and regarded as second-class citizens. As part of the civil rights movement and increasing concern for the rights of the handicapped, the concept of "normalization" was born, and, as patterns and conditions of everyday life were made accessible to them, handicapped individuals began to find a place in the mainstream of society. The past twenty years have brought legislation and court decisions allowing the developmentally disabled greater access to education and services. Although the new laws have been well intended, they have not reflected the crucial concepts of coordination and comprehensiveness of services, either in language or implementation.

It is not surprising, then, that the problems in meeting the needs of the developmentally disabled are fragmentation and duplication of services. Stated simply, the legislative

commitment over the past two decades to return developmentally disabled persons to the community has not been matched by any systematic effort to provide habilitative services at the community level. The purpose of this article is, therefore, to provide social workers with background information on federal legislation that has affected the deinstitutionalization movement. The intention is to make professional social workers aware that as planners, administrators, and providers of direct service, they must assume an active role in formulating and carrying out federal, state, and local policies in an attempt to help develop cohesive community services for the developmentally disabled. The importance of such an endeavor has been summarized by Garrett and Griffis:

> The human benefits both to the persons rehabilitated and to society cannot be measured in dollars and cents. They lie in the principles of Western civilization and of American democracy and in the belief that every man is of value in himself and that it is to his best interest and to society's to help him develop to his full potential.[1]

In looking at the adequacy of policy implementation that has taken place, the authors will specifically examine three areas of service development in the community: residential services, case management, and respite care.

A Brief History

One can begin to understand the problem of the fragmentation and duplication of services for the developmentally disabled by examining the definitions that have been used regarding the target population, the trends that have prevailed, and the services that have been proposed. The concept of developmental disabilities was first defined by Public Law (P.L.) 91-517, the Developmental Disabilities Services and Facilities Construction Amendments of 1970. At that time, a developmental disability was described as a severe and chronic disability attributable to various conditions, including mental retardation, cerebral palsy, epilepsy, and other neurological disorders, originating before age 18 and expected to continue indefinitely. Although services to the developmentally disabled existed prior to 1970, they had been categorical and directed toward individuals with a specific disabling condition.

In 1975, the Developmentally Disabled Assistance and Bill of Rights Act (P.L. 94-103) called for a study and a report to Congress concerning the definitions of developmental disabilities. This study resulted in the revised definition, which is currently being used, found in the Rehabilitation, Comprehensive Services, and Developmental Disabilities Amendments of 1978 (P.L. 95-602). The revised definition states that the term "developmental disability" refers to a severe, chronic disability that (1) is attributable to a mental or physical impairment or to a combination of mental or physical impairments; (2) is manifested before the individual attains age 22; (3) is likely to continue indefinitely; (4) results in substantial functional limitations in three or more of the following areas of major life activity: self-care, receptive and expressive language, learning, mobility, self-direction, capacity for independent living, and economic self-sufficiency; and (5) reflects the individual's need for a combination and sequence of

special, interdisciplinary or generic care, treatment, or other services that are of lifelong or extended duration and are individually planned and coordinated. The focus here was on the particular characteristics of the individual's disability and their influence on the individual's ability to function in society. The intent of the amendments was to have those in need of service identified according to their level of functioning. However, their actual impact was to reduce the number of persons eligible for services under the original 1970 legislation and to cause general confusion among service providers regarding exactly who was eligible. In 1978, prior to the enactment of the amendments, the developmentally disabled population in the United States was 5,265,894, as estimated by the Developmental Disability Planning Council. This estimate shrank by 26 percent, to 3,906,913, in 1980.[2] The decline in numbers seemed to continue through 1981, when the U.S. Council on the International Year of Disabled Persons reported 3.5 million disabled people living in this country.[3]

This apparent reduction may be ascribed to two factors: the largest portion (54.8 percent) of the developmentally disabled are mentally retarded, and approximately 89 percent of the retarded are mildly retarded and are not otherwise handicapped.[4] Because the mildly retarded are not normally identified as being substantially functionally limited and are not likely to seek or receive services available to the developmentally disabled, they are not likely to be identified as developmentally disabled under the 1978 amendments or to be included in any count of that population.

Many people with developmental disabilities have lived in institutions. But as a result of litigation during the 1970s concerning unsatisfactory conditions and the rights of residents, deinstitutionalization has become a central concept in the development of appropriate community services. Deinstitutionalization, defined as a planned reduction in the number of persons living in institutions, has also become popular because its effects are relatively easy to measure. The population of public institutions for the mentally retarded reached its peak between 1967 and 1970, at approximately 190,000 persons. An additional 65,000 individuals were living in private facilities at that time.[5] The President's Committee on Mental Retardation reported a 10.2 percent decrease in the residential population between 1970 and 1975 and suggested one main reason for this: the release of residents into the community.[6]

These figures may illustrate a national trend, but they also hide some important facts. Rather than declining, the institutionalized population may be changing. A study by Scheerenberger conducted in 1976 revealed that during Fiscal Year 1975-76, 80 percent of the 237 public residential facilities surveyed released individuals into the community, but 70 percent failed to show a net reduction in population because of new admissions.[7] Subsequently, an older, more severely handicapped group could be found in institutions. In addition, the study showed that many of those released were readmitted because their communities lacked appropriate local services.

Definition of Terms

Inherent in the concept of deinstitutionalization are two other concepts: habilitative services and the least restrictive alternative. Until developmental disabilities were defined by law, the term "rehabilitation" was used indiscriminately to refer to services to all disabled persons, regardless of the age at which they became disabled. However, rehabilitation is now usually differentiated from habilitation. Rehabilitative services are those intended to restore a person to his or her former level of functioning, which implies that this level was, at one time, sufficient for independent living. Habilitation, on the other hand, is a process of supporting and maintaining someone at his or her maximum level of functioning, without reference to a former or an ideal level of independence. Habilitative services have become associated with the developmentally disabled and with community services, and they generally include educational and psychological services as well as residential services, case management, and respite care.

When viewed absolutely in terms of dollars, the public cost of habilitative services for the developmentally disabled has been substantial. In 1965, the federal budget provided $225 million for direct and indirect services to the mentally retarded, and in 1971 the figure was $610 million.[8]

In 1976, the U.S. Department of Health, Education, and Welfare estimated that $2 billion were spent on the mentally retarded, $1 billion being spent for social services and another billion for income maintenance.[9] Cutbacks in the federal budget in 1981 and 1982 suggest that programs for the developmentally disabled are not as secure as they have been in the past. The last round of appropriations for Fiscal Year 1982 left programs for the developmentally disabled with approximately the same level of funding as in 1981. However, developmentally disabled individuals will still benefit from appropriations made in the area of vocational rehabilitation and from the new Social Services Block Grant.

Although it would appear that significant expenditures have been made on habilitation, when viewed relatively, the public cost of habilitative services has been small. The amount spent relative to total federal spending is a minute percentage, and the adequacy and effectiveness of these expenditures remain to be evaluated.

"Least restrictive alternative" is another term that frequently appears in legislation dealing with the developmentally disabled. It refers to the "environment which provides the minimum supervision necessary in the smallest living unit possible with the maximum integration into the mainstream of the community."[10] In residential or respite services, the least restrictive alternative is the individual's home. This is followed by a foster home, group living arrangement, and, finally, an institution. The concept of least restrictive alternative has also been applied to classroom placement, work settings, and recreational programs for the developmentally disabled. Its subjectivity, however, has been the source of much litigation.

Community-based services are considered the least restrictive alternative for the majority of the disabled population. Consequently, services of this kind have increased to a significant extent. From 1970 to 1975, community services represented the fastest growing segment of state budgets in the area of human services.[11] Steady growth in service development occurred from 1960 through 1977, apparently reflecting a legislative or judicial commitment to deinstitutionalization and to the establishment of an alternative that would be less restrictive than institutions.

In general, the success of any deinstitutionalization program depends on the range and quality of community services available. As defined by Horejsi, a comprehensive, community-based service system includes the following elements: community-based services under local control; comprehensive services that meet the needs of persons of all ages, disabilities, and background and are available whenever and wherever required; arrangements by which all physical units, staff, and equipment provide assistance and linkages between service components; and services that provide a continuum of care from a single, fixed point of referral.[12]

Scheerenberger's model of a community service system for the disabled includes all the services available to the general population.[13] However, as Scheerenberger points out, if setting up such arrangements were a requirement for deinstitutionalization, almost all handicapped persons would still be living in public or private residential facilities. Essentially, the model he describes contains four ingredients needed in the development of successful community programs:

1. A local board that is legally accountable to the programs and fully responsible for receiving and channeling funds.

2. An independent standard-setting and monitoring agency to evaluate programs that are to reflect the needs of service recipients only.

3. Substantial financial support, because high-quality services are costly, regardless of their setting.

4. An advocacy program to ensure the rights and maximum representation of clients.

Both Horejsi's and Scheerenberger's models of community service delivery portray an ideal situation. The reality in most, if not all, communities in this country falls short of this ideal, especially in regard to local coordination. Magrab and Elder have remarked that although the 1970s brought many positive steps toward meeting the needs of the developmentally disabled, there exists little effort to plan for orderly implementation of services.[14] Pollard, Hall, and Kiernan agree that there is a lack of communication and mutual respect among members of various professions, such as medicine, nursing, education, social work, and physical therapy, and present professionals with a challenge for the 1980s: the establishment of a coordinated human service delivery system.[15]

In regard to such an effort, Horejsi has stated that disabled persons need a changing combination of services over their lifetime and that these services must be planned and developed as a system, so that they are interdependent and interrelated.[16] The types of services he recommends include residential services, centralized coordination (for example, in the form of case management), and family support (such as respite care). These essential areas were among those delineated as priorities in the Developmental Disabilities Amendments of 1978, and they therefore received 65 percent of federal money spent by states on developmental programs. These particular services will now be examined in greater depth.

Residential Services

The legislation and litigation of the 1960s and 1970s had at their core a concern for the values of human dignity, equality, and justice for the developmentally disabled. Along with a growing desire for cost-effective alternatives to institutions, these values governed the formation of policy in the creation of community residences. Until 1965, few individuals who were institutionalized were ever released into the community. Once placed in an institution, most children tended to stay there because their families found it difficult or impossible to meet the needs of a disabled child in the community. After the policy changes that took place in the 1960s, many developmentally disabled persons were judged to be inappropriately placed and were released into the community. There they encountered residential programs that had recently received federal funding from an array of sources, including the U.S. Department of Health, Education, and Welfare and the U.S. Department of Housing and Urban Development. Each disbursement of funds came with its own set of regulations and eligibility requirements and a planning board.

To add to this potential confusion, only vague definitions of an "appropriate" community residence emerged over the years. The general concept of such a residence was of a community-based housing facility other than the individual's natural home that afforded living experiences appropriate to the current functioning level of the individual.[17] However, because a standardized classification system for community residences has never existed, beginning in the 1960s each community designed its own. Types of residences across the country ranged from small group homes for three to six persons to mini-institutions with more than twenty residents. These residences experienced steady growth from 1960 to 1977, and the number of group home programs in the United States doubled between 1973 and 1977. A study conducted by Bruininks, Hauber, and Kudla in 1977 of 4,427 community residences in all fifty states revealed that approximately twenty-nine persons per one hundred thousand were living in some form of community residence for the developmentally disabled.[18] The study also found that private, nonprofit agencies administered 54 percent of the homes, private corporations supported 38 percent, and government funds financed 8 percent. About 73 percent of the homes contained ten or fewer residents, which would suggest that policies supporting deinstitutionalization would promote the growth of smaller residences as community alternatives for the developmentally disabled.

Despite the trend toward community alternatives, many people remained in institutions, and most states were still supporting public facilities with state funds. As the states began setting up alternative living situations, they neglected a systematic approach to the development of services. Such an approach would have included efforts in the areas of vocational rehabilitation, social work services, education, case management, recreation, advocacy, and health care, all of which are necessary to maintain a person in the community. Other factors contributed to fragmentation. For example, most available federal funding was granted for short-term start-up costs. In Fiscal Year 1973–74, the President's Committee on Mental Retardation indicated that a lack of community services was the reason given for 50 percent of the readmissions reported in a study of 134 facilities.[19] Clearly, people were being released from institutions before coherent plans to serve them were in place. In commenting on the situation, Bradley has contended that many community services were designed primarily to use federal funds rather than to meet individual needs.[20] The cart was being placed before the horse in the development of community living alternatives for the deinstitutionalized population.

There are various theories to explain why so many attempts to develop adequate community residences failed, but advocates of deinstitutionalization blamed the federal government's failure to plan in a coordinated way for sufficient high-quality housing. In most states, residences were developed as funding was made available or as court decisions were issued, without regard for actual community resources or local needs. Although small family-style group homes were favored by most professionals and clients, the development of such homes was hindered by the imposition by the states of standards intended for institutions. Because potential operators of homes found that compliance with these regulations was expensive, the growth of nonprofit group homes was discouraged, and large corporations dominated the development of residential services in many communities. Proprietary interests seemed to have the financial savvy necessary to obtain federal money, but they had little interest in establishing small residences and no experience in providing services. Consequently, mini-institutions were developed in the community for profit, and the humanitarian intent of enacted legislation was lost in the pursuit of local funds.

Case Management

In the process of developing living arrangements for the disabled, most state and local agencies failed to establish comprehensive client management systems and relied instead on fragmentary support from various social service agencies. Social work services were available by law to institutionalized persons and their families. However, there was no system for providing social services to people living outside institutions. In general, service delivery to individuals in the community was ill defined and rarely implemented. Because no one was held accountable for the provision of services, many disabled people received duplicate services or, worse, no services at all. Indeed, lack of coordination of various community services is the reason most often cited for the failure of localities to meet the needs of their developmentally disabled citizens.[21]

The 1978 Developmental Disabilities Amendments reflected a recognition of the need for systematic service provision to clients. This legislation gave states the option to set up case management systems with their priority-area funds. Case management was defined as "a mechanism for linking and coordinating segments of the service delivery system to ensure the most comprehensive program for meeting a particular client's needs." The amendments also included provisions for maintenance of services to ensure a continuing relationship between the case manager and clients and the coordination of services to provide access, information, and support from a single point of contact.

In general, the functions of the case manager vary from rural to urban settings, but they usually include the coordination of an interdisciplinary team whose efforts produce an individualized habilitation plan for each client. Coordination is a difficult task

when a separate team and plan are required for each of the services an individual receives. For example, until recently quarterly team meetings and reviews of individual plans were required by the regulations governing, respectively, the Education for All Handicapped Children Act, Supplemental Security Income, vocational rehabilitation services, and Medicaid. According to the regulations, the case manager is responsible for coordinating services to facilitate the establishment of a comprehensive service system with a minimum of duplication and maximum amount of self-determination by the client.

Ideally, the case manager could elicit cooperation from every agency with which he or she worked. Not being affiliated with any one agency involved would enhance the manager's capacity for advocating for the client. However, as states instituted case management, they found that much of the funding they received was earmarked for service providers and that Title XX and the 1978 amendments, the two sources of funds, in fact moved the case manager into the delivery system. In addition, case managers found that they had more leverage for improving services and facilitating collaboration if they were actually part of the system.[22] Thus, in many states, objectivity and, possibly, confidentiality were sacrificed to assure cooperation and continuity of services for clients.[23]

At present, case management has not been in existence long enough to be adequately assessed; however, some roadblocks to its success have already been identified. For case management to work smoothly, caseloads must remain small, but this is unlikely to occur when staff cutbacks take place because of losses in funding. Case management also requires a commitment from all participating agencies to meet the needs of individuals rather than attend to issues concerning "turf." Finally, communication and agreement are necessary between the federal government and the states as well as among various local agencies concerning client eligibility criteria, responsibility for funding, and accountability procedures if the case manager's efforts are to succeed.

Respite Care

Deinstitutionalization was accomplished in most communities in two ways: by releasing institutionalized individuals into the community and by encouraging people to keep their disabled relatives at home. Studies found that between 27 and 40 percent of those already released from institutions returned to their homes, and in New York State in 1975, two out of every three placements involved the individual's natural home or a foster family.[24] However, it was also reported that the highest rate of readmission to public facilities stemmed from individuals returning from family care. Specifically, 30 to 48 percent of the placements made in clients' natural homes were not successful.[25] The most common reason was the lack of support in the community for the family.

In general, in order for a family to maintain a handicapped relative within their home successfully, gaps in the service system need to be filled. Respite care is one of the most frequently used services when it is available.[26] In this kind of care, the disabled individual is temporarily separated from his or her family and provided with supervision, thus relieving family members of the burden of care. Respite care takes many forms, ranging from the services of a trained sitter provided in the home to the temporary placement of the disabled person in a foster home or public residential facility. On a continuum of residential services, respite care is seen as the first line of defense against institutionalization, and participants at the 1970 White House Conference on Children agreed that the prevention of stress among the "high risk" families of the developmentally disabled was a top priority.[27]

However, respite care has received little legislative attention, and, consequently, the development of services in this area has not kept pace with need within local communities. Nevertheless, provision for respite care has sometimes been made. Title IV-B, Section 425 of the Social Security Act authorized formula grants to the states (for example, in the amount of $56.5 million in 1980) for the provision of "special care" to developmentally disabled children and children discharged from institutions. Such care could include foster care, day care, or homemaker services. In addition, Title XX funds have been used in many states to provide social services including child care for disabled persons or, as in Virginia, companion services for mentally retarded adults. Unfortunately, there have been barriers to the use of funds for respite programs, such as rigid licensing requirements for care providers and limits on the number of hours of care available to any particular family.

Medicaid funds pay for respite care to families in some states, such as Virginia, where regional training centers are used to provide care on an "as available" basis. However, even at a minimum cost of $62 per day per person, this arrangement is expensive for many states when it is compared to the more efficient sitter services set up by local agencies and available on an hourly or daily basis. The average cost of sitter services is $3.50 an hour or $48 a day, which is partially shared by the families using the services.[28]

Respite care represents one of the few inexpensive community services that are geared toward the prevention of institutional placements. This has finally been recognized in Congress, as evidenced by the October 1981 amendments to the Omnibus Reconciliation Act. Medicaid waivers are now available for respite care in many forms for the disabled or the elderly and their families. This arrangement constitutes a major step for those in need of respite services.

Social Work Role

The roles that social workers have assumed in the deinstitutionalization movement have been at least partially prescribed by law. In particular, social workers employed in publicly funded residential facilities must follow the regulations delineated within the Community Mental Health Centers Act and Title XIX Amendments of 1974. In addition to performing mandated roles, social workers involved in providing community services have readily adapted their professional skills and values to assisting disabled people and their families in locating and adjusting to alternatives to institutionalization.

Social workers in the field of developmental disabilities are found in a wide variety of roles in the service delivery system. In general, they perform traditional social work functions such as discharge planning, counseling, and the making of referrals. They are also administrators, researchers, and advocates for the disabled in fulfilling the intent of deinstitutionalization policies.

For example, workers undertaking case management adopt a systems approach in meeting a client's individual needs through a full range of services. Social workers equipped with skills in the area of team coordination, linkage among community resources, and advocacy for client self-determination find a natural opportunity for leadership in case management. Community residential programs employ social workers as administrators, planners, and providers of direct services who are involved in the placement and maintenance of individuals in group homes. In addition, as advocates of cost-effective family support services, social workers in respite care coordinate and train care providers.

Schodek and her associates suggest that although social workers have carried much of the burden of implementing deinstitutionalization, their lack of involvement in actual policy making has limited the profession's role.[29] In reviewing how deinstitutionalization policies have been implemented, the authors will examine this issue more closely.

Problems in Implementation

The development of community services for the developmentally disabled has been fraught with six identifiable problems:

1. *Resistance to deinstitutionalization.* The federal mandate for deinstitutionalization did not include a plan for the systematic release of individuals into the community. This lack of preparation by federal and state agencies was followed by community resistance and negativism toward the disabled that continue to this day. In addition, the parents of the institutionalized handicapped feared the return of their offspring and the burdens involved in their care in view of the scarce community supports available to them.[30]

2. *Lack of coordinated and adequate funding.* As a whole, the nation's program for the developmentally disabled had two major drawbacks in the area of funding: funding levels were inadequate to accomplish stated goals, and most of the funds were for start-up costs only, not for continual operating expenses of newly constructed facilities. As a result, some new community programs were deprived of funds almost as soon as they got under way. Burdensome federal regulations and requirements for strict accounting procedures also created problems. Finally, what often appeared to be constantly changing federal priorities and criteria discouraged the states to such an extent that they found it easier to spend their money on upgrading existing institutions than on developing community-based alternatives.

3. *"Too much bureaucracy."* More than half the coordinators of state programs for the developmentally disabled cited bureaucratic red tape as an obstacle to the delivery of services.[31] Consequently, programs were developed at the local level to meet federal or state priorities and funding requirements without regard to community needs or long-term planning. The authority of state offices in the field of developmental disabilities also varied greatly, some offices being substantially involved in decision making, as in Massachusetts, others acting as mere figureheads, as in Virginia. Multilayered state bureaucracies often precluded accountability for programs, especially when no centrally responsible office was assigned the task of monitoring or follow-up.

4. *Lack of interagency coordination.* Goals of local programs were often defined in terms of each agency's objectives rather than the needs of clients. A lack of clearly delineated roles and responsibilities for each service provider resulted in bickering and competition for funds among local agencies. This was directly related to the lack of systematic planning in most communities, which was in turn accompanied by insufficient re-

sources and authority over the integration of services.

5. *Lack of attention to clients' needs.* All the problems enumerated thus far contributed directly to the inability of the individual client to receive the housing, job training, education, and financial assistance needed to survive in the community. The absence of a coordinated national policy, the fragmented service systems, the multiple yet inadequate funding sources, and the lack of accountability ultimately impaired the ability of the developmentally disabled person to live in the least restrictive environment in the community.

State and local governments are not lacking in models of comprehensive service delivery at the community level. However, as reflected by other national policies such as health planning, the federal government failed to plan systematically for legislative contingencies and to take the individual recipient into consideration in the implementation of its plans. As a result, a well-intended policy failed to provide adequate services to any given individual and neglected the larger segment of the target population, namely, those who remain at home.

6. *Lack of social work involvement at the policy level.* Coordinating community services, matching them to clients' needs, and facilitating community and family adjustments are all vital components of a successful deinstitutionalization program. Social work involvement in these areas has been significant but limited to the implementation of services. Social work professionals now need to extend themselves beyond these boundaries to assume leadership in making policy.

Schodek and her associates have indicated that the following three steps would enable social workers and others to become participants in planning for deinstitutionalization: (1) the expansion of social work roles at the level of service delivery to include planning functions, (2) the appointment of former service providers to policy planning positions on the state and local level, and (3) the initiation of regular communication between social workers and administrators and officials whose functions include planning for deinstitutionalization.[32] Social work professionals have much to offer in the way of knowledge, abilities, and familiarity with ethical guidelines in the development of community services for the disabled. The failure to maximize social work's potential contribution may perhaps have hindered the development of coordinated service systems in many localities. Social workers must not continue to underutilize their talents in meeting the needs of the disabled in the community.

Every person who spends a lifetime in an institution costs taxpayers more than one million dollars.[33] The potential financial saving to be realized would alone justify the movement toward deinstitutionalization and the parallel development of community programs. Nevertheless, maintaining the developmentally disabled in their homes or communities is not simply an economic question but a social responsibility that has been reflected in the laws enacted over the past twenty years.

Maryanne P. Keenan, MSW, is Senior Staff Associate in Health Policy, National Association of Social Workers, Silver Spring, Maryland, and a doctoral student, School of Hygiene and Public Health, Johns Hopkins University, Baltimore, Maryland. Doris R. Parker, MSW, is a consultant with the National Association of Social Workers, Silver Spring, Maryland.

Notes and References

1. J. F. Garrett and B. W. Griffis, "The Economic Benefits of Rehabilitation for the Mentally Retarded," *Welfare in Review,* 9 (1971), p. 1.

2. R. Lee Henney, *The Impact of the Amendment of the Definition of "Developmentally Disabled" on the D. D. Program in FY '79 and FY '80* (Washington, D.C.: Institute for Comprehensive Planning, 1980).

3. Lynn Wikler, "Social Work Practice in Developmental Disabilities." Unpublished manuscript, Madison, Wis., March 1981.

4. R. Lee Henney, *The Impact of the Amend-*

ment of the Definition of "Developmentally Disabled" on the D. D. Program in FY '79 and FY '80; and ibid.

5. R. C. Scheerenberger, "A Model for Deinstitutionalization," *Mental Retardation,* 12 (December 1974), p. 3.

6. President's Committee on Mental Retardation, *MR: Trends in State Services* (Washington, D.C.: U.S. Government Printing Office, 1976).

7. R. C. Scheerenberger, *Public Residential Services for the Mentally Retarded* (Madison, Wis.: National Association of Superintendents of Public Residential Facilities for the Mentally Retarded, 1976).

8. President's Committee on Mental Retardation, *MR: Century of Decision—A Report to the President* (Washington, D.C.: U.S. Government Printing Office, 1974).

9. Robert M. Gettings, Harold A. Tapper, and Myrl Weinberg, *Income Maintenance and the Developmentally Disabled: An Analysis of Policy Issues* (Arlington, Va.: National Association of State Mental Retardation Program Directors, December 1977), p. 10.

10. B. Willer, R. C. Scheerenberger, and J. Intagliata, "Deinstitutionalization and Mentally Retarded Persons," *Community Mental Health Review,* 3 (1978), pp. 3–12.

11. President's Committee on Mental Retardation, *MR: Trends in State Services.*

12. Charles Horejsi, *Deinstitutionalization and the Development of Community Based Services for the Mentally Retarded: An Overview of Concepts and Issues* (Missoula, Mont.: Project on Community Resources and Deinstitutionalization, 1975), p. 6.

13. Scheerenberger, "A Model for Deinstitutionalization."

14. Phyllis Magrab and Jerry O. Elder, eds., *Planning Services to Handicapped Persons: Community, Education, Health* (Baltimore, Md.: Paul H. Brooks, Publishers, 1979), preface.

15. A. Pollard, H. Hall, and T. Kiernan, "Community Service Planning," in ibid.

16. Horejsi, *Deinstitutionalization and the Development of Community Based Services for the Mentally Retarded.*

17. President's Committee on Mental Retarda-

tion, *MR '74: A Friend in Washington* (Washington, D.C.: U.S. Government Printing Office, 1975).

18. Robert H. Bruininks, Florence A. Hauber, and Mary J. Kudla, "National Survey of Community Residential Facilities: A Profile of Facilities and Residents in 1977," *American Journal of Mental Deficiency,* 84 (March 1980), pp. 470–478.

19. President's Committee on Mental Retardation, *MR: '74: A Friend in Washington.*

20. Valerie J. Bradley, *Deinstitutionalization of Developmentally Disabled Persons: A Conceptual Analysis and Guide* (Baltimore, Md.: University Park Press, 1978).

21. See ibid; Magrab and Elder, *Planning Services to Handicapped Persons;* and C. B. Smith and L. L. Cooney, *Illinois: Case Management Study,* Vol. 1: *Executive Summary* (Springfield, Il.: Society for Autistic Children, April 1979).

22. Bradley, *Deinstitutionalization of Developmentally Disabled Persons.*

23. Jerry O. Elder, "Coordination of Service Delivery Systems," in Magrab and Elder, *Planning Services to Handicapped Persons.*

24. See Willer, Scheerenberger, and Intagliata, "Deinstitutionalization and Mentally Retarded Persons."

25. Ibid.

26. Ibid.

27. Ann Castle, "A Study of the Importance of Respite Care and the CAPS Respite Home Project." Unpublished thesis, Marymount College of Virginia, July 1980.

28. Ibid.

29. Kay Schodek et al., "The Regulation of Family Involvement in Deinstitutionalization," *Social Casework,* 61 (February 1980), pp. 67–73.

30. Willer, Scheerenberger, and Intagliata, "Deinstitutionalization and Mentally Retarded Persons."

31. President's Committee on Mental Retardation, *MR: Trends in State Services.*

32. Schodek et al., "The Regulation of Family Involvement in Deinstitutionalization."

33. H. Carl Haywood, "Presidential Address: Reducing Social Vulnerability Is the Challenge of the Eighties," *Mental Retardation,* 19 (August 1981), p. 16.

Afterword

This collection of articles emphasizes the range of opportunities for social workers in the field of developmental disabilities and the diversity of services they can provide. It combines basic information on service delivery to disabled people with the application of specific social work skills and values. The variety of approaches covered by these selections, from individual psychotherapy to family counseling to community change, will make this volume relevant to practitioners at every level.

In the wake of deinstitutionalization, the primary focus of the field has shifted to community-based care and support for families with a disabled member. Articles such as those by Coyne, Weber, and Baerward have described methods for facilitating the movement of disabled people into alternative living arrangements in the community. The impact that caring for a developmentally disabled person has on a family and the special needs of families regarding the early identification of disabilities and the management of stress were discussed by Parks, Wikler, Kurtz, and others. Underlying all of this is the need for families and professionals in the field to understand federal policies and court decisions as well as the ethical dilemmas they themselves face. These issues were explored by Gelman, Keenan and Parker, and Adams. The organization of the material in this collection, with its attention to the needs of individuals, families, and groups, should help to facilitate this understanding.

As illustrated throughout, professional social workers have already assumed an active role in the developmental disabilities field. In addition to performing their more traditional roles, social workers have begun to be more active advocates for the disabled within the community and in the development of policy. As more social workers come into contact with developmentally disabled people in the community and those already involved in this area become increasingly sophisticated about the subject, the profession's ability to effect change will increase. Social workers will be able to assist in the refinement of standards and the pursuit of the goals of normalization and community care.

Because of the recent and rapidly expanding dimensions of the field, social workers are now adding their contributions to the literature. The compilation of articles included in this volume represent the best and the latest resource material available to practitioners.

I would like to offer my congratulations to the editors for their efforts in compiling this collection. Both young professionals, they have already accumulated significant experience and expertise in the field of developmental disabilities. It is my hope that they will maintain the essential linkage between the fields of social work and developmental disabilities, as well as make continuing contributions to the literature.

EDWARD NEWMAN
Director, Developmental Disabilities Center
and
Professor of Social Administration
Temple University
Philadelphia, Pennsylvania
August 1983